GUIDE TO THE SOCIAL SERVICES

SOCIAL POLICY & LEGISLATION EXPLAINED

2002/2003

GUIDE TO THE SOCIAL SERVICES

SOCIAL POLICY & LEGISLATION EXPLAINED

2002/2003

90th edition

Published by
Waterlow Professional Publishing
Paulton House, 8 Shepherdess Walk, London N1 7LB
Tel: 020 7490 0049 *Fax:* 020 7608 1163
DX: 122030 Finsbury 3

Contents

Publisher
Polly Avgherinos

Head of Editorial
Bethan Cater

Editor
Claudia Rios

Editorial Assistant
Oliver Kitchingman

Production Manager
Keith Hawkins

Senior Marketing Executive
Michelle Gyan

Group Sales Manager
Jennifer Guy

Senior Sales Manager
Paula Murphy

Professional Portfolio Sales Manager
Nicola Hymos

Classified Co-ordinator
Julia McNulty

Researcher
Richard Flower

Editorial:
Tel: 020 7490 0049 *Fax:* 020 7608 1163 *DX:* 122030 Finsbury 3

Orders and Advertising:
Customer Services Department, Waterlow Professional Publishing
Tel: 020 7490 0049 *Fax:* 020 7608 1163

ISBN 1 85783 903X

a division of Wilmington Business Information Ltd 2002
Paulton House, 8 Shepherdess Walk, London N1 7LB
E-mail: crios@waterlow.com Web: http://www.connectinglegal.com

Printed in the UK by Polestar Wheatons, Exeter, Devon

Introduction

This Guide first appeared in 1882, when it formed the introduction to the first edition of the 'Charities Register and Digest', published by the Charity Organisation Society. It was subsequently published separately, entitled 'How to Help Cases of Distress' and subtitled 'A handy reference book for almoners, almsgivers and others'. It was the view of its author, Charles Loch, then secretary of the Charity Organisation Society, that when 'trying to help those in distress, the would-be helper is often led to wish that he could learn what this or that public body could do, or what the law or regulation may be on some point'. His book was intended to meet that need for information. Now it is even more important that social work practitioners, social work students and all the various advocates of 'people in distress' have as much basic information about the resources provided by statutory and other bodies as can be made available in one compact volume. The tremendous increase in the scope of social service provision since the beginning of the nineteenth century, particularly in recent years, with the emphasis on a pluralist approach to provision and with a fast rate of change in the pattern and nature of statutory services, means that everyone coming into contact with statutory and voluntary social work and administration must have access to basic information about the services available.

There is currently very little agreement about what the 'social services' constitute. For the purposes of this Guide, 'social' refers to the fact that the services are provided by the community to meet certain individual needs. It excludes those services which are provided primarily for a profit.

ORGANISATION OF THE GUIDE

The book is divided according to services provided, rather than the categories of people who make use of them or the needs they meet. This method has the advantage of placing the information given in the context of local and central government departments: it also has the drawback of splitting some provision between chapters, according to the supplier of a service, but the subject index seeks to assist in finding such multiple references.

LEGISLATION

In the first edition, Loch drew the users' attention to the 'grave difficulties that have to be met or allowed for in any attempt to put down shortly the leading features of the legal provisions regarding intricate subjects'. These difficulties seem ever greater now, with the vast increase in both the number and complexity of Acts of Parliament which govern the provision of social services. It is vital, however, that those who want to help others make use of the services should themselves know something of the legal basis and prescription for their work. Wherever possible, therefore, the statutes governing services have been specified. Attention has been given to recent legislation which is described in some detail. We have also added a Legislation List which is intended to act as a pointer to those recent Acts and Bills currently before Parliament of relevance to users of the Guide. Many of the Acts are part-way through the lengthy process of implementation and their effects will necessarily affect the accuracy of the Guide.

GEOGRAPHICAL SCOPE OF THE GUIDE

In the main, the services described and the information given in this Guide refer to England and Wales. The law and the legal system in Scotland differ in many ways and services are organised differently. Northern Ireland has its own legislation and administrative structure and, although its social services are kept broadly in line with those in the rest of the UK, nevertheless it should be noted that legislation for Great Britain does not necessarily apply to Northern Ireland. Where the legislation referred to in the Guide is also applicable to Scotland and Northern Ireland, this is indicated.

Preface

Welcome to the 2002/2003 edition of the Guide to the Social Services. This is the seventh year that Waterlow has published the Guide in association with the Family Welfare Association (FWA). As always, the Guide provides details on a wide range of areas of social care, fulfilling the needs of advisers, information workers and families. The Citizens Advice Bureaux directory continues to appear as an appendix to the entire volume.

Any comments or suggestions regarding this or any other Waterlow publication or the service we provide will be gratefully received.

This edition was largely prepared in July 2002. At the time of going to print, Waterlow has ensured that this edition is as accurate as possible with help from the relevant Government departments. Where corrections were unobtainable, the text remains the same as the previous edition. However, legislation will be passed and procedure may be emended during the production of the Guide or during the coming year. This may render some information provided within the Guide immediately obsolete. Where possible, in-coming legislation is mentioned in the text, and the Legislation List should provide an indicator of those Acts and Bills likely to affect the content over the coming year. Readers are reminded that the Guide is of necessity *not* an absolutely detailed or infallible description of all social services and sources of information; it is intended to be a good introduction to the field, providing signposts to sources of more help. For specialist needs and cases, more detailed advice is likely to be necessary.

Acknowledgements

We would particularly like to thank the following contributors who have generously given us their valuable advice and time to help update this edition:

David Baldwin (Lord Chancellor's Department) *Law and Legal Services*
John Chater (Binley's) *for writing the Health section*
Mark Donnelly (Department for Work and Pensions) *Welfare Benefits and Pensions, Education*
Paul Lipscombe (Department for Transport, Local Government and the Regions) *Housing*
Chris Myant (Commission for Racial Equality) *Equality and Citizenship*
Cathy Spence (Department for work and Pensions) *Employment*
Dominic Stuttaford (Norton Rose) *Tax*

Ending Child Poverty – Is Work the Answer?

Of all new Labour's pledges, none is more far-reaching than the Prime Minister's pledge to end child poverty within a generation. For Britain's poorest families, this is welcome indeed. But is the Government putting action – and investment – behind its words?

For this Government, the answer to ending family poverty lies squarely in helping the unemployed to return to paid work. And much has been done to reduce the number of workless households and to make work pay. In 1997, for example, only 44% of lone parents were in paid work. Today the figure stands at over 50% - and the Government has an ambitious target to have 70% of lone parents in paid work by the end of the decade. The financial gains from paid work have been improved – thanks to initiatives like the minimum wage and the working families tax credit. The National Childcare Strategy has made it possible for more parents to undertake part-time or fulltime work. And the New Deal programmes have offered support and advice to those who may be returning to the labour market after unemployment, or perhaps entering it for the first time.

The comprehensive scale of the attack on worklessness should not be underestimated. But have the initiatives reached the most excluded, and enabled them to enter and progress at work? And what of those - including some lone parents, carers, the sick and disabled – for whom paid work may not be the answer?

The Government's intention is that the rollout of Jobcentre Plus will concentrate energies on these harder questions, bringing together in one place help and advice for those who can work, and support for those who cannot. Meantime, changes to the system of tax credits, with the new child tax credit and working tax credit due to be introduced in 2003, offer the opportunity to make further significant progress in tackling poverty, for working families and for parents undertaking fulltime care of their children. And the money announced in the Spending Review for investment in a network of children's centres will help to address one of the main barriers still facing many parents thinking about a return to work.

But still there are large gaps to fill. Childcare places exist for only 1 in 7 children under the age of 8. Performance under the New Deals remains patchy, and more needs to be invested in education and training to ensure access to better-paid jobs and good prospects (nearly half of lone parents not in work have no academic qualifications). Still too many families find themselves struggling to make ends meet, struggling to meet housing costs (housing benefit administration in too many parts of the country remains deeply unsatisfactory), unable to access the Social Fund in times of crisis.

Certainly much has been achieved to improve employment prospects and to tackle child poverty. But much more is needed to reach the poorest and most excluded families, to secure their wellbeing and prospects, and offer security and opportunity for their children. The Government has begun on a radical programme of social change to tackle disadvantage. Now it must see it through.

Kate Green is the Director of the National Council for One Parent Families
Lone parent helpline: 0800 018 5026
www.oneparentfamilies.org.uk

Current Legislation

RECENT ACTS OF PARLIAMENT AND PUBLIC BILLS CURRENTLY BEFORE PARLIAMENT (JUNE 2002)

The following Acts of Parliament and Public Bills are listed on the grounds that they are of relevance to the content of this book and therefore to the readers. Full lists of Public Bills before Parliament in the current session are available on the government website at **www.legislation.hmso.gov.uk/acts.htm**. This list does not reflect the full list of Acts passed in the last twelve months.

Adoption and Children Bill

Commonhold and Leasehold Reform Act 2002

Divorce (Religious Marriages) Act 2002

Education Bill

Employment Act 2002

Finance Bill

Homlessness Act 2002

National Health Service Reform and Health Care Professionals Act 2002

National Insurance Contributions Act 2002

Nationality, Immigration and Asylum Bill

State Pension Credit Act 2002

Tax Credits Act 2002

Travel Concessions (Eligibility) Act 2002

GUIDE TO THE SOCIAL SERVICES

THE ORGANISATION AND ADMINISTRATION OF THE SOCIAL SERVICES

Successive acts of Parliament have made central and local government in England and Wales responsible for the provision of a wide range of social services. The main services provided by local authorities as outlined in this book are personal social services, education, housing and consumer protection. Central government retains responsibility for the National Health Service, employment services, the probation and after-care service and the national system of social security. This chapter describes how central and local government are organised to provide these services and the main agencies involved.

CENTRAL GOVERNMENT SERVICES

The services outlined in this section are the direct responsibility of central government departments. Although they may be administered at local level, they are financed almost wholly by central government revenues and there is little possibility of local authorities varying the provision of services. Thus the Department of Work and Pensions (DWP) is directly responsible for the national system of social security benefits and allowances. Both national insurance and other benefits, including income support, are administered through local social security offices by civil servants. The DWP is also responsible through Jobcentre Plus for employment and self-related services. Much of the administration of services is now undertaken by agencies, self-contained units within government departments, and this is a trend which the present government intends to continue.

The National Health Service in England and Wales is the responsibility of the Secretaries of State for Health and for Wales respectively. It is administered through the agency of Regional and District Health Authorities (RHAs and DHAs) in England, District Health Authorities only in Wales. These are statutory bodies accountable to the Secretary of State (in England the DHAs' accountability is at present through the RHA) and consist of members drawn from a variety of backgrounds.

The Probation and After-care service in England and Wales is the responsibility of the Home Office, which is advised by an Advisory Council for Probation and After-Care. The service is administered at local level by area probation and after-care committees composed of local magistrates and co-opted members with legal and specialist interests.

Responsibility for the administration of justice in England and Wales rests with the Lord Chancellor and the Home Secretary, the former being concerned with court procedure and responsible for the administration of all courts other than magistrates' courts. The Lord Chancellor is also concerned with law reform and the supervision of the legal aid and advice scheme. The Home Secretary is concerned with the criminal law and is responsible for the prevention of crime, apprehending offenders and the penal system.

Service First - the New Charter Programme

Service First was launched on June 30 1998 as the Government's new programme to raise the quality of public services and make them more responsive to their users. It builds on the achievements of the Citizen's Charter, but gives a new emphasis to four main themes: response, quality, effectiveness and working together.

These themes are reflected in hundreds of national (and thousands of local) charters, which explain the levels of service to which you are entitled and what to do if you have a suggestion for improvement or a complaint.

RELATIONSHIP BETWEEN CENTRAL AND LOCAL GOVERNMENT

The powers and responsibilities of local authorities are defined by Parliament and local authorities are responsible to their electorates for the way in which they discharge their functions. In addition, however, central government is answerable to Parliament for policies concerning the services provided by local authorities. Parliament passes legislation which is normally drafted and introduced by central government, but private members' Acts or amendments to legislation can impose new obligations on central government departments.

The legislation prescribing for Local Authority Services divides broadly between that imposing duties on local authorities, mandatory legislation, and that empowering them to do particular things; permissive legislation. The mandatory legislation is often couched in very general terms, which leaves wide scope for local interpretation. Thus, for example, under the Chronically Sick and Disabled Persons Act 1970, the extent of the service provided depends on the local authorities' perception of need. However, legislation also gives specific powers to central government for controlling the work of local authorities in relation to certain services, such powers being largely aimed at ensuring a degree of uniformity in standards of service. For some services, the supervisory powers of central government are wide, for others strictly limited or non-existent. The supervisory and advisory responsibilities of central government towards local authorities are summarised later in this chapter.

On 1 April 2002, The Electoral Commission took over the functions of the Local Government Commission for England (LGCE), which reviewed local authority electoral arrangements, including the number and boundaries of wards, and the number of councillors to be elected. A new Boundary Commission for England has been established within The Electoral Commission to assume this role, and the former LGCE staff have been transferred to the new organisation. For further information visit the website (www.electoralcommission.gov.uk).

The main task of the LGCE between 1992 and 1995 was to review the structure of local government in the shire counties, assessing the case for unitary (single tier) authorities. This review has been completed and the Electoral Commission is currently in the midst of a programme of periodic electoral reviews that should result in all local authorities in England having revised and updated electoral arrangements in place by 2005. The Commission makes recommendations to the Secretary of State for any changes to the electoral arrangements; i.e.. the total number of councillors to be elected to the council; the number and boundaries of electoral areas and the number of councillors to be elected for each electoral area; and the name of any electoral area.

Financial control

Local authorities in England and Wales can only lawfully spend money in the exercise of functions authorised by legislation. The income to meet this expenditure comes from three sources:

- central government grant (RSG, SSA Reduction Grant, Police Specific Grant, and other specific grants and special grants);
- national non-domestic rates (NNDR), redistributed on the basis of population; and
- revenue raised by local authorities from the council tax.

Central government controls the level of revenue support grant and the national non-domestic rate. Local authorities set their own budgets, in which they may also use income from fees and charges and money drawn from their reserves. They also set the level of council tax for each of the property bands in their area. There are, however, new reserve powers which the Secretary of State can use to protect local taxpayers in authorities where council taxes rise unacceptably. The new reserve powers are more flexible and discriminating than the previous capping powers. For example, when deciding whether to use the reserve powers, the Government will be able to look at increases over two years. They will also allow councils with limited increases to reduce their budgets in a following year rather than always requiring them to make the full adjustment in one year.

Money for capital expenditure comes from a number of sources, the most significant of which is borrowing. This is controlled by the issue of credit approvals. Basic Credit Approvals (BCAs) are issued annually to each local authority by the Office of the Deputy Prime Minister. These cover all services and are based on the total of Annual Capital Guidelines issued by each service department, less a proportion of the usable capital receipts available to each authority. Resulting BCAs are then reallocated to those authorities with the least receipts and a higher need to spend. In addition, any Minister of the Crown may issue Supplementary Credit Approvals to allow local authorities to borrow for specific projects or programmes.

Inspectorates and advisors

Some services are subject to scrutiny from inspectors who are directly responsible to a government department, for example OFSTED and SSI. The education service's inspectors (OFSTED) act as monitors and advisors to local education authorities (LEAs) in England. In the Department of Health (DoH), the Social Services Inspectorate (SSI) advises local authority social services departments in England on the local implementation of national policy and on practice, and also advises the DoH on local conditions and developments. A Social Work Service is organised by the Welsh National Assembly, which has similar functions in respect of Welsh Authorities, listed at the end of this introductory chapter.

In July 1999 a Best Value Inspectorate Forum was established, made up of the Heads of Inspectorates involved in improving local services under Best Value: OFSTED, BFI, HMFSI, SSI and the Audit Commission. This Forum has created a basis for policy discussion between the major professional inspectorates who will carry out Best Value inspections. It aims to establish a consistent and workable inspection methodology across all inspection functions, providing the means to develop an integrated inspection system for local government and is working together with all areas of central government in shaping the new policy. A similar forum has been established in Wales.

Government circulars

The ways in which local authorities are expected to carry out their duties are defined in circulars. They are issued by all departments of central government and can be mandatory or merely advisory. The circulars are used to instruct, give general policy guidance and advice, to explain new legislation and to exhort.

ORGANISATION OF LOCAL GOVERNMENT

England and Wales are divided into areas, each with an elected council of representatives (who are only paid expenses) and a staff of full-time officials. The basic two-tier division is that of counties, most of which are in turn divided into districts. In most parts of England and Wales, counties and districts have their own separate councils and paid staff, with county authorities normally providing services requiring wider areas of administration, while districts are responsible for the more local ones. However, in six English counties (heavily populated and known as Metropolitan authorities) the county authorities were abolished under the Local Government Act1985. In these, responsibility for nearly all services now rests with the district authorities, acting either individually or jointly. The six are Greater Manchester, Merseyside, South Yorkshire, Tyne and Wear, West Midlands and West Yorkshire. In addition to the 32 Boroughs and the City of London, the Capital is also governed by the Greater London Authority (GLA). The authority comprises a directly elected Mayor and 25 separately elected Assembly members. The GLA's role is primarily a strategic one, promoting co-ordination and pan-London initiatives in conjunction with the Boroughs.

Local government in the non-metropolitan areas was, until 1995, provided everywhere by a two-tier system of county councils and, within each county, a number of smaller district councils. The local government review of 1992-95 led to the replacement of two-tier arrangements with unitary authorities in some areas, especially the larger cities or areas with a particularly strong historical tradition. As a result there are now 34 upper-tier county councils, 240 lower-tier district councils, and 46 unitary councils in the shire areas in addition to the existing unitary authorities in Metropolitan areas and in London. There is no separate class of unitary authorities; they are legally district councils with the exception of the Isle of Wight, which is a county council. These unitary authorities have responsibility for all the services in their areas, as Metropolitan authorities either individually or jointly with neighbouring authorities.

Parish councils make up a third tier of local government, predominantly in rural areas and small towns. They have only limited power and may operate on a very small scale. In Wales, community councils have powers almost identical to those of parishes in England. Some district councils use the term 'borough' or 'city'; similarly, certain parish councils are styled town or city councils. This makes no difference to their functions.

Following the creation of the National Assembly for Wales and the Scottish Parliament, local government arrangements may change during the year for which this book is relevant.

LOCAL AUTHORITY SERVICES

Local authorities provide a wide range of services, from refuse collection to planning. They are controlled by elected councillors and, to some extent, by central government as outlined above. The elected council of a local authority is responsible for all the services provided by its staff.

Under current statute, each council establishes committees to deal with the business of one or more services. Where the council is responsible for social services they must, by law, establish a social services committee. Otherwise, the council can set up whatever other committees it chooses. Committees in turn can set up sub-committees to deal with part of their work and, in most cases, can co-opt non-councillors with expert knowledge. Under proposals in the Local Government Act, the committee system will cease to apply to the majority of council functions, including social services. Councils will instead have to adopt executive arrangements whereby a small executive would be responsible for implementing the policy framework and budget agreed by full council. The executive will in turn be held to account by overview and scrutiny committees who can co-opt non-councillors onto their committees. When councils adopt executive arrangements they will no longer be required to establish a social services committee.

An executive may arrange for the discharge of its functions by an individual member of the executive, a committee of the executive, an officer of the authority, by an area committee, a joint committee with another authority, another local authority, or contract out functions. The table below shows the functions of the principal authorities in England. In Wales, the allocation of functions between county and district councils is broadly the same as that in non-metropolitan areas of England, but there are some differences: refuse disposal is a district council function; subject to county council consent district councils may provide on-street as well as off-street parking; and district councils may, by order, be constituted library authorities.

A wide range of local authority services were previously subject to Compulsory Competitive Tendering (CCT), whereby local authorities could only carry out certain functions in-house if the work had first gone to tender and been won in open competition.

Compulsory Competitive Tendering was revoked by the Local Government Act 1999 which took effect from 2nd April 2000, and was replaced by a duty of Best Value. Best Value requires authorities to secure continuous improvement in the way in which their functions are exercised, having regard to a combination of economy, efficiency and effectiveness. Under Best Value authorities will have to review the provision of all their services, conducting these reviews on a five year cycle, through consultation, comparison, competition and through challenging the status quo. Where possible, inspection of each service will take place after the review has been carried out. Authorities are also required to prepare an annual Best Value Performance Plan for the year and a summary of their review programme.

Function of local authorities in England

	Met/London* Authorities			**Shire/Unitary Authorities**		
	Joint Authorities	*Met Council*	*London Boroughs*	*District Council*	*Unitary Authorities England & Wales*	*County Councils*
Education		•	•		•	•
Housing		•	•	•	•	
Planning Applications		•	•	•	•	
Strategic Planning		•	•		•	
Transport Planning		•			•	•
Passenger Transport	•				•	•
Highways		•	•		•	•
Fire	•				(1)•	•
Social Services		•	•		•	•
Libraries		•	•		•	•
Leasure & Recreation		•	•	•	•	
Waste Collection		•	•	•	•	
Waste Disposal	•	•	•		•	•
Environmental Health		•	•	•	•	
Revenue Collection		•	•	•	•	

Notes

1 Joint fire authority operate in Counties with Unitary Authorities in them. These are combined fire authorities, there are three combined fire authorities in Wales.

***Greater London Authority (GLA) functions:** *Transport:* control the underground and London buses, taxis, DLR and most main roads (the London Boroughs remain the highway & traffic authorities for 95% of roads). *Environment:* work with the boroughs on air quality, waste etc. *Planning:* set the overall strategic framework for the development of London (the boroughs will continue to deal with local planning matters). *Fire:* the London Fire & Emergency Planning Authority is responsible for London's fire service (9 members are drawn from the GLA). *Economic Development:* attract new investment. *Culture:* play a leading part in developing London's tourism, culture and sport. *Health:* has a duty to promote the improvement of the health Londoners.

LOCAL AUTHORITY SOCIAL SERVICES STAFF

Local authority social services are the responsibility of the elected members, but the various services are administered and delivered to the public by local authority employees. Senior staff of the various departments are primarily involved in organising and planning the services and, in many authorities, they form part of a corporate management team under the leadership of a chief executive. The practical work of providing the services and the day-to-day contact with the public are the responsibility of the following staff:

Social workers

In the context of local authority social services departments, 'social worker' is a generic term used to describe staff working with families and individuals who need assistance with personal, practical and emotional problems. Some social workers work with a whole range of people and problems; others may specialise in work with particular client groups, e.g., people with visual or hearing impairment. Increasingly, local authority social services departments employ social work staff in specific roles such as adoptions officer, intermediate treatment officer and welfare rights officer.

Hospital social workers

Social work staff in general and specialist hospitals are employed by the local authority and not by District Health Authorities. Although most of their work is with hospital patients, hospital social workers are also concerned with the patient's family and community.

Psychiatric social workers

These are concerned with the problems of people who are emotionally disturbed or have mental health problems, whether in the community or in hospital. Some are employed by local education authorities in their special schools or child guidance clinics, while others are employed by the local social services department in a hospital or community setting.

Education welfare officers

Local education authorities employ education welfare officers to carry out responsibilities under the various Education Acts. Their work ranges from advising teachers and parents about services and benefits available to children of school age to enforcing regulations concerning non-attendance at school. The work of education welfare officers varies throughout the country.

Housing welfare officers

Some local authority housing departments have staff with specific responsibility for giving advice and help to local authority tenants with particular housing problems. They may also be responsible for giving help and advice to homeless families.

ROLE OF VOLUNTARY AND NON-STATUTORY ORGANISATIONS

The main purpose of this book is to guide the reader through statutory services, but throughout the chapters reference is made to voluntary and non-statutory organisations which make a considerable contribution to the provision of services. The voluntary sector, made up of thousands of varied organisations, complements, supplements, extends and influences the informal and statutory systems. Many present-day services were pioneered by the voluntary sector over the last century and financial support was first given to voluntary bodies by central government in 1914. Current funding from central government totals approximately £2.4 billion. Voluntary organisations may receive grants from either central or local government to maintain their administrative and organisational structure, for particular short-term projects or in payment for specific services. In the immediate post-war years, when state involvement in the provision of services was on a more universal and wide-ranging scale than hitherto, it seemed that the contribution of voluntary organisations ought no longer to be necessary and that they would gradually disappear as the statutory services became established. Over time, the continuing value and even growing necessity of voluntary organisations in service provision, interest groups, information provision, campaigning and lobbying has been confirmed. The period since the 1950s has been one of increased activity and expansion for the voluntary sector. Many of the older established organisations have adapted by initiating new and varied ways of working with individuals and families and many new ones have been formed in response to evolving needs.

Today, voluntary and non-statutory bodies act as pressure groups for social reform, co-operate with local authorities in formulating policy and plans, provide support services and fill some of the gaps in statutory provision. Legislation and government policy in the past few years have brought voluntary organisations centre stage in much service provision and this is a trend which will continue and intensify: one key area in which this change is demonstrated is in the use by health and local authorities of formal contracts for the provision of services by voluntary organisations.

Details of many voluntary organisations are given throughout this book, in relation to particular services. The last chapter on sources of advice contains additional information. There are many guides and directories of charities and voluntary groups. Waterlow Professional Publishing, Paulton House, 8 Shepherdess Walk, London N1 7LB Tel: 020 7490 0049, publishes *Charities Digest* each December, listing hundreds of national and regional charities and giving lists of addresses nationwide of key local services and reference points such as Citizens Advice Bureaux and councils for voluntary service.

SOCIAL SERVICES IN SCOTLAND

Scottish local government has always developed on lines distinct from those in England and Wales. Following the setting up of the Scottish Parliament (which assumed full powers on 1 July 1999) the responsible Minister for Scotland is the Minister for Health and Social Care who works through the Scottish Executive, St Andrews House, Regent Road, Edinburgh EH1 3DT Tel: 0131 556 8400. Further information can be obtained from the website address www.Scotland.gov.uk

The structure of local government in Scotland was reorganised with effect from 1 April 1996 when the existing 12 mainland and island authorities were replaced by 32 new all purpose authorities. These changes are defined in the Local Government etc. (Scotland) Act 1994.

Personal social services

Under the provisions of the Social Work (Scotland) Act 1968, as amended by the Local Government etc. (Scotland) Act 1994, local authorities are no longer required by statute to establish committees solely for social work. Some authorities have social work committees whilst others have combined these functions with other services such as education and housing. Where authorities have chosen a different departmental structure which does not involve the appointment of a professionally qualified Director of Social Work it is necessary for that authority to appoint a professionally qualified Chief Social Work Officer. Social Work Departments, in whatever form they exist, include the functions of the Probation Service. Instead of the English system of youth courts, there is a system of children's hearings. The Minister for Health and Community Care has overall responsibility for social work as well as specific statutory functions under the terms of the Social Work (Scotland) Act 1968. The implementation of the social work policy is administered by the relevant Scottish Executive Policy Division and the Social Work Services Inspectorate (SWSI) who provide the First Minister with advice on that policy and on the exercise of his/her functions under the Act. They also provide policy and practice guidance to local authorities. These responsibilities include child care, community care and Social Work Services in the criminal justice system. SWSI also inspects and evaluates services nationally.

Personal health services

There are 15 Area Health Boards directly responsible to the Minister for Health and Community Care; there are no family practitioner committees in Scotland; the Common Services Agency carries out some of the functions which the Regional Health Authorities perform in England; Scottish health and social work authorities are not required to establish joint liaison committees, but the social work departments are required to consult the appropriate Area Health Boards on matters of common interest to clients and patients; and the public interest is represented by local health councils. Under the provisions of the Mental Health (Scotland) Act 1984, judicial responsibility over procedure for compulsory admission to hospital lies with the Sheriff. The Mental Welfare Commission for Scotland protects the interests of individual patients. Under the Act, the term 'mental disorder' in Scotland distinguishes two forms of mental health problems: 'mental illness' and 'mental handicap'. The Scottish Executive Health Department (SEHD) is reponsible for health policy and the administration of the National Health Service in Scotland.

Housing

Departmental and local government housing functions are similar to those in England and Wales. The councils of islands, areas and districts are housing authorities. The Minister responsible is the Minister for Social Justice working through The Scottish Executive. Housing legislation for Scotland reflects the country's different housing history and therefore its provisions are not always the same as for England and Wales.

Education

The Education (Scotland) Acts 1939 and 1974 contain provision for educational services like those in England and Wales. The councils of regions and of island areas are the education authorities. The central government department responsible is **The Scottish Office Education and Industry Department,** Victoria Quay, Leith, Edinburgh EH6 6QQ Tel: 0131 556 8400.

The law and legal services

In Scotland, criminal and civil jurisdiction are exercised by courts, some of which specialise in one or other branch of the law and some of which deal with both. There are also administrative tribunals. The organisation of the legal profession in Scotland is substantially the same as in England and Wales. This apart, the law, and the organisation and procedure of courts in Scotland, differ widely from English law and procedure. Provisions are made for a legal aid and advice service which closely resembles that in England and Wales.

LOCAL AUTHORITY SOCIAL SERVICES DEPARTMENTS AND THE SOCIAL SERVICES INSPECTORATE

Headquarters addresses and telephone numbers are listed below, starting with shire counties and metropolitan districts in England, the London boroughs, the Welsh counties, Scottish regions and Northern Irish area boards. Central and regional addresses for the Social Services Inspectorate are given at the end of this section.

England *Shire Counties*

Bedfordshire.................... Tel: 01234 228391
County Hall, Cauldwell Street
Bedford MK42 9AP

Berkshire (abolished)

Buckinghamshire .... Tel: 01296 395000
County Hall
Aylesbury HP20 1EZ

Cambridgeshire .... Tel: 01223 718211
Castle Court, Shire Hall, Castle Hill
Cambridge CB3 0AP

Cheshire.......................... Tel: 01244 602424
County Hall, Castle Drive
Chester CH1 1SF

Cornwall & Isles of Scilly.. Tel: 01872 323658
County Hall, Station Road
Truro TR1 3AY

Cumbria .... Tel: 01228 607080
3 Victoria Place
Carlisle CA1 1EH

Derbyshire .... Tel: 01629 580000
County Offices
Matlock DE4 3AG

Devon .... Tel: 01392 382000
County Hall, Topsham Road
Exeter EX2 4QR

Dorset................................ Tel: 01305 251000
County Hall, Colliton Park
Dorchester DT1 1XJ

Co Durham .... Tel: 0191-386 4411
County Hall
Durham DH1 5UG

East Sussex .... Tel: 01273 481000
County Hall
St Anne's Crescent
Lewes BN7 1SW

Essex .... Tel: 01245 492211
PO Box 297, County Hall
Chelmsford CM1 1YS

Gloucestershire................ Tel: 01452 426868
Quayside House, Shire Hall
Gloucester GL1 2RH

Hampshire .... Tel: 01962 841841
Trafalgar House, Trafalgar
Winchester SO23 8UQ

Hereford & Worcester (abolished)

Hertfordshire .... Tel: 01438 737400
County Hall, Pegs Lane
Hertford SG13 8DP

Hull .... Tel: 01482 300300
Brunswick House
Strand Close, Kingston-upon-Hull
HU2 9DB

Isle of Wight .... Tel: 01983 520600
Fairlee House
17 Fairlee Road, Newport
Isle of Wight PO30 2EA

Kent .... Tel: 01622 671411
Sessions House, County Hall
Maidstone ME14 1XQ

Lancashire.......................... Tel: 01772 254868
PO Box 162, East Cliff County Offices
Preston PR1 3EA

Leicester City .... Tel: 0116 253 1191
New Walk Centre, Welford Place
Leicester LE1 6ZG

Leicestershire .... Tel: 0116 232 3232
County Hall, Glenfield
Leicester LE3 8RL

Lincolnshire .... Tel: 01522 552222
Wigford House, Brayford Wharf East
Lincoln LN5 7BH

Norfolk .... Tel: 01603 222222
County Hall, Martineau Lane
Norwich NR1 2DH

Northamptonshire .... Tel: 01604 236236
County Hall, Guildhall Road
Northampton NN1 1AY

Northumberland .... Tel: 01670 533000
County Hall
Morpeth NE61 2EF

North Yorkshire .... Tel: 01609 780780
County Hall
Northallerton DL7 8DD

Nottinghamshire................ Tel: 0115 982 3823
County Hall, West Bridgford
Nottingham NG2 7QP

Oxfordshire .... Tel: 01865 815854
County Hall, New Road
Oxford OX1 1ND

Rutland .... Tel: 01572 722577
Rutland County Council, Catmose, Oakham
Rutland LE15 6HP

Shropshire .... Tel: 01743 251000
The Shirehall, Abbey Foregate
Shrewsbury SY2 6ND

Somerset .... Tel: 01823 355455
County Hall
Taunton TA1 4DY

Staffordshire .... Tel: 01785 223121
St Chad's Place
Stafford ST16 2LR

Suffolk .... Tel: 08456 023023
Customer First, Whitehouse Road
Ipswich IP1 5NX

Surrey .... Tel: 020 8541 8800
A C Court, High Street
Thames Ditton KT7 0QA

Warwickshire .... Tel: 01926 410410
Shire Hall, PO Box 48
Warwick CV34 4RD

West Sussex .... Tel: 01243 777100
Grange Block, County Hall, Tower Street
Chichester PO19 1QT

Wiltshire .... Tel: 01225 713000
County Hall, Bythesea Road
Trowbridge BA14 8LE

Worcestershire .... Tel: 01905 763763
County Hall, Spetchley Road
Worcester WR5 2NP

Unitary Authorities

Bath & NE Somerset .... Tel: 01225 477000
7 North Parade Building, Bath
BA1 1NY

Blackburn & Wrekin .... Tel: 01952 202100

Blackpool .... Tel: 01273 477666

Bournemouth .... Tel: 01202 458702
Town Hall, Bournemouth
BH2 6DY

Bracknell Forest .... Tel: 01344 424642

Brighton & Hove .... Tel: 01273 290000
Town Hall, Bartholomew Square
Brighton
BN1 1JA

Bristol .... Tel :0117 922 2000
Council House, College Green
Bristol BS1 5TR

Darlington .... Tel: 01325 346200
Town Hall, Darlington
DL1 5QT

Derby City .... Tel: 01332 293111
The Council House, Corporation Street
Derby
DE1 2FS

East Riding of Yorkshire .. Tel: 01482 887700
County Hall
Beverley HU17 9BA

Halton .... Tel: 0151 424 2061

Hartlepool .... Tel: 01429 266522
Civic Centre, Victoria Road
Hartlepool TS24 8AY

Herefordshire .... Tel: 01432 260000
35 Hafod Road
Hereford HR1 1SH

Kinston upon Hull .... Tel: 01482 300300
The Guildhall, Alfred Gelder Street
Hull HU1 2AA

Leicester .... Tel: 0116 254 9922
New Walk Centre, Welford Place
leicester LE1 6ZG

Medway Towns .... Tel: 01634 306000
Civic Centre, Strood
Rochester ME2 4AU

Middlesbrough .... Tel: 01642 245432
3rd Floor Civic Centre, Corporation Road
Middlesbrough TS1 1QL

Milton Keynes .... Tel: 01908 691691
Lloyds Court, 21 North Tenth Street
Central Milton Keynes MK9 3AA

North East Lincolnshire .... Tel: 01472 313131
Fryston House, Fryston Corner
Grimsby DN34 5BB

North Lincolnshire .... Tel: 01724 296296
The Angel, Market Place
Brigg DN20 8LD

North Somerset .... Tel: 01934 888888
PO Box 52, Town Hall
Weston-super-mare BS23 1ZY

Nottingham .... Tel: 0115 915 5555
The Guildhall, South Sherwood Street
Nottingham NG1 4BT

Peterborough .... Tel: 01733 563141
Town Hall, Bridge Street
Peterborough PE1 1HG

Plymouth .... Tel: 01752 668000
Civic Centre, Armada Way
Plymouth PL1 2EW

Poole .... Tel: 01202 633633
Civic Centre
Poole BH15 2RU

Portsmouth .... Tel: 023 9282 2251
Civic Offices, Guildhall Square
Portsmouth PO1 2AL

Reading .... Tel: 0118 939 0900
Civic Offices, Civic Centre
Reading RG1 7TD

Redcar & Cleveland .... Tel: 01642 444000
Council Offices, Kirkleatham Street,
P.O. Box 85
Redcar TS10 1SP

Slough .... Tel: 01753 552288
Town Hall, Bath Road
Slough SL1 3UQ

South Gloucestershire .... Tel: 01454 865900
St Lukes Close, Emersons Way, Emersons Green
Bristol BS17 7AL

Southampton .... Tel: 023 8022 3855
Civic Centre
Southampton SO14 7LY

Stockton-on-Tees .... Tel: 01642 393939
Church Road
Stockton-on-Tees TS18 1LD

Stoke-on-Trent .... Tel: 01782 234567
Civic Centre, Glebe Street
Stoke-on-Trent ST4 1HH

Swindon .... Tel: 01793 463000
Civic Offices, Euclid Street
Swindon SN1 2JN

Telford & Wrekin .... Tel: 01952 202100

Warrington .... Tel: 01925 444400
Town Hall, Sankey Street
Warrington WA1 1UH

West Berkshire .... Tel: 01635 42400
Market Street
Newbury RG14 5LD

Windsor & Maidenhead .... Tel: 01628 798888
St. Ives House
Maidenhead SL6 1RF

Wokingham .... Tel: 0118 974 6000

York .... Tel: 01904 613161
P.O. Box 402, Customer Advice Centre
George Hudson Street
York YO1 6ZE

Metropolitan Districts *Greater Manchester*

Bolton .... Tel: 01204 333333
Le Mans Crescent, Civic Centre
Bolton BL1 1SA

Bury .... Tel: 0161 253 5000
Craig House
Bank Street Bury BL9 0BA

Manchester .... Tel: 0161 234 5000
P.O. Box 536, Town Hall Extension
Manchester M60 2LA

Oldham .... Tel: 0161 911 0300
Civic Centre, West Street
Oldham OL1 1UW

Rochdale .... Tel: 01706 647474
P.O. Box 67, Municipal Offices
Smith Street
Rochdale OL16 1YQ

Salford .... Tel: 0161 794 4711
Crompton House
100 Chorley Road, Swinton
Manchester M27 4BP

Stockport .... Tel: 0161 480 4949
1st Floor Ponsonby House
Edward Street
Stockport SK1 3UR

Tameside .... Tel: 0161 342 8355
Council Offices, Wellington Road, Ashton-under-Lyne
Tameside OL6 6DL

Trafford .... Tel: 0161 912 1212
P.O. Box 77, Talbot Road, Stretford
M32 0TH

Wigan .... Tel: 01942 244991
Civic Centre
Millgate
Wigan WN1 1YD

Merseyside

Knowsley .... Tel: 0151 489 6000
Council Offices, Archway Road, Huyton
Liverpool L36 9UX

Liverpool .... Tel: 0151 225 4966
1-7 Brougham Terrace, West Derby Road
Liverpool L6 1AE

St Helens .... Tel: 01744 456000
Personal Services Department, The Gamble Institut, Victoria Square
St Helens WA10 1DY

Sefton .... Tel: 0151 922 4040
Merton House, Stanley Road, Bootle
Liverpool L20 3UU

Wirral .... Tel: 0151 666 3600
Social Services Headquarters, Westminster House, Hamilton Street
Birkenhead, Wirral CH41 5FN

South Yorkshire

Barnsley .... Tel: 01226 770770
WellingtonHouse, 36 Wellington Street
Barnsley S70 1WA

Doncaster .... Tel: 01302 737777
P.O. Box 251, The Council House, College Road
Doncaster DN1 3DA

Rotherham .... Tel: 01709 382121
Crinoline House, Effingham Square
Rotherham S65 1AW

Sheffield .... Tel: 0114 272 6444
Redvers House, Union Street
Sheffield S1 2JQ

Tyne and Wear

Gateshead .... Tel: 0191 433 3000
Civic Centre
Gateshead NE8 1HH

Newcastle upon Tyne...... Tel: 0191 232 8520
Civic Centre, Barras Bridge
Newcastle upon Tyne NE1 8PA

North Tyneside .... Tel: 0191 200 6565
Town Hall, High Street East, Wallsend
Newcastle upon Tyne NE28 7RR

South Tyneside................ Tel: 0191 427 1717
Kelly House, Campbell Park Road
Hebbarn NE31 2SR

Sunderland .... Tel: 0191 553 1000
50 Fawcett Street
Sunderland SR1 1RF

West Midlands

Birmingham .... Tel: 0121 303 9944
Louisa Ryland House, 44 Newhall Street
Birmingham B3 3PL

Coventry .... Tel: 024 7683 3333
New Council Offices, Earl Street
Coventry CV1 5RR

Dudley .... Tel: 01384 818181
Ednam House, St James Road
Dudley DY1 3JJ

Sandwell .... Tel: 0121 569 2200
Lombard Street West
West Bromwich B70 8EB

Solihull .... Tel: 0121 704 6000
PO Box 32, The Council House
Solihull B91 3QY

Walsall .... Tel: 01922 650000
Civic Centre, Darwall Street
Walsall WS1 1RG

Wolverhampton .... Tel: 01902 556556
The Civic Centre, St Peter's Square
Wolverhampton WV1 1RT

West Yorkshire

Bradford .... Tel: 01274 752918
Alicana House, Chapel Street
Bradford BD1 5RE

Calderdale .... Tel: 01422 363561
Horsfall House, Skircoat Moor Road
Halifax HX3 0HJ

Kirklees .... Tel: 01484 221000
Oldgate House, 2 Oldgate
Huddersfield HD1 6QF

Leeds .... Tel: 0113 247 8630
Leeds City Council Social Services Department
Selectapost 9, Merrion House, 110 Merrion Centre
Leeds LS2 8QB

Wakefield .... Tel: 01924 307701
8 St Johns North
Wakefield WF1 3QA

London Boroughs

Barking & Dagenham .... Tel: 020 8592 4500
Civic Centre, Dagenham
Essex RM10 7BY

Barnet .... Tel: 020 8359 2000
1255 High Road, Whetstone
London N20 0EJ

Bexley .... Tel: 020 8303 7777
Bexley Civic Offices, Broadway, Bexleyheath
Kent DA6 7LB

Brent .... Tel: 020 8937 1234
Mahatma Gandhi House, 34 Wembley Hill Road, Wembley
Middx HA9 8AD

Bromley .... Tel: 020 8464 3333
Bromley Civic Centre, Stockwell Close, Bromley
Kent BR1 3UH

Camden .... Tel: 020 7278 4444
79 Camden Road
London NW1 9ES

Corporation of London .... Tel: 020 7606 3030
PO Box 270, Guildhall
London EC2P 2EJ

Croydon .... Tel: 020 8686 4433
Taberner House, Park Lane, Croydon
Surrey CR9 2BA

Ealing .... Tel: 020 8825 5000
Ealing Civic Centre
14-16 Uxbridge Road, Ealing
London W5 2HL

Enfield.............................. Tel: 020 8366 6565
Civic Centre, Silver Street, Enfield
Middx EN1 3XA

Greenwich .... Tel: 020 8854 8888
Nelson House, 50 Wellington Street, Woolwich
London SE18 6PY

Hackney .... Tel: 020 8356 5000
205 Morning Lane
London E9 6LG

Hammersmith and Fulham Tel: 020 8748 3020
145 King Street, Hammersmith
London W6 9XY

Haringey .... Tel: 020 8489 0000
40 Cumberland Road, Wood Green
London N22 7SG

Harrow .... Tel: 020 8863 5611
PO Box 7, Civic Centre, Station Road, Harrow
Middx HA1 2UL

Havering .... Tel: 01708 434343
Whitworth Centre, Noak Hill Road, Harold Hill, Romford
Essex RM3 7YA

Hillingdon .... Tel: 01895 250111
Civic Centre, High Street, Uxbridge
Middx UB8 1UW

Hounslow .... Tel: 020 8583 2000
The Civic Centre, Lampton Road, Hounslow
Middx TW3 4DN

Islington .... Tel: 020 7527 2000
Highbury House, 4 Highbury Crescent
London N5 1RW

Kensington and Chelsea . Tel: 020 7937 5464
The Town Hall, Hornton Street
London W8 7NX

Kingston-upon-Thames ... Tel: 020 8546 2121
Guild Hall, The High Street
Kingston-upon-Thames, Surrey KT1 1EU

Lambeth .... Tel: 020 7926 4786
Mary Seacole House, 91 Clapham High Street
London SW4 7TF

Lewisham .... Tel: 020 8695 6000
Lawrence House, 1 Catford Road, Catford
London SE6 4SW

Merton .... Tel: 020 8543 2222
Civic Centre, London Road, Morden
Surrey SM4 5DX

Newham .... Tel: 020 8534 4545
Broadway House, 322 High Street
Stratford London E15 1AJ

Redbridge .... Tel: 020 8478 3020
17-23 Clements Road, Ilford
Essex IG1 1BL

Richmond-on-Thames .... Tel: 020 8891 1411
42 York Street, Twickenham
Middx TW1 3BZ

Southwark .... Tel: 020 7525 5000
Mabel Goldwin House, 49 Grange Walk
London SE1 3DY

Sutton .... Tel: 020 8770 5000
Civic Offices, St Nicholas Way, Sutton
Surrey SM1 1EA

Tower Hamlets .... Tel: 020 7364 5000
Mulberry Place, 5 Clove Crescent
London E14 2BG

Waltham Forest .... Tel: 020 8527 5544
Municipal Offices, High Road, Leyton
London E10 5QJ

Wandsworth .... Tel: 020 8871 6000
104 Wandsworth High Street, London
SW18 4LA

Westminster .... Tel: 020 7641 6000
PO Box 240, City Hall, 64 Victoria Street
London SW1E 6PQ

Wales

Anglesey .... Tel: 01243 750057
Council Offices
Llangefni LL77 7TW

Blaenau Gwent .... Tel: 01495 350555
Municipal Offices
Civic Centre
Ebbw Vale NP2 6XB

Bridgend .... Tel: 01656 642200
Council Offices, Sunnyside
Bridgend CF31 4AR

Caerphilly .... Tel: 01495 226622
Hawtin Park, Gellihaf
Blackwood NP2 2PZ

Cardiff .... Tel: 029 2087 2000
County Hall, Atlantic Wharf
Cardiff CF10 4UW

Carmarthenshire .... Tel: 01267 234567
3 Spilman Street
Carmarthenshire SA31 1LE

Ceredigion .... Tel: 01545 570881
Min-Aeron, Rhiw Goch
Aberaeron SA46 0DY

Conwy .... Tel: 01492 574060
Builder Street
Llandudno LL30 1DA

Denbighshire .... Tel: 01824 706655
Ty Nant, Nant Hall Road
Prestatyn LL19 9LG

Flintshire .... Tel: 01352 702555
County Hall
Mold CH7 6NN

Gwynedd .... Tel: 01286 672255
County Offices
Caernarfon LL55 1SH

Merthyr Tydfil .... Tel: 01685 725000
Ty Keir Hardie, Riverside Court, Avenue De Clichy
Merthyr Tydfill CF47 8XE

Monmouthshire .... Tel: 01633 644644
County Hall
Cwmbran NP44 2XH

Neath Port Talbot .... Tel: 01639 763333
Civic Centre
Port Talbot SA13 1PJ

Newport .... Tel: 01633 244491
Civic Centre
Newport NP20 4UR

Pembrokeshire .... Tel: 01437 764551
County Hall
Haverfordwest SA61 1TP

Powys .... Tel: 01597 826000
County Hall
Llandrindod Wells LD1 5LG

Rhondda Cynon Taff .... Tel: 01443 424000
The Pavilions, Cambria Park
Clydach Vale CF40 2XX

Swansea .... Tel: 01792 636000
County Hall
Swansea SA1 3SN

Torfaen .... Tel: 01633 648777
County Hall
Cwmbran NP44 2XH

Vale of Glamorgan .... Tel: 01446 700111
St. Hilary Court, Copthorne Way
Culverhouse Cross CF5 6UA

Wrexham .... Tel: 01978 292000
The Guildhall
Wrexham LL11 1WF

Scotland *Regional Offices*

Borders .... Tel: 01835 824000
St Dunstan's, Melrose
Roxburghshire TD6 0SA

Central .... Tel: 01786 471177
Drummond House, Wellgreen Place, Langgarth
Stirling FK8 2EG

Dumfries and Galloway .... Tel: 01387 260000
8 Gordon Street
Dumfries DG1 1EG

Grampian .... Tel: 01224 682222
Woodhill House, Burn Road
Aberdeen AB6 5GB

Highland .... Tel: 01463 702000
Kinmylies Building, Leachkin Road
Inverness IV3 6NN

Lothian .... Tel: 0131 554 4301
Shrubhill House, Shrub Place
Edinburgh EH7 4PD

Strathclyde .... Tel: 0141 227 2300
Strathclyde House, 20 India Street
Glasgow G2 4PF

Tayside .... Tel: 01382 433712
Tayside House, 28 Crichton Street
Dundee DD1 3RM

Island Councils

Orkney Islands .... Tel: 01856 873535
School Place, Kirkwall
Orkney KW15 1NY

Shetland Islands .... Tel: 01595 693535
92 St Olaf Street, Lerwick
Shetland ZE1 0EN

Western Isles .... Tel: 01851 703773
Council Offices, Sandwick Road, Stornoway
Isle of Lewis HS1 2BW

Northern Ireland *Health and Social Services Boards*

Eastern .... Tel: 028 9032 1313
12-22 Linenhall Street
Belfast BT2 8BS

Northern .... Tel: 028 2565 3333
County Hall, 182 Galgorm Road
Ballymena BT42 1QB

Southern .... Tel: 028 3752 2381
20 Seagoe Industrial Area, Portadown
Co Armagh BT63 5QD

Western .... Tel: 028 7186 0086
15 Gransha Park, Clooney Road
Londonderry BT47 6FM

Isle of Man

Isle of Man .... Tel: 01624 686179
Isle of Man Government Social Services Division, Hillary House, Prospect Hill
Douglas IM1 1EQ

Social Services Inspectorate *Central Government*

SSI Headquarters

Region .... Tel: 020 7972 2000
Richmond House, 79 Whitehall
London SW1A 2NL

Branch Enquiries:

SSI-Management Support Group .... Tel: 020 7972 2000
Wellington House, 135-155 Waterloo Road
London SE1 8UG

SSI-Child Care Group .... Tel: 020 7972 2000
Wellington House, 135-155 Waterloo Road
London SE1 8UG

SSI-Community Care and Ageing Group .... Tel: 020 7972 2000
Wellington House, 135-155 Waterloo Road
London SE1 8UG

SSI-Mental Health and Disabilities .... Tel: 020 7972 2000
Wellington House, 135-155 Waterloo Road
London SE1 8UG

SSI-TR GP .... Tel: 020 7972 2000
Training Resources and General Policy Group
Wellington House, 135-155 Waterloo Road
London SE1 8UG

Regional Offices in England

North West Group .... Tel: 0161 876 2400
11th Floor, Westpoint, 501 Chester Road
Old Trafford, Manchester M16 9HU

North East Group .... Tel: 0191 490 3400
Tyne Bridge Tower, Church Street, Gateshead
Tyne and Wear NE8 2DU

Central Group .... Tel: 0115 950 4799
J Rothschild House, Castel Olnay Boulevard
Nottingham NG7 1FW

South West .... Tel: 0117 941 6500
40 Barclay Square, Clifton
Bristol BS8 1HP

London West Group .... Tel: 020 7972 2000
Hannibal House, Elephant and Castle
London SE1 6TE

London East Group .... Tel: 020 7972 2000
Hannibal House, Elephant and Castle
London SE1 6TE

Inspection Resource Group ....
.... Tel: 0113 254 5000
16th Floor - West Riding House, 67 Albion Street
Leeds LS1 5AA

North of England Policy and
Business Region .... Tel: 0113 243 0906
16th Floor - West Riding House
67 Albion Street, Leeds LS1 5AA

Central England Policy and
Business Region .... Tel: 0121-631 4622
6th Floor – Ladywood House
Stephenson Street, Birmingham B2 4DF

South England Policy and
Business Region .... Tel: 020 7972 2000
Hannibal House, Elephant and Castle
London SE1 6TE

London Policy and Business
Region .... Tel: 020 7972 2000
Hannibal House, Elephant and Castle
London SE1 6TE

Wales *Y Swyddfa Gymreig*

London Office .... Tel: 020 7270 0543
Gwydr House, Whitehall
London SW1A 2ER

Cardiff Office .... Tel: 029 2082 5111
Crown Building, Cathays Park
Cardiff CF10 3NQ

Scotland *Social Work Services Inspectorate*

Enquiries .... Tel: 0131 556 8400
Victoria Quay
Edinburgh EH6 6QQ

Northern Ireland

Department of Health and
Social Services .... Tel: 028 9052 0500
Dundonald House
Upper Newtownards Road
Belfast BT4 3SF

CHAPTER ONE

Family and Community:

THE PERSONAL SOCIAL SERVICES

Section One: Children and Families

Section Two: Care and the community

CHAPTER ONE

Family and Community

Section One: Children and Families

INTRODUCTION

Central Government responsibility for the provision of care and social services for children and families is spread across a number of departments:

- Department of Health (www.doh.gov.uk) - for all matters concerning health and wellbeing.
- Department for Education and Skills (www.dfes.gov.uk) for education, day care and childminding.
- Home Office (www.homeoffice.gov.uk) for the probation service.
- Department of Work and Pensions (www.dwp.gov.uk) for welfare benefits.

The Department of Health provides statistical information on the number of children in society that are in need of care and social service provision. The Children in Need report (www.doh.gov.uk/cin/cin2001results.htm) summarises the results of a national survey carried out annually to determine how many children in the country can be defined as "in need." It also details the activity and expenditure by social services in their efforts to tackle these problems. In 2001 there were approximately 376,000 children in need in England with social services providing some kind of help for about 250,000 of them. The single main need for social service help is cases of neglect or abuse, which account for 55% of all cases. Social services spend, on average, about £50 million a week on these children, a rise of 26% from the £40.1 million that was spent last year.

The management of personal social services in England and Wales has been undertaken by local authority social services departments since the Local Authority Social Services Act 1970. The work that social services do on behalf of children is underpinned by the legislative framework of the Children Act 1989 and The Government's Objectives for Children's Social Services 1999. This Act and all others from 1988 onwards are available online from Her Majesty's Stationery Office website (www.hmso.gov.uk). Since the implementation of the Children Act 1989 a number of schemes, initiatives, programmes, organisations, Bills and further legislation have added to the services available to care for and protect children in society. This chapter will present information on the following:

- Legislation Overview - a brief outline of major legislation and official reports/ documents.
- Organisations and Programmes Overview - a brief outline of the major organisations, bodies, schemes and programmes.
- Protection Legislation - a more detailed looked at legislation for the protection of children.
- Care and Protection Orders and Processes - a more detailed look at the actions that courts and the social services can take to care for and protect children.
- Provision of Care in Society - including information on Quality Protects, Sure Start, fostering, adoption and day care services.
- Voluntary Organisations - contact details for the major voluntary organisations involved with the care and protection of children and families.

At the time of going to press (July 2002), The Victoria Climbié Inquiry was still ongoing. The official inquiry was set up to learn lessons from the death of Victoria Climbié, who died in February 2000. It is looking into why social services, the police and the NHS failed to prevent her death. It is considered likely that the chairman of the Inquiry, Lord Laming, will implement many reforms to local authority child protection services.

LEGISLATION AND REPORTS OVERVIEW

Children Act 1989, The

This Act, implemented on 14th October 1991, completely replaced some parts and amended others of previous childcare laws and legislation. The Act provides local authorities with powers and duties to assist children and families and to take action to protect children.

Protection of Children Act 1999, The

The Protection of Children Act 1999 transformed the vetting and registration of people deemed unsuitable for work with children.

Care Standards Act 2000, The

The Care Standards Act 2000 provided for the establishment of a National Care Standards Commission, responsible for regulation, setting standards and arranging for the inspection of the whole range of residential and domiciliary services. It also established a General Social Care Council to regulate both the conduct and training of all social care staff.

Valuing People: A New Strategy for Learning Disability for the 21st Century

This was published in March 2001 as a White Paper and includes a chapter on children which set out the Government's proposals for maximising opportunities for disabled children and supporting young people's transition into adult life. Provision for disabled children is now a priority in the work of the Children's National Service Framework.

Carers and Disabled Children Act 2000, The

Implemented on 1 April 2001, this Act gave local councils greater powers to make assessments and subsequently supply certain services direct to carers. Local councils were also given the right to make direct payments to carers and parents of disabled children to meet the assessed needs. In addition, this Act gave councils the right to make direct payments to 16 and 17 year old disabled young people.

Children (Leaving Care) Act 2000, The

This Act came into force in October 2001. Its principal aim is to improve the chances of young people living in and leaving local authority care.

Adoption and Children Bill, The

This Bill was introduced in October 2001 and will modernise the existing legal framework for domestic and inter-country adoption.

Learning to Listen (Core Principles on the Involvement and Engagement of Children and Young People)

This report was published by the Children and Young People's Unit (CYPU) in November 2001 and Government departments are required to produce action plans to implement them. Related developments to enhance the voice and rights of children include the establishment of a Children's Rights Director, a strengthening of advocacy services and improvements to complaints procedures.

Choice Protects

A major review of place choice and fostering services was announced in March 2002. The review focuses on helping councils commission and deliver effective placements and services for looked after children.

Children Act Report 2001, The

Published in July 2002 the Children Act Report 2001 provides an overview of the impact of the Act and progress by the service towards the achievement of the 11 objectives set out in The Government's Objectives for Children's Social Services 1999.

Government's Objectives for Children's Social Services 1999, The

Published in September 1999 these objectives are:

- To ensure that children are securely attached to carers capable of providing safe and effective care for the duration of childhood.
- To ensure that children are protected from emotional, physical and sexual abuse and neglect.
- To ensure that children in need gain maximum life chance benefits from educational opportunities, health care and social care.
- To ensure that looked after children gain maximum life chance benefits from educational opportunities, health care and social care.
- To ensure that young people leaving care are not isolated and participate socially and economically as citizens.
- To ensure that children with specific social needs are living in families or other appropriate settings.
- To ensure that referral and assessment processes discriminate effectively between different types and levels of need and produce a timely service response.
- To actively involve users and carers in planning services and in tailoring individual packages of care and to ensure effective mechanisms are in place to handle complaints.
- To ensure through regulatory powers and duties that children in regulated services are protected from harm and poor care standards.
- To ensure that social care workers are appropriately skilled, trained and qualified.
- To maximise the benefit service users from the resources available.

Special Educational Needs and the Disability Act 2001, The

This Act strengthens the right of children with specific educational needs to be educated in mainstream schools and from September 2002 protects them from discrimination on grounds of their disability in access to education.

Safeguarding Children Involved in Prostitution Guidance

The purpose of this guidance is to enable all agencies to work together to recognise the problem of child prostitution; help and protect those involved from further abuse; work together to prevent it; provide alternative opportunities; and investigate and prosecute those who coerce, exploit and abuse children through prostitution.

Private Fostering Review

A review of the existing legislation framework for private foster care (Part IX of theChildren Act 1989) was announced in January 2002. Recommendations will be made by the end of the year.

ORGANISATIONS AND PROGRAMMES

Children's National Service Framework - www.doh.gov.uk/nsf/children

On 28th February 2001, the Secretary of State announced a new Children's National Service Framework. This major programme of work is being overseen by the Children's Taskforce and was established to improve services for children. The Children's NSF will produce new national standards across the NHS and social services.

The Children's Taskforce - www.doh.gov.uk/nsf/children/taskforce.doc

The Children's Taskforce was established in October 2000 to support implementation of the NHS Plan. Its members are drawn from the NHS, social services and voluntary sector. The Mission of the Children's Taksforce is to improve the lives and health of children and young people through the delivery of appropriate, integrated, effective, evidence-based and needs-led services, and to improve their satisfaction with the services provided for them.

The work of the Taskforce has included the following projects:

- Development of the Children's National Service Framework;
- Quality Protects;
- Health inequalities;
- Disabled children;
- Adoption;
- Child and adolescent mental health;
- Cross-government support for children and families;
- Safeguarding children.

Children's Fund - www.cypu.gov.uk

Administered by the CYPU the Children's Fund is for children aged 5-13. Its aim is to extend preventive services and contribute to a local preventive strategy across the agencies. It is currently in place in two thirds of the country and will be nationwide by April 2004. The Fund emphasises the importance of involving children, young people and their families in the design and delivery of services. It also recognises the significant role the voluntary and community sectors can play in enhancing local services.

Children and Young People's Unit (CYPU) - www.cypu.gov.uk

By forming the Unit the Government is now able to take an overall, cross departmental view of children and young people. It is administered by the DfES and has its own Minister who is directly responsible. The role of the CYPU is to administer the Children's Fund and to take a strategic view of children and young people's welfare across government.

The General Social Care Council (GSCC) - www.gscc.org.uk

Set up under the Care Standards Act 2000, the General Social Care Council is the guardian of standards for the social care workforce, with the aim of increasing the protection of service users, their carers and the general public. The General Social Care Council has responsibility for agreeing and issuing statutory codes of conduct and practice, setting up a register of social care workers, dealing with matters of conduct and regulating and supporting social work education and training.

The National Care Standards Commission (NCSC) - www.carestandards.org.uk

The National Care Standards Commission is a new, independent public body set up under the Care Standards Act 2000, to regulate social care and private and voluntary health care services throughout England. From 1st April 2002 the NCSC took responsibility for the registration and inspection of services - replacing the existing system of inspection by local authority and health authority inspection units. The following services are required to register with the NCSC: Care Homes, Children's Homes, Domiciliary Care Agencies, Residential Family Centres, Voluntary Adoption Agencies, Independent Fostering Agencies, Private and Voluntary Hospitals and Clinics, exclusively private Doctors and Nurses Agencies. The Commission is also responsible for inspecting local authority fostering services, local authority adoption services and the welfare aspects of boarding schools.

Quality Protects - www.doh.gov.uk/qualityprotects

A five year programme begun in 1999 to transform services for children in need, including children looked after by local authorities, children in need of protection and disabled children. Its aim is to improve the governance, management and delivery of children's services.

The Social Care Institute for Excellence (SCIE) - www.scie.org.uk

SCIE creates and disseminates best practice guidelines in social care, with the aim of improving the quality and consistency of social care practice and provision. SCIE is a not for profit company limited by guarantee and works closely with government, with the new regulatory bodies - including the General Social Care Council and the National Care Standards Commission - and with other social care organisations, practitioners and users.

Sure Start - www.surestart.gov.uk

The aim of Sure Start is to tackle the problem of child poverty and social exclusion through the provision of services for young children. By setting up local programmes across the country it is hoped that this aim will be achieved.

PROTECTION LEGISLATION

Protection of Children Act 1999, The

The Protection of Children Act 1999 transformed the vetting and registration of people deemed unsuitable for work with children. The Act made four principal changes to the law and was further enhanced by in the Care Standards Act 2000 and the Criminal Justice and Court Services Act 2000.

1. It places the existing Department of Health Consultancy Service Index (a list of persons considered to be unsuitable to work with children) onto a statutory basis. To be known as the Protection of Children Act List (PoCA List).

2. It enables the Department for Education and Skills to identify people who are put on List 99 (DfES List) because they are not fit and proper persons to work with children.

3. It enables the Criminal Records Bureau to disclose information about people on the Protection of Children Act List or List 99 along with their criminal records.

4. It requires child care organisations proposing to employ someone in a child care position to ensure that individuals are checked through the CRB against the POCA List and List 99, and not to employ anyone who is included on either list.

Employment of Children

The main provisions governing the employment of children are contained in the Children and Young Persons Act 1933 although further amendments have been added in the Children and Young Persons Act 1963 and the Employment Act 1989. The conditions laid down by these pieces of legislation are as follows:

- Employment is limited to those aged 13 and over including those involved in light horticultural and agricultural work.
- No child under Minimum School Leaving Age (MSLA) may be employed before seven a.m. or after seven p.m. on any day or for more than two hours on any school day (only one of which may be before school) or Sunday.
- Children must have a minimum of two weeks free of work during the summer holidays and may only work up to 12 hours per week during term time.
- Children under the age of 15 may work a maximum of five hours a day on Saturdays and school holidays subject to a maximum of 25 a week. Those aged 15 and over may work a maximum of 8 hours on Saturdays and school holidays subject to a maximum of 35 a week.
- Employers must notify the local authority within eight days of a young person starting work of the hours and conditions of a child's employment and guarantee it will not endanger their health nor render them unfit to obtain proper benefit from their education. The local authority will issue a work permit in respect of the child.
- Work in television, theatre, film or similar performance activities such as modelling is regulated by the Children (Performances) Regulations 1968, as amended. Different criteria apply to htose of child employment bu a child must have a license issued by the relevant local authority to take part in a performance or activity.

The Care Standards Act 2000

This Act set up two new organisations to regulate and establish standards for the provision of social services: The National Care Standards Commission and The General Social Care Council.

The Act also added the following provisions to the Protection of Children Act 1999 regarding the official register of people not suitable to work with children.

1. Organisations other than child care organisations can refer names to the Protection of Children Act List.
2. Permission for the Secretary of State to consider the transfer of names currently held on the DH Consultancy Service Index to be transferred to the Protection of Children Act List.
3. Organisations can access the List without first going through the Criminal Records Bureau.

The Children (Leaving Care) Act 2000

The Act is intended to improve the opportunities available to young people leaving care and its progress will be monitored by the Department of Health. The legislation obliges Councils to assess and meet the needs of young people aged 16 and 17 whether they stay in care or leave before they are 18. They must also stay in touch with these young people until they are at least 21 and continue to help them financially or with training and support throughout this period. The Government hopes to raise achievement and reduce social exclusion of care leavers through the Children (Leaving Care) Act 2000. It amends the leaving care provisions contained in section 24 of the Children Act 1989 although the overall legal framework of the 1989 Act remains. Essentially, the Act should get local authorities to:

- Look after young people until they are ready to leave care.
- Maintain good relationships with them and their carers or family during and after the care period.

- Prepare looked after young people for life after being in care.
- Provide placements, employment assistance, accommodation, support and skills training for care leavers.
- Involve young people in all assessment, planning, review and decision making that goes on about their future.
- Continue to support the young person after they have left care.
- Monitor and evaluate the success of the scheme.

Any local authority has the right, under the terms of the Act, to request assistance in the discharge of the duties that have been set for it, from any of the following authorities; education, housing, health, primary care, NHS, and any person authorised by the Secretary of State.

Criminal Justice and Court Services Act 2000

The CJCS Act came into force in June 2001 and was designed to safeguard the health and safety of children in society. It sets out procedures and practice to be adopted by the police, the probation service, the CPS, those involved in the administration of justice in the courts, the prison services and any other organisations that may be involved in making a disqualification order. A disqualification order is part of a sentence imposed by a court and prevents the offender from working with children.

- The child protection provisions in the CJCSA are part of an integrated system for the protection of children. The Education Reform Act 1988, the Education Act 1996 and the Protection of Children Act 1999 provide the key building blocks on which the child protection provisions of CJCSA are founded.
- The CJCSA contains 4 main provisions with regard to the protection of children.

1. They create a new way for the courts to disqualify unsuitable people from working with children.
2. They provide a review process for the disqualified person.
3. They provide strong criminal sanctions against those who breach the disqualification.
4. They provide a new comprehensive definition of working with children.

The Act also gives guidelines for those responsible for recruitment. Recruiters and others will be committing an offence if they, knowing someone to be disqualified, offer work in a regulated position to them, or procure work in a regulated position for them.

Safeguarding Children Involved in Prostitution Guidance

The purpose of this guidance is to enable all agencies to work together to recognise the problem of child prostitution; help and protect those involved from further abuse; work together to prevent it; provide alternative opportunities; and investigate and prosecute those who coerce, exploit and abuse children through prostitution. Although the primary concern of the Government is to treat children involved in prostitution as victims of abuse, if the child continues to voluntarily persist in prostitution after all possible advice and support has been given, they will be entered into the criminal justice system in the same way as any other offender. This guidance is issued under section 7 of the Local Authority Social Services Act 1970 which means that such organisations are legally required to comply with it. It is also issued by the Home Office to the police under a Home Office circular to replace Home Office Circular 109/59 in respect of those aged under 18 who are involved in prostitution and how to deal with them. In summer 2001 the Government commissioned work to review how the guidance is being implemented. The results of this are expected late summer 2002.

CARE AND PROTECTION ORDERS AND PROCESSES

The welfare of children is a responsibility of the entire local authority working in partnership with other public agencies, the voluntary sector and service users and carers. Stated under section 47 of The Children Act 1989, a key objective for social services departments is to ensure that children are protected from significant harm. They also provide a wide range of care and support for children and in fact all members of the community. Social services also have a duty to make enquiries if they have reason to suspect that a child in their area is suffering, or likely to suffer significant harm, to enable them to decide whether they should take any action to safeguard or promote the child's welfare. A number of orders from the courts can be used in the task of protecting children at risk in society. When such orders are issued the child's interests are represented in court by a Children's Guardian. Prior to April 2001 these Children's Guardians were know as Guardian Ad Litem. The Children's Guardian will appoint a solicitor to speak for the child and is involved throughout the case.

Care Order

A care order places a child in the care of the local authority to safeguard and promote the child's welfare. The local authority holds Parental Responsibility for children placed under care orders, sharing responsibility with the parents. Children should still be allowed contact with their parents unless the court specifies otherwise. Care orders last until the child reaches 18 or earlier if the order has been discharged by the court.

Supervision Order

Under a supervision order the child is not taken into care and parents do not lose their parental responsibility. It places the child under the supervision of the local authority or a probation officer (under s.35). The order usually lasts for one year but can be extended.

Education Supervision Order

If a court considers a child is not being properly educated it can make an order (under s.36) putting the child under the supervision of a particular education authority, as long as the child is not in local authority care. These orders are usually made for up to one year, but can be extended.

Child Assessment Order

The local authority should make all reasonable efforts to persuade parents to co-operate with s.47 enquiries. If the parents continue to refuse access to a child for the purpose of establishing basic facts about the child's condition - but concerns about the child's safety are not so urgent as to require an emergency protection order - a local authority may apply to the courts for a child assessment order (s.43). The court may direct the parents/carers to co-operate with an assessment of the child, the details of which should be specified. The order does not take away the child's own right to refuse to participate in an assessment, so long as he or she is of sufficient age and understanding.

Emergency Protection Order

The court may make an emergency protection order under s.44 of the Children Act 1989 if it is satisfied that there is reasonable cause to believe that a child is likely to suffer significant harm if:

- He or she is not removed to accommodation; or
- He or she does not remain in the place in which he or she is then being accommodated.

An emergency protection order may also be made if s.47 enquiries are being frustrated by access to the child being unreasonably refused to a person authorised to seek access, and the applicant has reasonable cause to believe that access is needed as a matter of urgency. An emergency protection order gives authority to remove a child and place him or her under the protection of the applicant for a maximum of eight days - with a possible extension of up to seven days.

Under s.46, where a police officer has reasonable cause to believe that a child would otherwise be likely to suffers significant harm, s/he may:

- Remove the child to suitable accommodation and keep him or her there; or
- Take reasonable steps to ensure that the child's removal from any hospital or other place in which the child is then being accommodated is prevented.

No child may be kept in police protection for more than 72 hours.

Secure Accommodation Order

The Court can make a secure accommodation order when:

- A young person has a history of running away and is likely to run away from any other kind of home or children's unit and when running away places him/herself in danger; or

- If the young person is not kept in secure accommodation, he/she is likely to injure himself or other people.

A child cannot be placed in secure accommodation for running away only. The Court has to be satisfied that the child is at risk of significant harm when he or she runs away. Secure accommodation is used for the purposes of protecting children or others from them, not for the purposes of punishment. On the first application the Court can make an order for up to three months. After this, the Court can allow social services to keep a child in secure accommodation for up to six months.

The Role of Area Child Protection Committees (ACPC)

ACPCs are made up of representatives from each of the main agencies tasked with ensuring the safety of children. Typically this could be the Local Education Authority, social services, health services, the police, the Probation Service, NSPCC, the Domestic Violence Forum or the Armed Services. The specific responsibilities of an ACPC are:

- Develop and agree local policies and procedures for inter-agency work to protect children.
- Audit and evaluate how well local services work together to protect children.
- Put in place objectives and performance indicators for child protection.
- Encourage and develop effective working relationships between different services and professional groups.
- Get different agencies to agree upon operational definitions and thresholds for intervention.
- Share knowledge gained through national and local experience and research.
- Undertake case reviews where a child has died or been seriously harmed and where abuse or neglect are confirmed or suspected.
- Communicate clearly to individual services and professional groups their shared responsibility for protecting children and how each of them can contribute.
- Improve the quality of child protection work and inter-agency working through inter-agency training and development.
- Raise awareness within the wider community of the need to safeguard children and promote their welfare.

All local authorities that have social service responsibilities have to produce a Children's Service Plan. These plans look at the needs of local children and the ways in which local services should work together to meet these needs. The local authority should also consider how all of the services that it offers such as education, social services, housing, youth groups, culture and leisure contribute to this. Different services should work together to plan action on particular matters for example substance misuse, domestic violence or youth offending.

The Initial Child Protection Conference

The initial child protection conference brings together family members, the child where appropriate, and those professionals most involved with the child and family following s.47 enquiries. Its purpose is twofold:

- To bring together and analyse in an inter-agency setting the information which has obtained about the child's health, development and functioning.
- To decide on future action - agreeing an outline child protection plan.

The Child Protection Plan

The main aim of this plan is to safeguard the child from further harm. The plan should describe the identified needs of the child and the services required. The plan should set out clearly the roles and responsibilities of those professionals in routine contact with the child and ensure that progress reviews are timetabled.

The Child Protection Review Conference

This should be held within three months of the initial child protection conference and further reviews should be held at intervals of not more than six months for as long as the child's name remains on the child protection register. It is at these reviews that a child's name may be removed from the register if it is judged that the child is no longer at continuing risk of significant harm requiring safeguarding by means of a child protection plan.

The Child Protection Register

A central register is maintained for each area covered by a social services department. The register should list all the children resident in the area who are considered to be at continuing risk of significant harm and for whom there is a child protection plan. The Department of Health hold lists of custodians of child protection registers.

FAMILY PROCEEDINGS

Part II of the Children Act 1989 covers matters within families where there will not generally be local authority involvement. In cases where there is a dispute about a child's welfare under these circumstances, the courts can make certain orders. Applicants for such orders can be the parent or guardian of the child, someone the child has lived with for three years or others with an interest in the child.

Residence Order

This order decides where the child/children should live. It is possible to apply for a joint residence order, but the courts do not usually like to make such orders especially if it will mean the child will have to divide their time between two homes. Parents that have a Residence Order are allowed to take the children out of the country for less than one month at a time without the other partner's consent. Permanent residence abroad generally requires partner consent and/or permission from the court.

Contact Order

A contact order allows for the parent who does not look after the child/children full-time to request a visit or stay for short periods, such as weekends or part of the holidays. The order can also decide who should collect and deliver the children for contact visits, where the contact visit should take place and at what time.

Family Assistance Order

This order means that a social worker will have occasional contact with the family. The court can only make a family assistance order if the family consents and it will not last for longer than six months.

Specific Issue Order

This order is given when parents or guardians cannot decide about other issues to do with the children, for example, what school they should go to, whether to change their surname, whether they should have a major operation etc. The parent or guardian applies to the court and lets them decide.

Prohibited Steps Order

A parent or guardian can apply to the court for a prohibited steps order if they think their partner is likely to try and take the child/children away. This order is also used to contest one partner taking the children to live abroad. If the child/children have already been taken out of the country this order may be used to help get them back but this depends on which country they have been taken to.

PROVISION OF CARE

This section will cover a range of programmes, schemes and standards that have been put in place to ensure that children are cared for in our society. It includes information on Quality Protects, Sure Start, Day Care and Childminding, Fostering and Adoption.

Quality Protects (QP) - www.doh.gov.uk/qualityprotects

The QP scheme is a large, national campaign that aims to work with the most disadvantaged and vulnerable children in society. It forms part of the Government's wider strategy for reducing social exclusion. QP was launched in September 1998 with the aim of providing the right specific help to ensure that disadvantaged children and young people are able to take maximum advantage of the services available. The key elements of the QP programme are:

- New national Government objectives for children's social services.

- An important role for local councillors in delivering the programme.
- Annual evaluation of councils QP Management Action Plans which set out how they intend to improve their services.
- Partnership between and within central and local government and with the health service and the voluntary sector.
- A new children's service grant of £885 million over five years.

There are a number of workstreams under QP, taking forward activity to deliver different parts of the objective's for children's social services. These include:

Children's Participation
This part of QP aims to encourage the participation of children young people and their families in the planning and delivery of services and in decisions that will affect their lives. The Government holds Make It Happen national events to bring young people in the care system into an environment where they can give feedback on the way the QP scheme impacts on their everyday lives.

Section 64
Section 64 of the Health Services and Public Health Act 1968 gives the Secretary of State for Health power to make grants to voluntary organisations in England, whose activities support the Department of Health's policy objectives relating to health and personal social services. The QP scheme works closely with groups that provide advocacy services for children and helps to assess applicants for new funding and evaluating priority projects.

Young People's Reference Group
This is a group that meets three times a year to seek children and young people's opinions about how QP should be making changes across all aspects of children's day to day lives. The ultimate aim being to guarantee that children's opinions are at the heart of the QP programme. This group was established at the Make It Happen participation event and it contains members representative of all the different groups of people in care such as those who are disabled or from an ethnic minority.

Teenagers to Work
Started by the QP programme last year, Teenagers to Work is an innovative participation project which enables local councils to put corporate parenting into practice. It offers young people in care the opportunity to participate in work experience at their local council or with a local employer.

Galleries/QP and Sport
These schemes were set up in the hope of giving people in need or in care the chance to develop their creative talents and increase their access to sport and leisure facilities. The Department of Health has combined with the Departments of Culture, Media and Sport and the Hayward Gallery to improve participation, achievement and innovation by those involved.

Framework for the Assessment of Children in Need and Their Families
The aim of this project is to ensure that referral and assessment processes discriminate effectively between different types and levels of need and produce a timely service response.

Leaving Care
The QP Project Team on Leaving Care was set up to help young people leaving care find work. Part of their work is to make sure that local authorities assess and meet the needs of care leavers aged 16 and over up to the age of 21. The Children (Leaving Care) Act was developed as part of this programme.

Disabled Children and Young People
This project is intended to get disabled children the maximum benefit they possibly can from education opportunities as well as health and social care. Benefits made available to disabled people include family support services (to enable them to go on short-term breaks); inclusive play and leisure services; extra information for parents; equitable access to healthcare; and supported inclusion in mainstream schooling.

Health Project Group
The Health Project Group was initiated to review the work already underway by various organisations targeted at improving the health of children in care or in need. From this position

they can plan and develop work to fill the gaps they have identified and advise local authorities and health authorities of the best steps to take to meet the specified targets.

Education of Looked After Children Project Group
Since February 1999 this section of QP has been helping local authorities meet the Government's objectives in relation to the educational opportunities that are available to children in need or in care. The aim of the Government is to increase to 75% by 2003 the proportion of children leaving care with at least one GCSE or GNVQ equivalent.

The group issued a guidance booklet "The Education of Children and Young People in Public Care" in May 2000. The key features of this guide were:

- All local authorities are now required to provide all children in care with a Personal Education Plan within 20 days of them joining a new school.
- Appoint a teacher in each school designated to act as a resource and advocate for children in care by linking with social services on their behalf.
- Placing deadlines within which local authorities must secure educational placements for children in care.
- Making it a requirement for local authorities to make it possible for Local Education Authorities and social service departments to share relevant, up-to-date information.
- An education implementation team is helping local authorities implement the guidance.

Black and Ethnic Minority Children and Their Families
This programme aims to ensure the provision of appropriate services for black and ethnic minority children and to influence future policy developments. It has set up four demonstration projects which will incorporate the views of black and ethnic minority children.

Children's Social Services Core Information Requirements
All 150 councils in England are to be brought to a minimum satisfactory capability in collecting and using information by this QP project. It is intended that this will bring together the process for assessment, planning intervention, reviewing and recording information for all children in need.

Costs and Resources Project Team
This project team will act on the information gathered by the Children in Need Data Collection to create a means whereby all local authorities can discover where their effort and expenditure is directed. Then, if necessary, they can make changes to their methodology in order to make their actions more effective in the future.

Reducing Offending Among Looked After Children
The purpose of this project is to cut the proportion of children aged 10-17 who have received a final warning or conviction while in care by one third from the September 2000 position. Local authorities will be expected to work closely with their Youth Offending Teams to try and achieve this task and to report their progress as part of their Quality Protects management action plans.

Make it Happen in Art
This project was established last year to focus on involving young people in art by promoting access to art galleries, museums and other similar cultural activities. Young people are given the chance to work with prominent artists and to develop skills in a range of media such as photography and sculpture.

Sure Start - www.surestart.gov.uk

Sure Start brings together services for young children with the aim of tackling child poverty and social exclusion. Sure Start is overseen by a steering group involving ministers from ten Government departments. At the time of going to press (July 2002) the steering group is chaired by Yvette Cooper, Parliamentary Under-Secretary of State for Public Health, and represented in Cabinet by Estelle Morris, Secretary of State for Education and Skills.
Sure Start programmes are run by local partnerships which include Local Education Authorities, social services departments, local arms of the NHS, voluntary and community organisations and parents. To date 260 programmes have been approved and another 177 are in the planning

process. The sixth round of programmes is set to add another 85 to the Sure Start scheme. The local programmes work with parents to improve children's life chances through better access to:

- Family support
- Advice on children's development
- Health Services
- Early learning

Objectives and Targets
Long-term objectives are set out in a Public Services Agreement (PSA), with further targets for implementation being detailed in the accompanying Service Delivery Agreement (SDA).

Objective 1: improving social and emotional development
PSA - To achieve by 2004 in the 500 Sure Start areas, a 20 percent reduction in the number of children aged 0-3 who are re-registered within the space of 12 months on the child protection register.
SDA

- All local Sure Start programmes to have agreed and implemented, in a culturally sensitive way, ways of caring for and supporting mothers with post-natal depression.
- One hundred per cent of families with young children to have been contacted by local programmes within the first two months of birth.

Objective 2: improving health
PSA - To achieve by 2004 in the 500 Sure Start areas, a ten per cent reduction in mothers who smoke in pregnancy.
SDA

- Parenting support and information to be available for all parents in Sure Start areas.
- All local programmes to give guidance on breast feeding, hygiene and safety.
- A ten per cent reduction in children in the Sure Start area aged 0-3 admitted to hospital as an emergency with gastro-enteritis, a respiratory infection or a severe injury.

Objective 3: improving children's ability to learn
PSA - To achieve by 2004 in the 500 Sure Start areas, a five percent reduction in the number of children with speech and language problems requiring specialist intervention by the age of four.
SDA

- All children in Sure Start areas to have access to good quality play and learning opportunities, helping progress towards early learning goals when they get to school.
- Increased use of libraries by parents with young children in Sure Start areas.

Objective 4: strengthening families and communities
PSA - To achieve by 2004 in the 500 Sure Start areas, a reduction of at least 12 per cent in the number of 0-3 year old children living in households where no-one is working.
SDA

- 75 per cent of families reporting personal evidence of an improvement in the quality of services providing family support.
- All Sure Start programmes to have parent representation on the local programme board.
- All Sure Start programmes to have developed local target for ensuring links between the local Sure Start partnership and Jobcentre Plus.

- All Sure Start programmes to work with their Early Years Development Childcare Partnership (EYDCP) to help close the gap between the availability of accessible childcare for 0-3 year olds in Sure Start Areas and other areas.

Core Services

The design and content of local Sure Start programmes will vary according to local needs. However, the following core services are expected:

- Outreach and home visiting.
- Support for families and parents.
- Support for good quality play, learning and childcare experiences for children.
- Primary and community health care, including advice about family health and child health and development.
- Support for children and parents with special needs, including help getting access to specialised services.

Key Principles

To ensure a consistent approach, every programme works from a shared set of key principles. Sure Start services must:

- Co-ordinate, streamline and add value to existing services in the Sure Start area.
- Involve parents, grandparents and other carers in ways that build on their existing strengths.
- Avoid stigma by ensuring that all local families are able to use Sure Start services.
- Ensure lasting support by linking Sure Start to services for older children.
- Be culturally appropriate and sensitive to particular needs.
- Promote the participation of all local families in the design and working of the programme.

Sure Start Plus

Sure Start Plus is a pilot programme providing personal support and advice for pregnant teenagers. Its aim is to enable them to make well informed decisions about their pregnancy and provide young parents-to-be with co-ordinated packages of support tailored to individual needs. There are 20 pilot areas and Sure Starts programmes in these areas are expected to work closely with Sure Start Plus.

***To contact* Sure Start:**
Level 2, Caxton House
Tothill Street
London SW1H 9NA
Tel: 020 7273 4830
Fax: 020 7273 5182
sure.start@dfes.gsi.gov.uk
www.surestart.gov.uk

Day Care and Childminding

As part of the Government's commitment to promote the welfare and development of all young children, the National Childcare Strategy was launched in 1998. The aim of this strategy is to ensure that all childcare services provide a secure and safe environment for children. Under provisions in Part VI of the Care Standards Act 2000, responsibility for the regulation of day care and childminding has transferred from local authorities to OFSTED in the summer of 2001.

New National Standards for day care and childminding were published on 8th May 2001. The National Standards came into force from 2nd July 2001 for new applications for registration for day care or childminding to be made to OFSTED and from 1st September 2001 for providers who are already registered by a Local Authority under Part X of the Children Act 1989. There are five different types of day care and childminding provision that are covered by the 14 National Standards.

- Full day care
  Defined as facilities that provide day care for children under eight for a continuous period of four hours or more in any day in premises, which are not domestic premises.

- Sessional day care
  Defined as facilities that provide day care for children under eight for a session which is less than a continuous period of four hours in any day in premises which are not domestic premises.

- Crèches
  Defined as facilities that provide occasional care for children under eight and are provided on particular premises on more than five days a year. They need to be registered where they run for more than two hours a day, even where individual children attend for shorter periods. Some are in permanent premises and care for children while parents are engaged in particular activities, e.g. shopping or sport. Others are established on a temporary basis to care for children while their parents are involved in time-limited activities, e.g. a conference or exhibition.

- Out of school care
  Defined as facilities that provide day care for children under eight, which operate before or after school or during the school holidays. The total care provided is for more than two hours in any day and for more than five days a year.

- Childminders
  A childminder is registered to look after one or more children under the age of eight to whom they are not related on domestic premises for reward and for a total of more than two hours in any day.

The National Standards

1. Suitable - Adults providing day care, looking after children or having unsupervised access to them are suitable to do so.
2. Organisation - The registered person meets required adult child ratios, ensures that training and qualifications requirements are met and organises space and resources to meet the children's needs effectively.
3. Care, learning and play - The registered person meets children's individual needs and promotes their welfare. They plan and provide activities and play opportunities to develop children's emotional, physical, social and intellectual capabilities.
4. Physical environment - The premises are safe, secure and suitable for their purpose.
5. Equipment - Furniture, equipment and toys are provided which are appropriate for their purpose and help to create an accessible and stimulating evironment.
6. Safety - The registered person takes positive steps to promote safety within the setting and on outings and ensures proper precautions are taken to prevent accidents.
7. Health - The registered person promotes the good health of children and takes positive steps to prevent the spread of infection and appropriate measures when they are ill.
8. Food and drink - Children are provided with regular drinks and food in adequate quantities for their needs.
9. Equal opportunities - The registered person and staff actively promote equality of opportunity and anti-discriminatory practice for all children.
10. Special needs - Steps are taken to promote the welfare and development of the child within the setting in partnership with the parents and other relevant parties.
11. Behaviour - Adults caring for children are able to manage a wide range of children's behaviour in a way, which promotes their welfare and development.

12. Working in partnership with parents and carers - The registered person and staff work in partnership with parents to meet the needs of the children, both individually and as a group.

13. Child protection - The registered person complies with local child protection procedures approved by the Area Child Protection Committee.

14. Documentation - Records, policies and procedures, which are required for the efficient and safe management of the provision, are maintained.

Full details of the National Standards are available online at www.dfes.gov.uk/daycare/index.shtml and in print from:

DfES Publicaitons
PO Box 5050
Shrewood Park
Annesley
Nottingham NG15 0DJ
T: 0845 6022260 F: 0845 6033360
dfes@prolog.uk.com

Consultation

The Government is currently in the middle of a consultation process regarding early years and childcare regulation. In particular, how to regulate childcare facilities in independent and maintained schools and how to regulate childcare for the over sevens. Currently schools are not required to have childcare facilities registered and inspected by OFSTED. The DfES is proposing a scheme whereby OFSTED will issue over sevens childcare providers with a certificate confirming suitability to look after children. The consultation on this proposal ended on 24th May 2002 with results expected to be published later in 2002. For further information visit www.dfes.gov.uk/consultations.

Fostering and the Commissioning of Placements

On 20th March 2002 Health Minister Jacqui Smith announced a major review of fostering and placement choice, "Choice Protects". The aim of this government review is to help local authorities provide stability for looked after children through the commissioning of placements and a better framework of reward and support for foster carers. The review will look at the following areas:

- All aspects of commissioning, such as assessing need, market management, and commissioning skills and practices;
- Roles and status of foster care, including training and support, reward, recruitment and retention.

The review will ensure that the commissioning and provision of placements sits well alongside the work already being done to reform and develop Adoption services such as the work of the Adoption and Permanence Taskforce, and the provisions in the Adoption and Children Bill going through Parliament in 2002.

The National Care Standards Commission is responsible for inspecting a range of registered organisations, using the regulations and standards published in April 2002. In children's services, these include Children's Homes, Fostering Services, the welfare arrangements for Boarding Schools, Residential Special Schools and F.E. colleges accommodating students under 18.

Adoption - www.doh.gov.uk/adoption

Adoption Register for England and Wales - www.adoptionregister.net

This is a free service available to local councils and voluntary adoption agencies launched in England in August 2001 with the Welsh section following shortly after. It was established under existing legislation and will be underpinned by the Adoption and Children Bill. It is intended to eliminate delays in linking children needing new families with people waiting to adopt. The Register is a computer database that holds information on children and parents and suggests possible links. This service is fully funded by the government and is operated by Norwood Ravenswood on behalf of the Department of Health and the National Assembly for Wales. With the national infrastructure in place it is hoped that the waiting time between entry and care will be reduced from the current average of two years and ten months. Children who are older, disabled or part of a sibling group may have to wait even longer. Local councils in

England and Wales are required to place details of all children waiting to be adopted and all approved adoptive families on the Register after obtaining their informed consent. Once a child or family has been placed on the register social workers will search for an adoptive family locally for three months and if this is unsuccessful they will use the Register to broaden their search area. Once a match has been agreed, social workers will inform the Register so that its records can be updated.

Adoption and Children Bill 2001
This is a radical overhaul of adoption law intended to replace the Adoption Act 1976 and modernise the existing legal framework for domestic and international adoption. The government aims to increase the number of adoptions of children in care by 40% by 2004/5. Currently 70% of them leave care at 16 without any qualifications and the beneficial effects of putting them in a stable family environment cannot be underestimated. The Bill includes provisions to:

- Align adoption law with the Children Act 1989 so that the welfare of the child is the paramount consideration in all decisions.
- Encourage more people to adopt by making extra support available if needed.
- Enable the Secretary of State to establish an independent review mechanism for applicants to adopt who feel they are being turned down unfairly.
- Reduce potentially damaging hold-ups in the process by implementing measures that make it a requirement for courts to draw up timetables for adoption.
- Co-ordinate the release of information about adopted people and birth families so that it happens in the correct way and their views are taken into consideration as much as possible.
- Improve the legal controls on international adoption as well as strengthening the safeguards on arranging adoptions and advertising children for adoption.
- Introduce a new special guardianship order to provide permanent care for those children for whom adoption is not the best option.
- £66.5 million to improve services and support for children and their adoptive family.

If the Bill is approved by Parliament its main provisions will be brought into force in 2004. However, some parts, such as those providing adoption support for new adoptive families and the independent review mechanism will be introduced as early as April 2003.

National Adoption Standards for England
These were published in August 2001 and they help ensure that children, prospective adopters, birth families and others know what they can expect from the adoption service.

Adoption and Permanence Taskforce
The Taskforce helps councils to deliver better adoption services and spread best practice. It supports their efforts to improve performance on planning and delivering permanent homes for children in care. It encourages the use of adoption as an option for meeting the needs of these children and providing effective support to all parties involved. Delays in the court system are also a major problem so the government intends to increase the number of judges able to deal with family work and make better use of those already trained in such matters.

VOLUNTARY ORGANISATIONS

Services for children and families were pioneered by voluntary organisations in the 19th century. They may be grant-aided by central or local government, but most rely considerably on voluntary income as well. They vary in size and objectives and provide between them a very wide range of childcare services. A number of organisations exist at both local and national level to give advice and support specifically to lone parent families. Some of the major ones are listed below and many more services are listed in Waterlow's annual publication, Charities Digest.

Barnado's
Tanner's Lane, Barkingside, Ilford, Essex IG6 1QG Tel: 020 8550 8822
Barnado's is engaged in community work and the care of children in their own families and adoptive homes.

BPAS - British Pregnancy Advice Service
Head Office, Austy Manor, Wootton Wawen, Solihull, West Midlands B95 6BX
Tel: 01564 793225 Fax: 01564 794935 Actionline: 08457 30 40 30
info@bpas.org www.bpas.org
BPAS, established in 1968, is a registered non-profit organisation, with over 30 consultation centres and 12 clinics and daycare units nationwide. BPAS treats all clients with dignity and respect and provides confidential non-judgmental services.

Catholic Child Welfare Council
Child Care Secreatry of the Council, St Josephs, Watford Way, Hendon, London NW4 4TY
Tel: 020 8203 6323
A federation of the Catholic agencies concerned with childcare. The Council promotes the welfare of children and families, offers advice and training and encourages high standards of professional practice. A wide variety of services for children and families are provided by Catholic Children's Societies and diocesan caring agencies around the country.

Children's Society
Edward Rudolf House, 69-85 Margery Street, London WC1X 0JL Tel: 020 7841 4400
The Children's Society provides a comprehensive programme of childcare, including preventative work involving field social workers and community based projects, residential care, adoption and fostering.

The Church of England
Church House, Great Smith Street, London SW1P 3NZ Tel: 020 7898 1000
The Church of England offers a service for lone parents in some dioceses. A number of diocesan agencies are also registered adoption societies. Information about their work can be obtained from the Social Policy Committee of the Board for Social Responsibility at the above address.

Daycare Trust
21 St George's Road, London SE1 6ES Tel: 020 7840 3350 Fax: 020 7840 3355
www.daycaretrust.org.uk
Daycare Trust provides information to parents, employers and policy-makers about childcare issues.

Families Need Fathers
134 Curtain Road, London EC2A 3AR Tel/fax: 020 7613 5060 www.fnf.org.uk
Families Need Fathers promotes research into the problems facing children and parents from divided families.

Family Rights Group
The Print House, 18 Ashwin Street, London E8 3DL Tel: 020 7923 2628
An independent national organisation which advises families, whether involved in child protection procedures, or with children in accommodation or care, or receiving support from social services. It has lists of agencies and solicitors who are willing to act in care proceedings, panels of professional experts willing to prepare independent reports for the courts and details of support and self-help groups.

Family Service Units
207 Old Marylebone Road, London NW1 5QP Tel: 020 7402 5175
The Units study the influences which may cause or prevent family breakdown and provide a comprehensive family welfare service from local FSUs in England and Scotland for families under strain.

Family Welfare Association
501-505 Kingsland Road, London E8 4AU Tel: 020 7254 6251 Fax: 020 7249 5443
FWA.headoffice@fwa.org.uk
The FWA provides social care and financial support. Centres within London, the South East, East Anglia and the Midlands offer a variety of services, including work with families of abused or potentially abused children, support for people with mental health problems and practical help for carers. FWA's range of counselling services include well-family work in GP practices. Financial support for families in exceptional need is available throughout the UK.

Gingerbread
7 Sovereign Court, London E1W 3HW Tel: 020 7488 9300 Advice Line: 0800 018 4318
Gingerbread was started in 1970 and is a leading support organisation for lone parent families in England and Wales. A network of local groups provides practical help and emotional support on a mutual aid basis.

Gingerbread Ireland
29-30 Dame Street, Dublin 2, Republic of Ireland Tel: 00 353 1 671 0291

Gingerbread Northern Ireland
169 University Street, Belfast BT7 1HR Tel: 028 9023 1417

Gingerbread Scotland
1307 Argyle Street, Glasgow G3 8TL Tel: 0141 576 5085/7976

Home-Start UK
2 Salisbury Road, Leicester LE1 7QR Tel: 0116 233 9955
Home-Start UK promotes the welfare of families with a child under five years old. Local Home-Starts operate through trained volunteers who befriend and support in the family home to prevent crisis and breakdown.

National Council for One Parent Families
255 Kentish Town Road, London NW5 2LX Tel: 020 7428 5400 Helpline: 0800 018 5026
Info@oneparentfamiles.org.uk
The National Council for One Parent Families runs an information service for lone parents, other organisations, local authorities and the media. It also campaigns and lobbies to change the law and improve provisions for lone parent families.

National Council of Voluntary Child Care Organisations (NCVCCO)
Unit 4, Pride Court, 80-82 White Lion Street, London N1 9FF Tel: 020 7833 3319 Fax: 020 7833 8637 www.ncvcco.org
NCVCCO is the umbrella organisation for voluntary child care organisations in England to ensure the well being and safeguarding of children by promoting the voluntary sector's contribution to the provision of services.

National Early Years Network
77 Holloway Road, London N7 8JZ Tel: 020 7607 9573
The national umbrella group for organisations concerned with the early years and social provision.

National Society for the Prevention of Cruelty to Children (NSPCC)
National Centre, 42 Curtain Road, London EC2A 3NH Tel: 020 7825 2500 24 hour helpline: 0800 800 500
The NSPCC is the UK's leading charity specialising in child protection and the prevention of cruelty to children. It operates over 150 Child Protection Teams and various projects including a national programme offering training to childcare professionals.

NCH Action for Children
85 Highbury Park, London N5 1UD Tel: 020 7226 2033
NCH provides a comprehensive service for children and young people in various forms of residential and community care. Much of the work is concentrated on new forms of childcare outside state provision.

One Parent Families Scotland
13 Gayfield Square, Edinburgh EH1 3NX Tel: 0131 556 3899 Helpline: 0800 018 5026 Fax: 0131 557 7899 Info@opfs.org.uk www.opfs.org.uk
One Parent Families Scotland has been working since 1944 to help lone parents. A national voluntary organisation, registered as a charity whose members include individual lone parents, various organisations working with lone parents and others who just simply want to support the cause of lone parents.

PARENTLINE Plus
Unit 520 Highgate Studios, 53-57 Highgate Road, London NW5 1TL Tel: 020 7289 5500 Helpline: 0808 800 2222
Parentline Plus is a network of helplines for parents having any kind of problem with a child.

Parents Online
21 Universal Marine, Crableck Lane, Sarisbury Green, Southampton, Hants SO31 7ZN info@parents.org.uk www.parents.org.uk
The UK website for parents by parents covering all aspects or parenting including education, leisure and health.

RPS Rainer
Rectory Lodge, High Street, Brastead, Westerham, Kent TN16 1JF Tel: 01959 578200
RPS Rainer works exclusively with young people aged between 10 and 25 in trouble or need. The work is project-based and offers schemes for young offenders and housing projects for homeless people.

Save the Children Fund
Mary Datchelor House, 17 Grove Lane, London SE5 8RD Tel: 020 7703 5400
Save the Children is an independent international organisation, professionally staffed, whose purpose is to achieve lasting benefits for children within the communities in which they live and promote children's rights in the UK and overseas.

Shared Parenting Information Group (SPIC) UK
28 Garraways, Wotten Bassett SN4 8LL Tel: 01793 851544
SPIC promotes responsible shared parenting after separation or divorce by making available information research and resources to all concerned.

Section Two: Care and the Community

INTRODUCTION

This section is concerned with personal social services available to older people and those with a physical disability, a learning disability or mental health problems. The term physical disability, as used here, includes conditions caused by illness, injury or birth defect and includes sensory impairments such as blindness or deafness.
After a brief outline of the legislation and bodies involved in providing care for these groups of people, general information on services is provided. This is followed by information on services specific to particular groups and the relevant Government policies are presented in the following order:

- Physical disability including visual and hearing impairments
- Learning disability
- Mental health
- Older people

A brief outline then follows of the provision of training for personal social services staff. Finally, many of the social care arrangements made by social services for the groups of people highlighted above require the co-operation of voluntary organisations. These organisations have in many cases pioneered such services at national and local level and this chapter finishes with a list of them and their contact details.

LEGISLATION

Full information on all legislation passed since 1988 is available from the website of Her Majesty's Stationery Office www.hmso.gov.uk.

The National Assistance Act 1948

This Act laid the foundations for the present system of welfare services. It empowered local authorities to make arrangements in effect for older people and those with physical or learning disabilities or mental health problems.

Chronically Sick and Disabled Persons Act 1970

This Act extended the provisions for people with a disability defined in Section 29 of the 1948 Act. Section one place authorities under a duty to inform themselves of numbers and needs and to publish information on services provided. Section 2 places authorities under a duty to arrange non-residential services for people where they are satisfied that it is necessary to do so.

The National Health Service Act 1977

This Act consolidates the powers of local authorities to provide for the prevention of illness and for the care and after-care of persons who are, or have been, suffering from illness.

The Residential Homes Act 1980

This Act empowered district authorities to provide meals and recreation for older people in their own homes or elsewhere.

The Mental Health Act 1983

This Act deals with detention in hospital or guardianship, normally by local authorities, or people suffering from defined mental health problems and with consent to provide after-care services for patients who have been detained under certain section of the Act. At the time of going to press the draft **Mental Health Bill 2002**, which will replace much of this legislation, was in consultation. This bill will be discussed further in this chapter.

The Registered Homes Act 1984

This Act consolidated previous legislation on nursing homes and on the registration, inspection and conduct of voluntary and private residential homes. Please refer to the Care Standards Act 2000 as it supersedes much of this legislation.

Disabled Persons (Services, Consultation and Representation) Act 1986

This Act was intended to improve services for people with a physical disability, learning disability or mental health problem, adding to the provision of the 1970 Act for assessment, the provision of information and advocacy. Sections 1, 2, 3 and 7 have been superseded by the NHS and Community Care Act 1990.

NHS and Community Care Act 1990

This Act provides the legislative base for the provision of community care services, and in particular section 47 places a duty on authorities to assess the needs of people who may be in need of community services.

The Carers (Recognition and Services) Act 1995

This Act came into effect on 1 April 1996. It requires local authorities to assess the circumstances of a carer providing substantial care on a regular basis to an adult in need or a child with a disability, at that carer's request. The assessment must inform the care plan for the person in need.

Disability Discrimination Act 1995

The Disability Discrimination Act became law in November 1995 and many of its main provisions came into force on 2 December 1996. The Act has introduced new rights and measures aimed at ending the discrimination, which many disabled people face. Disabled people now have new rights in the areas of employment; getting goods and services; and buying or renting property. Further rights of access to goods and services to protect disabled people from discrimination will be phased in. These require service providers to make reasonable adjustments to policies, procedure and practices; to provide auxiliary aids and services and, where premises are inaccessible, to provide these services by a reasonable alternative means; and to make reasonable adjustments to premises (from 2004). Under the Act, schools, colleges and universities must provide information for disabled people and their parents. The Act also allows the Government to draw up regulations which will require all new public transport vehicles and systems to be accessible. For information on the Disability Discrimination Act visit the website www.disability.gov.uk/dda/.

Community Care (Direct Payments) Act 1996

This came into effect on 1 April 1997. It empowers authorities to provide cash payments for those assessed as needing community care services. People between the ages of 18 and 65 are provided with the funds to purchase and manage their own care if they are competent and wish to do so.

Care Standards Act 2000

The Care Standards Act 2000 is the culmination of two white papers published by the Government in November 1998 and March 1999 detailing proposals for social services in England and Wales. In summary this act:

- Initiates a new independent regulatory body for social care and private and voluntary healthcare services in England known as the National Care Standards Commission (NCSC);
- Provides for an arm of the National Assembly for Wales to be the regulatory body for such services in Wales;
- Sets up new Councils to register social care workers, sets standards in social care work and regulates the education and training of social workers in England and Wales;
- Establishes an office of the Children's Commissioner for Wales;
- Reforms the regulations of childminders and day care provision for young children;
- Provides for the Secretary of State to maintain a list of individuals who are considered unsuitable to work with vulnerable adults.
- Remove the exemption on the requirement to register in the case of small private children's homes (those that provide care for less than four children).

The main purpose of the act is reform of the regulatory system for care services in England and Wales so that for the first time, local authorities will be required to meet the same standards as independent sector providers. The new arrangements will replace those set out in the Registered Homes Act 1984 and those provisions in the Children Act 1989 which deal with the regulation of voluntary children's homes and registered children's homes. Community homes will now be regulated, as will local authority fostering and adoption services. The National Care Standards

Commission will carry out this monitoring. The General Social Care Council will register social care workers, regulate the training of social workers and raise standards in social care through publishing codes of conduct and practice.

OFFICIAL BODIES

National Care Standards Commission (NCSC)

This became fully operational in April 2002, replacing the now disbanded implementation team in the Department of Health. The NCSC is a national, independent body established by the Care Standards Act 2000 to improve the quality of care services in England and improve the protection of vulnerable people using these services. It is responsible for care homes, children's homes, domiciliary care agencies, independent fostering agencies, private and voluntary hospitals and clinics and nurses' agencies as well as inspecting local authority fostering and adoption and the welfare of boarding school pupils. The duties of the NCSC will include:

- Inspecting regulated services against a set of regulations and National Minimum Standards.
- Investigating complaints and concerns.
- Taking action against those who fail to comply with the regulations.
- Making information about their services available to the public.
- Providing advice, guidance, and support to service providers.
- Reporting regularly to the Secretary of State for Health on the range and quality of services in England.

On 19th April 2002 the Secretary of State for Health announced plans to establish two new independent inspectorates, the Commission for Social Care Inspection and the Commission for Healthcare Audit and Inspection. These new bodies will further strengthen the system for inspecting health and social care, ensure clearer public accountability and rationalise the number of bodies regulating health and social care.

The Commission for Social Care Inspection will create a single comprehensive Inspectorate for social care, bringing together the inspection functions of the Social Services Inspectorate and the National Care Standards Commission and including the regulation of social care providers.

The National Care Standards Commission and the Social Services Inspectorate will continue their existing work until the new body goes live. Legislation to establish the new inspectorates will be introduced as soon as Parliamentary time allows.

General Social Care Council (GSCC)

On 1 October 2001 the first regulatory body for the social care profession in England was launched. Set up under the Care Standards Act 2000, the GSCC aims to increase the protection of service users, their carers and the general public. It has responsibility for agreeing and issuing statutory codes of conduct and practice, setting up a register of social care workers, dealing with matters of conduct and regulating and supporting social work education and training. The GSCC describes its objectives as:

- To create a well-trained and accountable social care workforce.
- To make public and private sector employers responsible and accountable.
- To increase public confidence through higher standards.
- To ensure good practice.
- To move social care up the political agenda.
- To improve the public image of the profession.

In order to achieve this the GSCC will set up a comprehensive register of social care workers; launch a new degree in social work to raise professional standards; and embark on a rigorous regulatory regime. Similar organisations will perform these roles in Wales (Care Council for Wales), Northern Ireland (Northern Ireland Social Care Council) and Scotland (Scottish Social Services Council).

Social Care Institute for Excellence (SCIE)

The Department of Health and the National Assembly for Wales set up SCIE as part of the government's Quality Strategy for Social Care. It will work closely with government and the new regulatory bodies (the GSCC, Social Services Inspectorate and NCSC) to produce best practice guidelines in social care. These guidelines will be widely available and should help to produce better training and organisational development.

Social Services Inspectorate (SSI)

The SSI gives every local authority a star rating to help people judge how well their council is performing its duty to provide social services. These ratings range from three stars (excellent) to zero stars (poor) in the same way as is used to assess NHS authorities. The best-rated councils will receive more freedoms while those that are under performing will be subject to special restrictive measures. For example, three star councils will have access to their share of the social services Performance Fund by right while councils with one or zero stars will need to have their schemes approved in advance. Councils such as this have to produce an action plan explaining how they are going to improve performance and provide regular monitoring information to the SSI. An annual review meeting is held between each council and the SSI to bring out strengths, areas for development and actions for the coming year. Following this meeting the SSI inspector drafts a letter to the Director of Social Services describing the performance of the council during the previous year. This letter is later published on the Department of Health website along with the star rating that each local authority received. This gives people the opportunity to compare the performance of their local authority with others throughout the country.

GENERAL SERVICES

Community Nurses and Health Visitors

Community nurses visit people at home to give nursing care. They also arrange for aids and equipment for home nursing to be provided. Health visitors support families with disabled children.

GP Services

General Practitioners provide general medical care and can refer patients to other NHS professionals. Many practices offer a range of services such as health promotion clinics as well as routine consultations.

Occupational Therapists

Occupational therapists work with people of any age with physical or mental health problems to promote their independence in caring for themselves, in employment and in leisure activities.

Physiotherapists

Physiotherapists have specialist skills in the treatment and rehabilitation of people. They work widely in hospitals and the community, often as part of a multi-disciplinary rehabilitation team, offering a range of therapies to enable sick, elderly or disabled people to function as well as possible.

Social Workers/Care Managers

Social workers work within the community or in hospitals. They assess needs and provide services and equipment to patients. They also provide support, help with welfare benefits, and any other issues that concern the patient.

Speech and Language Therapists

Speech and language therapists treat children and adults with communication difficulties from a wide range of different causes. When it is not possible to achieve spoken language, they provide instruction in other methods such as signing or the use of technological aids.

Day Care Centres

These are facilities for recreation and training to help people back to work. They may offer some supported employment, educational and sporting activities, and provide an opportunity to meet socially.

Equipment and Adaptations

Social services provide a range of aids and equipment for people to use at home. They work with housing departments and associations to provide adaptations, usually following an assessment from an occupational therapist.

Home Care

Home care or home help services can help people with their personal and domestic care needs.

Meals on Wheels

This scheme delivers hot meals to people in their homes who are incapacitated and unable to cook for themselves.

Residential Care

The care assessment of a patient may result in a decision to provide residential accommodation in a residential care home or a nursing home. If so, the local authority will either provide a place in one of its own homes or contract with an independent home to provide a place. When an authority places someone in a home, it assesses on a means tested basis the ability of the resident to contribute to the cost.

PHYSICAL DISABILITY

The wide range of personal social services for people with a physical disability can be divided broadly into those which are designed to help people live as independently as possible in the community and those which provide residential care. Although the local authority is required to keep a register of all people with a physical disability in its area, registration is voluntary and not a prerequisite for help. Although it is entirely voluntary, people with a disability are encouraged to register, as this provides information on the incidence of disability and assists in the planning of appropriate services.

Disability Rights Commission

The Disability Rights Commission (DRC) is an independent body set up by the Government to help secure civil rights for disabled people. Its statutory duties are:

1. To work to eliminate discrimination against disabled people.
2. To promote equal opportunities for disabled people.
3. To encourage good practice in the treatment of disabled people.
4. To advise the Government on the working of disability legislation (the Disability Discrimination Act (DDA) 1995 and the Disability Rights Commission Act 1999).

The Disability Rights Commission has launched a public consultation on recommendations for changes to the Disability Discrimination Act - its first review of the legislation. The recommendations include:

- making it easier for disabled people, particularly mental health service users, to get protection under the DDA
- preventing employers from making disability-related enquiries before a job is offered (except in a few specified circumstances)
- calling for an EU Directive to prevent discrimination on the grounds of disability in relation to a broad range of goods and services.

Responses to the consultation must be received by 16th August 2002.

DRC Helpline
Freepost MID 02164
Stratford-upon-Avon
CV37 9HY
Tel: 08457 622 633 Fax 08457 778 878
Textphone 08457 622 644
www.drc-gb.org

Blind or Visually Impaired

Blind or visually impaired people are entitled to equipment and alterations in their homes, machines for playing talking books, training in the use of Braille or Moon (simplified raised print), a television licence at reduced cost as well as social worker support for themselves and their families. Please see the section on voluntary organisations for further help and information.

Deaf or Hearing Impaired

Deaf or hearing impaired people are entitled to home equipment and alterations such as textphones, flashing doorbells and loop systems for listening to television. Social services should also provide them with information on interpreter services and lip reading classes as well as social worker support form themselves and their families. Please see the section on voluntary organisations for further help and information.

Deafblind

Deafblindness is a term used to refer to those who suffer from a combined sight and hearing impairment. The dual sensory loss may make it difficult or impractical for them to benefit from mainstream services or those that are aimed primarily at deaf or blind people who rely on one sense to compensate for the loss of another. Social services for disabled adults are normally provided by the National Assistance Act 1948 in conjunction with the Chronically Sick and Disabled Persons Act 1970. According to this and the Deafblind Circular (Local Authority Circular LAC (2001) 8), local authorities should take the following action with regards to deafblind people:

- Identify, make contact with and keep a record of deafblind people in their catchment area.
- Ensure that when an assessment is required or requested, it is carried out by a specifically trained person or team.
- Guarantee that the services provided to deafblind people are appropriate.
- Give them access to specifically trained one-to-one support workers if they need one.
- Provide information about services in formats and methods that are accessible to them.
- Assign overall responsibility for deafblind services to one member of the senior management team.

From 2001-02, a new Promoting Independence Grant replaces the previous Partnership and Prevention Special Grants. This fund could be a suitable source of funding for providing deafblind services. It incorporates an additional £100 million for social services announced on 27 November 2000. The total Grant in 2001-02 is £296 million.

LEARNING DISABILITY - www.doh.gov.uk/learningdisabilities

Social services departments, the NHS, housing agencies, the education services, and voluntary and community organisations provide services and information for people with learning disabilities. The Department of Health has worked with several other Government Departments on a White Paper, *Valuing People: A New Strategy for Disability in the 21st Century*, designed to improve support for people with learning disabilities and their families.

Valuing People: A New Strategy for Disability in the 21st Century

Published on 20th March 2001, this was the first white paper on learning disability for 30 years and it sets out a programme of action for improving services. It is based on four key principles: civil rights, independence, choice and inclusion. Valuing People takes a lifelong approach, beginning with an integrated approach to services for disabled children and their families and then providing new opportunities for a full and purposeful life as adults. The proposals are intended to produce improvements in education, social services, health, employment, housing and support.

The Learning Disability Task Force and Implementation Support Team

In December 2001, Health Minister Jacqui Smith appointed the Learning Disability Task Force to oversee implementation of the proposals set out in the White Paper *Valuing People; A New Strategy for Learning Disability for the 21st Century.* For further information on the task force, refer to the website.

The Learning Disability Development Fund (LDDF)

The LDDF was created in April 2002 by the Valuing People White Paper to provide an estimated £30 million to assist local authorities in paying for improved services for people with learning difficulties as well as the Implementation Support Team.

Carers and Disabled Children Act 2000

This Act enables local authorities to offer support to carers in their area who may need assistance looking after someone with a long-term illness or a disability. Since 1996 when the Carers (Recognition and Services) Act 1995 came into force, carers who provide a substantial amount of care on a regular basis have been entitled, on request, to an assessment of their ability to care. The results of this assessment are taken into account when decisions are made about the type and level of community care services to be provided for the person cared for. This Act makes several changes to the law and gives local authorities the power to supply certain services, which help the person cared for, direct to their carer following assessment. It also allows them to make direct payments to carers and parents of disabled children for the services that meet their own assessed needs. For carers to get the opportunity to take a break from their care duties, the Act provides voucher schemes that provide cover while they take a short break.

The Learning Disability Helpline - www.mencap.org.uk

Launched on 3 December 2001, the Learning Disability Helpline is available on Freephone 0808 808 1111. It is jointly funded by the Department of Health and Mencap and it provides information and advice on a range of issues such as support, welfare benefits, health, housing, learning and employment for people with disabilities as well as parents, carers and professionals working in the learning disability field. The helpline can also link enquirers up with organisations or services in their own area by making use of Mencap's local knowledge and network of contacts nationwide.

Adult Placement (AP) Schemes

AP carers offer people aged 18 and over an alternative and highly flexible form of accommodation and support. They give the opportunity to live an ordinary domestic life as part of the AP carers' family. An AP carer can give short or long term accommodation for between one and three adults. They have all the opportunities for personal development such as a variety of work, education and training and a range of leisure activities together with the chance to develop and maintain personal and family relationships. AP schemes ensure that the choice of adult placement is based upon a prior assessment of the prospective service user's needs. Service users are involved in the selection of AP carers and there is a written placement agreement for each service user placed with an AP carer.

Joint Investment Plans - www.doh.gov.uk/jointunit

In April 2001, Joint Investment Plans for learning disabilities and welfare to work for disabled people was introduced. The objective of the Joint Investment Plan for people with learning disabilities is to promote the provision of integrated services that will help adults with learning disabilities achieve and sustain maximum independence. Health and local authorities supervise the Joint Investment Plans, which are three-year rolling programmes.

The British Institute of Learning Disabilities - www.bild.org.uk

BILD is involved in a number of projects, programmes and initiatives for people with learning disabilities.

1. **Support for Older Carers**
   This project has been exploring how local authorities can provide support for the family carers of older people with a learning disability. BILD is working with authorities in six localities across England to set up groups for older carers to explore topics such as: planning for the future; new services in the pipeline; welfare benefits for people with a learning disability and their carers; changing supports as needs change with increasing age.

2. **Physical interventions**
   As part of an ongoing programme of work to improve practice around the use of physical interventions BILD is:

   - Working with training organisations to develop a core curriculum for training staff in physical interventions.
   - Developing a training proposal to measure the impact of training on staff performance.
   - Preparing model policies for Local Education Authorities and for special schools (funded by the Department of Education and Skills).
   - Preparing risk assessment protocols to assist teachers in responding to the

risk posed by the challenging behaviours presented by pupils in special schools (funded by the Department of Education and Skills).

3. **Citizen Advocacy**
The BILD Citizen Advocacy Project currently working with local advocacy groups and organisations to produce common guidelines and explore the benefits of local affiliations between advocacy groups. Another aim of this project is to map the existing provision of advocacy groups across the UK.

4. **Access to Health Services**
BILD is working with Sandwell Health Authority and the University of Birmingham to find out what helps people with a learning disability to get access to good quality health care. As a part of this work Sandwell Health Authority is consulting with staff families and service users before introducing changes which will make it easier for people with a learning disability to get the healthcare they need.

5. **Development of the National Electronic Library for Learning Disability**
In collaboration with the NHS Information Authority, The National electronic Library for Health (NeLH) has as its aim the delivery of best current knowledge, using web based browser technology. NeLH has core collections, and will also have a network of virtual branch libraries. BILD has developed a beta test site for a virtual branch library for learning disability (www.minervation.com/ld). The site structure is based on some of the key headings from Valuing People.

MENTAL HEALTH - www.doh.gov.uk/mentalhealth

At any one time one adult in six suffers from mental illness, which makes it as common as asthma. Most people with mental health difficulties are cared for by their GP, although nine in every 100 need to be referred for specialist treatment. At the time of going to press (July 2002) the consultation period on the draft Mental Health Bill had begun. This process is due to finish on 16th September 2002 so it is likely that in late 2002 and 2003 provision for people with mental health problems will be changed.

Draft Mental Health Bill 2002

In December 2000 the Government published a white paper on the need for reform to mental health legislation (*Reforming the Mental Health Act*) which set out their plans to underpin improvements to mental health services with reforms to mental health law. The purpose of this bill is to introduce a new legal framework covering the compulsory care and treatment of people who are suffering from mental disorders, including mentally disordered offenders. The Bill provides guidance on determining when and how treatment for mental disorder may be provided on a compulsory basis in the best interests of the patient or to prevent serious harm to other people. It will replace most of the Mental Health Act 1983 in that it introduces one broad definition of "mental disorder" to ensure that all forms of mental illness, disorder or disability come within the scope of the Bill. The Government's strategy for mental health services has three elements:

- Increased investment making mental health a key priority
- Implementation of National Service Frameworks and the NHS Plan
- An up-to-date legal framework which promotes patients' rights, protects their safety and protects the safety of the public.

NSF for Mental Health - www.doh.gov.uk/nsf

The National Service Framework for Mental Health details the Government's objectives in this area, how services should be developed and delivered and how to measure performance across the country. The NSF expands on policies announced in the White Paper *Modernising Mental Health Services* and is part of the Government's agenda to improve quality and reduce unacceptable variations in health and social services. It was developed with advice from health and social care professionals, service users and carers, health and social service managers and partner agencies. In the NHS the standards are set by the National Institute for Clinical Excellence; delivered by clinical governance; underpinned by self-regulation and life-long learning; and monitored by the Commission for Health Improvement, the new National Performance Assessment Framework and the National Survey of Patients. The NSF assesses the mental health needs of working age adults up to the age of 65 as well as touching upon the needs of children and young people, though these are generally addressed through separate service development programmes across the NHS and social services.

Mental Health Information Strategy

This is the plan for the way in which the information systems and underpinning work required to support modern mental health care delivery will be carried out. The strategy is a product of the programme to implement Information for Health and it is intended that the improved information will support service user empowerment and safer care. Essentially, the strategy has these main goals:

- Integrated service user information - Making information available in electronic form across social and health boundaries will support co-ordinated care.
- Local service and access information - Each health and social care community will develop a local directory of services and facilities for people with mental health problems so that they have easy access to what is available in their area.
- Consumer information - Current, relevant information on mental health will be made available to the public in easily accessible form.
- The evidence base - An up to date evidence base about effective treatments and care will be provided by the National electronic Library for Mental Health (NeLMH).
- Quality and management information - Data about which services are in place, what care work they undertake, the quality of care and what impact services have is necessary to support effective mental health clinical governance and management. The framework through which national comparisons can be made will be provided by the National Service Mapping and the Mental Health Minimum Dataset.

Mental Health Promotion Project

As part of the NSF, the Mental Health Task Force created the Mental Health Promotion Project. The project has been established to lead policy development and support implementation around mental health promotion and suicide prevention. Other objectives are as follows:

- Raising awareness of mental health issues with a view to reducing misunderstanding and discrimination.
- Promote greater opportunities in employment, education, benefits, training and financial services for people with mental health problems.
- Encourage and support international co-operation in sharing good practice in mental health promotion.
- Reduce the suicide and undetermined death rate of those with mental health problems by at least one-fifth by 2010.

Modernisation Board

In order for the NSF to achieve what was set out in the *Modernising Mental Health Services* White Paper they have established a Modernisation Board. The board is chaired by the Secretary of State for Health, Alan Milburn and is made up of representatives from leading healthcare organsiations, NHS employees and patient and citizen delegates. The board's role is to ensure and monitor the progress of achieving the aims of the NSF. The Modernisation Board is the first time that an independent group representing the many different interests involved in health and social services has had an influence over health policy and its implementation.

Mental Health Task Force

The Mental Health Task Force has a key role to play in terms of maintaining the momentum of developing mental health services as well as encouraging change and providing advice on implementation. The membership of the taskforce brings together a wide range of expertise, knowledge and experience with the aim to:

- Treat individuals living with mental health problems with dignity and encourage their full involvement in their care.
- Respect cultural and ethnic diversity and tackle discriminatory practices.
- Acknowledge the role and skills of carers, recognising them as partners in care and supporting them in this.

- Promote positive mental health and take effective steps to reduce stigma and discrimination.
- Make the best and most effective treatments available, when and where they are needed.
- Respond appropriately to need so that people get the right care for them at the right time.
- Emphasise safety, particularly of the service users themselves.
- Ensure the workforce is skilled, of high morale and able to adopt new ways of working.

This taskforce is one of 11 established by the Secretary of State for Health to drive forward the Government's programme of modernisation through implementation of the NHS Plan (Published in July 2000). So far the Mental Health Task Force has created 170 assertive outreach teams, 500 extra secure beds and 320 24-hour staffed beds. In the future it plans to introduce more of these plus crisis resolution teams, extra staff and improvements to conditions for mentally ill prisoners.

Community Mental Health Teams (CMHT)

CMHTs play an important role in supporting service users and families in community settings. The service is intended for adults of working age with the full range of mental health problems. Most patients treated by the CMHT have limited disorders and will be referred back to their GP after a period of a few weeks or months. However, a substantial minority will remain for ongoing treatment, care and monitoring for periods of several years. Generally, this encompasses those with serious psychological problems; victims of previous poor treatment; potentially dangerous patients; anyone requiring skilled or intensive treatment; those who may need intervention (under the Mental Health Act 1983); or sufferers of severe personality disorders. With all patients the CMHT carries out three distinct functions: they advise professionals on the management of those with mental health problems and then provide treatment and care. In some areas these functions are provided by separate teams on behalf of the CMHT but whatever structure is adopted the aim is to:

- Increase capacity within primary care through collaboration.
- Reduce the stigma associated with mental health care.
- Ensure that care is delivered in the least restrictive and disruptive manner possible.
- Stabilise social functioning and protect community tenure.

By working with GPs to assess all cases and organise referrals the CMHT is working towards fully integrated health and social care. Weekly team meetings are held to review the progress and outcomes of the scheme.

Discharge and Transfer - After treatment by a CMHT patients are normally discharged back to primary care as promptly as is feasible once they have recovered. They are given a comprehensive discharge letter indicating current treatment and procedures for re-referral if necessary or if more complicated care is needed a liaison meeting will be carried out before discharge. Should a patient need to be transferred from one CMHT to another there is a meeting held to discuss arrangements before the transfer takes place and no disengagement will occur until the new team has established a relationship.

OLDER PEOPLE

In Britain the number of people aged over 65 has doubled in the last 70 years and the number of people aged over 90 is set to double in the next 25 years. Older people are more likely to need health and social care services and the increasing numbers of them means that more effective services are needed. In order to address this the Government has taken a number of steps:

- It has established a Cabinet Committee on Older People.
- It has appointed Professor Ian Philip as the first National Director for Older People.
- It has published the National Service Framework for Older People.

The National Service Framework

The NSF for Older People is a ten-year plan that came into place in March 2001. It will focus on:

- Reducing disability and the need for long-term care.
- Maximising independent living and social functioning.
- Enhancing the well being of older people and their carers.
- Informing the choices of individual users of health and social care.
- Promoting understanding of the needs of older people from black and ethnic minority communities.
- Providing those who deploy health and social care resources with knowledge about the most cost-effective and equitable means of carrying them out.
- Encouraging the development and evaluation of innovative practice in health and social care.

The NSF sets the new national standards of care for all older people and it is backed by £1.4 billion to be invested every year by 2004 in better services. The additional resources will be used to finance the following:

- 200 more consultants, 7,800 extra nurses and 2,500 therapists and health professionals.
- £120 million to modernise old, open plan or mixed sex wards and replace them with individual single sex accommodation.
- £105 million to provide community equipment such as hoists, grab rails and chair lifts.
- 5,000 more intermediate care beds.
- Better care and support for those with mental health problems and their families.
- Fairer access to effective drugs for conditions such as Alzheimer's.
- Widespread flu vaccination.

The NSF also outlines the Single Assessment Process. This is an initiative set up to ensure that agencies work together so that assessment and subsequent care planning is effective and co-ordinated.

Research on Ageing and Older People

In November 2001 the Health Minister, Lord Philip Hunt announced an £8 million research project into ageing and old age by the Research Councils. The funding will be used for research projects set up by the Government to aid active recovery and rehabilitation and prevent loss of independence for older people.

- £2 million has been awarded by the Department of Health and the Medical Research Council for research to evaluate intermediate care services for older people.
- £2 million will be spent on the Engineering and Physical Sciences Research Council's Enabling Independence in Old Age programme.
- A further £4 million will be available under the Biotechnology and Biological Sciences Research Council's Experimental Research on Ageing initiative.

CAREdirect - www.caredirect.gov.uk – 0800 444 000

CAREdirect is a new service being developed by the Department of Health in partnership with local councils for people aged 60 and over and their carers and relatives. It is the result of consultation with older people, carers, their representative organisations and service providers from across the public, voluntary and private sectors. Its aim is to make it easier for older people to get information and help when they need it. CAREdirect provides older people or their carers with information about social care, health, housing and social security benefits and offers practical help to get in touch with the organisations that provide these services. Contact can be by phone or in person.

CAREdirect is currently being piloted and evaluated in Plymouth, Somerset, Bournemouth, Gloucestershire, Bristol and Devon. Ministers will decide in the light of the evaluation outcome and other developments if the service is to be rolled out beyond the pilot sites.

The SSI and the Elderly

The Social Services Inspectorate has an important role to play in identifying and preventing abuse of elderly people whether this is at home or in a residential care environment. They have published several guidance documents *(Confronting Elder Abuse, No Longer Afraid, In Safe Hands)* designed to help local authorities to be more successful in their attempts to combat instances of abuse. This guidance seeks to encourage improved protection through increased co-operation between various agencies such as health, social services and the police. The Care Standards Act 2000 has laid the legal basis for the establishment of a General Social Care Council with powers to regulate the social care workforce and of a National Care Standards Commission. The SSI has studied all reports of elderly people published since 1994 and has produced a summary of responses that includes examples of good practice in order to give examples of what councils should be seeking to achieve. The new Social Care Institute for Excellence has considerable potential for connecting SSI findings from this research with comparable best practice.

TRAINING FOR THE PERSONAL SOCIAL SERVICES

General Social Care Council - www.gscc.org.uk

The Central Council for Education and Training in Social Work (CCETSW) was replaced on 1 October 2001 with the General Social Care Council (GSCC) in England; the Care Council for Wales (CCW) in Wales; the Scottish Social Services Council (SSSC) in Scotland and the Northern Ireland Social Care Council (NISCC) in Northern Ireland. The GSCC will undertake responsibility at the present time for administering post-graduate bursaries in England, Scotland and Wales (DHSSPS (NI) will continue to administer Northern Ireland bursaries).

The General Social Care Council approves social work education and training by validating the quality of the training being offered by universities and colleges to ensure high quality education and consistency. This includes both qualifying training - the diploma or degree in social work - and post-qualifying training.

New Degree in Social Work

The Department of Health announced in March 2001 that a new degree in social work would be introduced in England from autumn 2003. This new degree will eventually replace the Diploma in Social Work (DipSW). (Other arrangements apply in Scotland, Northern Ireland and Wales). During the phasing out of the DipSW, DipSW courses will continue to be run. The Diploma, and other predecessor qualifications, will continue to be recognised as valid social work qualifications. A list of universities accredited by the General Social Care Council to offer the new degree in social work will be published on the GSCC website (www.gscc.org.uk) in late 2002. Universities will be taking applications from February 2003, with courses starting in September 2003. For further information about the new degree, visit www.doh.gov.uk/swqualification. Information on careers and training can be obtained from the Department of Health at www.socialworkcareers.co.uk from their recruitment hotline on 0845 604 6404.

TOPSS - www.topss.org.uk

Training Organisation for the Personal Social Services provides a coherent education and training strategy to underpin the delivery and the development of social work, social care and related activities.
Their mission is to improve:

- employers' confidence in the competence of their workforce.
- employees' confidence in their own knowledge and skills.
- service users' confidence in the quality of service they are receiving.

TOPSS is licensed by the Secretary of State for Education and Skills as a National Training Organisation, to take responsibility for the overall coherence of training and education in the social care sector. As a National Training Organisation, TOPSS is led by the employers - not only the 150 local authority social services departments, but also some 25,000 private and voluntary sector bodies. It is the employers, ultimately, who implement social care work policy and decide day-to-day priorities, so the supply of trained and qualified staff must meet the employers' requirements. Their view is complemented among the membership of TOPSS England by representatives of professional associations, trades unions, training providers and, of course, the voice of service users themselves.

TOPSS is not alone in its work. As well as its partnership with government - particularly the Departments of Health and for Education and Skills - it has a number of alliances to which it contributes and through which it is supported. TOPSS England became structurally and financially independent of CCETSW in April 2000. The closure of CCETSW in September 2001 has led to new partners for TOPSS England, in particular:

- the General Social Care Council which, by requiring various categories of social care worker to be registered, will demonstrate the importance of the education and training which TOPSS is to develop;
- the National Care Standards Commission, to take over from registration and inspection functions of social services and health trusts;
- the Social Care Institute for Excellence (SCIE), will provide research as evidence of 'what works' best in particular social care settings.

TOPSS works in partnership with a huge range of training and education bodies in the social services field, such as the awarding bodies for NVQs in Care, 'social inclusion' NTOs, the Quality Assurance Agency, the Qualifications & Curriculum Authority and the funding sources for higher and further education. Regional Development Agencies, the Learning and Skills Councils and the Small Business Services are also key partners for TOPSS England, particularly for Regional Training Forums.

The Institute of Welfare

Progressing towards charitable status. The Institute of Welfare (IOW) is a professional body for freelance, public and private sector welfare practitioners engaged in occupational, social care and welfare and voluntary settings. It offers one of the few professional accreditation schemes in the UK to meet the Government's requirements for an accredited welfare work qualification in the field of social care and welfare. Members, who must adhere to the IOW's Codes of Ethics and Practice, are entitled to use the professional designation **Registered Welfare Officer** in addition to qualifying letters relevant to their level of membership. The IOW's Certificate and Diploma in Welfare Studies are recognised at NVQ Levels 3 and 4 respectively by the Qualifications and Curriculum Authority. These are open to welfare practitioners and members of the public alike and delivered at 40 Further Education colleges throughout the UK.

The Institute of Welfare
(Founded in 1945 as the Institute of Welfare Officers)
Newland House, 137-139 Hagley Road, Birmingham B16 8UA
Tel: 0121 454 8883 Fax: 0121 454 7873
info@insituteofwelfare.co.uk
www.instituteofwelfare.co.uk

VOLUNTARY ORGANISATIONS

Blind / Visually Impaired

Guide Dogs for the Blind
Hillfields, Burghfield
Reading RG7 3YG
Tel: 0870 600 2323
guidedogs@guidedogs.org.uk
www.guidedogs.org.uk

The Partially Sighted Society
P.O. Box 322
Doncaster DN1 2XA
Tel: 01302 323132
www.leeder.demon.co.uk

Royal National Institute for the Blind
105 Judd Street
London WC1H 9NE
Tel: 020 7388 1266
www.rnib.org.uk

St Dunstan's
12-14 Harcourt Street
London W1H 4HD
Tel: 020 7616 7930 Fax: 020 7262 6199
enquiries@st-dunstans.co.uk
www.st-dunstans.co.uk

Deaf / Hearing Impaired

British Deaf Association
1-3 Worship Street
London EC2A 2AB
Tel: 020 7588 3520 Fax: 020 7588 3526
www.britishdeafassociation.org.uk

Link Centre for Deafened People
19 Hartfield Road
Eastbourne
East Sussex BN21 2AR
Tel: 01323 638230 Fax: 01323 642968
Textphone: 01323 739998
Linkcntr@dircon.co.uk
www.linkcentre.org

Royal National Institute for Deaf People
19-23 Featherstone Street
London EC1Y 8SL
Tel: 020 7296 8000 Fax: 020 7296 8199
www.rnid.org.uk

Deafblind

Deafblind UK
100 Bridge Street
Peterborough PE1 1DY
Tel: 01733 358100 Fax: 01733 358356
www.deafblind.org.uk

Sense
11-13 Clifton Terrace
London N4 3SR
Tel: 020 7272 7774 Fax: 020 72727 6012
www.sense.org.uk

Learning Disability

Association for Residential Care
ARC House, Marsden Street
Chesterfield
Derbyshire
S40 1JY
Tel: 01246 555043 Fax: 01246 555045
contactus@arcuk.org.uk
www.arcuk.org.uk

CARE – Cottage and Rural Enterprises Limited
9 Weir Road
Kibworth
Leicestershire LE8 0LQ
Tel: 0166 279 3225
www.care-ltd.co.uk

Central England People First Limited
P.O. Box 5200
Northampton NN1 1ZB
United Kingdom
Tel: 01604 721 666 Fax: 01604 721 611
northants@peoplefirst.org.uk
www.peoplefirst.org.uk

ENABLE – Scottish Society for the Mentally Handicapped
6th Floor, 7 Buchanan Street
Glasgow G1 3HL
Tel: 0141 226 4541
www.enable.org.uk

Home Farm Trust
Merchants House, Wapping Road
Bristol BS1 4RW
Tel: 0117 927 3746
www.hft.org.uk

MENCAP
The Royal Society for Mentally Handicapped Children and Adults
123 Golden Lane
London EC1Y 0RT
Tel: 020 7454 0454 Fax: 020 7696 5540
information@mencap.org.uk
www.mencap.org.uk

Rathbone Community Industry
4th Floor, Churchgate House
56 Oxford Street
Manchester M1 6EU

SCOVO - Standing Conference of Voluntary Organisations for People with a Learning Disability in Wales
5 Dock Chambers
Bute Street
Cardiff CF10 5AG
Tel: 029 2049 2443
www.scovo.org.uk

Mental Health

MACA (Mental After Care Association)
25 Bedford Square
London WC1B 3HW
Tel: 020 7436 6194
www.maca.org.uk

MIND (The National Association for Mental Health)
Granta House, 15-19 Broadway
Stratford
London E15 4BQ
Tel: 020 8519 2122
www.mind.org.uk

Rethink Severe Mental Illness *(formerly National Schizophrenia Fellowship)*
28 Castle Street
Kingston-upon-Thames
Surrey KT1 1SS
Tel: 020 7330 9100
Advice line: 020 8974 6814 *(open Mon, Wed, Fri from 10am to 3pm and Tue and Thur from 10am to 1pm)*
www.nsf.org.uk

Richmond Fellowship for Community Mental Health
80 Holloway Road
London, N7 8JG
Tel: 020 7697 3300 Fax: 020 7697 3301
enquiries@richmondfellowship.org.uk
www.richmondfellowship.org.uk

Older People

Action on Elder Abuse
Astral House, 1268 London Road
London SW16 4ER
Tel: 020 8765 7000 Fax: 020 8679 4074
www.elderabuse.org.uk

Age Concern
Astral House, 1268 London Road
London SW16 4ER
Tel: 020 8679 8000 Fax: 020 8679 6069
www.ageconcern.org.uk

Centre for Policy on Ageing
25-31 Ironmonger Row
London EC1V 3QP
Tel: 020 7253 1787 Fax: 020 7553 6501
www.cpa.org.uk

Counsel and Care
Lower Ground Floor, Twyman House
16 Bonny Street
London NW1 9PG
Tel: 020 7485 1550
www.counselandcare.org.uk

Elderly Accommodation Counsel
3rd floor, 89 Albert Embankment
London SE1 7TP
enquiries@e-a-c.demon.co.uk
www.housingcare.org
Elderly Accommodation Counsel is a registered charity that maintains a nationwide database of all forms of accommodation for older people - sheltered housing for sale and rent, residential care homes, nursing homes and close care schemes. Staff also give guidance, advice and detailed information to help callers choose and fund the accommodation most suited to their needs.

Help the Aged
207-221 Pentonville Road
London N1 9UZ
Tel: 020 7278 1114 Fax: 020 7278 1116
info@helptheaged.org.uk
www.helptheaged.org.uk

Pensioners Voice
National Federation of Retirement Pensions Associations
Melling House, 14 St Peter Street
Blackburn
Lancashire BB2 2HD
Tel: 01254 52606

Pre-Retirement Association of Great Britain and Northern Ireland
26 Frederick Sanger Road
Surrey Research Park
Guildford, Surrey GU2 5YD
Tel: 01483 301170

Physical Disability

Action Research
Vincent House, North Parade
Horsham
West Sussex RH12 2DP
Tel: 01403 210406
www.actionresearch.co.uk

Arthritis Care
18 Stephenson Way
London NW1 2HD
Tel: 020 7916 1500
www.arthritiscare.org.uk

Association for Spina Bifida and Hydrocephalus (ASBAH)
ASBAH House, 42 Park Road
Peterborough
Cambridgeshire PE1 2UQ
Tel: 01733 555988
www.asbah.org

Association to Aid the Sexual and Personal Relationships of People with a Disability
286 Camden Road
London N7 0BJ
Tel: 020 7607 8851

BREAK (formerly Davison Morley Trust)
1 Montague Road
Sheringham
Norfolk NR26 8LN
Tel: 01263 822161 Fax: 01263 822181
Office@break-charity.org
www.break-charity.org

British Council of Disabled People
Litchurch Plaza
Litchurch Lane
Derby DE24 8AA
Tel: 01332 295551 Fax: 01332 295580
www.bcodp.org.uk

Capability Scotland
22 Corstorphine Road
Edinburgh EH12 6HP
Tel: 0131 337 9876
www.capability-scotland.org.uk

Crossroads (Association of Care Attendant Schemes Ltd)
10 Regent Place
Rugby
Warwickshire CV21 2PN
Tel: 01788 573653 Fax: 01788 565498
www.crossroads.org.uk

Disability Alliance
Universal House, 88-94 Wentworth Street
London E1 7SA
Tel: 020 7247 8776 Fax: 020 7247 8765
www.disabilityalliance.org

Disability Law Service (registered as Network for the Handicapped Ltd)
Room 241, 2nd Floor, 49-51 Bedford Row
London WCIR 4LR
Tel: 020 7831 8031 Fax: 020 7831 5582
www.mkurrein.co.uk/work/disablaw.html

Disabled Living Centres Council
Redbank House, 4 St Chad's Street
Cheetham
Manchester M8 8QA
Tel: 0161 834 1044 Fax: 0161 839 0802
dlcc@dlcc.org.uk
www.dfcc.org.uk

Disabled Living Foundation
380-384 Harrow Road
London W9 2HU
Tel: 020 7289 6111 Fax: 020 7266 2922
www.dlf.org.uk

Epilepsy Action
New Anstey House, Gateway Drive
Yeadon LS19 7XU
Tel: 0113 243 9393
Helpline: 0808 800 5060
www.epilepsy.org.uk

Invalid Children's Aid Nationwide (I CAN)
4 Dyer's Buildings
Holborn
London EC1N 2QP
Tel: 0870 0104066 Fax: 0870 0104067

Multiple Sclerosis Society of Great Britain and Northern Ireland
372 Edgware Road
Staples Corner
London NW2 6ND
Tel: 020 8438 0700
www.mssociety.org.uk

Muscular Dystrophy Group of Great Britain and Northern Ireland
7-11 Prescott Place
London SW4 6BS
Tel: 020 7720 8055
www.muscular-dystrophy.org

National Children's Bureau – Council for Disabled Children
8 Wakley Street
London EC1V 7QE
Tel: 020 7843 6000 Fax: 020 7278 9512
www.ncb.org.uk

Parkinson's Disease Society of the United Kingdom
215 Vauxhall Bridge Road
London. SW1V 1EJ
Tel: 020 7931 8080 Fax: 020 7233 9908 / 020 7963 9360
enquiries@parkinsons.org.uk
www.parkinsons.org.uk

RADAR (Royal Association for Disability and Rehabilitation)
12 City Forum, 250 City Road
London EC1V 8AF
Tel: 20 7250 3222
www.radar.org.uk

Reach – The Association for Children with Hand or Arm Deficiency
PO Box 54
Helston
Cornwall TR13 8WD
Tel: 0845 1306225 Fax: 01872 262098
reach@reach.org.uk
www.reach.org.uk

Royal British Legion
48 Pall Mall
London SW1Y 5JY
Tel: 020 7973 7200
www.britishlegion.org.uk

SCOPE (formerly The Spastics Society)
6 Market Road
London N7 9PW
Tel: 0808 800 3333
cphelpline@scope.org.uk
www.scope.org.uk

The Scottish Spina Bifida Association
190 Queensferry Road
Edinburgh EH4 2BW
Tel: 0131 332 0743
www.ssba.org.uk/

FAMILY AND COMMUNITY

A J BOND & CO
Universal House, 1 Walters Yard, High Street, Bromley, Kent BR1 1QA
Tel: 020 8464 2229 ***Fax:*** 020 8466 6009
Docx: 117606 BROMLEY 7

AARONSON & CO
308 Earls Court Road, London SW5 9BA
Tel: **020 7373 9516** *Fax:* **020 7835 1014**
Docx: **400750 EARLS COURT 1**

Legal Aid franchise adn block contracts in immigration family law, housing and welfare benefits. Members of Law Society Family Law Panel, Immigration Law Practitioners Association adn Personal Injury Panel.

AIDAN WOODS & CO
238 Stapleton Road, Eastville, Bristol BS5 0NT
Tel: 0117 952 2006 ***Fax:*** 0117 935 4115
Email: Enquiries@Aidanwoods.co.uk

ASTON CLARK
225-227 High Street, Acton, London W3 9BY
Tel: 020 8752 1122 ***Fax:*** 020 8752 1128
Docx: 80267 ACTON
Email: aston@clark1996.fsnet.co.uk

ATKINS HOPE
74-78 North End, Croydon, Surrey CR9 1SD
Tel: 020 8680 5018 ***Fax:*** 020 8688 8347
Docx: 2629 CROYDON 1
Email: enquiries@atkinshope.co.uk
Web: www.atkinshope.co.uk

BAILEY WIGHT & CO
Guildhall Buildings, Navigation Street, Birmingham, West Midlands B2 4BT
Tel: 0121 244 6600 ***Fax:*** 0121 244 6611
Email: solicitors@baileywright.com

BONE& PAYNE
55, Madoc Street, Llandudno, Conwy LL30 2TW
Tel: 0492 876354 ***Fax:*** 01492 874531
Docx: 11354 LLANDUDNO
Email: enquiries@boneandpayne.co.uk

BROOMHEAD & SAUL
11 & 13 East Street, Ilminster, Somerset TA19 0AE
Tel: 01460 57056 ***Fax:*** 01460 54846
Docx: 95803 ILMINSTER
Email: enquiries@broomhead-saul.co.uk
Web: www.broomhead-saul.co.uk

Community
Legal Service

CARVERS (PART OF THE WILKES PARTNERSHIP)
10 Coleshill Road, Hodge Hill, Birmingham, West Midlands B36 8AA
Tel: 0121 784 8484 ***Fax:*** 0121 783 4935
Docx: 27434 HODGE HILL
Email: legal@carverslaw.co.uk
Web: www.carverslaw.co.uk

CHANCELLORS LEA BREWER
246 Broadway, Bexleyheath, Kent DA6 8BB
Tel: 020 8303 0077 ***Fax:*** 020 8304 4023
Docx: 31800 BEXLEYHEATH
Email: athomas@chancellors.com

COSTERTONS
Family Law, 186 High Street, Sutton, Surrey SM1 4JP
Tel: **020 8661 1177** *Fax:* **020 8643 8919**
Email: **costertons@freeserve.co.uk**

CROCKETT & CO
260 Harehills Lane, Leeds, West Yorkshire LS9 7BD
Tel: 0113 226 0111 ***Fax:*** 0113 226 0110
Docx: 26434 LEEDS PARK SQUARE
Email: hcrockettsols@aol.com

D J GRIFFITHS HARVEYS
Reliance House, 3 Sherman Road, Bromley, Kent BR1 3JH
Tel: 020 8460 6668 ***Fax:*** 020 8460 1249
Docx: 5751 BROMLEY 1
2 Members of the Law Society Family Law Panel. 1 Member of the Law Society Children Panel. 2 Members of Accident Line.

DANIEL & CRUTTWELL
The Family Law Centre, 21-22 Bath Street, Frome, Somerset BA11 1DL
Tel: 01373 463311 ***Fax:*** 01373 461765
Docx: 43801 FROME
Email: info@danielcruttwell.co.uk

DINGLE BURD WRIGHT
30 Hamilton Square, Birkehhead, Merseyside CH41 6AZ
Tel: **0151 666 2210** *Fax:* **0151 666 2537**
Docx: **17868 BIRKENHEAD**
Email: **sd@dbw-law.com**

DREW JONES
17 Queens Road, Coventry, West Midlands CV1 3EG
Tel: 024 7655 5511 ***Fax:*** 024 7655 5577
Docx: 706791 COVENTRY 9
Email: law@drewjones.co.uk

FIELD SEYMOUR PARKES
The Old Coroner's Court, PO Box 174 No 1 London Street, Reading RG1 4QW
Tel: 0118 951 6200 ***Fax:*** 0118 950 2704
Docx: 4001 READING
Email: enquiry@fsp-law.com

FOSTER & PARTNERS
1st Floor Office Suite, 48 Corn Street, Bristol BS1 1HQ
Tel: **0117 922 0229** *Fax:* **0117 929 8621**
Docx: **7867 BRISTOL 1**
Email: **pfoster@fostersbristol.co.uk**

We are one of the leading firms of solicitors specialising in public law relating to children in the South West. We deal with all aspects of childrens law and care proceedings.

FRASER BROWN
13 Borough Street, Castle Donington, Leicester DE74 2LA
Tel: 01332 810189 ***Fax:*** 01332 853132
Docx: 22431 CASTLE DONNINGTON
Email: dspiers@proweb.co.uk

HACKWELL ASHWORTH & CO
100 Market Street, Stalybridge, Greater Manchester SK15 2AB
Tel: 0161 338 8808 ***Fax:*** 0161 338 2616
Docx: 15573 STALYBRIDGE

HARRY BOODHOO & CO
21 Copson Street, Withington, Greater Manchester M20 3HE
Tel: 0161 445 0588 ***Fax:*** 0161 445 4949
Docx: 28608 WITHINGTON
Email: harryboodhoo@harryboodhoo.co.uk
Criminal Defence Specialists, Housing Problems, Famliy Law.

HARTLEY & WORSTENHOLME
10 Gillygate, Pontefract, West Yorkshire WF8 1PQ
Tel: 01977 732222 ***Fax:*** 01977 600343
Docx: 22256 PONTEFRACT
Email: info@hartley-worstenholme.co.uk
Web: www.hartley-worstenholme.co.uk

HARTNELLS
Oriel House, Southernhay Gardens, Exeter, Devon EX1 1NP
Tel: 01392 421777 ***Fax:*** 01392 421237
Docx: 8388 EXETER
Email: enquiries@hartnell.co.uk
Web: www.hartnell.co.uk
A specialist team of Family Lawyers and a Welfare Benefits Expert who are able to deal with the full range of family related issues. We act for parents and children. We also represent Guardians Ad Litem in care proceedings having three Child Panel Members.

HATCHER ROGERSON
25 Castle Street, Shrewsbury, Shropshire SY11 1DA
Tel: 01743 ***238545 Fax:*** 01743 242879
Email: mail@hr-law.co.uk
Websitemail: www.hr-law.co.uk

HENRIQUES GRIFFITHS
18 Portland Square, Bristol BS2 8SJ
Tel: 0117 909 4000 ***Fax:*** 0117 942 0017
Docx: 122076 BRISTOL 11
Email: info@henriquesgriffiths.com

HENRY Y SMITH & CO
152-154 Essex Road, London N1 8LY
Tel: 020 7704 2881 ***Fax:*** 020 7704 2436
Docx: 58279 ISLINGTON

HOPKIN MURRAY BESKINE
Tower House, 149 Fonthill Road, London N4 3HF
Tel: **020 7272 1234** *Fax:* **020 7272 4050**
Docx: **57474 FINSBURY PARK**

JAMES MURRAY SOLICITORS
41 Merton Road, Liverpool, Merseyside L20 7AP
Tel: 0151 933 3333 ***Fax:*** 0151 933 3343
Docx: 18807 BOOTLE 1
Email: info@jamesmurray.law.co.uk

KTP SOLICITORS
KTP Chambers, Dinas Isaf Industrial Estate, Williamstown, Pontypridd, Rhondda Cynon Taff CF40 1NY
Tel: 01443 424800 ***Fax:*** 01443 441194
Email: ktpsolicitors@aol.com

LAMBERTS
Prospect House, 1 Prospect Street, Caversham, Reading RG4 8JB
Tel: 0118 947 8638 ***Fax:*** 0118 946 1092
Docx: 84152 CAVERSHAM

LEEDS DAY
7/8 Market Hill, Huntingdon, Cambridgeshire PE18 6NT
Tel: 01480 454301 ***Fax:*** 01480 412825
Docx: 80905 HUNTINGDON
Email: law@leedsday.co.uk
Web: www.leedsday.co.uk

LEEDS DAY
1A South Street, St Neots, Cambridgeshire PE19 2BW
Tel: 01480 474661 ***Fax:*** 01480 473610
Docx: 100305 ST NEOTS
Email: law@leedsday.co.uk
Web: www.leedsday.co.uk

LEVENES SOLICITORS
Ashley House, 235-239 High Road, Wood Green, London N22 8HF
Tel: **0800 118899** *Fax:* **020 8889 63**
Docx: **135576 WOOD GREEN 4**
Email: **info@levenes.co.uk**
Web: **www.levenes.co.uk**

LINDSAY & JOKELSON
169a Walworth Road, London SE17 1RW
Tel: 020 7701 9898 ***Fax:*** 020 7701 1525
Docx: 34905 WALWORTH

MAIDMENTS
St Johns Court, 74 Gartside Street, Manchester, Greater Manchester M3 3EL
Tel: 0161 834 0008 ***Fax:*** 0161 832 4140/01
Docx: 14307 MANCHESTER 1
Email: info@maidments.co.uk
Web: www.maidments.com

MARTIN MURRAY & ASSOCIATES
56 High Street, Slough SL1 1EL
Tel: 01753 551313 ***Fax:*** 01753 552237
Docx: 3401 SLOUGH
Miss Jyoti Singh and Mr Laurence Klass - Children Panel Members. Specialists in Childcare, Matrimonial and Family Law. Offices also at West Drayton and Reading.

MASON & MOORE DUTTON
Kirkton House, Hunter Street, Chester, Cheshire CH1 2AS
Tel: 01244 348881 ***Fax:*** 01244 351513
Docx: 22151 CHESTER NORTHGATE
Email: law@masonmooredutton.co.uk

MOTLEY & HOPE
The Manor House, 11 Shortmead Street, Biggleswade, Bedfordshire SG18 0AT
Tel: 01767 600600 ***Fax:*** 01767 317939
Docx: 37151 BIGGLESWADE
Email: paulmotley@motleyandhope.co.uk
Paul Motley is an experienced Child Care Lawyer who has been a member of the Law Society's Panel since its inception and is also a member of the Association of Children's Lawyers. Paul works regularly in the care field for parents, grandparents and children individually or through a Childrens' Guardian. Recent care work has included representation in both the Court of Appeal and House of Lords.

MOWBRAY WOODWARDS
3 Queen Square, Bath, Bath & North East Somerset BA1 2HG
Tel: 01225 485700 ***Fax:*** 01225 445064
Docx: 8023 BATH
Email: admin@mowbraywoodwards.co.uk

NAUNTON LYNCH HALL
Oakley Lodge, 20 Liverpool Gardens, Worthing, West Sussex BN11 1RY
Tel: 01903 234556 ***Fax:*** 01903 212162
Docx: 3746 WORTHING 1
Email: nlh@dial.pipex.com

OLIVER & CO
Booth Mansion, 30 Watergate Street, Chester, Cheshire CH1 2LA
Tel: 01244 312306 ***Fax:*** 01244 350261
Docx: 19977 CHESTER
Email: oliverlaw@aol.com

PHILCOX GRAY & CO
61 Peckham High Street, London SE15 5RU
Tel: 020 7703 2285 ***Fax:*** 020 7708 1285
Docx: 34253 PECKHAM

PRITCHARD JOYCE & HINDS
St Brides House, 32 High Street, Beckenham, Kent BR3 1AY
Tel: 020 8658 3922 ***Fax:*** 020 8658 8694
Docx: 40601 BECKENHAM
Email: postmaster@pj-h.co.uk

R J FELLOWES & SON
21 Church Hill, Walthamstow, London E17 3AD
Tel: 020 8520 7392 ***Fax:*** 020 8509 0759
Docx: 32011 WALTHAMSTOW
Email: fellowesca@aol.com
Est'd 1932 - A personal and specialist service.

RAMSDENS
1/3 Ramsden Street, Huddersfield, West Yorkshire
Tel: 01484 821500 ***Fax:*** 01484 510446
Docx: 710094 HUDDERSFIELD 8
Email: prj@ramsdens.co.uk
Representation in all areas of family law both public nd private including Children Act Proceedings.

SAS LAWYERS
30 Greek Street, Stockport, Greater Manchester SK3 8AD
Tel: 0161 480 1221 ***Fax:*** 0161 480 4246
Docx: 22603 STOCKPORT 2
Email: help@saslawyers.co.uk
Web: www.saslawyers.co.uk

SIMPSON DUXBURY
2 Tyrrel Street, Bradford, West Yorkshire BD1 1RJ
Tel: 01274 734166 ***Fax:*** 01274 390182
Docx: 11709 BRADFORD
Email: lawyers@simpsonduxbury.co.uk

SMITH LLEWELYN PARTNERSHIP
18 Princess Way, Swansea SA1 3LW
Tel: 01792 464444 ***Fax:*** 01792 464726
Docx: 92051 SWANSEA 3
Email: mainofficeslp@virgin.net

STUART SMITH & BURNETT
16 Wellington Road, Bridlington, East Riding of Yorkshire YO15 2BG
Tel: 01262 678128 ***Fax:*** 01262 400012
Docx: 61900 BRIDLINGTON
Email: burnetts@lineone.net

SYDNEY MITCHELL
Chattock House, 346 Stratford Road, Shirley, Solihull, West Midlands B90 3DN
Tel: 0121 746 3300 ***Fax:*** 0121 745 7650
Docx: 13856 SHIRLEY 2
Email: enquiries@sydneymitchell.co.uk
Website: www.sydneymitchell.co.uk
Specialists in Family Law work. Areas include divorce, separation agreement and mediation, children matters, injunctions, property disputes, CSA calculation, Financial Issues. Offices also in Sheldon (0121 722 2969) and City Centre (0121 698 2200). Legal Aid Franchise in family work.

T V EDWARDS
Park House, 29 Mile End Road, Tower Hamlets, London E1 4TP
Tel: 020 7791 1050 ***Fax:*** 020 7790 5101
Docx: 300700 TOWER HAMLETS

TAYLOR POOLE
61 Highfield Road, South Shore, Blackpool FY4 2JE
Tel: 01253 348142 ***Fax:*** 01253 348149

THE SETHI PARTNERSHIP SOLICITORS
The Barn House, 38 Meadow Way, Eastcote,
Middlesex HA4 8TB
Tel: 020 8866 6464 ***Fax:*** 020 8866 3232
Docx: 35159 EASTCOTE
Email: ritu@sethi.co.uk
Web:www.sethi.co.uk

THOMPSON SMITH & PUXON
4-5 North Hill, Colchester, Essex CO1 1EB
Tel: **01206 574431** *Fax:* **01206 563174**
Docx: **3617 COLCHESTER**
Email: **info@tsplegal.com**
Web: **www.tsplegal.com**

CHAPTER TWO

Health

CHAPTER TWO

Health

THE CHANGING NHS

April 2002 was a watershed in the Government's push to modernise the NHS:

- Changes to the structure of the service came into effect, with the creation of 28 strategic health authorities and the further empowerment of primary care trusts;
- *Delivering the NHS Plan – next steps on investment, next steps on reform* was published, describing action and progress on the NHS Plan;
- Significant increases in NHS funding were announced in the Budget.

There are over 300 primary care trusts in England. They manage and deliver primary care services and are now responsible for many of the powers of the defunct health authorities. The intention is that PCTs will create efficient working arrangements with health and social care providers, matching service delivery to patient needs.

By 2004, primary care trusts will manage three-quarters of NHS expenditure, managing budgets for local services and commissioning hospital care for patients.

What is envisaged is the creation of a near central-bureaucracy free local health service, controlled by health care practitioners and accurately reflecting local conditions. The creation of patient forums (subject to legislation) in every PCT and NHS trust, with a member serving on the trust board, is also expected to create a service where changing patient needs can be recognised and acted upon. The target is an ambitious one, imposing considerable administrative duties on already over-stretched health care providers.

It would be wrong to conclude from the 'big-push' to PCTs that the Government and the Department of Health are to divest themselves of overall control of the service. Along with the drive to prioritise primary care is an increasing backdrop of national standards and targets, set, for example, by the national service frameworks, the performance assessment framework and the National Institute for Clinical Excellence. Also, the newly created strategic health authorities, though only exceptionally becoming involved in the delivery of local services, hold primary care trusts to account for their performance.

Such is the rate of change in the NHS that any description of it can at best be temporary, requiring almost immediate updating. The task is made more difficult by the volumes of information the NHS itself generates, seeking to keep both health care providers and the public informed of developments. The present picture of the NHS, then, is of a service in a state of flux, being driven from the centre into local autonomy.

THE STRUCTURE OF THE NHS IN ENGLAND

The Department of Health

The Health Secretary

The Secretary of State for Health *(also known as the Health Secretary)* leads the NHS in England. A cabinet minister, the Health Secretary is accountable to Parliament for the overall running of the NHS. Because of the high public profile of the office, the role is one of the most politically sensitive in Government.

The present Health Secretary is Alan Milburn, MP for Darlington.

The Department of Health ministerial team
A ministerial team assists the Health Secretary, each minister is accountable for different policy areas.

The current ministerial team is made up of:

John Hutton - Minister of State for Health, MP for Barrow and Furness
- Ministerial responsibilities include:
  - NHS human resources
  - Access to services
  - Primary care services

Jacqui Smith - Minister of State for Health, MP for Redditch

- Ministerial responsibilities include:
  - Long-term care for the elderly, nursing and residential care
  - General personal social services
  - Mental health services

Lord Hunt of King's Heath - Parliamentary Under Secretary of State (Lords)

- Ministerial responsibilities include:
  - NHS performance management
  - Clinical quality
  - Medicines and medical devices

Hazel Blears – Parliamentary Under Secretary of State for Public Health, MP for Salford

- Ministerial responsibilities include:
  - Public health protection
  - Cancer
  - Coronary heart disease and stroke
  - Maternity
  - Children's health
  - Teenage pregnancy

David Lammy – Parliamentary Under Secretary of State, MP for Tottenham

- Ministerial responsibilities include:
  - Emergency care
  - Patients focus issues
  - Health action zones
  - Pharmacy services

The Department of Health Civil Service and Key Specialists

As with all Government departments, the DoH is staffed by the civil service. At the top of the DoH civil service is the NHS Chief Executive (also the Permanent Secretary). The Chief Executive reports directly to the Health Secretary and is also the most senior member of the Department Board (which is responsible for the day to day management of the work of the DoH). The present Chief Executive/Permanent Secretary is Nigel Crisp, appointed in November 2000.

Experts, or key specialists, are appointed to the DoH to provide expert knowledge in specific fields of health and social care. They advise the DoH and contribute to the formation of health care policy, as well as making up part of the DoH Board. Key specialists include:

The Chief Medical Officer (CMO)

The CMO is the Government's senior medical advisor and is also the professional head of all medical staff in England. He has responsibilities for developing policy, protecting and improving public health, and leading the implementation of clinical governance. The present CMO, Professor Liam Donaldson, was appointed in 1998.

The Chief Nursing Officer (CNO)

The CNO is the main advisor to the DoH on nursing, midwifery and health visiting, and leads over 420,000 nurses, midwives and health visitors. Sarah Mullally was appointed CNO in 1999.

The Chief Social Services Inspector (CSSI)

The CSSI provides professional advice on social services matters to Government, assisting the DoH to carry out its personal social services responsibilities. Denise Platt CBE was appointed CSSI in 1998.

Regional Offices and the Regional Directors of Public Health

The DoH is supported in its management of the NHS by eight regional offices, which are accountable to the DoH for the regional performance of the NHS.

The regional office tier of the DoH will be abolished from April 2003, its role being replaced by four regional directors of health and social care, who will act between the DoH and the NHS. The regional directors will be responsible for the development of NHS and social care. They will also ensure that adequate partnership arrangements are in place between health and social care providers.

Strategic Health Authorities

Since April 2002, 28 strategic health authorities (StHAs) have been responsible for the performance of the local NHS and for setting strategies within which the national framework set out by the DoH can be achieved. StHAs have assumed many of the duties of the former health authorities.

The average StHA's population is around 1.5 million. They manage performance agreements, which hold PCTs and NHS trusts to account, support performance improvement and help trusts deliver NHS initiatives.

Primary Care Trusts

Primary care groups (PCGs) and primary care trusts (PCTs) were created to improve levels of service within the local NHS, and to deliver efficiencies. General practitioners, nurses and other health professionals play the lead part in running primary care organisations.

The first PCGs appeared in April 1999 (numbering 481). They replaced the previous system of structuring GP services (GP fundholding). In April 2000, the first PCTs were established (numbering 17). From April 2002 there were 303 PCTs and only one PCG remaining.

PCTs provide primary care (services provided by GPs and in the local community, such as community nurses) and commission hospital services, employing community health staff, e.g. district nurses and health visitors. They may run community hospitals and are responsible for building strong links with the local health and social care community.

An important PCT function is the development of the local health improvement and modernisation plan (HIMP), agreed between the PCT and other local health care providers. The HIMP operates on a three-year cycle and sets out local targets for the delivery of national priorities, the intentions of which are to reduce inequalities and improve health. PCTs take the lead in developing the HIMP, which is constructed in conjunction with other local organisations, e.g. hospital trusts and local authorities. Accountability for the delivery of the HIMP is to the local strategic health authority.

PCTs are controlled by a board, which sets the PCT strategy and monitors performance against the health improvement and modernisation plan. The board also verifies the work of the PCT executive committee (responsible for the day to day running of the PCT). The PCT board accounts to the strategic health authority for the PCT's performance.

PCTs are the lead NHS organisations and are expected to become responsible for the flow of the majority of NHS funding (75% by 2004). In line with their increased funding role is an increase in responsibility for commissioning services. It is intended that the majority of commissioning of health care will be done by PCTs. This includes commissioning hospital and community health services. To effectively commission services PCTs need to assess population health needs, and develop plans and service agreements to provide the required services.

PCTs receive a single sum for the provision of their services – the unified budget – rather than separate amounts for separate items of activity. The budget is allocated direct to the PCT and not through the strategic health authority. The budget is cash-limited – if one area is overspent a cutback in another has to be made.

The majority of expenditure is on commissioning hospital and mental health services (three-quarters of the budget). Running costs, community services provision and infrastructure make up approximately 10% of expenditure, and prescribing 15%.

The budget is arrived at by consideration of prior expenditure, the responsibilities of the PCT and any other relevant factors that may affect expenditure (e.g. tackling local health inequalities).

Care trusts and local authorities

Care trusts are an important step forward in the coordination of local health and social care services. They will deliver and commission primary/community health care and social care for various client groups, including older people.

Underpinning care trusts is the desire to focus attention on the patient's journey, rather than on the individual agencies that provide care (e.g. an elderly person leaving hospital may require well coordinated NHS and social services care). They will work to allow local services to be supplied in partnership, thereby delivering efficiencies, and will build upon existing NHS/local authority partnerships.

PCTs form an ideal basis for care trusts; however, to accommodate local variation the care trust framework is adaptable to conditions. Factors such as the size of the PCT(s) and the number of local authorities within the catchment area are relevant.

The local authority remains accountable for its own services, provided as the social care component of a care trust, and will have significant influence in the supervision and management of the care trust itself (the board of the care trust will include a social care representative).

Care trusts can be formed following an application to the Health Secretary from a PCT, a local authority or specialist NHS trust. Care trusts have been set up to run from 2002.

NHS Trusts – Hospital Services

In England there are approx 275 NHS trusts – each run by its own board of directors. Types of trust include:

- Acute hospital trusts (which provide care in the hospital setting)
- Community trusts (e.g. employing health visitors and district nurses, and providing learning disability services – these functions are now often carried out by primary care trusts)
- Mental health trusts
- Ambulance service trusts

Trusts must match national targets, successfully partner other primary care providers and agencies, and provide efficient services.

NHS trust income is obtained through a combination of service agreements with PCTs (which set out services to be provided by the trust in return for funding), the provision of undergraduate/ postgraduate training, private health care and limited commercial activities (e.g. car parks). There are three main types of hospital:

District general hospitals (DGHs)
DGHs provide hospital clinical services such as outpatient and inpatient treatment and surgery. They serve average populations of 200,000 – 300,000 and provide the majority of emergency (A&E) and elective (pre-booked) services. Linked to DGHs are smaller hospitals, which serve populations of up to 100,000, yet do not provide the full range of emergency services. The 'traditional' DGH begins to look dated as services become increasingly specialised. Inpatient stays are progressively shorter, with many patients receiving day care or outpatient treatment that does not require an overnight stay.

Specialist tertiary centres
Tertiary care centres provide treatment for complex conditions, e.g. they provide specific cancer therapies. Patients are admitted after referral by a hospital consultant.

Community hospitals
Community hospitals, also sometimes called 'cottage hospitals', provide minor injury, rehabilitation and respite care. Minor surgery and maternity services may also be provided, with local hospital consultants and local GPs providing medical expertise. They have an important role in providing care for older people who no longer require hospitalisation, yet are unable to return home.

QUALITY IN NHS SERVICES

The Department of Health is committed to prioritising quality and effectiveness in NHS services – quality issues are now pervasive and not just a factor of service delivery. The commitment to quality includes improving clinical care, using resources efficiently and raising standards of care generally.

Measures to improve services include clarifying evidence-based guidelines and standards so that the quality agenda can be clearly understood, and supporting the delivery of quality services through effective professional standards.

The clinical governance agenda was introduced to underpin the drive to raise standards in NHS organisations. Clinical governance is a concept or philosophy that should form a part of all service decisions.

Clinical governance is defined as: A framework through which the NHS is accountable for improving the quality of services and safeguarding high standards of care by creating an environment in which best practice in clinical care will flourish.

The National Institute for Clinical Excellence

The National Institute for Clinical Excellence (NICE) was launched in 1999 as a special health authority. NICE employs expert teams to produce NHS guidance on the:

- Use of new and existing health technologies (technology appraisals)
- Management and care of specific conditions (clinical guidelines)
- Safe and effective use of new surgical procedures (interventional procedures)
- Lessons learnt following investigation of deaths and serious incidents in specific clinical circumstances (confidential enquiries)

NICE appraises some 30 technologies annually. The criteria for selection include whether or not the technology is of considerable importance to public health, and its cost and efficiency in use. Evaluation is made primarily on the basis of the clinical effectiveness of the technology under consideration, which will need to be supported by clinical trials that demonstrate its effectiveness. Costs to the NHS are also a main factor.

Clinical guidelines are derived from both expert opinion and the best clinical evidence available. Again, cost is a significant factor, as recommendations must be cost as well as clinically effective. Clinical guidelines cover all aspects of care – from self-care by the patient, through to care provided by health professionals in hospital and community settings.

Guidance issued by NICE derives from its clinical guidelines advisory committee, which sources guidance through the national collaborating centres. The centres issue best practice clinical guidelines and audit advice for the NHS in England and Wales in acute care, chronic conditions, nursing and supportive care, mental health, primary care, and women and children's health.

In April 2002 NICE assumed responsibility for the Safety and Efficacy Register of New Interventional Procedures (SERNIP), which develops guidance for the NHS on the safe and effective use of new surgical procedures (interventional procedures).

NICE also has responsibility for four nationwide confidential enquiries, which collect data from the NHS on the deaths of mothers and babies in childbirth, the death of infants, deaths during and within 30 days of surgery, and suicides/homicides.

Though NICE guidance is not mandatory, the anticipation is that the NHS will follow its advice, and this has proven to be the case in practice. Importantly, from 2002, the NHS in England has three months from the publication of a NICE technology appraisal to make funds available for the provision of the approved technology, if a physician considers it appropriate.

NICE is extremely influential, as its decisions as to the suitability or otherwise of the use of a technology (medicine) by the NHS has obvious implications for the NHS, patients and the pharmaceutical industry. Its decisions are therefore high profile, commanding considerable attention not just in health care but also in the media.

The Commission for Health Improvement

The Commission for Health Improvement (CHI), described as the Government's watchdog on health, was set up in 1999 to monitor clinical standards in the NHS in England and Wales. CHI is an independent body, reporting to Lord Hunt, the DoH Under Secretary to the Lords. Its remit is to prioritise the patients' experience of the NHS, to ensure that health care providers have effective quality systems in place, and to work to eliminate bad practice.

CHI aims to inspect all PCTs and NHS trusts every four years. It can also carry out spot-checks or investigate in response to a request. After inspection a report is published and any necessary remedial action agreed upon. The responsibility for ensuring that the inspected trust follows CHI recommendations currently rests with the relevant NHS regional office (strategic health authorities are due to take on this role in 2002).

So far, CHI has completed over 100 clinical governance reviews. Nearly three-quarters of NHS trusts have been reviewed and the evaluation of primary care, mental health services and ambulance trusts is underway. Additionally, CHI has conducted eight investigations into serious NHS service failures.

A CHI investigation is an important event in the life of a trust, as its decisions have control and funding implications. Also, CHI decisions are often reported in the media. Should an investigation indicate severe problems, then CHI can go so far as to recommend the dismissal of the responsible board.

CHI reviews are based upon the best currently available evidence. CHI also ensures that NHS providers use the latest available technologies that correspond with national guidance and advice (e.g. it works with the Audit Commission to monitor implementation of the national service frameworks).

The NHS Reform and Health Care Professions Bill (at the time of publication before Parliament) will, when made law, change the role of CHI. Subject to the new act, CHI will:

- Be able to review all aspects of health care, not just clinical governance
- Recommend measures to improve standards
- Produce for the Health Secretary an annual report on the state of the NHS in England and Wales, which will be laid before Parliament
- Set up a new office for information on healthcare performance, which will be involved in performance assessment and the publication of a trust rating system

CHI and functions of the Audit Commission and the National Care Standards Commission will merge – possibly in 2003 – to form the Commission for Healthcare Audit and Inspection (see below).

The Commission for Healthcare Audit and Inspection

The accountability of NHS organisations will be strengthened by the creation of a new inspectorate – the Commission for Healthcare Audit and Inspection (CHAI) – announced in April 2002 (*Delivering the NHS Plan – next steps on investment, next steps on reform*).

CHAI will be an independent body, responsible for the audit/inspection of the performance of both the public and private health care sectors. It will merge the existing Commission for Health Improvement with the health value-for-money role of the Audit Commission, and the private healthcare role of the National Care Standards Commission.
CHAI will:

- Inspect all NHS hospitals
- License the provision of private health care
- Conduct national value-for-money audits of the NHS
- Validate published performance statistics on the NHS, e.g. waiting lists
- Publish star ratings for NHS organisations and recommend special measures if problems persist
- Publish reports on the performance of NHS organisations
- Scrutinise patients' complaints
- Publish an annual report on the NHS to Parliament

It is currently anticipated that CHAI will be set up to run in 2003.

The national performance assessment framework

The performance assessment framework (PAF) is a tool used to assess NHS performance and indicate areas where services can be improved.

Performance and clinical indicators, developed in partnership with health care experts and NHS managers, facilitate the framework. The indicators are used to assess local services against set standards, and highlight areas where action or investigation may be required. Indicators are also used by PCTs and NHS trusts in constructing health improvement and modernisation plans. The latest sets of NHS performance indicators were published in February 2002.

The PAF was used in 2001 as a basis for issuing the first star ratings for acute NHS trusts. The star ratings system awards stars to NHS organisations on the basis of their performance. At the extremes, the best performing hospitals are awarded the full three stars: the worst performing no stars.

Under-performing hospitals are given a deadline to improve performance to an acceptable level. The rating a hospital receives carries with it funding and autonomy ramifications –

effectively, high performing hospitals are entrusted with more money and are given greater freedom over how funds are spent. It is anticipated that, in 2002, assessment will be extended to all NHS organisations.

The national service frameworks

The national service frameworks (NSFs) are a programme of Government initiatives targeted on major health and disease areas. They set standards and objectives that apply across the NHS in England and Wales and indicate the appropriate services that ought to be available in primary care and secondary care. The aim is to ensure that high standards of care are achieved and variations in service eradicated.

The Commission for Health Improvement, in its routine inspection of NHS organisations, scrutinises progress on the implementation of NSF objectives. To date, three NSFs have been published:

NSF for mental health (published September 1999)
Includes – prioritising services for working age adults suffering from mental illness, mental health promotion, access to mental health services in primary care, supporting carers, and the prevention of suicide.

NSF for coronary heart disease (published March 2000)
Includes – prevention, diagnosis and treatment of CHD, effective rehabilitation, improving ambulance response times, and increasing the prescription of aspirin, beta-blockers and statins following heart attack.

NSF for older people (published March 2001)
Includes – combating age discrimination in the NHS (ensuring resources are made available irrespective of age), tackling stroke and falls, reinstating single sex wards, and improving services for older people with mental health problems.

A cancer plan, an NSF in effect if not in name, was published in September 2000. It aims to consolidate cancer care services such as research, prevention, screening, diagnosis and treatment. Main objectives are to reduce smoking, improve waiting times for treatment and augment hospice care.

NSFs in the pipeline include:

- The NSF for diabetes – standards were published in December 2001 and the full NSF is expected in 2002
- The NSF for renal services
- The NSF for children
- The NSF for long-term health conditions

DELIVERING THE NHS PLAN

Delivering the NHS Plan – next steps on investment, next steps on reform was published in April 2002 and described the stages being undertaken to reform the NHS in line with the NHS Plan (published July 2000 and setting out the Government's 10-year plan to modernise the NHS).

To summarise the main objectives of *Delivering the NHS Plan*:

Primary care

- Primary care trusts (PCTs) will be able to purchase care from public sector, private or voluntary providers
- There will be 500 more primary care centres
- Separate surgical units or 'diagnostic and treatment centres' will provide more elective surgery outside of the hospital setting
- Each PCT will publish a prospectus, informing its resident population of the type and quality of services offered.

Secondary care

- A system will be introduced so that hospitals can be paid according to results
- To combat waiting times, cash incentives will be used to increase elective surgery
- 40 new hospitals are planned
- Waiting times for operations will fall from a maximum of 15 months in 2002 to 12 months by 2003, 6 months by 2005 and 3 months by 2008.

Despite earlier controversy, the first NHS foundation hospitals will be established, possibly in 2002. They will have control over their assets and have more autonomy in employing and rewarding staff. They will also devise their own board arrangements, so as to involve not only staff, but patients and the public.

New measures will tackle the problem of bed-blocking (which occurs where patients, mainly elderly people, unnecessarily occupy hospital beds because there are not adequate social care facilities to allow them to be discharged, e.g. nursing home care or home help). As an incentive to ensuring sufficient post-hospital care, local authorities will be made accountable for hospital bed-blocking costs. Conversely, charges will be made on hospitals which discharge patients prematurely, leading to avoidable emergency readmission.

Patient power

- Patients will be able to opt for treatment at alternative hospitals, so as to benefit from shorter waiting lists
- Patients waiting for at least six months for heart surgery will be able to choose their own hospital – in the public or private sector

NHS staff targets for 2008

- 15,000 additional GPs and consultants
- 30,000 additional therapists and scientists
- 35,000 additional nurses, midwives and health visitors

The Commission for Healthcare Audit and Inspection

See individual entry under 'Quality in NHS services'.

FUNDING THE NHS

The Budget 2002

In the April 2002 Budget, significant additional funds were promised for the NHS:

- A further £2.4 billion to be allocated to UK health spending in 2003-04

- A commitment that UK NHS spending will grow 7.4% a year (7.5% in England) to 2007- 08 – an increase of 45%, after inflation
- UK health care expenditure will be 9.4% of GDP by 2007-08

Funding for the increase in spending is being met by:

- An increase in national insurance contributions from April 2003
- Freezing the personal allowance for under 65s in 2003/04

Projected UK NHS expenditure following the April 2002 Budget

Year	2003/04	2004/05	2005/06	2006/07	2007/08
£ billion	72.1	79.3	87.2	95.9	105.6

Spending on social services in England is planned to increase by 6% a year, in real terms, up to 2006 (an additional personal social services allocation of £0.4 billion will be made in 2003/04).

Projected personal social services expenditure in England following the April 2002 Budget

Year	2003/04	2004/05	2005/06
£ billion	12.5	13.4	14.6

The Wanless report

The Chancellor's review of NHS expenditure in the Budget was informed by the review, *Securing our Future Health: Taking a Long-Term View*, also known as the Wanless report (after Derek Wanless, who undertook the report), published April 2002.

The report was an independent review of the likely trends affecting the UK health service over the next 20 years. Its aim was to ascertain the resources required to deliver a publicly funded, quality service, not based upon ability to pay.

The report concluded that:

- Delivering the envisaged service would require not only further resources but also the reform of the existing system
- More of the UK's resources should be devoted to health care
  - From 7.7% of GDP at present to around 10.6%-12.5% in 20 years
  - Growth in UK NHS spending of 4.2%-5.1% per annum, in real terms, over the next 20 years
- A short-term boost in funding was required to improve standards as quickly as possible
- In later years, significant increases in the NHS workforce will be required to sustain and implement changes.

DEVOLUTION IN THE UK

The provision of health care across the UK has been significantly affected by the creation of the Scottish Parliament, Welsh Assembly and Northern Ireland Assembly. Each country of the UK is now, to a degree, responsible for the provision of health care within its own borders, with the English Parliament only retaining control of a few UK-wide policy areas, e.g. for abortion and human genetics.

The Scottish Parliament

In Scotland, a referendum held in September 1997 – in which the majority voted in favour of devolution – led to the UK government introducing legislation allowing for the creation of the Scottish Parliament.

The enabling act - the Scotland Act 1998 – received Royal Assent in November 1998 and provided for the establishment of the Scottish Parliament. The Scottish Parliament is able to pass laws that affect Scotland on a range of issues (including health) and raise or lower the basic rate of income tax by up to 3 pence in the pound.

The first elections to the Scottish Parliament were in May 1999 – there are 129 Scottish MPs – and the Parliament took up its full powers in July 1999.

The Welsh Assembly

In September 1997, a referendum in Wales gave consent to the implementation of the Government's proposals for devolution in Wales (as set out in the white paper, *A Voice for Wales*). The Government of Wales Act 1998 established the National Assembly for Wales, and the National Assembly for Wales (Transfer of Functions) Order 1999, enabled the transfer of devolved powers and responsibilities to the Assembly in July 1999.

The National Assembly for Wales develops and implements policies, and allocates funding from the Treasury.

The Northern Ireland Assembly

The Belfast (Good Friday) Agreement instigated devolution and established the Northern Ireland Assembly with the election of 108 members in 1998.

There are 10 separate departments of government, concerned with the development of policy, and an executive committee, which is made up of a first minister and deputy, and ten ministers with responsibility for the departments. The departments of government were agreed by the Assembly in February 1999 and fully implemented in December of the same year, when power was devolved.

HEALTH CARE ACROSS THE UK

The NHS in Scotland

The Scottish Parliament is responsible for the NHS in Scotland, including public health and mental health. The Parliament controls the structure of the service, and is able to determine the configuration of health boards, trusts and other health care groups.

The Scottish Executive Health Department (SEHD) supports ministers, develops strategy, allocates resources, implements policy and manages NHS performance.

The SEHD oversees the work of:

- 15 area health boards, which are responsible for health service planning
- 28 self-governing NHS trusts, which are responsible for providing services to patients

In each of the health board areas a single unified NHS board is responsible for overseeing the local NHS. The boards work with NHS trusts to develop local health services.

There are both primary care and acute hospital trusts in Scotland. Primary care trusts provide family health care, community and mental health services. In PCTs, GPs may form local health care cooperatives, which are bodies of health care professionals from different localities, working to improve primary care services. The co-operatives may control budgets for primary and community services.

Acute hospital trusts provide hospital services in Scotland, and are commissioned by the health boards.

The NHS in Wales

The Health and Social Services Committee of the National Assembly for Wales sets policy and allocates funds to the NHS in Wales.

Five regional health authorities buy services from health care professionals in primary care, secondary care, tertiary care (specialist hospitals which treat a limited range of conditions), and community care.

Local health groups, committees of the health authorities, currently exist in each local authority area. They provide health and social care through a combination of the health professions, other agencies, and the public. Local health groups take responsibility for improving health, clinical governance, and commissioning hospital and community services.

From 2003 local health groups will become local health boards, statutory bodies with a wider range of powers. Twenty-two local health boards will be established.

There are nearly 2,000 GPs in Wales, providing primary care services, as well as the full range of other primary care professionals. The future of primary care in Wales underwent consultation in 2001, with new ideas and recommendations to improve primary services being considered. Responses to the consultation are currently being considered, with an announcement on progress due in 2002.

Fifteen NHS trusts (including the one ambulance trust) manage 135 hospitals, containing approximately 15,000 beds. Some hospital services, e.g. minor injuries, and minor elective surgery are increasingly being undertaken in partnership with primary and community services.

The NHS in Northern Ireland

In Northern Ireland, the Department of Health, Social Services and Public Safety (DHSSPS) is responsible for health and personal social services (primary and secondary care, community health and personal social services), and public health. (The public safety role is concerned with the fire authority, food safety and emergency planning.) The DHSSPS is charged with improving the health of the public and setting priorities for healthcare delivery.

Four health and social services boards commission health and social care services. They assess local needs, negotiate contracts and arrange services. They are also responsible for ensuring that services are provided to a high standard and are clinically and cost effective.

Nineteen trusts in Northern Ireland provide the services agreed through the commissioning arrangements with the health and social services boards. The trusts provide hospital (acute and psychiatric), community and social services, either individually or in combination. A single trust is responsible for the Northern Ireland ambulance service.

GP fundholding arrangements came to an end in Northern Ireland in April 2002, with the creation of local health and social care groups (LHSCG) – of which there will be 15. LHSCGs are centred around GP practices and are expected to create partnership opportunities between primary care providers and other agencies/groups, including the public. It is expected that they will manage a budget for commissioning by April 2003.

Fifteen acute hospitals in Northern Ireland provide hospital services to patients. A number of community hospitals also provide a range of non-emergency services, and are often supervised by GPs.

A report into the future of acute hospital services in Northern Ireland was published in June 2001. It made far-reaching recommendations, including the reconfiguration of services, additional funding and changes to the primary care/hospital interface. The results of a consultation exercise on the report's conclusions are due for announcement in 2002.

John Chater, Development Manager
Binley's – health & care information specialist, www.binleys.com

HEALTH

Primary Care Trusts

Data supplied by Binleys (Beechwood House Publishing Ltd)

Aberdeen & North LHCC
Bridge of Don Health Clinic, Cairnfold Road, Aberdeen, Aberdeenshire AB22 8LD
Tel: 01224 227831

Aberdeen Inner City LHCC
Denburn Health Centre, Rosemount Viaduct, Aberdeen, Aberdeenshire AB25 1QB
Tel: 01224 555252

Aberdeen West LHCC
Forester Hill Health Centre, Westburn Road, Aberdeen, Aberdeenshire AB25 2AY
Tel: 01224 559909

Adur, Arun and Worthing Primary Care Trust
1 The Causeway, Goring-by Sea, Worthing, West Sussex BN12 6BT
Tel: 01903 708419

Airdrie Local Health Care Co-operative
Adam Avenue Clinic, South Nimmo Street, Airdrie, Lanarkshire ML6 6DN
Tel: 01236 769291

Airedale Primary Care Trust
Airedale House, 21A Mornington Street, Keighley, West Yorkshire BD21 2EA
Tel: 01535 690416

Amber Valley Primary Care Trust
Babington Hospital (Meadow Suite), Derby Road, Belper, Derbyshire DE56 1WH
Tel: 01773 525099

Anglesey Local Health Group
17 High Street, Llangefni, Anglesey, LL77 7LT
Tel: 01248 751229

Angus LHCC
Whitehills Hospital, Station Road, Forfar, Angus DD8 3DY
Tel: 01307 464551

Annandale and Eskdale LHCC
Lochmaben Hospital, Lockmaben, Lockerbie, Dumfriesshire DG11 1RQ
Tel: 01387 811743

Anniesland/Bearsden/Milngavie LHCC
85 Milngavie Road, Bearsden, Glasgow, Lanarkshire G61 2DN
Tel: 0141 211 5627

Arbroath & Friockheim LHCC
c/o Arbroath Infirmary, Arbroath, Angus DD11 2AT
Tel: 01241 872584

Argyll & Bute LHCC
Lorn Medical Centre, Soroba Road, Oban, Argyll PA34 4HE
Tel: 01631 570082

Ashfield Primary Care Trust
The Ashfield Business Centre, Idlewells Precinct, Sutton-in-Ashfield, Nottinghamshire NG17 1BP
Tel: 01623 559568

Ashford Primary Care Trust
Unit 3, Eurogate Business Park, Thomson Road, Ashford, Kent TN24 8XW
Tel: 01233 655800

Ashton, Leigh & Wigan Primary Care Trust
Bryan House, 61 Standishgate, Wigan, Lancashire WR1 1AH
Tel: 01942 772711

Ayr Prestwick & Troon LHCC
Ailsa Hospital Campus, Dalmellington Road, Ayr, Ayrshire KA6 6AB
Tel: 01292 268983

Badenoch & Strathspey LHCC
St Vincent's Hospital, Kingussie, Inverness-Shire PH21 1EX
Tel: 01540 661219

Banff & Buchan LHCC
Chalmers Hospital, Clunie Street, Banff, Aberdeenshire AB45 1JA
Tel: 01261 819048

Barking and Dagenham Primary Care Trust
Clock House, East Street, Barking, Essex IG11 8EY
Tel: 020 8532 6285

Barnet Primary Care Trust
Hyde House, The Hyde, Edgware Road, London, NW9 6QQ
Tel: 020 8201 4700

Barnsley Primary Care Trust
Hilder House, 49/51 Gawber Road, Barnsley, South Yorkshire S75 2PY
Tel: 01226 779922

Basildon Primary Care Trust
The Hatherley, Basildon, Essex SS14 2QJ
Tel: 01268 441622

Bassetlaw Primary Care Trust
Retford Hospital, North Road, Retford, Nottinghamshire DN22 7XF
Tel: 01777 274400

Bath & North East Somerset Primary Care Trust
c/o St Martins Hospital, Midford Road, Bath, Avon BA2 5RP
Tel: 01225 831800

Bebington & West Wirral Primary Care Trust
Administration Block, St Catherine's Hospital, Church Road, Tranmere, Wirral, Merseyside CH42 0LQ
Tel: 0151 651 3979

Bedford Primary Care Trust
Gilbert Hitchcock House, 21 Kimbolton Road, Bedford, Bedfordshire MK40 2AW
Tel: 01234 795714

Bedfordshire Heartlands Primary Care Trust
1 & 2 Doolittle Mill, Froghall Road, Ampthill, Bedfordshire MK45 2NX
Tel: 01525 631153

Bexhill & Rother Primary Care Trust
Bexhill Hospital, Holliers Hill, Bexhill-on-Sea, East Sussex TN40 2DZ
Tel: 01424 735600

Bexley Primary Care Trust
221 Erith Road, Bexleyheath, Kent DA7 6HZ
Tel: 020 8298 6000

Billericay Brentwood & Wickford Primary Care Trust
Highwood Hospital Site, Geary Drive, Ongar Road, Brentwood, Essex CM15 9DY
Tel: 01277 302516

Birkenhead & Wallasey Primary Care Trust
The Admin Block, St Catherines Hospital, Church Road, Birkenhead, Merseyside CH42 0LQ
Tel: 0151 651 0011

Birmingham North East Primary Care Trust
Suite 20, Waterlinks House, Richard Street, Birmingham, West Midlands B7 4AA
Tel: 0121 333 4113

Blackburn with Darwen Primary Care Trust
Guide Business Centre, School Lane, Blackburn, Lancashire BB1 2QH
Tel: 01254 267000

Blackpool Primary Care Trust
Blackpool Technology Management Centre, Faraday Way, Blackpool, FY2 0JW
Tel: 01253 473637

Blackwater Valley & Hart Primary Care Trust
Winchfield Lodge, Old Potbridge Road, Winchfield, Hook, Hampshire RG27 8BT
Tel: 01252 849000

Blaenau Gwent Local Health Group
16a Market Square, Brynmawr, Gwent NP23 4AJ
Tel: 01495 313838

Bolton Primary Care Trust
St Peters House, Silverwell Street, Bolton, Lancashire BL1 1PP
Tel: 01204 377000

Bootle & Litherland Primary Care Trust
First Floor, Merton House, Stanley Road, Bootle, Merseyside L20 3DL
Tel: 0151 288 5300

Borders LHCC
Borders Primary Care NHS Trust, Newstead, Melrose, Roxburghshire TD6 9DB
Tel: 01896 825508

Borders West LHCC
Hay Lodge Health Centre, Neadpath Road, Peebles, Peeblesshire EH45 8JG
Tel: 01721 723710

Bournemouth Primary Care Trust
Trust Headquarters, 11 Shelley Road, Boscombe, Bournemouth, Dorset BH1 4JQ
Tel: 01202 443700

Bracknell Forest Primary Care Trust
51/52 Turing Drive, Bracknell, Berkshire RG12 7SR
Tel: 01344 823250

Bradford City Primary Care Trust
1st Floor, Joseph Brennan House, Sunbridge Road, Bradford, West Yorkshire BD1 2SY
Tel: 01274 424780

Bradford South & West Primary Care Trust
Queensbury Health Centre, Russell Road, Queensbury, Bradford, West Yorkshire BD13 2AG
Tel: 01274 321800

Brent Primary Care Trust
Wembley Health & Care Centre, 116 Chaplin Road, Wembley, Middlesex HA0 4UZ
Tel: 020 8795 6000

Bridgend Local Health Group
North Court, David Street, Bridgend Industrial Estate, Bridgend, Mid Glamorgan CF31 3TP
Tel: 01656 754400

Bridgeton LHCC
Bridgeton Health Centre, 201 Abercromby Street, Glasgow, Lanarkshire G40 2DA
Tel: 0141 531 6540

Brighton & Hove City Primary Care Trust
6th Floor, Vantage Point, New England Road, Brighton, East Sussex BN1 4GW
Tel: 01273 295490

Bristol North Primary Care Trust
King Square House, King Square, Bristol, Avon BS2 8EE
Tel: 0117 900 2677

Bristol South & West Primary Care Trust
Central Health Clinic, Tower Hill, Bristol, Avon BS2 0JD
Tel: 0117 929 1010

Broadland Primary Care Trust
The Octagon, St Michaels Hospital, Cawston Road, Aylsham, Norwich, Norfolk NR11 6NA
Tel: 01263 738600

Bromley Primary Care Trust
Global House, 10 Station Approach, Hayes, Bromley, Kent BR2 7EH
Tel: 020 8315 8315

Broxtowe & Hucknall Primary Care Trust
Priory Court, Derby Road, Nottingham, NG9 2TA
Tel: 0115 875 4900

Burnley, Pendle & Rossendale Primary Care Trust
31-33 Kenyon Road, Nelson, Lancashire BB9 5SZ
Tel: 01282 619909

Burntwood Lichfield & Tamworth Primary Care Trust
Guardian House, Rotten Row, Lichfield, Staffordshire WS13 6JB
Tel: 01543 410020

Bury Primary Care Trust
21 Silver Street, Bury, Lancashire BL9 0LN
Tel: 0161 762 3100

Caerphilly Local Health Group
Ystrad Mynach Hospital, Caerphilly Road, Ystrad Mynach, Hengoed, Mid Glamorgan CF82 7XU
Tel: 01443 862056

Caithness LHCC
Riverview Practice, Wick Medical Centre, Martha Terrace, Wick, Caithness KW1 5EL
Tel: 01955 602355

Calderdale Primary Care Trust
School House, 56 Hopwood Lane, Halifax, West Yorkshire HX1 5ER
Tel: 01422 397300

Cambridge City Primary Care Trust
Heron Court, Ida Darwin, Block 23, Fulbourn, Cambridge, Cambridgeshire CB1 5EE
Tel: 01223 885700

Camden Primary Care Trust
4th Floor East, St Pancras Hospital, St Pancras Way, London, NW1 0PE
Tel: 020 7530 3500

Camglen LHCC
130 Stonelaw Road, Glasgow, Lanarkshire G73 2PQ
Tel: 0141 531 6000

Cannock Chase Primary Care Trust
Coppice Suite, c/o Cannock Chase Hospital, Brunswick Road, Cannock, Staffordshire WS11 2XY
Tel: 01543 576595

Canterbury & Coastal Primary Care Trust
Chesterfield Medical Centre, Reeves Way, Chesterfield, Whitstable, Kent CT5 3QU
Tel: 01227 794777

Cardiff Local Health Group
Trenewydd, Fairwater Road, Llandaff, Cardiff, South Glamorgan CF1 2LD
Tel: 029 2055 2212

Carlisle & District Primary Care Trust
The Coppice, Cumwhinton Drive, Carlisle, Cumbria CA1 3SX
Tel: 01228 602727

Carmarthenshire Local Health Group
Glanmor Terrace, Burry Port, Carmarthen, Carmarthenshire SA16 0NE
Tel: 01554 834962

Carrick & Doon Valley LHCC
West Lodge, Ailsa Hospital, Dalmellington Road, Ayr, Ayrshire KA6 6AB
Tel: 01292 289564

Carrick Primary Care Trust
The Old Nurses Home, City Hospital, Infirmary Hill, Truro, Cornwall TR1 2HZ
Tel: 01872 354499

Castle Point & Rochford Primary Care Trust
12 Castle Road, Rayleigh, Essex SS6 7QF
Tel: 01268 464500

Central Aberdeenshire LHCC
Inverurie Hospital, Upper Boat Road, Inverurie, Aberdeenshire AB51 3UL
Tel: 01467 672752

Central Cheshire Primary Care Trust
Barony Court, Barony Road, Nantwich, Cheshire CW5 5QU
Tel: 01270 415300

Central Cornwall Primary Care Trust
The Old Nurses Home, City Hospital, Infirmary Hill, Truro, Cornwall TR1 2HZ
Tel: 01872 354499

Central Derby Primary Care Trust
118 Osmaston Road, Derby, Derbyshire DE1 2RD
Tel: 01332 203102

Central Liverpool Primary Care Trust
Hartington Road Family Health Clinic, Hartington Road, Liverpool, Merseyside L8 0SQ
Tel: 0151 734 5832

Central Manchester Primary Care Trust
1st Floor Mauldeth House, Mauldeth Road West, Chorlton, Manchester, M21 7RL
Tel: 0161 958 4000

Central Suffolk Primary Care Trust
Stow Lodge Centre, Chilton Way, Stowmarket, Suffolk IP14 1SZ
Tel: 01449 616346

Ceredigion Local Health Group
First Floor Offices, Natwest Bank, 37 High Street, Lampeter, Dyfed SA48 7BD
Tel: 01570 423983

Charnwood & North West Leicestershire PCT
53 Baxter Gate, Loughborough, Leicestershire LE11 1TH
Tel: 01509 838696

Chelmsford Primary Care Trust
Wood House, St Johns Hospital, Wood Street, Chelmsford, Essex CM2 9BG
Tel: 01245 295000

Cheltenham & Tewkesbury Primary Care Trust
Unit 43, Central Way, Arle Road, Cheltenham, Gloucestershire GL51 8LX
Tel: 01242 548800

Cherwell Vale Primary Care Trust
Oxford Road, Banbury, Oxfordshire OX16 9GE
Tel: 01295 819 500

Cheshire West Primary Care Trust
1829 Building, Countess of Chester Heath Park, Liverpool Road, Chester, Cheshire CH2 1HJ
Tel: 01244 650300

Chesterfield Primary Care Trust
Scarsdale, Newbold Road, Chesterfield, Derbyshire S41 7PF
Tel: 01246 231255

Chiltern & South Bucks Primary Care Trust
Chiltern District Council Offices, King George V Road, Amersham, Buckinghamshire HP6 5AW
Tel: 01494 732020

Chingford, Wanstead & Woodford Primary Care Trust
1st Floor Chingford Health Centre, 109 York Road, Chingford, Essex E4 8LF
Tel: 020 8928 7000

Chorley & South Ribble Primary Care Trust
Dob Bridge Cottage, Twin Lakes Park, Bretherton Road, Croston, Preston, Lancashire PR26 9RF
Tel: 01772 602800

City and Hackney Primary Care Trust
St Leonard's, Nuttall Street, London, N1 5LZ
Tel: 020 7301 3000

Clydebank LHCC
Clydebank Health Centre, Kilbowie Road, Clydebank, Glasgow, G81 2TQ
Tel: 0141 531 6328

Clydesdale Local Health Care Co-operative
Roadmeetings Hospital, Goremire Road, Carluke, Lanarkshire ML8 4PS
Tel: 01555 772271

Coatbridge Local Health Care Co-operative
Coathill Hospital, Hospital Street, Coatbridge, Lanarkshire ML5 4DN
Tel: 01236 707702

Colchester Primary Care Trust
Health Offices, North Essex Health Authority, Turner Road, Colchester, Essex CO4 5JR
Tel: 01206 288500

Conwy Local Health Group
Glyn Colwyn, 19 Rosemary Avenue, Colwyn Bay, Conwy LL29 7PU
Tel: 01492 536586

Cotswold & Vale Primary Care Trust
Corinium House, Cirencester Hospital, Tetbury Road, Cirencester, Gloucestershire GL7 1UX
Tel: 01285 884694

Coventry Primary Care Trust
Christchurch House, Greyfriars Lane, Coventry, West Midlands CV1 2GQ
Tel: 024 7624 6016

Craven, Harrogate & Rural District PCT
1 Sceptre House, 2 Hornbeam Square North, Hornbeam Park, Harrogate, North Yorkshire HG2 8PB
Tel: 01423 815150

Crawley Primary Care Trust
Fairfield Annexe, West Green Drive, West Green, Crawley, West Sussex RH11 7DH
Tel: 01293 600460

Croydon Primary Care Trust
Knollys House, 17 Addiscombe Road, Croydon, Surrey CR0 6SR
Tel: 020 8401 3900

Cumbernauld/Kilsyth LHCC
Central Health Centre, North Carbrain Road, Cumbernauld, G67 1BJ
Tel: 01236 731771

Dacorum Primary Care Trust
The Isbister Centre, Chaulden House Gardens, Off Chaulden Lane, Hemel Hempstead, Hertfordshire HP1 2BW
Tel: 01442 840950

Darlington Primary Care Trust
Valley House, Valley Street North, Darlington, Co Durham DL1 1TJ
Tel: 01325 487773

Dartford, Gravesham & Swanley Primary Care Trust
The Livingstone Hospital, East Hill, Dartford, Kent DA1 1SA
Tel: 01322 622369

Daventry & South Northants Primary Care Trust
Danetree Hospital, London Road, Daventry, Northamptonshire NN11 4DY
Tel: 01327 705610

Deeside LHCC
Glen O'Dee Hospital, Corsee Road, Banchory, AB31 5RX
Tel: 01330 826924

Denbighshire Local Health Group
Ty Livingstone, HM Stanley Hospital, St Asaph, Denbighshire LL17 0RS
Tel: 01745 589601

Denniston LHCC
Townhead Health Centre, 16 Alexandra Parade, Glasgow, G31 2ES
Tel: 0141 531 6510

Derbyshire Dales & South Derbyshire PCT
Repton Health Centre, Askew Grove, Repton, Derbyshire DE65 6SH
Tel: 01283 703407

Derwentside Primary Care Trust
Top Floor, Tower Block, Shotley Bridge Hospital, Consett, Co Durham DH8 0NB
Tel: 01207 214371

Doncaster Central Primary Care Trust
Central House, St Catherines Hospital, Tickhill Road, Doncaster, South Yorkshire DN4 8QN
Tel: 01302 796800

Doncaster East Primary Care Trust
Barclay Court, Heavens Walk, Doncaster, South Yorkshire DN4 5HZ
Tel: 01302 381940

Doncaster West Primary Care Trust
West Lodge, St Catherine's Hospital, Tickhill Road, Balby, Doncaster, South Yorkshire DN4 8QN
Tel: 01302 796796

Drumchapel LHCC
Drumchapel Health Centre, 80-90 Kinfauns Drive, Drumchapel, Glasgow, G15 7TS
Tel: 0141 211 6070

Dudley Beacon & Castle Primary Care Trust
Russel House, 1 The Inhedge, Dudley, West Midlands DY1 1RR
Tel: 01384 459500

Dudley South Primary Care Trust
Trust Headquarters, Ridge Hill, Brierley Hill Road, Stourbridge, West Midlands DY8 5ST
Tel: 01384 457373

Dumfries & Nithsdale LHCC
Nithbank, Dumfries, DG1 2SD
Tel: 01387 244404

Dundee LHCC
Liff House, Liff Hospital, Dundee, DD2 5NF
Tel: 01382 423088

Dunfermline LHCC
Carnegie Clinic, Inglis Street, Dunfermline, Fife KY12 7AX
Tel: 01383 733740

Durham & Chester-Le-Street Primary Care Trust
Federation House, Green Lane, Old Elvet, Durham, Co Durham DH1 3JY
Tel: 0191 333 3917

Durham Dales Primary Care Trust
16 Tentern Street, Bishop Auckland, Co Durham DL14 7AD
Tel: 01388 458835

Ealing Primary Care Trust
1 Armstrong Way, Southall, Middlesex UB2 4SA
Tel: 020 8893 0303

Easington Primary Care Trust
Health Partnership Centre, Council Offices, Seaside Lane, Easington, Peterlee, Co Durham SR8 3TN
Tel: 0191 554 5700

East Ayrshire LHCC
Strathlea Cottages, Holmes Road, Kilmarnock, KA1 1TW
Tel: 01563 537243

East Cambridgeshire & Fenland Primary Care Trust
Fenland View, Alexander Road, Wisbech, Cambridgeshire PE13 1HQ
Tel: 01945 469400

East Devon Primary Care Trust
Dean Clarke House, Southernhay East, Exeter, Devon EX1 1PQ
Tel: 01392 205205

East Elmbridge & Mid Surrey Primary Care Trust
Cedar Court, Guildford Road, Leatherhead, Surrey KT22 9RX
Tel: 01372 227300

East Hampshire Primary Care Trust
3rd Floor, Raebarn House, Hulbert Road, Waterlooville, Hampshire PO7 7GP
Tel: 023 9224 8800

East Highland LHCC
Maywood, Ferry Road, Dingwall, IV15 9QS
Tel: 01349 863313

East Kent Coastal Primary Care Trust
Protea House, New Bridge, Marine Parade, Dover, Kent CT17 9HQ
Tel: 01304 205706

East Kilbride LHCC
Greenhills Health Centre, 20 Greenhills Square, East Kilbride, G75 8TT
Tel: 01355 234325

East Leeds Primary Care Trust
Oaktree House, 408 Oakwood Lane, Leeds, West Yorkshire LS8 3LR
Tel: 0113 391 8300

East Lincolnshire Primary Care Trust
c/o Boston Borough Council, Municipal Buildings, West Street, Boston, Lincolnshire PE21 8QR
Tel: 01205 314353

East Lothian LHCC
Eden Hall Hospital, Pinkieburn, Musselburgh, East Lothian EH21 7TZ
Tel: 0131 536 8000

East Staffordshire Primary Care Trust
The Outwoods Site, Belvedere Road, Burton-on-Trent, Staffordshire DE13 0QL
Tel: 01283 593151

East Surrey Primary Care Trust
St Johns Court, St Johns Road, Redhill, Surrey RH1 6DS
Tel: 01737 780209

East Sutherland LHCC
Lawson Memorial Hospital, Station Road, Golspie, Sutherland KW10 6SS
Tel: 01408 664031

East Yorkshire Primary Care Trust
33 Lairgate, Beverley, East Yorkshire HU17 8ET
Tel: 01482 862832

Eastbourne Downs Primary Care Trust
3rd Floor, Greencoat House, 32 St Leonards Road, Eastbourne, East Sussex BN21 3UT
Tel: 01323 41774

Eastern Birmingham Primary Care Trust
Suite 20, Waterlinks House, Richard Street, Aston, Birmingham, B74 1AA
Tel: 0121 333 4113

Eastern Cheshire Primary Care Trust
Toft Road Surgery, Toft Road, Knutsford, Cheshire WA16 9DX
Tel: 01565 621071

Eastern Glasgow LHCC
Shettleston Health Centre, 420 Old Shettleston Road, Glasgow, G32 7JZ
Tel: 0141 531 6280

Eastern Hull Primary Care Trust
Netherhall, Wawne Road, Sutton, Hull, East Yorkshire HU7 4YG
Tel: 01482 335400

Eastern Leicester Primary Care Trust
1st Floor Mansion House, 41 Guild Hall Lane, Leicester, Leicestershire LE1 5FR
Tel: 0116 295 1400

Eastern Wakefield Primary Care Trust
Friarwood House, Friarwood Lane, Pontefract, West Yorkshire WF8 1UA
Tel: 01977 602000

Eastleigh & Test Valley Primary Care Trust
The Mount Hospital, Bishopstoke, Hampshire SO50 6ZB
Tel: 023 8065 2537

Eastwood LHCC
Clarkston Clinic, 56 Busby Road, Glasgow, G76 7AT
Tel: 0141 300 1299

Eden Valley Primary Care Trust
8 Tynefield Drive, Penrith, Cumbria CA11 8JA
Tel: 01768 245317

Ellesmere Port & Neston Primary Care Trust
5 Civic Way, Ellesmere Port, Cheshire CH65 0AX
Tel: 0151 373 4900

Enfield Primary Care Trust
Holbrooke House, Cockfosters Road, Barnet, London, EN4 0DL
Tel: 020 8272 5500

Epping Forest Primary Care Trust
Birchwood House, St Margarets Hospital, The Plain, Epping, Essex CM16 6TN
Tel: 01992 902010

Erewash Primary Care Trust
Ilkeston Health Centre, South Street, Ilkeston, Derbyshire DE7 5PZ
Tel: 0115 951 2300

Exeter Primary Care Trust
Dean Clarke House, Southernhay East, Exeter, Devon EX1 1PQ
Tel: 01392 207522

Fareham & Gosport Primary Care Trust
Unit 180 Fareham Reach, 166 Fareham Road, Gosport, Hampshire PO13 0FH
Tel: 01329 233447

Flintshire Local Health Group
c/o North Wales Health Authority, Preswylfa, Hendy Road, Mold, Flintshire CH7 1PZ
Tel: 01352 744103

Forth Valley South LHCC
Old Denny Road, Larbert, FK5 4SD
Tel: 01324 404175

Fylde Primary Care Trust
16-18 St Georges Road, St Annes, Lancashire FY8 2AE
Tel: 01253 789170

Gateshead Primary Care Trust
Unit 12 Enterprise House, Kingsway, Team Valley Trading Estate, Gateshead, Tyne & Wear NE11 0SR
Tel: 0191 491 5713

Gedling Primary Care Trust
Arnot Hill House, Civic Centre, Arnot Hill Park, Arnold, Nottingham, NG5 6LU
Tel: 0115 859 9090

Glenrothes LHCC
Cos Lane Surgery, Woodside Road, Glenrothes, Fife KY7 4AQ
Tel: 01592 769090

Great Yarmouth Primary Care Trust
Astley Cooper House, Estcourt Road, Great Yarmouth, Norfolk NR30 4JH
Tel: 01493 856156

Greater Derby Primary Care Trust
5 Stuart Street, Derby, Derbyshire DE1 2EQ
Tel: 01332 298700

Greater Shawlands LHCC
Pollockshaws Clinic, 35 Wellgreen, Glasgow, G43 1RR
Tel: 0141 577 7734

Greater Yardley Primary Care Trust
Suite 20, Waterlink House, Richard Street, Birmingham, B7 4AA
Tel: 0121 333 4113

Greenwich Primary Care Trust
1 Hyde Vale, Greenwich, London, SE10 8QG
Tel: 020 8694 7300

Guildford & Waverley Primary Care Trust
The Jarvis Centre, Stroughton Road, Guildford, Surrey GU1 1LJ
Tel: 01483 783116

Gwynedd Local Health Group
Eryldon, Campbell Road, Caernarfon, Gwynedd LL55 1HU
Tel: 01286 672451

Halton Primary Care Trust
North Cheshire Health, Lister Road, Artmoor West Estate, Runcorn, Cheshire WA7 1TW
Tel: 01928 593000

Hambleton & Richmondshire Primary Care Trust
Duchess of Kent Hospital, Horne Road, Catterick Garrison, North Yorkshire DL9 4DF
Tel: 01748 834908

Hamilton/Blantyre LHCC
Udston Hospital, Farm Road, Burnbank, Hamilton, Lanarkshire ML3 9LA
Tel: 01698 723200

Hammersmith and Fulham Primary Care Trust
5-7 Parsons Green, London, SW6 4UL
Tel: 020 8846 7836

Haringey Primary Care Trust
St Ann's Hospital, St Ann's Road, Tottenham, London, N15 3TH
Tel: 020 8442 6000

Harlow Primary Care Trust
Level 16, Terminus House, Terminus Street, Harlow, Essex CM20 1XE
Tel: 01279 694747

Harrow Primary Care Trust
Grace House, Harrovian Business Village, Bessborough Road, Harrow, Middlesex HA1 3EX
Tel: 020 8422 6644

Hartlepool Primary Care Trust
Third Floor, Mandale House, Harbour Walk, The Marina, Hartlepool, Cleveland TS24 0UX
Tel: 01429 285079

Hastings & St Leonards Primary Care Trust
P O Box 124, St Leonards, TN38 9WH
Tel: 01424 457100

Havering Primary Care Trust
Bentley Suite, St Georges Hospital, The Willows, 117 Suttons Lane, Hornchurch, Essex RM12 6RS
Tel: 01708 465000

Heart of Birmingham Teaching Primary Care Trust
The Carnegie Centre, Hunters Road, Hockley, Birmingham, B19 1DR
Tel: 0121 255 7695

Herefordshire Primary Care Trust
Belmont Abbey, Belmont, Hereford, Herefordshire HR2 9RP
Tel: 01432 344344

Hertsmere Primary Care Trust
The Elms Clinic, High Street, Potters Bar, Hertfordshire EN6 5DA
Tel: 01707 647586

Heywood & Middleton Primary Care Trust
c/o Citizens Advice Bureau, Milton Street, Middleton, Manchester, M24 5TU
Tel: 0161 643 6900

High Peak & Dales Primary Care Trust
Newholme Hospital, Baslow Road, Bakewell, Derbyshire DE45 1AD
Tel: 01629 812525

Hillingdon Primary Care Trust
Kirk House, 97-109 High Street, Yiewsley, West Drayton, Middlesex UB7 7HJ
Tel: 01895 452000

Hinckley and Bosworth Primary Care Trust
Heath Lane Surgery, Earl Shilton, Leicester, Leicestershire LE9 7PB
Tel: 01455 851189

Horsham and Chanctonbury Primary Care Trust
New Park House, North Street, Horsham, West Sussex RH12 1RL
Tel: 01403 215129

Hounslow Primary Care Trust
Phoenix Court, 531 Staines Road, Hounslow, Middlesex TW4 5DP
Tel: 020 8321 2211

Huddersfield Central Primary Care Trust
St Lukes House, Blacknorefoot Road, Crossland Moor, Huddersfield, West Yorkshire HD4 5RH
Tel: 01484 344221

Huntingdonshire Primary Care Trust
The Priory, Priory Road, St Ives, Cambridgeshire PE27 5BB
Tel: 01480 308222

Hyndburn & Ribble Valley Primary Care Trust
Red Rose Court, Clayton Business Park, Clayton-Le-Moors, Accrington, Lancashire BB5 5JR
Tel: 01254 380400

Inverclyde LHCC
Greenock Health Centre, 20 Duncan Street, Greenock, Renfrewshire PA15 4LY
Tel: 01475 724477

Inverness LHCC
c/o Royal Northern Infirmary, Inverness, IV3 5SS
Tel: 01463 715479

Ipswich Primary Care Trust
Second Floor, St Clements Building, Foxhall Road, Ipswich, Suffolk IP3 8LS
Tel: 01473 329050

Irvine Kilwinning & Dundonald LHCC
Pavillion 7, c/o Ayrshire Central Hospital, Kilwinning Road, Irvine, KA12 8SS
Tel: 01294 323579

Isle of Arran LHCC
Arran War Memorial Hospital, Lamlash, Isle of Arran KA27 8LF
Tel: 01770 600777

Isle of Wight Primary Care Trust
c/o Whitecroft, Sandy Lane, Newport, Isle of Wight PO30 3ED
Tel: 01983 535455

Islington Primary Care Trust
c/o Insull Wing, 110 Hampstead Road, London, NW1 2LJ
Tel: 020 7853 5353

Kennet and North Wiltshire Primary Care Trust
Postern House, Cherry Orchard, Marlborough, Wiltshire SN8 4AS
Tel: 01672 517643

Kensington & Chelsea Primary Care Trust
2nd Floor, 125 Old Brompton Road, London, SW7 3RP
Tel: 020 8237 2520

Kincardine LHCC
Arduthrie Lodge, Kincardine Community Hospital, Kirkton Road, Stonehaven, AB39 2NJ
Tel: 01569 792056

Kingston Primary Care Trust
Woodroffe House, Tolworth Hospital, Red Lion Road, Surbiton, Surrey KT6 7QU
Tel: 020 8390 0102

Kirkcaldy & Levenmouth LHCC
c/o Randolph Wemyss Memorial Hospital, Wellesley Road, Buckhaven, Leven, Fife KY8 1HU
Tel: 01592 719044

Knowsley Primary Care Trust
Moregate Road, Knowsley Industrial Park, Kirkby, Liverpool, Merseyside L33 7XU
Tel: 0151 477 4700

Lambeth Primary Care Trust
1 Lower Marsh, London, SE1 7NT
Tel: 020 7716 7000

Langbaurgh Primary Care Trust
Langbaurgh House, Bow Street, Guisborough, Cleveland TS14 7AA
Tel: 01287 284400

Leeds North East Primary Care Trust
South Wing St Mary's House, St Mary's Road, Chapletown, Leeds, West Yorkshire LS7 3JX
Tel: 0113 295 2432

Leeds North West Primary Care Trust
2nd Floor Mill House, Troy Road, Horsforth, Leeds, West Yorkshire LS18 5TN
Tel: 0113 305 7120

Leeds West Primary Care Trust
Armley Park Court, Stanningley Road, Leeds, West Yorkshire LS12 2AE
Tel: 0113 387 4500

Leicester City West Primary Care Trust
Ground Floor, Mansion House, 41 Guildhall Lane, Leicester, Leicestershire LE1 5FR
Tel: 0116 295 1100

Levern Valley LHCC
201 Main Street, Barrhead, Glasgow, G78 1SA
Tel: 0141 880 4149

Lewisham Primary Care Trust
Elizabeth Blackwall House, Wardals Grove, Avonley Road, London, SE13 5ER
Tel: 020 8297 0707

Lincolnshire South West Primary Care Trust
Annexe C, Council Offices, Eastgate, Sleaford, Lincolnshire NG34 7EP
Tel: 01529 304438

Liverpool North Primary Care Trust
Cottage Number 7, New Hall Campus, Longmore Lane, Liverpool, Merseyside L10 1LD
Tel: 0151 293 1900

Lochaber LHCC
Belford Hospital, Belford Road, Fort William, Inverness-Shire PH33 6BS
Tel: 01397 702481

Lomond LHCC
Hartfield, Latta Street, Dumbarton, Dunbartonshire G82 2DB
Tel: 01389 604526

Luton Teaching Primary Care Trust
Nightingale House, 94 Inkerman Street, Luton, Bedfordshire LU1 1JD
Tel: 01582 528840

Maidstone Weald Primary Care Trust
Preston Hall, Forstal Ward, Aylesford, Kent ME20 7NJ
Tel: 01580 720537

Maldon & South Chelmsford Primary Care Trust
Administration Block, St Peter's Hospital, 32a Spital Road, Maldon, Essex CM9 6EG
Tel: 01621 727300

Mansfield District Primary Care Trust
Ransom Hall,Ransom Wood Bus Prk, Southwell Road West, Rainworth, Mansfield, Nottinghamshire NG21 0ER
Tel: 01623 414114

Maryhill/Woodside LHCC
Woodside Health Centre, Barr Street, Glasgow, G20 7LR
Tel: 0141 531 9224

Medway Primary Care Trust
Admirals Offices, Historic Dock Yard, Chatham, Kent ME4 4TZ
Tel: 01634 810800

Melton, Rutland & Harborough Primary Care Trust
St Mary's Hospital, Thorpe Road, Melton Mowbray, Leicester, Leicestershire LE13 1SJ
Tel: 01664 855000

Mendip Primary Care Trust
St Aldhelm's Hospital, Green Lane, Frome, Somerset BA11 4JW
Tel: 01373 468010

Merthyr Tydfil Local Health Group
The Business Centre, Triangle Business Park, Merthyr Tydfil, CF48 4TQ
Tel: 01685 358500

Mid Devon Primary Care Trust
New Court House, Old Rydon Lane, Exeter, Devon EX2 7JU
Tel: 01392 449700

Mid Hampshire Primary Care Trust
Unit 3, Tilbury Farm, Bullington Cross, Sutton Scotney, Winchester, Hampshire SO21 3QQ
Tel: 01962 763940

Mid Sussex Primary Care Trust
Kleamwort, Haywards Heath Hospital, Butlers Green Road, Haywards Heath, West Sussex RH16 4BE
Tel: 01444 4757000

Middlesbrough Primary Care Trust
18 High Force Road, Riverside Park, Middlesbrough, Cleveland TS2 1RH
Tel: 01642 352370

Midlothian LHCC
Dalkeith Health Centre, 24 St Andrew Street, Dalkeith, Midlothian EH22 1AP
Tel: 0131 561 5531

Milton Keynes Primary Care Trust
Standing Way, Eaglestone, Milton Keynes, Buckinghamshire MK6 5NG
Tel: 01908 243933

Monmouthshire Local Health Group
Chepstow Community Hospital, Tempest Way, Chepstow, Monmouthshire NP16 5YX
Tel: 01291 636400

Moray LHCC
Spynie Hospital, Duffus Road, Elgin, IV30 5PW
Tel: 01343 567832

Morecambe Bay Primary Care Trust
Tenterfield, Brigsteer Road, Kendal, Cumbria LA9 5EA
Tel: 01539 797800

Motherwell Local Health Care Co-operative
c/o Motherwell Health Centre, Windmill Hill Street, Motherwell, ML1 1TB
Tel: 01698 254601

Nairn/Ardersier LHCC
c/o The Lodge Hill Clinic, Lodge Hill Road, Nairn, IV12 4RF
Tel: 01667 452096

Neath & Port Talbot Local Health Group
Suite A, Britannic House, Llandarcy Neath, Neath, SA10 6JQ
Tel: 01792 326500

New Forest Primary Care Trust
8 Stern Road, Tatchbury Mount, Calmore, Southampton, Hampshire SO40 2RZ
Tel: 023 8087 4270

Newark & Sherwood Primary Care Trust
65 Northgate, Newark, Nottinghamshire NG24 1HD
Tel: 01636 700238

Newbury and Community Primary Care Trust
Newbury Community Hospital, Andover Road, Newbury, Berkshire RG14 6LS
Tel: 01635 32500

Newcastle Primary Care Trust
Benfield Road, Walkergate, Newcastle Upon Tyne, NE6 4PF
Tel: 0191 219 6000

Newcastle-under-Lyme Primary Care Trust
Bradwell Hospital, Talke Road, Chesterton, Newcastle-under-Lyme, Staffordshire ST5 7NJ
Tel: 01782 425440

Newham Primary Care Trust
c/o Plaistow Hospital, Samson Street, London, E13 9EH
Tel: 020 8586 6200

Newport Local Health Group
9 Clytha Park Road, Newport, Gwent NP20 4US
Tel: 01633 256853

North & East Cornwall Primary Care Trust
Lamellion Hospital, Station Road, Liskeard, Cornwall PL14 4DG
Tel: 01579 335340

North Birmingham Primary Care Trust
Blakeland House, 400 Aldridge Road, Perry Barr, Birmingham, West Midlands B44 8BH
Tel: 0121 332 1900

North Bradford Primary Care Trust
Eccleshill Clinic, Rillington Mead, Harrogate Road, Bradford, West Yorkshire BD10 0ED
Tel: 01274 322190

North Devon Primary Care Trust
12 Boutport Street, Barnstaple, Devon EX31 1RW
Tel: 01271 327779

North East Edinburgh LHCC
Mill Lane Clinic, 5 Mill Lane, Edinburgh, EH6 6TJ
Tel: 0131 536 8801

North East Fife LHCC
North East Fife LHCC, St Andrews Memorial Hospital, Abbey Walk, St Andrews, Fife KY16 9LG
Tel: 01334 476206

North East Lincolnshire Primary Care Trust
Scartho Hall, Diana Princess of Wales Hospital, Scartho Road, Grimsby, Lincolnshire DN33 2BA
Tel: 01472 874111ext 1280

North East Oxfordshire Primary Care Trust
Bicester Community Hospital, Kings End, Bicester, Oxfordshire OX26 6DU
Tel: 01869 604040

North Eastern Derbyshire Primary Care Trust
St Mary's Court, St Mary's Gate, Chesterfield, Derbyshire S41 7TD
Tel: 01246 551158

North Forth Valley LHCC
Forth Valley Primary Care NHS Trust, Old Denny Road, Larbert, FK5 4SD
Tel: 01324 404285

North Glasgow LHCC
Springburn Health Centre, 200 Springburn Way, Glasgow, Lanarkshire G21 1TR
Tel: 0141 531 6746

North Hampshire Primary Care Trust
c/o Executive Suite, Parklands Hospital, Basingstoke, Hampshire RG24 9RH
Tel: 01256 376300

North Herts & Stevenage Primary Care Trust
Solutions House, Dunhams Lane, Letchworth, Hertfordshire SG6 1BE
Tel: 01462 708470

North Kirklees Primary Care Trust
12 Central Arcade, Cleckheaton, West Yorkshire BD19 5DN
Tel: 01274 865568

North Lincolnshire Primary Care Trust
Health Place, Wrawby Road, Brigg, North Lincolnshire DN20 8GS
Tel: 01652 659659

North Manchester Primary Care Trust
2nd Floor, Newton Silk Mill, Holyoak Street, Newton Heath, Manchester, M40 1HA
Tel: 0161 219 9400

North Norfolk Primary Care Trust
Kelling Hospital, Cromer Road, Holt, Norfolk NR25 6QA
Tel: 01263 710611

North Peterborough Primary Care Trust
St John's, Thorpe Road, Peterborough, Cambridgeshire PE3 6JG
Tel: 01733 882288

North Sheffield Primary Care Trust
Welfare House, North Quadrant, Firth Park, Sheffield, South Yorkshire S5 6NU
Tel: 0114 226 4031

North Somerset Primary Care Trust
1st Floor, The Court House, Old Weston Road, Flax Bourton, Bristol, BS48 1UL
Tel: 01275 465200

North Stoke Primary Care Trust
Haywood Hospital, High Lane, Burslem, Stoke-on-Trent, Staffordshire ST6 7AG
Tel: 01782 817709

North Surrey Primary Care Trust
West Elmbridge Borough Office, c/o Walton Community Hospital, Rodney Road, Walton-on-Thames, Surrey KT12 3LD
Tel: 01932 220060

North Tees Primary Care Trust
Tower House, Teesdale South, Thornaby Place, Thornaby, Stockton-on-Tees, Cleveland TS17 6SF
Tel: 01642 352297

North Tyneside Primary Care Trust
Benfield Road, Walkergate, Newcastle, Tyne & Wear NE6 4PF
Tel: 0191 219 6000

North Warwickshire Primary Care Trust
139 Earls Road, Nuneaton, Warwickshire CV11 5HP
Tel: 024 7664 2200

North West Ayrshire & Cumbrae LHCC
LHCC Office - Pavillion 7, Ayrshire Central Hospital, Kilwinning Road, Irvine, KA12 8SS
Tel: 01294 323579

North West Edinburgh LHCC
Corstorphine Hospital, 136 Corstorphine Road, Edinburgh, EH12 6TT
Tel: 0131 334 5472

North West Sutherland LHCC
Lawson Memorial Hospital, Station Road, Golspie, Sutherland KW10 6SS
Tel: 01408 664031

Northampton Primary Care Trust
Highfield, Cliftonville Road, Northampton, Northamptonshire NN1 5DN
Tel: 01604 615202

Northamptonshire Heartlands Primary Care Trust
Isebrook Hospital, Nene House, Irthlingborough Road, Wellingborough, Northamptonshire NN8 1LP
Tel: 01536 494134

Northumberland Primary Care Trust
Merley Croft, Loansdean, Morpeth, Northumberland NE61 2DL
Tel: 01670 394400

Norwich Primary Care Trust
St Andrew's House, Northside, St Andrew's Bus Park, Thorpe St, Andrew, Norwich, Norfolk NR7 0HT
Tel: 01603 307334

Nottingham City Primary Care Trust
Linden House, 261 Beechdale Road, Aspley, Nottingham, Nottinghamshire NG8 3EY
Tel: 0115 942 6000

Oldbury & Smethwick Primary Care Trust
c/o Kingston House, 438 High Street, West Bromwich, West Midlands B70 9LD
Tel: 0121 500 1500

Oldham Primary Care Trust
Westhulme Avenue, Oldham, Lancashire OL1 2PL
Tel: 0161 622 6500

Oxford City Primary Care Trust
The Ritchards Building, Old Road, Hedington, Oxford, Oxfordshire OX3 7LG
Tel: 01865 226900

Paisley LHCC
Larch Grove, Dykebar Hospital, Grahamston Road, Paisley, Renfrewshire PA2 7DE
Tel: 0141 884 5122

Pembrokeshire Local Health Group
Penffynnon, Hawthorn Rise, Haverfordwest, Pembrokeshire SA61 2AZ
Tel: 01437 765865

Perth & Kinross LHCC
Perth Royal Infirmary, Perth, Perthshire PH1 1NX
Tel: 01738 473537

Plymouth Primary Care Trust
Building One, Derriford Business Park, Brest Road, Derriford, Plymouth, Devon PL6 5QZ
Tel: 01752 315315

Poole Primary Care Trust
Parkstone Health Centre, Mansfield Road, Parkstone, Bournemouth, Dorset BH14 0DJ
Tel: 01202 710100

Portsmouth City Primary Care Trust
Finchdean House, Milton Road, Portsmouth, Hampshire PO3 6DP
Tel: 023 9283 5020

Powys Local Health Group
Mansion House, Bronllys, Brecon, Powys LD3 0LS
Tel: 01874 711661

Preston Primary Care Trust
Preston Business Centre, Sharoe Green Hosp, Sharoe Green Lane, Fulwood, Preston, Lancashire PR2 8DU
Tel: 01772 711774

Reading Primary Care Trust
57 - 59 Bath Road, Reading, Berkshire RG30 2BA
Tel: 0118 982 2760

Redbridge Primary Care Trust
Becketts House, 2-14 Ilford Hill, Ilford, Essex IG1 2QX
Tel: 020 8926 5335

Redditch & Bromsgrove Primary Care Trust
Crossgate House, Crossgate Road, Park Farm, Redditch, Worcestershire B98 7SN
Tel: 01527 507040

Renfrew LHCC
c/o The Health Centre, 103 Paisley Road, Renfrew, PA4 8LH
Tel: 0141 886 4044

Rhondda/Cynon Taf Local Health Group
Unit 17 & 18 Centre Court, Treforest Industrial Estate, Pontypridd, Mid Glamorgan CF37 5YR
Tel: 01443 824400

Richmond & Twickenham Primary Care Trust
Teddington Memorial Hospital, Hampton Road, Teddington, Middlesex TW11 0JL
Tel: 020 8408 8210

Rochdale Primary Care Trust
Unit 1 St James Place, 164 Yorkshire Street, Rochdale, Lancashire OL16 2DL
Tel: 01706 516900

Rotherham Primary Care Trust
Headquarters, Bevan House, Oakwood Hall Drive, Rotherham, South Yorkshire S60 3AQ
Tel: 01709 302009

Rowley Regis & Tipton Primary Care Trust
c/o Kingston House, 438 High Street, West Bromwich, West Midlands B70 9LD
Tel: 0121 500 1500

Royston, Buntingford & Bishops Stortford PCT
Rutherford House, Herts & Essex Hospital, Haymeads Lane, Bishops Stortford, Hertfordshire CM23 5JH
Tel: 01279 827228

Rugby Primary Care Trust
Central Surgery, Corporation Street, Rugby, Warwickshire CV21 3SP
Tel: 01788 550860

Rushcliffe Primary Care Trust
6 Bridgford Road, West Bridgford, Nottingham, Nottinghamshire NG2 6AB
Tel: 0115 914 3225

Salford Primary Care Trust
St James House, 2nd Floor, Pendleton Way, Salford, Lancashire M6 5FW
Tel: 0161 212 4800

Scarborough, Whitby & Ryedale Primary Care Trust
13 Yorkersgate, Malton, North Yorkshire YO17 7AA
Tel: 01653 602900

Sedgefield Primary Care Trust
Green Lane, Spennymoor, Co Durham DL16 6HD
Tel: 01388 824006

Selby & York Primary Care Trust
37 Monkgate, York, North Yorkshire YO31 7PB
Tel: 01904 623142

Sheffield South West Primary Care Trust
Old Station Yard, Off Archer Road, Millhouses, Sheffield, South Yorkshire S8 0LA
Tel: 0114 226 4020

Sheffield West Primary Care Trust
4 Dragoon Court, Hillsborough Barracks, Penistone Road, Sheffield, South Yorkshire S6 2GZ
Tel: 0114 285 6920

Shepway Primary Care Trust
8 Radnor Park Avenue, Folkestone, Kent CT19 5BN
Tel: 01303 222481

Shetland LHCC
Lerwick Health Centre, South Road, Lerwick, Shetland, Shetland Islands ZE1 0RB
Tel: 01595 743066

Shropshire County Primary Care Trust
William Farr House, Mytton Oak Road, Shrewsbury, Shropshire SY3 8XL
Tel: 01743 492401

Slough Primary Care Trust
First Floor, c/o Walk in Centre, Upton Hospital, Albert Street, Slough, Berkshire SL1 2BJ
Tel: 01753 635018

Solihull Primary Care Trust
20 Union Road, Solihull, West Midlands B91 3EF
Tel: 0121 711 7171

Somerset Coast Primary Care Trust
Riverside Office, Bridgwater Community Hospital, Salmon Parade, Bridgwater, Somerset TA6 5AH
Tel: 01278 436746

South and East Dorset Primary Care Trust
c/o Wimborne Clinic, Rowlands Hill, Wimborne, Dorset BH21 1AR
Tel: 01202 858370

South Birmingham Primary Care Trust
Trust Headquarters, Moseley Hall Hospital, Moseley, Birmingham, B13 4AL
Tel: 0121 687 4600

South Cambridgeshire Primary Care Trust
Heron Court, Block 23, Ida Darwin, Fulbourn, Cambridge, Cambridgeshire CB1 5EE
Tel: 01223 885700

South Central Edinburgh LHCC
Blackford Pavillion, Astley Ainslie Hospital, 133 Grange Loan, Edinburgh, EH9 2HL
Tel: 0131 537 9387

South East Edinburgh LHCC
Craigmiller Medical Centre, 106 Niddrie Mains Road, Edinburgh, EH16 4DT
Tel: 0131 536 9670

South East Glasgow LHCC
Govanhill Health Centre, 233 Calder Street, Glasgow, G42 7DR
Tel: 0141 531 8303

South East Hertfordshire Primary Care Trust
1-4 Limes Court, Conduit Lane, Hoddesdon, Hertfordshire EN11 8EP
Tel: 01992 706120

South East Oxfordshire Primary Care Trust
Wallingford Community Hospital, Reading Road, Wallingford, Oxfordshire OX10 9DU
Tel: 01491 208570

South East Sheffield Primary Care Trust
9 Orgreave Road, Handsworth, Sheffield, South Yorkshire S13 9LQ
Tel: 0114 226 4050

South Gloucestershire Primary Care Trust
c/o Avon Health Authority, King Square House, King Square, Bristol, BS2 8EE
Tel: 0117 900 2546

South Hams and West Devon Primary Care Trust
The Lescaze Offices, Shinner's Bridge, Dartington, Totnes, Devon TQ9 6JE
Tel: 01803 866665

South Huddersfield Primary Care Trust
St Lukes House, Blackmoorfoot Road, Huddersfield, West Yorkshire HD4 5RH
Tel: 01484 466000

South Leeds Primary Care Trust
Fountain Medical Centre, Little Fountain Street, Morley, Leeds, Yorkshire LS27 9EN
Tel: 0113 295 1648

South Leicestershire Primary Care Trust
Rosings, Forest Road, Narborough, Leicestershire LE9 5EQ
Tel: 0116 272 7790

South Liverpool Primary Care Trust
The Surgery, 1 Childwall Park Avenue, Liverpool, Merseyside L16 0JE
Tel: 0151 291 7359

South Manchester Primary Care Trust
1st Floor Home 4, Withington Hospital, Nell Lane, West Didsbury, Manchester, M20 2LR
Tel: 0161 445 8111

South Peterborough Primary Care Trust
St John's, Thorpe Road, Peterborough, Cambridgeshire PE3 6JG
Tel: 01733 882288

South Sefton Primary Care Trust
3rd Floor Burlington House, Crosby Road North, Waterloo, Merseyside L22 4QB
Tel: 0151 920 5056

South Somerset Primary Care Trust
South Petherton Hospital, Hospital Lane, South Petherton, Somerset TA13 5AR
Tel: 01460 243011

South Stoke Primary Care Trust
278 Duke Street, Fenton, Stoke-on-Trent, Staffordshire ST4 3NT
Tel: 01782 326708

South Tyneside Primary Care Trust
Imgham House, South Shields, Tyne & Wear NE33 3DP
Tel: 0191 401 4500

South Warwickshire Primary Care Trust
Westgate House, Market Street, Warwick, Warwickshire CV34 4DE
Tel: 01926 493491

South West Ayrshire LHCC
Davidson Hospital, The Avenue, Girvan, KA26 9DS
Tel: 01465 712571

South West Dorset Primary Care Trust
Castle House, 1a Acland Road, Dorchester, Dorset DT1 1JW
Tel: 01305 259366

South West Edinburgh LHCC
Sighthill Health Centre, 380 Calder Road, Edinburgh, Midlothian EH11 4AU
Tel: 0131 537 7169

South West Glasgow LHCC
Pollock Health Centre, 21 Cowglen Road, Glasgow, G53 6EQ
Tel: 0141 531 6800

South West Kent Primary Care Trust
c/o Sevenoaks Hospital, Hospital Road, Sevenoaks, Kent TN13 3PG
Tel: 01732 470200

South West Oxfordshire Primary Care Trust
First Floor - Administration Block, Abingdon Community Hospital, Marcham Road, Abingdon, Oxfordshire OX14 1AG
Tel: 01235 205555

South Western Staffordshire Primary Care Trust
Mellor House, Corporation Street, Stafford, Staffordshire ST16 3SR
Tel: 01785 220004

South Wiltshire Primary Care Trust
42-44 Chipper Lane, Salisbury, Wiltshire SP1 1BG
Tel: 01722 341319

South Worcestershire Primary Care Trust
Isac Maddox House, Shrubb Hill Road, Worcester, Worcestershire WR4 9RW
Tel: 01905 760010

Southampton City Primary Care Trust
Central Health Clinic, East Park Terrace, Southampton, Hampshire SO14 0YL
Tel: 023 8090 2500

Southend Primary Care Trust
Harcourt House, 5-15 Harcourt Avenue, Southend-on-Sea, Essex SS2 6HE
Tel: 01702 224600

Southern Norfolk Primary Care Trust
St Andrews House, Northside, St Andrews Business Park, Norwich, Norfolk NR7 0HT
Tel: 01603 307337

Southport & Formby Primary Care Trust
Hesketh Centre, 51-55 Albert Road, Southport, Merseyside PR9 0LT
Tel: 01704 530940

Southwark Primary Care Trust
Mabel Goldwin House, 49 Grange Walk, London, SE1 3DY
Tel: 020 7525 3793

St Albans and Harpenden Primary Care Trust
99 Waverley Road, St Albans, Hertfordshire AL3 5TL
Tel: 01727 831 219

St Helen's Primary Care Trust
Cowley Hill Lane, St Helens, Merseyside WA10 2AP
Tel: 01744 457221

Staffordshire Moorlands Primary Care Trust
Leek Moorlands Hospital, Ashbourne Road, Leek, Staffordshire ST13 5BQ
Tel: 01538 487141

Stewartry LHCC
67 Queens Street, Castle Douglas, DG7 1EG
Tel: 01556 502386

Stockport Primary Care Trust
c/o Stockport Health Authority, Springwood House, Poplar Grove, Hazel Grove, Stockport, Cheshire SK7 5BY
Tel: 0161 419 4600

Strathkelvin LHCC
Kenmure Medical Practice, 7 Springfield Road, Bishopbriggs, Glasgow, G64 1PJ
Tel: 0141 772 6309

Suffolk Coastal Primary Care Trust
Bartlett Hospital Annex, Undercliff Road East, Felixstowe, Suffolk IP11 7LT
Tel: 01394 458900

Suffolk West Primary Care Trust
Thingoe House, Cotton Lane, Bury St Edmunds, Suffolk IP33 1YJ
Tel: 01284 706930

Sunderland Teaching Primary Care Trust
Suites 9B & 10, Armstrong House, District 2, Washington, Tyne & Wear NE37 1PR
Tel: 0191 417 9404

Sussex Downs & Weald Primary Care Trust
36/38 Friars Walk, Lewes, East Sussex BN7 2PB
Tel: 01273 485310

Sutton & Merton Primary Care Trust
Hamilton Wing, Nelson Hospital, Kingston Road, Raynes Park, London, SW20 8DB
Tel: 020 8251 1111

Swale Primary Care Trust
Bramblefield, Grovehurst Road, Kemsley, Sittingbourne, Kent ME10 2ST
Tel: 01795 430794

Swansea Local Health Group
Raglan House, Charter Court, Phoenix Way, Swansea, West Glamorgan SA7 9DD
Tel: 01792 516300

Swindon Primary Care Trust
c/o Water Research Centre, Frankland Road, Blagrove, Swindon, Wiltshire SN5 8YF
Tel: 01793 818200

Tameside & Glossop Primary Care Trust
Century House, 107/109 Market Street, Hyde, Cheshire SK14 1HL
Tel: 0161 351 4000

Taunton Deane Primary Care Trust
Wellsprings Road, Taunton, Somerset TA2 7PQ
Tel: 01823 344401

Teignbridge Primary Care Trust
The Seminar Offices, Newton Abbot Hospital, East Street, Newton Abbot, Devon TQ12 4PT
Tel: 01626 357384

Telford & Wrekin Primary Care Trust
The Davidson Suite, The Health Centre, Wellington, Telford, Shropshire TF1 1PZ
Tel: 01952 226013

Tendring Primary Care Trust
Carnarvon House, Carnarvon Road, Clacton-on-Sea, Essex CO15 6QD
Tel: 01255 206060

The North Dorset Primary Care Trust
Forston Clinic, Herrison Road, Dorchester, Dorset DT2 9TB
Tel: 01305 361300

The Riverside LHCC
PO Box 16771, Glasgow, Lanarkshire G11 7WB
Tel: 0141 339 9235

Three Towns LHCC
Pavillion 7, Ayrshire Central Hospital, Kilwinning Road, Irvine, KA12 8SS
Tel: 01294 323579

Thurrock Primary Care Trust
c/o PO Box 83, Civic Offices, New Road, Grays, Essex RM17 6FD
Tel: 01375 406400

Torbay Primary Care Trust
Rainbow House, Avenue Road, Torquay, Devon TQ2 5LS
Tel: 01803 210910

Torfaen Local Health Group
Block B, Manhilad House, Manhilad Park Estate, Pontypool, Gwent NP4 0YP
Tel: 01495 752230

Tower Hamlets Primary Care Trust
Trust Offices, Mile End Hospital, Bancroft Road, London, E1 4DG
Tel: 020 8709 5000

Trafford North Primary Care Trust
The 2nd Floor, Oakland House, Talbot Road, Old Trafford, Manchester, M16 0PQ
Tel: 0161 873 9500

Trafford South Primary Care Trust
Ist Floor, Oaklands House, Washway Road, Sale, Cheshire M33 6FS
Tel: 0161 968 3700

Uttlesford Primary Care Trust
John Tasker House, 56 New Street, Great Dunmow, Essex CM6 1BH
Tel: 01371 878295

Vale of Aylesbury Primary Care Trust
Manor House, Bierton Road, Aylesbury, Buckinghamshire HP20 1EG
Tel: 01296 504200

Vale of Glamorgan Local Health Group
Hensol Castle Grounds, Pen-Y-llyn, Miskin, Pontyclun, Mid Glamorgan CF72 8YS
Tel: 01656 753498

Wakefield West Primary Care Trust
Trust Headquarters, Thornhill Street, Wakefield, West Yorkshire WF1 1NL
Tel: 01924 213050

Walsall Primary Care Trust
Uplands House, Litchfield Road, Walsall, West Midlands WS4 2HT
Tel: 01922 858473

Walthamstow, Leyton & Leytonstone PCT
Becketts House, 2-14 Ilford Hill, Ilford, Essex IG1 2QX
Tel: 020 8926 5236

Wandsworth Primary Care Trust
2nd Floor Re-hab Unit, Queen Mary's University Hospital, Roehampton Lane, London, SW15 5PN
Tel: 020 8355 2808

Warrington Primary Care Trust
Woolston Clinic, Holes Lane, Woolston, Warrington, Cheshire WA1 4NE
Tel: 01925 811058

Watford & Three Rivers Primary Care Trust
1a High Street, Rickmansworth, Watford, Hertfordshire WD3 1ET
Tel: 01923 713050

Waveney Primary Care Trust
6 Regent Road, Lowestoft, Suffolk NR32 1PA
Tel: 01502 533733

Wednesbury & West Bromwich Primary Care Trust
c/o Kingston House, 438 High Street, West Bromwich, West Midlands B70 9LD
Tel: 0121 500 1599

Welwyn Hatfield Primary Care Trust
Charter House, Parkway, Welwyn Garden City, Hertfordshire AL8 6JL
Tel: 01707 361204

West Cumbria Primary Care Trust
The Staff Hostel, West Cumberland Hospital, Hensingham, Whitehaven, Cumbria CA28 8JG
Tel: 01946 523802

West Fife LHCC
House 4, Lynebank Hospital, Halbeath Road, Dunfermline, Fife KY11 4UW
Tel: 01383 737577

West Gloucestershire Primary Care Trust
Unit 14 & 15, Highnam Business Centre, Newent Road, Highnam, Gloucester, Gloucestershire GL2 8DN
Tel: 01452 389400

West Hull Primary Care Trust
Brunswick House, Strand Close, Hull, East Yorkshire HU2 9DB
Tel: 01482 606644

West Lancashire Primary Care Trust
Ormskirk & General District Hospital, Wigan Road, Ormskirk, Lancashire L39 2JW
Tel: 01695 598084

West Lincolnshire Primary Care Trust
The Gatehouse, Long Leys Road, Lincoln, Lincolnshire LN1 1EJ
Tel: 01522 518500

West Norfolk Primary Care Trust
St James, Exton's Road, Kings Lynn, Norfolk PE30 5NU
Tel: 01553 816200

West of Cornwall Primary Care Trust
Josiah Thomas Memorial Hall, Trevithick Road, Camborne, Cornwall TR14 8LQ
Tel: 01209 886533

West Renfrewshire LHCC
Banchory Cottage, Merchiston Hospital, Brookfield, Johnstone, Renfrewshire PA5 8TY
Tel: 01505 384020

West Wiltshire Primary Care Trust
Unit A & B, Valentines, Epsom Square, White Horse Business Park, Trowbridge, Wiltshire BA14 0XG
Tel: 01225 754453

Wester Ross, Lochalsh & Skye LHCC
Dr Mackinnon Memorial Hospital, Broadford, Isle of Skye, IV49 9AA
Tel: 01471 822137

Western Sussex Primary Care Trust
1st Floor, Women & Childrens Block, St Richards Hospital, Chichester, West Sussex PO19 4SE
Tel: 01243 770770

Westminster Primary Care Trust
50 Eastbourne Terrace, London, W2 6LX
Tel: 020 7725 3333

Westone LHCC
Plean Street Clinic, 18 Plean Street, Glasgow, G14 0YJ
Tel: 0141 959 1329

Wigtownshire LHCC
Locality Office, Dalrymple Hospital, Stranraer, Wigtownshire DG9 7HX
Tel: 01776 889770

Windsor, Ascot & Maidenhead Primary Care Trust
King Edward VII Hospital, St Leonards Road, Windsor, Berkshire SL4 3DP
Tel: 01753 636801

Wishaw/Shotts/Newmains LHCC
Cleland Hospital, Bellside Road, Cleland, ML1 5NR
Tel: 01698 863238

Witham, Braintree & Halstead Primary Care Group
New Surgery, The Square, Notley Green, Great Notley Garden Village, Braintree, Essex CM7 8US
Tel: 01376 331549

Woking Area Primary Care Trust
Woking Community Hospital, Heathside Road, Woking, Surrey GU22 7HS
Tel: 01483 715911

Wokingham Primary Care Trust
Wokingham Hospital, Barkham Road, Wokingham, Berkshire RG41 2RE
Tel: 0118 949 5000

Wolverhampton City Primary Care Trust
Coniston House, West Entrance, Chapel Ash, Wolverhampton, West Midlands WV3 0XE
Tel: 01902 444888

Wrexham Local Health Group
Ellis House, Kingsmill Road, High Town, Wrexham, LL13 8RD
Tel: 01978 290883

Wycombe Primary Care Trust
Hawthornden Surgery, Wharf Lane, Bourne End, Buckinghamshire SL8 5RX
Tel: 01628 850754

Wyre Forest Primary Care Trust
7th Floor, Brook House, Kidderminster Hospital, Bewdley Road, Kidderminster, Worcestershire DY11 6RJ
Tel: 01562 863694

Wyre Primary Care Trust
Furness Drive, Poulton-le-Fylde, Lancashire FY6 8JT
Tel: 01253 303131

Yorkshire Wolds & Coast Primary Care Trust
First Floor, Beaver Lodge, Westwood Hospital, Beverley, East Yorkshire HU17 8BU
Tel: 01482 886679

CHAPTER THREE

Welfare Benefits and Pensions

Section One: the System

Section Two: the Details

CHAPTER THREE

Welfare Benefits and Pensions

Section One: The System

The Welfare Reform and Pension Act 1999 introduced major changes to the Social Security and Pension system. Following the General Election in 2001 the Department of Social Security and parts of the former Department for Education and Employment were merged to form the Department for Work and Pensions with its principal aim being the implementation of the Government's Welfare to Work strategy. This and the following section (Section Two: The Details) describe the national system of benefits and pensions which provides income support to individuals and families. This section outlines the background to the present system and the main features of the wide and complex range of benefits available. There is also some detail of the agencies which provide advice and information about benefits. In the next section, the benefits are classified and described in more detail.

There are many voluntary and charitable organisations which have limited funds available for families and individuals with particular needs. Organisations which provide significant help in their field are mentioned in the relevant chapter, but a full list is beyond the scope of this book. Many such organisations are listed in *Charities Digest* published by Waterlow Professional Publishing, Paulton House, 8 Shepherdess Walk, London N1 7LB Tel: 020 7490 0049.

BACKGROUND

The foundations of the current system of welfare benefits and pensions were laid in the immediate post-war years with the implementation of the main proposals of the Beveridge Report 'Social Insurance and Allied Benefits', published in 1942 in the National Insurance Act 1946 and the National Health Service Act 1946.

The principal Acts governing the present system of benefits are the Social Security Contributions and Benefits Act 1992 and the Social Security Administration Act 1992, which consolidated the previous legislation governing income-related and non income-related benefits, including the Social Security Act 1986. It is still a complex system and these chapters contain only a broad outline of income-related and non income-related benefits.

The Department for Work and Pensions (DWP) is the central government authority responsible for the national system of social security. Legislation in this field applies to Scotland as well as England and Wales; in Northern Ireland, some of the administrative arrangements differ, but in general the same benefits apply. District offices exist throughout the country to administer the system at local level. There are, however, many other benefits within the scope of this chapter which are administered by other central and local government agencies.

TYPES OF BENEFIT

Cash benefits and other forms of income support

It is important to distinguish between benefits which are paid in cash to those families and individuals eligible for them and those benefits which take the form of subsidising the cost of particular goods and services to those who can claim them. For example, retirement pension would fall into the first category because it consists of a cash payment unrelated to the provision or purchase of particular goods or services. An example of a benefit in the second category would be the free school dinners which are available to the children of parents in receipt of Income Support. Benefits which fall within the first category are usually known as social security benefits and are described in this chapter. In general, benefits falling within the second category are described elsewhere in this book in the chapter most relevant to the goods or service being described.

Contributory and non-contributory benefits

The main contributory benefits are retirement and widow's pensions and sickness, unemployment, invalidity and maternity benefits. The individual's right to these benefits depends his or her own participation or, in some cases, that of a husband in the national insurance scheme. The amount of benefit paid is then, to some extent, related to the number of contributions that have been paid into the scheme.

Non-contributory benefits do not depend on contributions but are payable to all who meet the conditions of benefit. The main ones are Income Support, Housing Benefit, Working Families Tax Credit and Child Benefit.

Income-related benefits

The second distinction to be made is between non-contributory benefits that are income-related and those that are not. With means-tested benefits, a statement of income of the individual or family has to be made to the agency supervising the benefit; entitlement to benefit and the amount paid depend upon income. The main income related benefits are Income Support, for those not in full-time work, Family Credit, for people who have children in work but with low incomes, and Housing Benefit, which can be paid in or out of work; there is also a whole range of other benefits in this category which are described in the next section of this chapter. Contributory benefits are not income-related.

Taxable benefits

The third distinction is between those benefits which are taxable and those which are not. Taxable benefits are added to a family's income for tax purposes. Where tax is payable by a family on earned income, the tax will be increased when a taxable benefit is paid. Retirement and widows' benefits are taxable, as well as benefits paid to unemployed people; not taxable are sick and maternity pay, invalidity and maternity allowance.

Levels of social security benefits

A feature of the current social security system is that many of the contributory national insurance benefits do not pay enough to cover basic needs as defined in the income support scheme. Thus those in receipt of such benefits and pensions may be able to claim income support in addition, once an assessment has been made on the basis of their income and requirements.

Take-up of benefits

Because of the complexity of the benefits system, many who could claim benefit do not, either because they do not realise that they have an entitlement to benefit or because, for one reason or another, they choose not to claim. For instance, the DSS estimates that in 1994/95 between £1,150 million and £1,840 million in income support went unclaimed as between 1,130,000 and 1,710,000 of those eligible failed to apply. Publicity about benefits and clarity of official forms and leaflets have both seen improvements, but voluntary organisations concerned with poverty are still working to raise awareness of entitlement and encourage better rates of take-up. New computer systems are being developed by the Benefits Agency which are intended to provide the public with swift and accurate decisions on entitlement to benefit and make it much easier for the public to obtain information concerning benefit entitlement.

The poverty trap

An increase in earnings can lead to the little gain or net loss in a family's income because of the extra tax paid and benefit withdrawn. This is because total deductions in income tax and national insurance contributions, as well as reduction in benefit entitlement, nearly match or exceed a wage increase. This is known as the 'poverty trap'. Measures introduced from April 1988 under the Social Security Act 1986 were intended to improve this situation. By assessing Family Credit and Housing Benefit on net rather than gross income that is, on the amount people have left after paying tax and national insurance contributions, some effects of the 'poverty trap' have been eliminated. An increase in wages should now mean a net increase in income for most families on income related benefits. The creation of a closer alignment between benefits available to those families in work and those out of work is intended to help families to be better off in work than when unemployed.

NATIONAL INSURANCE CONTRIBUTIONS

National Insurance Contributions are now, officially, handled by the Inland Revenue National Insurance Contributions Office. General enquiries about National Insurance can be directed to the National Insurance helpline 0191 213 5000. Generally, everyone aged between 16 and pension age, 65 for a man, 60 for a woman has to pay National Insurance Contributions when working, either as an employed or as a self-employed person earning more than a minimum amount. Employers also pay a contribution for each employee. Contributions go into the National Insurance Fund; benefits and a small part of the National Health Service are financed from the Fund. The leaflet NI 196 'Social Security Benefit Rates - Benefit Rates, earnings rules and National Insurance Contributions rates' gives details of rates and limits for all four classes of contributions. For full information visit the website www.inlandrevenue.gov.uk.

There are, broadly, four different classes of contributions: Class 1 contributions are paid by employees (Primary) and their employers (Secondary); Class 2 are flat-rate contributions paid by self-employed people earning less than £4,025 (2002/2003); Class 3 are voluntary flat-rate payments paid by men under 65 and women under 60 to top up their contributions and can be paid to enable a person to qualify for a basic retirement pension and widow's benefit; Class 4 contributions are paid by self-employed people in addition to Class 2 contributions on taxable profits exceeding £7,540. The rates below are for the 2002-2003 tax year.

Class 1 Contributions

These are paid if earnings are equal to or above £75 per week and will be deducted through the PAYE scheme with income tax. Since 1989, employees' contributions have been paid at an initial rate on earnings at the lower earnings limit, plus a main rate on earnings between the lower earnings limit (£75) and the upper earnings limit (£585). The employee's primary Class 1 rate is 10% of £89.01 to £585 per week. The employer's Class 1 secondary rate is 11.8% on earnings above £89 per week.

Class 1 (Employees) Contribution Rates

Earnings brackets for total weekly earnings of an employee	Not contracted-out contribution rate
0- £66	Nil
£75-£89	10%on earnings above the LEL*
£80.01-£585	10% on earnings above the LEL
over £585	10% on earnings above the LEL, up to and including the UEL*

*LEL = lower earnings limit
*UEL = upper earnings limit

Class 2 and Class 4 Self-employed Contributions

People who are self-employed have to pay Class 2 contributions at a rate of £2 per week, unless they earn less than £4,025 per year, in which case they may apply for a certificate of exception. In addition, Class 4 contributions are also payable at a rate of 7% on profits or gains. Those who are self-employed, and at the same time also work for an employer, are liable for both Class 1 and Class 2 and in some cases Class 4 contributions, up to an annual maximum sum.

Class 3 Voluntary Contributions

These may be paid at the rate of £6.85 per week either weekly or as a lump sum in order that a person may have a qualifying contribution record for certain benefits.

Credits

A credit may be available for each week of proven incapacity for work, unemployment or entitlement to maternity allowance and, in some cases, for approved courses of adult training. Between the ages of 16 and 18, young people are awarded credits for retirement and widow's benefits. Credits are available to a man for the tax years of his 60th birthday and the four following years, providing certain conditions are satisfied.

Leaflets with further information on contributions

The following leaflets (and all those relating to tax and/or National Insurance contributions) are available from the Inland Revenue - www.inlandrevenue.gov.uk/leaflets.

- CA 13: Married women
- CA 03: Self-employed people
- CA 02: National insurance contributions for people with small earnings from self-employment
- CA 01: Guide for employees
- NI 47: Share fishermen
- NI 51: Widows
- CA 08: Voluntary contributions
- CA 04: Direct debit – the easy way to pay.

SOCIAL SECURITY AGREEMENTS WITH OTHER COUNTRIES

Advice should be taken from the DWP before going abroad and attempting to obtain benefit. The European Community (EC) regulations on social security give equal treatment and protection of benefit rights to employed and self-employed people and their families moving within the European Economic Area (EEA). The EEA includes the countries of the European Community – Austria, Belgium, Denmark, Finland, France, Germany, Greece, Ireland, Italy, Luxembourg, the Netherlands, Portugal, Spain, Sweden and the UK *including Gibraltar* – as well as Iceland, Norway and Liechtenstein. From 1 June 2002 the EC regulations apply also to Switzerland. The regulations apply to nationals of these countries moving within the EEA and Switzerland. The UK also has reciprocal agreements with most EEA countries, and also Switzerland, that may apply to persons who do not benefit from the EC regulations.

In addition, the UK has reciprocal agreements with several countries outside the EEA. These countries are listed below, along with the explanatory leaflet giving further information about each agreement:

SA 43: Barbados
SA 23: Bermuda
SA 20: Canada
SA 12: Cyprus
SA 29: Iceland, Liechtenstein and Norway
SA 27: Jamaica
SA 4: Jersey and Guernsey
SA 11: Malta
SA 38: Mauritius
SA 8: New Zealand
SA 42: Philippines
SA 6: Switzerland
SA 22: Turkey
SA 33: USA
SA 17: Yugoslavia *applies to the Federal Republic of Yugoslavia (Serbia and Montenegro), Bosnia-Hercegovina, Croatia, Slovenia and the former Yugoslav Republic of Macedonia*

The Isle of Man is party to all of the reciprocal agreemtns, and Jersey and Guernsey to most; neither nationals of these terrritories nor their social security schemes are covered by the EC regualtions.

To obtain copies of these leaflets, write to the **Department of Work and Pensions**, International Pensions Centre, Tyneview Park, Benton, Newcastle upon Tyne NE98 1YX.

INFORMATION AND ADVICE

Detailed information and advice about the benefits available and how to claim them are available from both statutory and voluntary agencies, including those listed below. Freephone and helpline telephone services for specific queries are given in the next section of this chapter.

Local Authority social services departments: a few departments employ specialist Welfare Rights officers to advise both staff and clients on the benefits systems.

Citizens Advice Bureaux: there is a CAB in most towns; addresses will be found in the post office or telephone directory and a list is given later in this book.

Child Poverty Action Group, 94 White Lion Street, London N1 9PF Tel: 020 7837 79796, Fax: 020 7837 6414, known as CPAG, has many campaigning branches throughout the country. At its London office, it has a Citizens' Rights Office, which gives advice to advisers. CPAG publishes many useful books, leaflets and magazines, offers training to those involved in welfare benefits advice and membership for individuals and organisations. In particular, CPAG's annual *Welfare Benefits Handbook* with substantial and up-to-date detail on benefits. It also publishes handbooks on child support on the new child maintenance arrangements, on ethnic minorities' benefits, council tax and debt advice, disability rights and appeals.

Claimants' Union: local groups run by unemployed people exist in many areas of England, Scotland and Wales and are able to help with welfare rights problems. Addresses should be available from local Citizens Advice bureaux.

Disability Alliance, Universal House, 88-94 Wentworth Street, London E1 7SA Tel: 020 7247 8776 Fax: 020 7247 8765, **Benefits' Rights Advice Line** for claimants and advisors, *Monday* *and Wednesday from 2pm – 4pm* Tel: 020 7247 8763. Disability Alliance is a federation of organisations which aim to achieve a comprehensive income scheme for people with disabilities. It publishes a series of books on social security and disability as well as the *Disability Rights Handbook* and *Benefits for Disabled Children and their Families*.

Money Management Council, P O Box 77, Hertford SG14 2HW Tel: 01992 503448 does not offer individual counselling or casework, but it participates in training courses, especially in pre-retirement and redundancy preparation. It publishes reading lists and factsheets on savings, income tax, personal budgeting, etc.

Section Two: The Details

This section describes the benefits and pensions paid by government. All figures mentioned should be taken as guides. The system of welfare benefits and pensions was outlined in the previous chapter and here the benefits are split into the three main types mentioned in that chapter: contributory benefits under the National Insurance Scheme, non-contributory benefits and income-related benefits. Some benefits are described more fully in their relevant chapters: for instance, housing benefit and council tax benefit are mentioned in passing here but a full description is given in chapter four. Reference is made throughout to leaflets which provide full details of the various schemes. They can be obtained from post offices, Social Security offices, or from The Stationery Office (TSO), Broadgate, Chadderton, Oldham, Lancashire OL9 0JA. Leaflet FB 2, 'Which benefit?', gives basic information on the social security system of benefits and contains an order form for other leaflets.

Benefit Enquiry Line

Advice and information for people with disabilities and their carers about benefits is available on Tel: 0800 882200, Textphone Tel: 0800 243355. The Claim Line Completions Service Tel: 0800 441144.

Family Credit

see Working Families' Tax Credit below.

CONTRIBUTORY NATIONAL INSURANCE BENEFITS

Everyone working between the age of 16 and pension age has to pay national insurance contributions either as Class 1 contributions if an employee, or as Class 2 (possibly Class 4) contributions if self-employed. Additionally, voluntary (Class 3) contributions may sometimes be paid in order to secure certain benefits, where there would otherwise have been insufficient contributions for entitlement to benefit. The contributions paid affect the benefits obtainable and Table III shows which contributions count for each benefit. The reduced rate contributions which some married women and widows may still be paying do not count towards benefit.

Table III
Relationship of Contribution (By Class) to Benefits

Benefit	***Class 1***	***Class 2***	***Class 3***
Additional Pension	yes	no	no
Incapacity Benefit	yes	yes	no
Jobseekers Allowance	yes	no	no
Maternity Allowance	yes	yes	no
State Retirement Basic Pension	yes	yes	yes
Statutory Maternity Pay	yes	no	no
Statutory Sick Pay	yes	no	no
Widowed Mother's Allowance	yes	yes	yes
Widow's Payment	yes	yes	yes
Widow's Pension	yes	yes	yes

In certain cases, contributions of a husband count towards benefits obtainable by a wife. Retirement pension and Widow's benefit may be payable at a reduced rate if the contribution conditions are only partially satisfied. Earnings-related supplements are no longer payable. The new state pension scheme, an extension of the National Insurance benefits scheme, which began operating in April 1978 and has now been amended by the Social Security Act 1986, is described later in this chapter. Following any claim for benefit, the claimant will be told of the decision and how to contest it if necessary. Appeals are heard in the first instance by an independent local tribunal and finally by a Social Security Commissioner. Certain other bodies, eg industrial injuries medical boards, decide on some specific benefits; in these cases, appeals are made in writing to the local social security office.

STATUTORY SICK PAY, INCAPACITY BENEFIT

Statutory sick pay

Under the Social Security Contributions and Benefits Act 1992, most people who work for an employer and earn on average per week at least as much as the lower earnings limit for national insurance contributions, currently £75, a week get statutory sick pay (SSP) for up to 28 weeks in a period of incapacity for work. Employers who experience unusually high levels of sickness absence may recover part of their SSP costs under the Percentage Threshold scheme. This compares SSP payments in a tax month with total National Insurance liability for the same period. SSP is subject to PAYE income tax and national insurance contributions. Employees who are still sick after 28 weeks can then claim incapacity benefit. Employees earning below the lower earnings limit and certain other groups, such as those over 65 at the beginning of their sickness and those who do not have an employer, are not entitled to SSP but may claim incapacity benefit instead. Incapacity benefit is based on the employee's National Insurance record. The single rate of SSP from April 2002 is £63.25.

Every known employer in the country is sent the E14 Helpbook "What to do if your employee is sick". The more detailed "Statutory Sick Pay Manual for Employers" (Leaflet CA30) is available from the Orderline on 0845 7 646 646. Both are free of charge and further copies are available from the Orderline or on the CD-Rom in the Employer's annual pack or by looking at the Inland Revenue's website at www.inland-revenue.gov.uk/leaflets. There is also a leaflet for employees, "Employees' Guide to Statutory Sick Pay" (CA86)

Severe Disablement Allowance (SDA)

SDA has not been available to new claimants from 6 April 2001. From that date, disabled people, whose incapacity benefit began before the age of 20 (or 25 if in education or training before the age of 20), may be able to receive Incapacity Benefit without having to satisfy the National Insurance contribution conditions. Those already receiving SDA continue to receive it while they remain incapable of work. If they qualified for the allowance because of disability assessed at 80% that condition must also be satisfied. The weekly rate is £42.85 and age-related additions are payable for those dependants; £25.45 for an adult dependant, £9.65 for the first child and £11.35 for each other child. The rate may be reduced if other benefits or allowances are payable. It is not taxable. Further Information is available from Jobcentre Plus, ONE and Social Security offices.

Incapacity benefit

Incapacity Benefit replaced sickness benefit and invalidity benefit from April 1995. It is a contributory benefit and the contribution conditions are the same as those which applied to sickness benefit and invalidity benefit. People who are incapable of work because of an industrial accident or disease will not be deemed to satisfy the contribution conditions.

Incapacity Benefit has two elements: short-term and long-term incapacity benefit. Short-term benefit consists of a lower rate of £50.35 payable for the first 28 weeks of sickness to people not entitled to SSP, and a higher rate of £59.55 payable after 28 weeks. Long-term incapacity benefit will be payable after 52 weeks at £66.75. The long-term rate of incapacity benefit will be paid after 28 weeks to those who are terminally ill or in recipt of the highest rate care component of Disability Living Allowance.

Additional amounts will be payable to people whose incapacity begins early in life. Long-term incapacity benefit will be increased by £13.60 a week where incapacity commenced before the age of 35, £6.80 a week if before the age of 45. There will also be dependency increases for adults with dependent children and spouses aged 60 or over. Child dependency increases will also be payable with the higher rate of short-term incapacity benefit and long-term incapacity benefit. There is no earnings-related additional pension (AP) in incapacity benefit.

Those who receive invalidity benefit received incapacity benefit at the rates prevailing at the time of the change and these will continue to be uprated annually, except for the earnings-related addition which will be frozen.

When a person reaches state pension age, incapacity benefit will normally cease. Short-term incapacity benefit, however, may be payable for up to 52 weeks, based on entitlement to retirement pension, where sickness began before pension age. For those over pension age and in receipt of invalidity benefit before 13 April 1995, benefit may continue for up to five years after pension age.

The higher rate of short-term incapacity benefit and long-term incapacity benefit are taxable benefits. Those who were receiving invalidity benefit at the time of the change receive long-term incapacity benefit tax free.

A new medical incapacity test has been introduced. This is meant to provide a clearer assessment of the effect of the medical condition on a person's ability to carry out a range of work-related activities. The new test involves the claimant, their GP and a departmental doctor. After satisfying the new conditions, claimants will no longer need to obtain medical statements from their own doctor. The new test will also be used to assess entitlement to other social security benefits paid on the basis of incapacity for work. It will be applied to all existing claimants, except for those who are clearly incapable of work. This includes terminally ill people, those in receipt of the highest care component of Disability Living Allowance and those suffering from certain severe illnesses. People in receipt of Invalidity Benefit on 1 December 1993, when the changes were announced, and who were 58 or over in April 1995, will also not be subject to the new test.

JOBSEEKERS ALLOWANCE

Jobseekers Allowance (JSA) replaced unemployment benefit and income support in 1996. It is a single, unified benefit, with standard rates of payment based on current income support rates. There are two routes of entry into JSA, one based on contributions paid and one based on a means test. Those who have paid sufficient Class 1 National Insurance contributions may receive a personal rate of JSA for six months, irrespective of capital or a partner's earnings. Those who do not qualify, or whose needs are not met by contribution based JSA may qualify for income-based JSA for themselves and their dependents, if their income is insufficient for their needs. This help will continue to be provided for as long as it is needed, if the qualifying conditions continue to be met.

Jobseekers must be available for any work which they can reasonably be expected to do, for at least 40 hours a week, and they must actively seek work. A new condition of entitlement is the 'Jobseekers' Agreement', which will set out each person's plans to find work at the start of the claim.

JSA will be available to people aged between 18 and state pension age. It will also be available to 16 and 17 year olds in special circumstances.

Claimants must be out of work or working less than 16 hours a week. Partners of JSA and income support claimants will be able to work for up to 24 hours a week without losing entitlement to benefit.

Earnings are treated in the same way across JSA; most people will be allowed to earn £5 each week before benefit is reduced; for couples, this will be £10, benefiting those couples where only one partner works.

Claimants breaking benefit rules do not get benefit (automatically), but have to prove hardship. There will be no access to hardship payments and no access to the Social Fund for the first two weeks of a sanction except in cases of vulnerability (the sick, pregnant, or those with children or caring responsibilities). Claimants not fulfilling labour market conditions have no access to hardship payments at all or to the Social Fund, except in cases of vulnerability.

The amount of occupational pension which can be received before contribution-based JSA is reduced will be £50 and this reduction of benefit will apply whatever the age of the jobseeker.

Income-based JSA is very similar to income support. It consists of the personal allowance, premiums and mortgage interest payments appropriate to people's circumstances. People who are unemployed and in receipt of income-based JSA have automatic entitlement to other welfare benefits under arrangements similar to those which apply to income support.

A 'Back to Work Bonus' has been introduced. This will enable claimants who, if they (or their partner, if they are claiming for one) are working part-time, to build up a lump sum equivalent to half their part-time earnings after the disregard is deducted. The bonus, a maximum of £1,000, is payable when the claimant moves off benefit into work.

JSA has power to pilot rule changes locally before national implementation, to allow flexibility in developing work incentives in the social security system; pilot reductions benefit rates are ruled out.

Administration

JSA is delivered from Jobcentres. Staff are responsible for the labour market aspects of claims, and continue to offer help and advice to people who are unemployed on getting back to work. Benefit Agency staff are responsible for the financial aspects of the JSA, dealing with the calculation and payment aspects of the benefit, and are located, wherever possible, in Job Centre Plus offices.

STATUTORY MATERNITY PAY AND MATERNITY ALLOWANCE

Statutory Maternity Pay (SMP)

SMP is paid by employers for a maximum period of 18 weeks. A woman can qualify if the same employer has continuously employed her for at least 26 weeks ending in the 15th week before her expected week of childbirth. In addition her average weekly earnings for the eight weeks leading up to that week must be at or above the lower earnings limit applying to National

Insurance contributions (£75 per week for the 2002/3 tax year). You should note that this is not the same level as that at which National Insurance contributions start to be payable. The first six weeks of SMP are paid at an earnings related rate: 90% of her average weekly earnings. This is followed by a maximum of 12 weeks at the standard rate of £75 (April 2002 rate). She has to pay tax and National Insurance contributions on SMP.

Maternity Allowance

Women who are not entitled to SMP may qualify for Maternity Allowance (MA) from the Department of Work and Pensions (their local Social Security or Jobcentre Plus office). Like SMP, MA is paid for a maximum of 18 weeks. To qualify they must have been employed or self-employed in at least 26 weeks of the test period (the 66 weeks before the week the baby is due), and earn on average a minimum of £30 a week over a 13 week period within their test period. Women with average weekly earnings at least equal to the lower earnings limit (LEL) which applies at the beginning of their test period get standard rate MA (£75 a week from April 2002). Women earning at least £30, but below that LEL, will get 90% of their average weekly earnings (maximum £75 a week). Self-employed women paying Class 2 NI contributions get the same rate as employees.

When SMP and MA start and how to claim

Working women can start their maternity benefits at any time from the 11th week before the week the baby is due right up to the baby's birth. However if they fall sick with a pregnancy-related illness in the six weeks before the baby is due, their maternity benefits and leave will start automatically. SMP is not paid for any week in which the woman works for the employer paying it. Generally MA is not paid for any week in which a woman works.

A woman wishing to receive SMP or MA should obtain a maternity certificate (form MATB1) from her doctor or midwife not earlier than the twentieth week before the week in which her baby is expected. To get SMP, the woman should give her employer at least 21 days notice of the date she wants her SMP to start. The employer may want to be told in writing. She should also give her employer form MATB1. If she does not have an employer, she should send form MATB1 to her local social security office with a claim form MA1. If she has an employer but is not entitled to SMP, she should also send in form SMP1 from her employer. This explains why she cannot get SMP from her employer. Leaflet NI17A, "A guide to Maternity Benefits", gives full details of SMP and MA and is available through local social security and Jobcentre Plus Offices. The Department of Work and Pensions website: www.dwp.gov.uk. Leaflet URN 99/1191 is a more general guide to Maternity Rights covering maternity leave and other rights for pregnant women. It is available from Jobcentres and Jobcentre Plus offices and through the Department of Trade and Industry website: www.dti.gov.uk.

Sure Start Maternity Grants

A Sure Start Maternity Grant from the Social Fund may be made if either partner is getting Income Support, Income-based JobSeekers Allowance, Working Families Tax Credit or Disabled Person's Tax Credit. The grant is £500 for each baby born or expected on or after June 16th 2002. A grant may be claimed at any time from the eleventh week before the baby is due up until the child is three months old. If the mother has a partner, either can claim the grant but, if her partner claims, the name of the child's mother should be included. In adoption cases the baby must not be more than 12 months old. Married couples who have been granted a parental order in respect of a surrogate birth can also apply for a grant. A claim must be made within three months from when the adoption or parental order is granted. In order to be eligible the claimant or partner must also show that they have received advice on maternal and/or child health from a health professional. A person wishing to claim a Sure Start Maternity Grant should obtain a claim form SF100 from a local social security office. More information on the Social Fund is given in leaflet SB 16 and SSMG1.

BENEFITS RELATING TO THE DEATH OF A PARTNER OR PARENT

Bereavement benefits

These are the main benefits, with the old arrangements running concurrently where applicable:

- Bereavement payment (formerly the widow's payment);
- Widowed parent's allowance (formerly widowed mother's allowance);
- Bereavement Allowance;
- Widow's pension.

All those currently receiving widow's benefits will continue to qualify on the original terms. Only the late husband's contributions record counts towards widow's benefits. Claims should be made by completing the claim form BW1 and the certificate issued by the Registrar, form BD8, and taking it to a local social security office. All widow's benefits, except bereavement payment and child dependency increases, are taxable. An additional earnings related pension can be paid with widow's pension and widowed mother's allowance. All widow's benefits cease on remarriage and are suspended on living with a man as his wife.

Bereavement payment

Introduced in 1988 as the widow's payment, this is now a single tax-free lump sum payment of £2,000 following the recommendation of the Welfare Reform and Pensions Act 1999. It is not taxed. Help with funeral costs through the Social Fund is not ruled out by receipt of this payment. There are no increases for dependent children.

Widowed parent's allowance (formerly widowed mother's allowance)

Following the Welfare Reform and Pensions Act 1999, the conditions of entitlement to widowed mother's payments was extended to a spouse or partner of the opposite sex who was co-habiting with the deceased partner at the time of death, provided that the applicant is responsible for the child or children of the deceased. If widowhood occurred after 11 April 1988, the allowance is still payable to a widow/er entitled to child benefit for a qualifying child from the time of their partner's death. It is also paid if a widow is expecting a child by her late husband or as a result of artificial insemination or 'in vitro' fertilisation. The widowed parent receives a weekly, taxable, non-means-tested benefit which is equivalent to the widowed mother's allowance, still running concurrently. Widows and widowers with children will receive an extra sum, up to £15 per week, through a disregard of their widowed parent's allowance when negotiating entitlement to income-related benefits.

Bereavement Allowance and the Widow's Pension

The Welfare Reform and Pensions Act 1999 introduced an amendment to the widow's pension scheme whereby a bereaved partner aged 45 or over with no dependent children will receive a weekly, taxable, non-means-tested benefit for one year which is age-related on the basis of the widow's pension (as follows). Where widowhood occurred after 11 April 1988, widow's pension is payable from the outset of widowhood to widows aged 45 or over at widowhood and with no dependent children, or 45 or over when title to the widowed mother's allowance ceases. If widowhood occurred before 11 April 1988, the pension is payable to widows aged 40 or over at widowhood, with no dependent children, or 40 or over when title to the widowed mother's allowance ceases. The pension is payable on a scale which depends on the widow's age at her bereavement or at the time the widowed mother's allowance ceases. The following rates are based on 2002 figures.

Standard rate Widow's Pension	£75.50
Age-related Widow's Pension:	
45	£22.65
46	£27.94
47	£33.22
48	£38.51
49	£43.79
50	£49.08
51	£54.36
52	£59.65
53	£64.93
54	£70.22

Further information is available in leaflet NP 45, 'A guide to widows' benefits' and leaflet WRP 3, 'Widowhood -an introduction to state retirement pension'.

Child's special allowance

was abolished for all new claims where an ex-husband died on or after 6 April 1987. It will, however, still be paid to existing claimants. The weekly rate is £9.90 for an only, elder or eldest child, £11.30 for each subsequent child in addition to child benefit.

Funeral payments

from the Social Fund are available for those with good cause for arranging a funeral, but have insufficient funds for such a large expense. The payment covers the reasonable cost of some specified items including reasonable burial or cremation charges plus up to £600 for other funeral expenses. People who receive family credit, income support, income-based jobseekers allowance, disability working allowance, housing benefit or council tax benefit are eligible. Payments are recoverable from the deceased person's estate. Further information is available in leaflets SB 16, SFL 2 and D 49. These leaflets and claim form SF 200 can be obtained from local DSS offices.

RETIREMENT PENSION

Retirement pension is payable to men at the age of 65 and women at 60, provided they satisfy the contribution conditions and make a claim for the benefit. It should be noted that, since 1989, it has not been necessary to be retired from regular work in order to be eligible for a pension.

A married woman is entitled to a retirement pension on her husband's contributions, when he claims and draws his pension, provided she is then 60 or over. If a woman qualifies for a pension on her own and her husband's contributions, she receives whichever pension is the higher or she can combine the two up to a maximum of £45.20 per week.

Since 1978, there has been a state earnings-related pension scheme (SERPS). The standard weekly basic pension is £75.50; or, where a married woman qualifies on her husband's contributions, the standard rate is £45.20. Increases payable for dependants are: £45.20 for a spouse or person looking after children, and £9.90 for an only, elder or eldest child, £11.35 for each subsequent child. Pensioners have the option of bank payments every fourth or thirteenth week into most bank or building society accounts by credit transfer. The Welfare Reform and Pensions Act 1999 aims to reform SERPS, introducing the **Second State Pension** to boost the pensions of the lowest earners, carers and the disabled.

Stakeholder Pensions

Following the Welfare Reform and Pensions Act, there have been revisions to the above pension scheme, some of which have yet to be implemented. Stakeholder Pensions are designed to be accessible to everyone but they are targeted at those earning in excess of £9,000 per annum not participating in an occupational pension scheme. Up to £3,600 can be paid into such a scheme each year. Those employers not offering an occupational pension scheme should provide access and information to registered stakeholder pension schemes for their employees.

Increases of pension

By deferring claiming retirement pension beyond 65, 60 for a woman, extra pension can be earned, the amount of extra pension being dependent on how long a person defers claiming retirement pension up to a maximum of five years. A married woman earns extra pension based on the pension which she herself gives up, whether that is based on her contributions or those of her husband. A widow may also get any extra pension earned by her late husband. Anyone who receives retirement pension can give it up but only once at any time between 65 and 70, 60 and 65 for a woman, in order to earn extra pension.

Graduated pension (ceased 1975)

The amount payable depends only on the total of graduated contributions paid between 1961 and 1975 when graduated contributions ceased. A man gets 8.67 pence a week for each 'unit' of £7.50 of graduated contributions paid and a woman gets 8.67 pence a week for each 'unit' of £9 paid. Extra graduated pension can be earned where a person defers retirement pension.

Age addition

An extra weekly payment of 25 pence is made to all pensioners aged 80 or over.

Invalidity allowance

This may be paid in addition to retirement pension.

How earnings affect the pension

A person's retirement pension is no longer affected by any earnings s/he might have but dependency increases can be affected by a dependant's earnings, including the receipt of an occupational or personal pension. Any increase awarded before 16 September 1985 for a wife or a person looking after children who resides with the pensioner will be reduced by 5 pence for every 10 pence of earnings between £45.10 and £49. Above £49, 10 pence is deducted for every 10 pence earned until the increase is extinguished. Any increase awarded after 16 September 1985 for an adult dependant residing with a pensioner is not payable if the dependent person earns more than £51.40 per week. An increase for a separated dependant is not payable if s/he earns more than £39.95 per week. An adult dependant or partner's earnings may also affect the extra benefit payable for children (leaflet GL23). A male pensioner must declare any earnings of his spouse or person looking after children if he draws a dependency increase for her.

How to claim

A claim form, BR1, will normally be sent out by the DWP about four months before a man's 65th birthday and a woman's 60th. If a claim form has not been received three months before this birthday, the local benefits office should be notified. If the claim is late, benefit may be lost. Further information is available in leaflets NP 45, 'Guide to widow's benefit', NP 46, 'Guide to retirement pensions', NI 92, 'Giving up your right to earn extra retirement pension' and FB 6, 'Retiring?'.

Non-contributory retirement pension for people over 80

may be paid to anyone aged 80 or over who is not receiving a national insurance retirement pension or equivalent benefit or who is getting one at less than £39.95 a week. This is called a Category D pension. Certain residence conditions must be satisfied and previous residence in Gibraltar or in another member state of the European Community may help to satisfy these conditions. The weekly rate is £39.95. Further information is available in leaflet NI 184. Detailed information about these pensions is normally only available from a Social Security office.

State earnings-related pension scheme (SERPS)

The Social Security Act 1986 modified this scheme and introduced gradual changes from April 1988. Under this scheme, retirement, widow's and invalidity pensions are in two parts: a basic pension equivalent to the former flat-rate pension and an additional pension related to earnings. Following the 1999 Welfare Reform and Pensions Act, SERPS was revised to include a Second State Pension to boost the pensions of carers, certain categories of disabled people and low earners in general.

Employees who are members of an occupational pension scheme or a personal pension scheme may be contracted out of the additional pension for retirement and half the additional pension for widowhood. A contracted out occupational pension scheme assumes responsibility for providing that part of the additional pension. The state scheme provides the whole of any invalidity pension, basic widow's benefit, any balance of additional widow's benefits and any basic retirement pension. It also continues cover for sickness, unemployment, maternity and industrial injuries benefits.

Although the government does not expect occupational pension schemes to take on an open-ended commitment to inflation-proof guaranteed minimum pensions or annuities deriving from protected rights, schemes are now expected to accept inflation-proofing up to a given limit each year.

The additional pension is related to earnings between lower and upper earnings limits for contribution liability. These limits are reviewed annually. Additional pension is calculated as one-eightieth of these earnings for each year of contributions to the scheme up to a maximum of one-quarter of these earnings after 20 years of contributions. At present, all additional pension rights earned are calculated on a 25% basis. This will change to a 20% basis in respect of earnings in 1988-89 and later years, but everyone reaching the age of 60-65 before April 1999 will get an additional pension calculated on the original rate. The transition to the 20% basis will be phased in over 10 years, the rate being reduced by 0.5% each year from 1999-2000. So, for instance, someone reaching age 60-65 in 2003-04 will have an additional pension calculated at 23% of earnings since 1988, someone in 2007-08 21% and so on. In the case of guaranteed minimum pensions, the calculation differs for those reaching state pension age (SPA) by 5 April 1999 and for those who reach it later: the calculation is slightly different from the one applied to SERPS. Any shortfall arising from these differences will be paid to the individual through SERPS.

The state additional pension is now based on a notional working life of 20 years. With effect from April 1999, the state additional pension will be based on a person's earnings averaged over the number of years from 1978-79 or the tax year in which the age of 16 is reached, if that is earlier, to the last complete tax year before that in which pension age is reached. A legislative power exists which would allow years during which a person is caring for a child, a sick person or one with a disability, or is personally sick or has a disability, to be excluded: this would still be subject to earnings being averaged over 20 years. The legislation to cover this is not yet in place.

A widow will get any additional pension earned by her husband, along with her widowed mother's allowance or widow's pension. A widowed retirement pensioner will be able to add together the entitlements on her own and her husband's contributions up to the maximum that one person could have earned. A man whose wife dies when they are both over state pension age will also be able to inherit his wife's pension rights, in the same way as a widow. Certain people who have recently been widowed may be able to use their late spouse's earnings record for invalidity pension if this gives a more favourable result than their own. As of 2001, however, widows and older widowers are only able to add half their partner's additional pension to their own, subject to the same ceiling.

Contributions for employees will continue to depend on the amount earned, but the better pensions have to be paid for by higher contributions. The employee and employer are liable for contributions based on the employee's earnings. Women aged 60 or over and men of 65 or over are not liable for contributions. Newly married women can no longer choose to pay reduced rate contributions, but some married women and widows may, subject to certain conditions, retain their right to pay at the reduced rate.

Pensions and Divorce

Reforms of pensions following divorce are being implemented following the Welfare Reform and Pensions Act 1999. Couples are to be encouraged to settle their pension rights where they exist in both occupational pensions and SERPS by means of a 'pension share', to be settled finally by court order or divorce (or nullity) agreement. Pension share agreements will reflect family law systems as operated in England, Wales, Scotland and Northern Ireland and will only apply to those divorce proceedings beginning after the implementation of the policy.

Stakeholder Pensions

In response to various social factors, particularly changing working patterns and longer life expectancy, the Government has made it clear that more people will be expected to make greater provision for themselves in their retirement. By way of addressing this expectation, Stakeholder Pensions are a new type of private pension that will be simple, secure, low cost and highly flexible. Introduced by the Government on the 6th April 2001, they are intended to make it easier for people, particularly those on lower or middle incomes, to save for their own retirement, either on their own or as a supplement to a basic state retirement pension. The Government has set out strict criteria for Stakeholder Pensions that must be met by pension providers. For example, the charges and minimum contribution levels are subject to an upper ceiling that will be lower than for many existing types of pension. Equally anyone who contributes into a Stakeholder Pension will have total control over stopping, changing or re-starting their contributions without penalty. Stakeholder pensions are available from financial services companies such as insurance companies, banks, investment companies and building societies. Other organisations such as trade unions may also offer stakeholder schemes to their members. But, significantly, all employers have to offer stakeholder pensions by October 2001; only those with fewer than five employees are exempt.

The main features of Stakeholder Pensions are as follows.

- Maximum 1% annual charge.
- Minimum contribution level of £10.
- Anybody can contribute up to £3,600 a year to a stakeholder pension.
- Available to employed and self-employed people.
- Either supervised by trustees - in the style of occupational pensions - or run by authorised stakeholder managers - in the style of personal pensions.
- All employers have to offer stakeholder pensions - only those with fewer than five employees are exempt.
- Savers are able to stop and start contributions without penalty.
- Penalty free transfers from one stakeholder scheme to another.
- Obligatory issue of annual pension statements; listing contributions paid in, fund values and charges deducted.
- Members of occupational pension schemes earning less than £30,000 a year can pay into a stakeholder scheme and still remain in their occupational scheme.
- Up to 10% of stakeholder contributions can be earmarked for life assurance benefits.

- Contributions are always paid net of basic rate tax, irrespective of employment status.
- Stakeholder pension providers reclaim the tax deducted.
- Contributions of more than £3,600 can be paid up to the limits for personal pensions.

Advice line

There is a Pensions Customer Service Line 0191 218 2763 and a Pensions Overseas Customer Service Line 0191 218 7878, minicom 0191 218 7820 for advice on the transfer of pensions overseas, medical cover and making claims overseas.

Inflation proofing

Basic pension will at least keep up with the average increase in prices. Additional pension will be protected in two ways:

- the earnings on which additional pension will be based will be revalued in line with the general movement of earnings; and
- after pensionable age, the pension awarded will keep up with the average increase in prices.

Occupational schemes contracted out of the state scheme are now responsible for increasing guaranteed minimum pensions and all annuities deriving from protected rights, earned since April 1988, after award in line with prices up to a maximum of 3%.

Contracted out schemes

Occupational schemes can provide an alternative to SERPS. An employer operating such a scheme can contract out employees and take over the liability for payment of an additional pension. Employers and employees will then pay national insurance contributions (NICs) at a lower rate than normal on the earnings falling between the lower and upper earnings limits. If an employer's pension scheme is not contracted out, its benefits are additional to SERPS and NICs are due at the full rate. Further information is available in leaflet NP 46, 'A guide to retirement pensions'.

Contracted out schemes: incentive payment

The government's aim is to encourage a significant increase in the number of people with an occupational or personal pension. To assist this process, and give more flexibility and choice in pension provision, a 2% incentive payment, on earnings between the lower and upper limits, was given to personal pension holders and members of occupational pension schemes contracting out for the first time between January 1986 and April 1993. There has also, since April 1993, been a 1% age addition for people over 30 who are contracted out via a personal pension. To give scheme members greater security and choice, occupational schemes are now required to preserve the pension rights of anyone contributing for over two years. There is also greater flexibility for those wanting to transfer their pension rights into other occupational and personal pension schemes. The range of financial institutions providing personal pension schemes has been widened to insurance companies, building societies, banks, friendly societies and unit trusts. It is also possible to make additional voluntary contributions (AVCs) through occupational schemes and, through free-standing arrangements, to maximise benefits up to Inland Revenue limits. Additional contributions can also be made in personal pension schemes.

State Second Pension

The Child Support, Pensions and Social Security Act 2000 introduced the legislation needed to reform SERPS through the State Second Pension. State Second Pension is designed to:

- Give more help to employees on low and moderate earnings;
- Allow carers and long-term disabled people with broken work records to build up a second tier pension for the first time.

State Second Pension introduces three "Earnings Bands" and a new statutory Low Earnings Threshold – LET - £10,800 in 2002/03.

Low Paid Earners – employees whose earnings fall into Band 1 below are treated as having earnings at the Threshold. And as the accrual rate is twice that of SERPS, they will be at least twice as well off as they would have been under SERPS.

Moderate Earners – employees earning up to the upper limit of Band 2 (£26,400 in 2002/03) also gain over SERPS, but the gains taper off above the LET the more they earn.

Higher Earners – earning up to the Annual NI Upper Earnings Level (UEL) (£30,420 in 2002/03) will get the same benefits from S2P as they would have done from SERPS.

The State Second Pension Earnings Bands

	Bandwidth Formulae	% Rates 6/4/02 – 5/4/10*	% Rates From 6/4/10
Band 1	LEL to LET	twice prevailing SERPS percentage	40%
Band 2	LET+£1 to (3xLET-2xLEL)	half prevailing SERPS percentage	10%
Band 3	(3xLET-2xLEL) to UEL	prevailing SERPS percentage	20%

**reflects the reduction in the SERPS accrual rate from 1999*

Carers are treated as having earnings at the LET for each complete tax year they do not work at all, or earn less than the annual Lower Earnings Limit and they are looking after:

- A child under age six and get child benefit for that child; or
- An ill or disabled person **and** are entitled to Invalid Care Allowance or qualify for Home Responsibilities Protection (HRP).

Long-term ill/disabled people are treated as having earnings at the LET for each complete tax year they are entitled to long-term Incapacity Benefit or get Severe Disablement Allowance, as long as, at state pension age, they have worked and paid Class 1 NI contributions, or are treated as having paid Class 1 NI contributions for at least 1/10th of their working life since 1978.

Low and moderate earners who are contracted-out of State Second Pension also benefit from the extra help available. This is delivered by a combination of enhanced rebates to their private schemes and/or state scheme top-ups. This means there will be no difficult choices to make for certain groups as to whether they should remain in, or join, a private scheme.

Flat Rate Scheme

The Government has indicated that, once stakeholder pension schemes have become established, S2P will become a flat-rate scheme, with everybody treated as if they had earnings of £10,800 regardless of how much they actually earn. The flat-rate scheme will apply only to those with "a significant part of their working life ahead of them". Contracted-out rebates will remain earnings-related.

Inherited SERPS

From 6 October 2002, the maximum percentage of SERPS that a person can inherit from a late spouse will depend on their late spouse's date of birth:

SERPS Entitlement	Date of Birth: Men	Date of Birth: Women
Up to 100%	5/10/37 or earlier	5/10/42 or earlier
Up to 90%	6/10/37 to 5/10/39	6/10/42 to 5/10/44
Up to 80%	6/10/39 to 5/10/41	6/10/44 to 5/10/46
Up to 70%	6/10/41 to 5/10/43	6/10/46 to 5/10/48
Up to 60%	6/10/43 to 5/10/45	6/10/48 to 5/07/50
Up to 50%	6/10/45 or later	6/07/50 or later

NON-CONTRIBUTORY BENEFITS

This section is divided into benefits for children, for those injured at work, for people with disabilities and older people and for war pensioners.

CHILDREN

There are two non-contributory benefits relating to children:

- child benefit;
- guardian's allowance.

Child benefit

A tax-free cash benefit normally payable to a person responsible for a child. This can either be a person with whom the child is living or a person who contributes towards the child's support at a rate of not less than the weekly rate of child benefit payable for the child. The child must be under the age of 16, or under the age of 19 and receiving full time, non-advanced education.

Child benefit can also be claimed, for a limited period, for a child aged 16 or 17 who has left school recently and is registered for work or Training with Connexions or the Careers Service and has not been placed.

Payment of child benefit automatically qualifies the recipient for Home Responsibilities Protection (HRP). HRP helps to protect the pension of people who are not working, or who are working part-time and not paying enough NI contributions to count towards a basic Retirement Pension because they are bringing up children.

There is no entitlement to child benefit:

- if the person claiming is subject to immigration controls (unless they are a refugee, or granted leave to remain in the UK or settled status, or from a country covered by EU or bilateral agreements).
- for the first six months of residence in Great Britain unless the person claiming has lived in this country for more than 26 weeks in the 52 weeks before the date of claim or they are from a country covered by EU or bilateral agreements, or they intend to stay in the UK for more than six months and become employed or self-employed or they or their spouse received Child Benefit within the last three years.
- if one of a married or unmarried couple have income exempt from UK income-tax.

Child benefit is generally not payable (after the first eight weeks) when:

- a child is being looked after by a local authority and their accomodation and basic maintenance is funded out of local authority or other public funds.
- the person claiming and the child go abroad for a temporary period. Child Benefit is generally not payable (after the first 12 weeks) when a child goes abroad on their own for a temporary period.

The weekly rates (from April 2002) are £15.75 for the eldest qualifying child of a couple; £10.55 for all other children. Child benefit is not taxable. Claim forms are available in the "bounty packs" given to new mothers, or are available from social security offices. The claim form should be returned to the Child Benefit Centre with the child's birth (or adoption) certificate, though the claim should not be delayed if the certificate is not immediately available. Claims can only be backdated for up to three months. Child benefit can be paid (a) directly into a bank or building society account or (b) at a post office. All payments are normally made four weekly, but can be paid weekly at a post office where a family is receiving income support, or JobSeeker's Allowance (Income-based).

Further information is available from:

Department of Work and Pensions
The Child Benefit Centre (Washington)
P.O. Box 1
Newcastle-upon-Tyne
NE88 1AA
Tel: 0870 155 5540
Web: www.dwp.gov.uk

The following leaflets are revelant and available from the DWP:

CH11 Child Benefit for lone parents

CF411 Home Responsibilities Protection

Guardian's allowance

is a weekly tax-free payment to a person who takes an orphan into the family. To qualify it is not necessary to be the child's legal guardian, but the person claiming must be entitled to child benefit for the child. Normally both parents of the child must be dead, but the allowance can sometimes be paid where:

- one parent is dead and at the time of death the other parent was missing and cannot be traced
- the parents never married, the mother is dead and the father is not known
- one parent is dead and the other parent is serving a prison sentence of at least five years imposed after the date of death
- the parents were divorced, one parent is dead and the other did not have custody of, or pay voluntary maintenance for the child, and was not liable for custody or maintenance under a court order, or a child support assessment.

One of the child's parents must have satisfied a residence test. The weekly rate is £11.35, adjusted to £9.65 where either of the higher rate of child benefit are payable for the same child. The claim form BG1 is available from social security offices and should be returned to the Guardian's Allowance unit at the Child Benefit Centre with the death certificate(s). The claim should not be delayed if the certificates are not readily available as claims can only be backdated for up to three months.

Further information is available in leaflet NI14 Guardian's Allowance, or from the Guardian's Allowance Unit at the Child Benefit Centre.

Assistance from a local authority under the Children Act 1989

Section 17 of the Act confers a power on local authorities to offer financial assistance to children in need. The definition of children in need is individual to each social services department and there is as yet little clarity about the availability and use of such funds. Money can also be paid to assist a young person who has been accommodated by the local authority under section 23.

INJURY OR DEATH AT WORK

The benefits described here are:

- industrial injuries disablement benefit and associated increases;
- reduced earnings allowance;
- retirement allowance;
- industrial death benefit;
- the Pneumoconiosis, Byssinosis and Miscellaneous Diseases Benefit Scheme;
- the Workmen's Compensation *Supplementation* Scheme.

Industrial Disablement Pension

Disablement benefit can normally only be paid if there is disability assessed at 14%-100% resulting from an industrial accident or prescribed industrial disease except for certain respiratory diseases. It can be paid usually 15 weeks (90) days after the date of the accident or onset of disease. It is paid in addition to any social security benefit to which the claimant is entitled. The extent of any disability is assessed by a medical advisor.

A weekly pension is payable where the assessment of disability is between 14% and 100%. The rates vary from £22.58 (20% disability) to a maximum of £114.80 (100% disability) for beneficiaries over 18 or under 18 with dependants. For those under 18, weekly pensions range from £14.07 (20%) to £70.35. Assessments of 14% to 19% are payable at the 20% rate. If the assessment is over 20%, it will be rounded up or down to the nearest 10%. Industrial injuries disablement benefit is not taxable.

The following can be paid with disablement benefit:

Constant attendance allowance

This applies where disability is 100% or totals 100% including, in some circumstances, a number of injuries and the claimant needs constant care and attention as a result of the effects of the injury or disease. There are four rates payable up to £92 a week, depending upon the amount of attendance needed.

Exceptionally severe disablement allowance

This applies where constant attendance allowance is being paid at a rate of £69 or more a week or would be but for the fact that the claimant is in hospital and where the need for such attendance is likely to be permanent. The rate payable is £46 a week.

Reduced earnings allowance

This is a separate benefit which can be paid in addition to disablement benefit, provided the industrial accident occurred or the occupational disease started before 1 October 1990. It is paid where, as a result of the accident or disease, the claimant is unable to return to his or her regular job and cannot do work of a similar standard. Disablement benefit does not have to be in payment, but there must be a current assessment of disability of at least 1%. The maximum rate payable is £45.92 a week.

Retirement allowance

If the claimant is over minimum pension age and gives up regular employment, or ceases to receive sickness, invalidity or JobSeeker's Allowance, reduced earnings allowance is replaced by retirement allowance. The amount of retirement allowance is 25% of the reduced earnings allowance which was being paid provided it was at least £2 a week, or 10% of the maximum amount of disablement benefit, whichever is less. Further information is in leaflet GL23. There is also an 'unemployability supplement'.

Claim forms for basic disablement benefits are available from local Social Security offices. Further information is available in leaflets:

DB1: A guide to Industrial Injuries Schemes Benefits;

SD6: Ill or disabled because of a disease or deafness caused by work?

SD7: Disabled because of an accident at work?

SD8: Ill or disabled because of working with asbestos in your job?

Industrial death benefit

is a pension paid to women or men who were widowed before 11 April 1988 as a result of an industrial accident or prescribed disease. For a widow living with her husband, or being maintained by him at the time of his death, the weekly rates are either £75.50 or £22.65 depending on circumstances. Allowances are paid for the children of the deceased. When payable to the widow with the death benefit, the weekly rate is £9.65 for the eldest child and £11.35 for subsequent children. Industrial death benefit is also payable to widowers who were dependent on their wives at the time of death and are permanently incapable of self support. Industrial death pensions are taxable, but allowances for children are not.

Pneumoconiosis, byssinosis and miscellaneous diseases

Allowances may be paid to people who are suffering from pneumoconiosis or byssinosis, or certain other slowly developing diseases, due to employment which ended before 5 July 1948. They must not at any time have been entitled to benefit for the disease under the industrial injuries provisions of the social security Contributions and Benefits Act 1992 or compensation under the Workmen's Compensation Acts, or received damages through the courts. Further information is contained in leaflet DB1. If the disease was contracted from work on or after 5 July 1948, leaflet DB1 " A Guide to Industrial Injuries Schemes Benefits", gives information on how to claim.

Workmen's Compensation (Supplementation) Scheme

In certain cases, supplementation allowances are payable to people who are getting, or have a right to, compensation under the Workmen's Compensation Acts. These rights are in respect of accidents occurring or diseases due to employment before the industrial injuries scheme was introduced on 5 July 1948. Leaflet DB1 contains further information.

BENEFITS FOR PEOPLE WITH A PHYSICAL OR LEARNING DISABILITY

Under this category, the following non-contributory benefits are described:

- Disability Living Allowance, for people who need help with the extra costs arising from personal care and limitations on mobility;
- Attendance Allowance, available for people with severe disabilities over the age of 65;
- Disabled Person's Tax Credit, for working people whose disability puts them at a disadvantage in getting a job;
- Invalid Care Allowance, for someone who cares for a person with severe disability;
- Severe Disablement Allowance, only in payment to people who claimed before April 2001

Also described is the assistance obtainable from the Family Fund for families with a child with a severe disability. The non-contributory pension for the over-80s has been described above with other pensions for older people.

Disability Living Allowance (DLA)

In April 1992, this replaced Mobility Allowance and Attendance Allowance for those who became disabled before the age of 65 and who claim before they are 66. It is a non-contributory, tax-free benefit. It is intended to contribute to the extra costs incurred by people who need help with personal care, mobility or both. Those receiving the higher rate of the mobility component qualify for exemption from car tax. It is not normally affected by income or savings. There is a qualifying period of three months and the person claiming must be likely to need help for six months or more. If, however, a claimant is not expected to live longer than six months because of an illness, s/he will not have to wait three months and will qualify for help with personal care even if no help is needed. The weekly allowances are from 8 April 2002:

care component	*mobility component*
higher rate £56.25	higher rate £39.30
middle rate £37.65	lower rate £14.90
lower rate £14.90	

The lower rates of each component provide help for people whose disability did not meet the criteria for the previous benefits. Leaflet DS 704 has fuller information and there is a free Benefits Enquiry Line on Tel: 0800 882200 for England, Scotland and Wales, Tel: 0800 220674 for Northern Ireland, a DLA/AA Helpline for present clients on Tel: 08457 123456 and Benefit Enquiry Line Advisors can arrange help with form completion. The DLA claim pack, which includes form DLA 1, is available from Social Security Offices. Anyone with difficulty filling in the form can ask for help at a local advice agency or social security office or ask for a doctor to visit. There is a right of reconsideration and thereafter of appeal for anyone whose application for the allowance is rejected.

Attendance Allowance (AA)

Payable to people with a severe mental or physical disability which began after the age of 65. There are two rates, higher rate £56.25 and lower rate £37.65. To qualify for the higher rate, people must require attention by day and by night as follows: by day, frequent attention in connection with bodily functions or continual supervision to avoid substantial danger to themselves or others; and, by night, prolonged or repeated attention or someone awake for a long period to watch over them to avoid substantial danger to themselves or others. To qualify for the lower rate, a person must satisfy either one of the day conditions or one of the night conditions.

To receive Attendance Allowance, people must normally have needed help for six months. Anyone who is not expected to live longer than six months because of an illness will not have to wait to qualify and they will qualify for help with personal care even if no help is needed. Leaflet DS 702 gives more information about the allowance, leaflet HB 5, 'A guide to Non-Contributory benefits for Disabled People and their carers', is a detailed guide, and there is a free **Benefits Enquiry Line** 0800 882200.

Disabled Persons Tax Credit

From October 1999, the Disabled Persons Tax Credit replaced the Disability Working Allowance, and operates along much the same lines as the Working Families Tax Credit. The Tax Credit is administered by the Inland Revenue and aims to supplement wages (or money earned through working). Eligibility for DPTC is based on the disability affecting the individual's ability to work, and is based on their circumstances at the date of claim from which it will run for 26 weeks. To qualify for Disabled Person's Tax Credit (DPTC), the applicant must:

- be working at least 16 hours per week;
- have difficulty getting to work because of illness or disability;
- be in receipt of, or have recently received, a state benefit or invalid carriage because of their disability;
- be at least 16 years old and a UK resident;
- have a fairly low income;
- not have more than £16,000 savings.

DPTC includes a couples tax credit component and a disabled child's tax credit and the total of these components will add up to the maximum credit, with deductions of 55 pence for every £1 net earned over the threshold. There are separate thresholds for single people, couples and lone parents. Tax credits are paid into wages by employers, where applicable. The self-employed continue to receive tax credits directly from the Inland Revenue.

There is a Helpline for all DPTC enquiries: 0845 605 5858. There is also a Textphone for those with speech or hearing difficulties: Textphone 0845 608 8844.

Invalid Care Allowance (ICA)

Currently payable to people of working age who live in the UK and have given up the opportunity of full-time paid employment to care for a person with a severe disability. The allowance is available to those aged between 16 and 65 (see changes below) who are regularly and substantially engaged in caring for someone with a severe disability who receives Attendance Allowance, certain rates of constant attendance allowance or the Disability Living Allowance care component at the highest or middle rate. The carer must not be gainfully employed or undergoing full time education.

Changes: From 28 October 2002, carers age 65 or over will be able to qualify for ICA on the same basis as younger carers (claims will be accepted from 28 July, but entitlement will start from 28 October). Other benefits will continue to affect the payment of ICA because of the overlapping benefits rule. This means that ICA cannot be paid in addition to a State Retirement Pension of the same or greater amount. However, where the carer has an underlying entitlement to ICA, the carer premium of £24.80 a week can be paid with the income-related benefits, such as the Minimum Income Guarantee paid through Income Support.

At the same time the law will also change so that entitlement to ICA will continue for up to eight weeks for carers of all ages following the death of the severely disabled person. From April 2003, ICA will be renamed 'Carer's Allowance'; the rules will otherwise continue unchanged.

'Regularly and substantially engaged in caring' means spending at least 35 hours a week in caring for a person with a severe disability.

'Not gainfully employed' means that a person must not be doing any paid work with earnings of more than the Lower Earnings Limit for National Insurance Contributions (currently £75 a week) after deduction of allowable expenses. If earnings are more than the Lower Earnings Limit in any one week, the allowance will not normally be payable in the following week.

The weekly rate is £42.45 in addition to any increases which may be payable for dependants. ICA counts as taxable income.

Further information is contained in claim pack DS-700, which is available from local social security offices, and in leaflet SD4, 'Caring for someone?'. Anyone who may be entitled should claim as soon as possible, since payment of the allowance cannot be backdated for more than three months. The claim should be made even if the decision on the related DLA/AA claim is still awaited.

Severe Disablement Allowance

For people who have been incapable of work for at least 28 weeks and do not have enough national insurance contributions to qualify for incapacity benefit. Claims may be made between the ages of 16 and 65. Once someone has qualified, there is no upper age limit for receipt of the benefit. People who become incapable of work on or before their twentieth birthday can qualify on the basis of their incapacity alone. Anyone over that age must also have a disability assessed at least 80%. The weekly rate is £39.10 and age-related additions are payable for those who became incapable of work before their sixtieth birthday. Increases are payable for dependants; £21.95 for an adult dependant, £9.90 for the eldest child and £11.15 for each other child. The rate may be reduced if other benefits or allowances are payable. It is not taxable. Further information is given in claim pack SDA 1, which can be obtained from social security offices.

The Family Fund

Run by the Joseph Rowntree Memorial Trust for the government and its function is to help families caring for a child under the age of 16 with a severe physical or learning disability. Any family may apply for assistance with whatever is most needed; there is no set list to choose from and help is given towards, for instance, driving lessons, car hire, purchase of a washing machine, clothing, bedding, special footwear or holiday expenses. The Fund is discretionary within general government guidelines. There is no means test, although social and economic circumstances are taken into account. Further information and application forms can be obtained from The Family Fund, PO Box 50, York YO1 1UY Tel: 01904 621115.

Council tax

It should be noted that there is scope for a reduction in council tax if a person with a disability needs additional space for a wheelchair to be used indoors, or an extra room to meet special needs. In such cases, the council tax bill may be reduced to that of a property in a band lower in the valuation list. No reduction applies to dwellings in the lowest band, Band A. Council tax is covered in more detail in chapter four on housing.

WAR PENSIONERS

There are two types of pension available and both are paid completely free of income tax: the war disablement pension and a war widow's or a dependant's pension.

War Disablement Pension

Available for people with disabilities as a result of service at any time in the armed forces. Pensions may also be paid to other groups, for instance civilians or merchant seamen injured as a result of enemy action in World War Two. The amount of pension depends upon the severity of the disability. If the disability is not too severe, a gratuity may be paid rather than a pension. There are extra allowances according to the severity of the disability and circumstances, e.g., for care and attendance, unemployability and mobility. A person may not claim a War Disablement Pension if they are still serving in HM Armed Forces.

War Widow's / Widower's Pension

Payable to the widow of a man who died as a result of service at any time in the Armed Forces between 4 August 1914 and 30 September 1921 or since 2 September 1939 and to widows of certain other casualties, such as civilian or merchant seamen injured as a result of enemy action during World War Two. It is also paid on the death of a war pensioner who was in receipt of war pensioners' constant attendance allowance at the time of death, or would have been if not confined to hospital: or from 7 April, whose disablement was assessed at 80% more and was in receipt of unemployment allowance. The amount of the pension depends on the rank of the deceased and on the age of the widow. There are additions for children and for rent. Pensions are also payable to orphaned children and widowers although payment to the latter group depends on their financial circumstances. If you receive a War Pension, you may also be entitled to extra supplementary allowances, however some of these may affect the social services benefits you may receive.

War Pensions Helpline

General advice on new and ongoing claims is available Tel: 0800 169 2277.

INCOME RELATED BENEFITS

These benefits are paid depending on an individual's or a family's income. There are two main benefits which are intended as means of general financial support to people; these are working families' tax credit, for families where the man or woman works for 16 hours or more a week, and income support, where neither the man nor the woman is working for 16 hours or more a week and may or may not be receiving other benefits or pensions. Additionally, there is a NHS Low Income Scheme for providing help with National Health Service charges where entitlement is income related. Visit www.ppa.org.uk/ppa/low_income.htm for further details.

WORKING FAMILIES' TAX CREDIT

Working Families' Tax Credit (WFTC) replaced Family Credit in October 1999. WFTC is administered by the Inland Revenue, which operates a Helpline for information and advice Tel: 0845 609 5000. There is also a Textphone enquiry service for applicants with hearing or speech impairment: Textphone 0845 606 6668. Welsh language enquiries should be directed to the Welsh Helpline: 0845 766 0830.

WFTC consists of an adult tax credit, a child tax credit (for each child in the family, the quantity being dependant on the age of the child), a 30-hour tax credit and a child care tax credit (providing help towards child care costs).

Applicants qualify for WFTC if they are:

- a married couple.
- a lone parent.
- a woman and man who normally live together as if they are married.

and the applicant, or one of the couple:

- normally lives in Britain;
- works for 16 hours or more per week;
- is responsible for at least one child under 16, or under 19 and in full-time education studying for a qualification at or below NVQ level 3, A levels or Scottish Highers;
- does not have more than £8,000 in savings.

The amount paid depends on the number and age of the children in the family, the income of the household, the number of hours worked and the amount paid out in child care charges. The maximum amounts are as follows:

Working Families Tax Credit

One adult tax credit (one per household)		£62.50
plus		
Extra tax credit for working 30+ hours per week		£11.65
plus		
Tax credits for each child aged	0 - under 16	£26.45*
	16 - 18	£27.20 (if still in full-time non-advanced education)

**from June 2002*

For incomes exceeding £94.50 per week, the Inland Revenue deducts 55 pence in every £1 earned over £94.50. It is imperative that applicants (and their partners) have a National Insurance number for applications to be processed. Disabled applicants may be better off applying for Disabled Person's Tax Credit (DPTC) (see section above). The Inland Revenue produces leaflet WFTC6 to explain details of Working Families' Tax Credit. Other relevant leaflets include: WFTC1 (application form for Working Families' Tax Credit); WFTC501 (Income from self-employment and WFTC); WFTC502 (child care charges and WFTC) and TC500 (earnings enquiry form).

INCOME SUPPORT

Income Support is an income-related benefit for people aged 16 or over whose income is below a certain level. Income support claimants must be habitually resident in the United Kingdom, the Channel Islands, the Isle of Man or the Republic of Ireland or treated as habitually resident in the United Kingdom. People can claim income support if they are not expected to sign on as unemployed and they are:

- incapable of work due to sickness or disability.
- lone parent.

- 60 or over.
- looking after a disabled person (carer).
- registered blind - for people aged 60 or over Income Support is called Minimum Income Guaranteed.

Some people who are not in these groups may also be able to get income support. They may still be able to get income support if:

- they have got savings over £3,000 and up to £8,000 (£6,000 and £12,000 if they are aged 60 or over). If they have a partner, their savings are counted as well. Special rules apply for people who live in a residential care home or nursing home - see leaflet IS 50 'Help if you live in a residential care home or nursing home'.
- they have not paid National Insurance contributions.
- they work part time. They cannot get income support if they work, on average, for 16 hours a week or more (or if their partner works for 24 hours or more on average a week). However some people can still get it if they work more than these hours. Leaflet IS 20 'A guide to income support' explains who.

If they are 16 or 17 and in non-advanced education they may be able to get income support in certain circumstances. If they want to talk about claiming, ask at their social security office.

Special help

Before 1 April 1993 people living in a nursing home or in residential care may have got help with fees through Income Support. From 1 April 1993 when the Community Care Act was introduced the change in legislation meant Local Authority (LA) Social Services Departments (SSDs) or Social Work Departments (SWD's) in Scotland became responsible for customers entering residential care homes or nursing homes on or after that date. Help can also be considered towards the cost of prison visits for people in receipt of income support through the Assisted Prison Visits Unit and more information is in leaflet F 2022, available from social security offices.

Personal allowance

The adult allowance varies according to age, with dividing lines at ages 16, 18 and 25. Lone parents and couples receive the higher personal allowance from age 18. Allowances are also paid in respect of dependent children, with increased payments at 16 and 18. The 18-24 year old personal allowance is paid to 16-17 year olds forced to live independently because they are estranged from their parents and those who qualify for the disability premium.

Income Support from April 2002

Personal Allowances

Single	under age 18	£32.50
	under age 18 (higher rate)	£42.70
	age 18 to 24	£42.70
	age 25 or over	£53.95
Lone parent	under age 18	£32.50
	under age 18 (higher rate)	£42.70
	age 18 or over	£53.95
Couple	both 18 or over	£84.65
Dependent children	birth to September following 16th birthday	£33.50
	from September following 16th birthday to day before19th birthday	£34.30

Premiums

Family		£14.75
Family Premium (lone parent)		£15.90
Pensioner	single	£44.20
	couple	£65.15

Premiums

Pensioner *(enhanced)*	single	£44.20
	couple	£65.15
Pensioner (higher)	single	£44.20
	couple	£65.15
Disability	single	£23.00
	couple	£32.80
Severe disability	single	£42.25
	couple *(one qualifies)*	£42.25
	couple *(two qualifies)*	£84.50
Disabled child		£35.50
Carer		£24.80

Family premium

This is included in the income support of all those who have dependent children living with them as part of their family. It continues as long as the child remains in non-advanced education and is treated as dependent.

Family premium rate (lone parent)

From 6 April 1998, all lone parents making a new claim receive the ordinary family premium. If you were receiving Income Support which included the lone parent rate of family premium on 5th April 1998, you will continue to receive this higher rate unless your circumstances change. If, after that date, you stop claiming or you cease to qualify for the premium for any reason, you will receive the ordinary family premium on any subsequent claim.

Pensioner premiums

Three premiums are payable to pensioners. The pensioner premium is paid when the claimant or partner is aged 60 or over. The enhanced pensioner premium is paid when the claimant or partner is aged between 75 and 79. The higher pensioner premium is paid where the claimant or partner is aged 80 or over. In addition, this premium is payable when a person aged 60 or over receives attendance allowance, disability living or working allowance, incapacity benefit paid at the long-term rate or severe disablement allowance. It is also payable if a person is registered blind, or has an invalid vehicle or receives payment for such a vehicle under the War Pension Vehicle Scheme or Mobility Scheme. A person whose income support includes the disability premium on their sixtieth birthday will normally automatically qualify for the higher pensioner premium from that date.

Disability premium

This is awarded to people less than 60 who have been incapable of work for 364 days or longer (196 days if the claimant is terminally ill). It is also awarded to anyone who receives or whose partner receives incapacity benefit at the long-term rate, severe disablement allowance, attendance allowance, mobility allowance, mobility supplement or disability living or working allowance. Anyone who is registered blind also qualifies.

Disabled child premium

This is paid if a dependent child has a disability and receives disability living allowance or is registered blind.

Severe disability premium

This premium is paid to people living independently, who receive attendance allowance or the higher or middle rate of the care component of the disability living allowance and who do not have anyone receiving invalid care allowance in respect of their care needs.

Carer premium

This is paid if the claimant and partner, or one of them, is entitled to invalid care allowance. Normally only one premium, whichever is the higher, is paid. The family premium, but not the lone parent rate, disabled child premium, carer premium and severe disability premium, are paid in addition to other premiums.

Expenses

Expenses include water rates and residual housing costs such as maintenance and insurance for owner occupiers are expected to be met from personal allowances. Children under school age and expectant mothers are entitled to free milk and vitamins; children at school do not have to pay for school meals.

For owner occupiers, income support can include an amount towards interest payments on home loans. Help is available on loans that were taken out to purchase the home or for repairs and improvements that were necessary to maintain the home's fitness for habitation. No help can be given with capital repayments or with the premiums on an endowment policy. Eligible interest is normally calculated using a standard interest rate charged by the lender and payment is made directly to the lender. Housing costs may be restricted for one of the following reasons:

- when the outstanding loan, or loans, exceeds £100,000, income support can only help with the interest on that amount. Loans that relate to the specific needs of a person with a disability are exempt from this limit;
- the amount that is allowed for housing costs in income support can be restricted if the housing costs are considered excessive. This will only be done if it is reasonable to expect the claimant to move and the home is unnecessarily large for the family, or if it is in an unnecessarily expensive area, or the costs of the property are high compared with those of suitable alternative accommodation in the same area;
- anyone who buys the home which s/he previously rented while receiving income support may have the amount that is allowed for housing costs restricted to the amount that was previously allowable for housing benefit;
- anyone who takes out a new loan to purchase another home while receiving income support may have the amount that they are allowed for interest payments onthe new loan restricted to the amount that they were receiving to help with interest payments before taking out the new loan;
- if there are non-dependent members of the household for example, grown-up children, an amount may be deducted as an assumed contribution from them towards the housing costs.

Income support can also help with the following housing costs: some service charges, ground rent, feu duty, rent charge, payments under a co-ownership scheme, payments made by a Crown Tenant and, if the home is a tent, the site rent.

Waiting periods

Apart from income support claimants who are aged 60 years or more, there is a waiting period before help towards full loan interest, service charges, payments by way of ground rent, feu duty or rentcharge is available.

- New housing costs (loans taken out and agreements entered into since 2 October 1995). Nothing for the first 39 weeks.
- Existing housing costs (loans taken out and agreements entered into prior to 2 October 1995). Nothing for the first 8 weeks and 50% for the next 18 weeks.

Claimants in the following groups who have new housing costs will be treated as if they have existing housing costs:

- carers where the person being cared for is in receipt of, or has claimed Attendance Allowance or Disability Living Allowance with a care component at the highest or middle rate;
- people whose mortgage protection insurance policy will not pay because their claim is the result of a pre-existing medical condition or an HIV-related illness;
- prisoners in custody waiting on trial or sentence;
- people with children who have claimed Income Support because their partner has died or abandoned them.

Direct payments of mortgage interest

As the mortgage interest element of income support is provided specifically for IS recipients to pay to their lender, there is a scheme for it to be paid direct by the DWP to qualifying lenders. If the mortgage was taken before Oct 1995 the interest on the mortgage payable after six weeks will be 50%, and after 26 weeks 100%. If the mortgage was taken out after Oct 1995, no interest will be payable for 39 weeks. The scheme applies to all cases, whether or not there are arrears. A standard deduction can also be made, however, towards arrears of mortgage interest. Qualifying lenders have given assurances that they will not take any action to repossess while the full mortgage interest due is paid to them.

Deductions from Income Support

In general, IS recipients are free to spend their benefit as they see fit in the light of their individual needs and preferences and to make their own budgeting arrangements. It is only when there is a need for intervention that deductions from income support may be made to avoid a person losing their home, disconnection of essential supplies of fuel and water, eviction, seizure of goods or imprisonment. Deductions may be made from a claimant's income support for payment to third parties to recover debts and pay current charges of housing, fuel, water charges, some hostel and residential care or nursing home charges (current charges only), repayment of community charge or council tax debt, recovery of unpaid fines and payment of child support maintenance.

In calculating the amount of income support payable, note is taken of all sources of income and capital belonging to the claimant's family, subject to the following provisions:

The standard earnings disregard is £5 a week, £10 for couples, which is applied to earnings after deductions have been made for tax, national insurance contributions and half of any personal or occupational pension contributions. Where a couple both have earnings, the £5 disregard applies to each member individually. No allowances will be made for personal work related expenses e.g., fares to work, childminding fees, trade union dues etc, but any expenses incurred wholly, exclusively and necessarily in the performance of duties are disregarded, as are payments made by employers for such expenses.

There is a £20 disregard based on the same calculation of net earnings available to:

- lone parents entitled or with an underlying entitlement to the one-parent premium;
- people entitled or with an underlying entitlement to the disability premium, or entitled to the higher pensioner premium, but only if they were entitled to the disability premium before the higher pensioner premium was payable and where the work was continuous;
- where the above disregards apply to couples, the £20 is a joint amount.

There may be entitlement to the £20 disregard on other grounds as follows:

- a part-time firefighter; or
- a member of the crew of a lifeboat, or someone manning or launching a lifeboat, or;
- a member of the Territorial Army, the reserve forces; or
- a carer who is, or whose partner is, entitled to the carer premium; or
- an auxiliary coastguard involved in coast rescue duties.

Any earnings of a dependent child, other than earnings from remunerative work after s/he has left school, are disregarded in full. Earnings from remunerative work after a child has left school and any other income s/he has are disregarded to the extent that in total, after any other disregards have been applied, they exceed the amount of the child allowance and any disabled child premium.

Child benefit, one-parent benefit and most national insurance benefits will be taken fully into account. The first £10 of a war widow's pension, a war disablement pension and any equivalent foreign social security payment can be disregarded. There is an overriding £20 limit per family which also applies to regular charitable or voluntary payments.

Maintenance payments are fully taken into account.

Any occupational pension is taken fully into account. If the claimant and partner have more than £8,000 capital, no benefit will be payable. The first £3,000 is ignored, but a deduction from benefit of £1 is made for each £250 or part thereof above £3,000, up to the capital limit of £8,000. Where a dependent child has capital over £3,000, no personal allowance or disabled child premium is payable for that child. The family and any lone parent premium is unaffected.

If you or your present partner claim Income Support, and you are a parent with care of a child or children whose other parent lives elsewhere in the UK, you will be required to apply for child support maintenance if asked to do so by the CSA. An exception may be made where the CSA accepts that there is a risk of harm or undue distress occuring to you or any of the children who live with you if you are required to apply.

Trade disputes

Anyone involved in a trade dispute is not entitled to benefit for his or her own day to day living expenses and any benefit paid to their family is reduced by £29; however, up to £29 per week strike pay is ignored.

Fuel costs and fuel debts

Normal heating needs are intended to be met by weekly benefit. Since income support is a system of income maintenance which provides personal allowances based on age and family status, these are intended to cover everyday needs including normal heating costs. The extra premium payments described above for certain groups are assumed to help with extra needs. The principle intended to be embedded in this system of benefits is that recipients should control their money in the same way as any other member of the community and set their own priorities for expenditure. There may, however, be help available from the Social Fund treated in more detail below where there is a fuel debt and the possibility of disconnection of supply. Whilst help with the cost of mains fuel is excluded from budgeting loans and community care grants, Social Fund payments can be awarded as crisis loans for fuel costs in cases where it is the only means of preventing serious risk to the health or safety of a member of the family.

Budgeting loans can be arranged for non-mains fuel. Under the code of practice operated by the fuel industries for domestic customers, the industries have agreed to offer debtors repayment arrangements or, where safe and practicable, pre-payment meters, before disconnecting. They have also given an undertaking that pensioner households who cannot afford their bills will not be disconnected between 1 October and 31 March. If normal payment arrangements cannot be made between the fuel board and the customer, and disconnection is threatened or has taken place, the DWP can intervene on behalf of income support recipients by making deductions from a claimant's benefit before it is paid. These deductions are known as 'direct payments'. The amount of benefit withheld covers current fuel consumption and reduction of any outstanding debt and the money is periodically paid direct to the fuel suppliers. In return, the fuel suppliers undertake to maintain the supply.

Fuel oil and solid fuel are generally paid for on a different basis from mains fuel. They usually have to be bought in bulk and paid for on or shortly after delivery. For this reason direct payments, such as those used to pay for mains gas and electricity, are not made, but help may be given to applicants who have been in receipt of income support for 26 weeks through budgeting loans, to help spread the cost of a consignment over a longer period. In a case where serious risk to health or safety is recognised, a crisis loan may be made and this would not require the applicant to have been in receipt of income support for 26 weeks at the time of consideration of the application.

A standard cold weather payment of £8.50 will be available from the Social Fund for any period of seven consecutive days when the average temperature is 0°C or below. People who receive income support or income-based jobseekers allowance and who have a child under five or those whose benefit includes a pensioner or disability premium will automatically receive a payment. For details, see leaflet CWP 1 or ring the **Winter Warmth Line** on Tel: 0800 289404 UK, Tel: 0800 838587 Scotland, Tel: 0800 616757 Northern Ireland.

Winter Fuel Payments are one-off payments to help towards winter fuel bills. They are paid to eligible households that include someone who is age 60 or over and ordinarily resident in Great Britain during a particular week announced each year. We call this the qualifying week. They do not need to be getting any benefits. Winter Fuel Payments do not have to be paid back.

SOCIAL FUND

The Social Fund is divided into regulated payments and discretionary payments. The regulated maternity, funeral and cold weather payments are described on pages earlier in this chapter. Decisions on these regulated payments are made by Adjudication Officers and are subject to appeal to a Social Security Appeal Tribunal and subsequently to a Social Security Commissioner. They are not limited by a fixed Social Fund budget.

Discretionary payments fall into three categories:

Community care grants

For people on Income Support or income-based JobSeekers Allowance, community care grants are intended to:

- help people move into the community after a period in institutional or residential care, or to remain in the community rather than enter such care;
- ease exceptional pressures on families;
- help people set up home in the community, as part of a planned resettlement programme, following an unsettled way of life;
- care for a prisoner on release on temporary licence;
- meet certain essential travelling expenses.

These are grants and not loans and therefore are not repayable.

Budgeting loans

Interest-free loans for people who have been on income support or income-based jobseekers allowance for six months or more and need help with important intermittent expenses for which they cannot make provision from normal benefit. Repayment is made by deductions from benefit.

Crisis loans

Interest-free loans for people, whether or not on benefit, who as a result of an emergency or disaster, are without resources and have no other means of preventing serious risk or serious damage to their own health or safety or that of a member of their family.

Discretionary payments are decided by the Social Fund Decision Maker. Each office has a budget for grants and for loans. Social Fund Officers are expected to manage the budget so as to ensure that the highest priority needs are met whenever they occur in the financial year. Anyone who is dissatisfied with a Social Fund Officer's decision should ask the local social security office for a review and, if still dissatisfied, request a further review by an independent Social Fund Inspector. For community care grants and budgeting loans, savings of more than £500, £1,000 for those aged 60 or over, are taken into account; for crisis loans all savings are taken into account.

Further details are available in leaflet SB 16, 'A guide to the Social Fund', and SFL2, 'How the Social Fund can help you'.

HOUSING BENEFIT

Housing benefit is assessed on net income, with no account being taken of capital up to £3,000 or the income from it. No-one with capital of more than £16,000 is eligible for housing benefit. Income is compared with the claimant's 'applicable amount', which for most people will be the same as their income support 'applicable amount'. It should be noted, however, that the personal allowance for those under 18 and the family premium (lone parent) premium are higher in housing benefit. Most householders at the income support level will normally have their eligible rents met in full. Maximum housing benefit is reduced by a percentage (a taper) applied to the amount by which net income exceeds the claimant's 'applicable amount'.

STUDENTS AND BENEFIT

Most full-time students are not eligible to claim income-related Social Security benefits, including income support, income-based jobseeker's allowance, housing benefit and council tax. However, benefits continue to be available to certain students in vulnerable groups, including students with a dependent child and disabled students. Partners of students, who are not themselves students can claim on behalf of the couple. Part-time students remain eligible to claim benefits. Further information should be sought from a social security office, local authority or student adviser.

HELP WITH NHS COSTS

People and their dependants who are receiving income support, family credit or disability working allowance and had capital of £8,000 or less when DWA was claimed are automatically entitled to free NHS prescriptions, dental treatment, sight tests and wigs and fabric supports; maximum value of a voucher towards the costs of glasses or contact lenses; and a refund of reasonable travel costs to hospital for NHS treatment.

People who are not automatically entitled to help with NHS costs, but whose income whether from work or not is limited, can apply for help under the NHS 'low income scheme'. Assessment under the scheme follows the income support arrangements in comparing the requirements and income of a claimant and any dependants s/he might have.

Requirements consist of a personal allowance for day-to-day living expenses; premiums for specific needs such as age and disability; housing costs which include mortgage repayments, both interest and capital, rent less any housing benefit and council tax less any discounts or benefits. The amount of housing costs and council tax to be included will be the amount that someone is personally liable to pay. Income consists of anything a claimant and his or her dependants receives on a regular basis, including a student loan.

People whose requirements are equal to or more than their incomes are entitled to full help and are sent certificate HC2. Those whose requirements are less than their income are entitled to limited help from the scheme. They are sent certificate HC3, which shows how much they are expected to contribute to their health costs. If their contribution is higher than the NHS cost, they are expected to pay only their actual NHS costs. In the case of optical treatment, the amount on the HC3 would first be used to pay up to the NHS fee for a sight test and anything left would be used to reduce the value of the appropriate optical voucher. The value of the optical voucher depends on the strength of the patient's optical prescription. No help is available to people with capital of more than £8,000.

Further information can be obtained from leaflet HC11, 'Help with NHS costs', available from benefit agency offices and post offices. It includes a claim form. People who are unemployed should claim on form B1 from unemployment benefit offices. Detailed information can be found in leaflet IS 20, 'A Guide to Income Support'.

WELFARE,BENEFITS AND PENSIONS

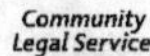

AARONSON & CO
308 Earls Court Road, London SW5 9BA
Tel: **020 7373 9516** *Fax:* **020 7835 1014**
Docx: **400750 EARLS COURT 1**

Legal Aid franchise adn block contracts in immigration family law, housing and welfare benefits. Members of Law Society Family Law Panel, Immigration Law Practitioners Association and Personal Injury Panel.

BROMLEY HYDE & ROBINSON
50 Wellington Road, Ashton-under-Lyne, Greater Manchester OL6 6XL
Tel: 0161 330 6821 ***Fax:*** 0161 343 1719
Docx: 25616 ASHTON-UNDER-LYNE
Email: bromleys@bromleys.co.uk
Web: www.bromleys.demon.co.uk

DREW JONES
17 Queens Road, Coventry, West Midlands CV1 3EG
Tel: 024 7655 5511 ***Fax:*** 024 7655 5577
Docx: 706791 COVENTRY 9
Email: law@drewjones.co.uk

HOWARD & OVER
114 & 116 Albert Road, Devonport, Devon PL2 1AF
Tel: 01752 556606 ***Fax:*** 01752 607101
Docx: 120027 PLYMOUTH 12
Email: howard-over.co.uk
Web: www.howard-over.co.uk

LEVENES SOLICITORS
Ashley House, 235-239 High Road, Wood Green, London N22 8HF
Tel: **0800 118899** *Fax:* **020 8889 63**
Docx: **135576 WOOD GREEN 4**
Email: **info@levenes.co.uk**
Web: **www.levenes.co.uk**

OLIVER & CO
Booth Mansion, 30 Watergate Street, Chester, Cheshire CH1 2LA
Tel: 01244 312306 ***Fax:*** 01244 350261
Docx: 19977 CHESTER
Email: oliverlaw@aol.com

Community
Legal Service

SMITH LLEWELYN PARTNERSHIP
18 Princess Way, Swansea SA1 3LW
Tel: 01792 464444 ***Fax:*** 01792 464726
Docx: 92051 SWANSEA 3
Email: mainofficeslp@virgin.net

T V EDWARDS
Park House, 29 Mile End Road, Tower Hamlets, London E1 4TP
Tel: 020 7791 1050 ***Fax:*** 020 7790 5101
Docx: 300700 TOWER HAMLETS

Benefits Agency Offices

Aberdare
Crown Buildings, Greenbach, Aberdare, Rhondda Cynon Taff, CF44 7HU
Tel: 01685 887200
Fax: 01685 887201

Aberdeen
Greyfriars House, Gallowgate, Aberdeen, AB10 1ZU
Tel: 01224 618000
Fax: 01224 618181

Aberystwyth
Crown Buildings, Northgate Street, Aberystwyth, Ceredigion, SY23 2JS
Tel: 01970 653800
Fax: 01970 653801

Accrington
Melbourne House, Melbourne Street, Accrington, Lancashire, BB5 6PU
Tel: 01254 355800
Fax: 01254 355801

Acton (GBC)
Government Buildings, Bromyard Avenue, London, W3 7HY
Tel: 0845 377 0001
Fax: 0845 377 0143

Airdrie Customer Service Point
86 Graham Street, Airdrie, Lanarkshire, ML6 6AT
Tel: 01236 502800
Fax: 01236 502808

Aldershot
South Western House, Station Road, Aldershot, Hampshire, GU11 1HP
Tel: 01252 356500
Fax: 01252 319106

Alexandria Public Caller Office
9 Mitchell Way, Alexandria, Glasgow, G83 0LW
Tel: 0141 951 3100
Fax: 0141 951 3101

Ammanford
Llys Afon, Park Street, Ammanford, Carmarthenshire, SA18 2NT
Tel: 01269 815500
Fax: 01269 815501

Andover
6 London Street, Andover, Hampshire, SP10 2PE
Tel: 01264 826000
Fax: 01264 826001

Arbroath
8 Grant Road, Arbroath, Angus, DD11 1AP
Tel: 01241 446000
Fax: 01241 446001

Ashford
International House, Dover Place, Ashford, Kent, TN23 1HT
Tel: 01233 208000
Fax: 01233 208004

Ashington
Rieverdale House, Woodhorn Road, Ashington, Northumberland, NE63 9YU
Tel: 01670 840000
Fax: 01670 840092

Ashton
Crown Buildings, Booth Street, Ashton-Under-Lyne, Greater Manchester, OL6 7PN
Tel: 0161 253 3000
Fax: 0161 253 3001

Aylesbury
Sunley House, Oxford Road, Aylesbury, Buckinghamshire, HP19 3EZ
Tel: 01296 314700
Fax: 01296 314701

Ayr
Wallacetoun House, John Street, Ayr, South Ayrshire, KA8 0BX
Tel: 01292 666000
Fax: 01292 666002

Balham Irene House
Irene House, 218 Balham High Road, Balham, London, SW12 9BX
Tel: 020 8682 8000
Fax: 020 8682 8190

Balham Steel house
Steel House, 177 Balham High Street, Balham, London, SW12
Tel: 020 8682 8000
Fax: 020 8682 8337

Banbury
Crown Buidlings, Southam Road, Banbury, Oxfordshire, OX16 7EX
Tel: 01295 455000
Fax: 01295 455001

Bargoed (One Stop Shop)
Charleston House, 44-46 High Street, Bargoed, Caerphilly, CF8 8RD
Tel: 029 204 24300

Barking
Phoenix House, 12-14 Wakering Road, Barking, Essex, IG11 8QB
Tel: 01708 774000
Fax: 020 8258 8700

Barnet Hill (Caller Office)
Raydean House, 15 Western Parade, Barnet, Hertfordshire, EN5 1AH
Tel: 020 8258 6500
Fax: 020 8258 6589

Barnoldswick (Caller Office)
Station Road, Barnoldswick, Lancashire, BB8 5NA
Tel: 01282 473200
Fax: 01282 473310

Barnsley
John Rideal House, 29 Shambles Street, Barnsley, South Yorkshire, S70 2SA
Tel: 01226 777222
Fax: 01226 777333

Barnstaple
Princess House, Queen Street, Barnstaple, Devon, EX32 8HD
Tel: 01271 395300
Fax: 01271 395353

Barrow
Phoenix House, Stephen Street, Barrow-in-Furness, Cumbria, LA14 1BY
Tel: 01229 842700
Fax: 01229 842701

Barry
Provincial House, Kendrick House, Barry, Merthyr Tydfil, CF62 8UF
Tel: 01446 731700
Fax: 01446 731701

Basildon
Great Oaks House, Great Oaks, Basildon, Essex, SS14 1JE
Tel: 01268 363000
Fax: 01268 363001

Basingstoke
Crown Building, Winchester Road, Basingstoke, Hampshire, RG21 8ES
Tel: 01256 726400
Fax: 01256 726420

Bath
Kingsmead House, James Street West, Bath, Bath & North East Somerset, BA1 2DG
Tel: 01225 498200
Fax: 01225 498201

Bathgate
Government Buildings, Whitburn Road, Bathgate, West Lothian, EH48 1HG
Tel: 01506 772000
Fax: 01506 772001

Bedford
Wyvern House, 53 - 57 Bromham Road, Bedford, Bedfordshire, MK40 2EH
Tel: 01234 361500
Fax: 01234 361501

Bellshill Benefit Office
417 Main Street, Bellshill, ML4 1HU
Tel: 01236 502800
Fax: 01698 484101

Berwick
Norham House, 15 Walkergate, Berwick-upon-Tweed, Northumberland, TD1 1DS
Tel: 01289 356000
Fax: 01289 356001

Beverley (Caller Office)
Crosskill House, Hull, Kingston upon Hull,
Tel: 01482 584444

Bexley (Thameside)
Westminster House, 186-194 Broadway, Bexleyheath, Kent, DA6 7BB
Tel: 020 8218 4700
Fax: 020 8218 4922

Birkenhead
Hordan House, 35 Price Street, Birkenhead, Merseyside, L41 6NU
Tel: 0151 649 1000
Fax: 0151 649 1002

Birmingham Coventry Road
2104 Coventry Road, Sheldon, Birmingham, West Midlands, B26 3JQ
Tel: 0121 722 7000
Fax: 0121 722 7085

Birmingham Edgbaston
Clarendon House, Duchess Road, Edgbaston, Birmingham, West Midlands, B16 8NU
Tel: 0121 452 8000
Fax: 0121 452 8155

Birmingham Erdington
224-232 High Street, Erdington, Birmingham, West Midlands, B23 6ST
Tel: 0121 377 4600
Fax: 0121 377 4605

Birmingham Handsworth
Temple Row House, 25-45 Soho Road, Handsworth, Birmingham, West Midlands, B21 9SL
Tel: 0121 507 8000
Fax: 0121 507 8002

Birmingham Ladywood
65-77 Summer Row, Ladywood, Birmingham, West Midlands, B3 1LB
Tel: 0121 237 8300
Fax: 0121 237 8305

Birmingham Northfield
946 Bristol Road South, Birmingham, West Midlands, B31 2NL
Tel: 0121 480 8000
Fax: 0121 480 8005

Birmingham Perry Barr
307 Walsall Road, Perry Barr, Birmingham, West Midlands, B42 1TZ
Tel: 0121 332 4000
Fax: 0121 332 4002

Birmingham Poplar Road
Poplar Road, Sparkhill, Birmingham, West Midlands, B11 1UP
Tel: 0121 722 7000
Fax: 0121 722 7344

Birmingham Ravenhurst
42 Moseley Road, Birmingham, West Midlands, B12 0HH
Tel: 0121 766 4300
Fax: 0121 766 4305

Birmingham Washwood Heath
St Margarets Road,
Birmingham, West Midlands,
B8 2DJ
Tel: 0121 253 5500
Fax: 0121 253 5625

Bishop Auckland
Vinovium House, Saddler Street, Bishop Auckland, Co. Durham, DL14 7AG
Tel: 01388 456000
Fax: 01388 456001

Bishops Stortford (Caller Office)
Council Offices, The Causeway, Bishop's Stortford, Hertfordshire, CM23 2EN
Tel: 01279 758036
Fax: 01279 758036

Blackburn
Orchard House, Penny Street, Blackburn, Lancashire, BB1 6HA
Tel: 01254 343600
Fax: 01254 343602

Blackpool North
Mexford House, Mexford Avenue, Blackpool, FY2 0XN
Tel: 01253 502000
Fax: 01253 502222

Blackpool South
Westmorland House, 29-31 Orchard Road, Lytham St Annes, Lancashire, FY8 1UO
Tel: 01253 783500
Fax: 01253 783501

Blackwood
Newbridge House, 75-77 High Street, Blackwood, Caerphilly, NP2 1YY
Tel: 01495 232600
Fax: 01495 232601

Bloomsbury (London Bankside)
Tavis House, 1-6 Tavistock Square, London, WC1H 9NB
Tel: 020 7200 6000
Fax: 020 7200 6198

Blyth
Bridge House, Percy Street, Blyth, Northumberland, NE24 2DF
Tel: 01670 541000
Fax: 01670 541111

Bognor
Gloucester House, High Street, Bognor Regis, West Sussex, PO21 1HH
Tel: 01243 846300
Fax: 01243 865095

Bolton
Elizabeth House, 21 Back Spring Gardens, Bolton, Greater Manchester, BL1 1SJ
Tel: 01204 367000
Fax: 01204 367010

Boston
Crown House, Lincoln Lane, Boston, Lincolnshire, PE21 8SJ
Tel: 01205 313000
Fax: 01205 313020

Bournemouth
20-28 Cotlands Road, Bournemouth, BH1 3RS
Tel: 01202 446000
Fax: 01202 446300

Bracknell
Fitzwilliam House, Skimped Hill, Bracknell, Bracknell Forest, RG12 1JX
Tel: 01344 744800
Fax: 01344 744884

Bradford East
373 Leeds Road, Bradford, West Yorkshire, BD3 9LT
Tel: 01274 336200
Fax: 01274 336201

Bradford South
Law Russell House, 63 Vicar Lane, Bradford, West Yorkshire, BD1 5SX
Tel: 01274 336 200
Fax: 01274 336 750

Bradford West
Westfield House, 85 Manningham Lane, Bradford, West Yorkshire, BD1 3BE
Tel: 01274 336200
Fax: 01274 336524

Braintree
Government Buildings, Panfield Lane, Braintree, Essex, CM7 7TR
Tel: 01376 557200
Fax: 01376 557209

Bridgend
Crown Buildings, Angel Street, Bridgend, CF31 4AA
Tel: 01656 762000
Fax: 01656 762050

Bridgwater
Hanover House, Northgate, Bridgwater, Somerset, TA6 3HG
Tel: 01278 435100
Fax: 01278 435101

Bridlington
Crown Buildings, Quay Road, Bridlington, East Riding of Yorkshire, YO16 4LR
Tel: 01262 623000
Fax: 01262 623001

Brighton
Windsor House, 30-35 Edward Street, Brighton, Brighton & Hove, BN2 2LN
Tel: 01273 647400
Fax: 01273 647615

Bristol East
Lodge House, Fishponds Road, Fishponds, Bristol, BS16 3HZ
Tel: 0117 958 9400
Fax: 0117 958 9409

Bristol Lipscombe House (Neighbourhood Office)
Lipscombe House, Portland House, Bristol, BS2 8RR

Bristol Quayside
Eagle House, St Stephens Street, Bristol, BS1 1EN
Tel: 0117 938 8100
Fax: 0117 938 8259

Bristol South
St Catherine's House, St Catherine's Place, Bedminster, Bristol, BS3 4HQ
Tel: 0117 953 6000
Fax: 0117 953 6085

Bristol Southmead (Caller Office)
256 Greystoke Avenue, Southmead, Bristol, BS10 6BQ

Brixton (BBC)
246 Stockwell Road, Brixton, London, SW9 9YX
Tel: 0845 377 1001
Fax: 0845 377 4826

Broadstairs
2-4 St Peters Park Road, Broadstairs, Kent, CT10 2BP
Tel: 01843 873000
Fax: 01843 873100

Bromley (Caller Office)
1 Westmoreland Road, Bromley, Kent, BR2 0TS
Tel: 020 8315 4000
Fax: 020 8315 4043

Burnley
Brun House, Kingsway, Burnley, Staffordshire, BB11 1AG
Tel: 01282 473200
Fax: 01282 473310

Burton-on-Trent
Crown House, New Street, Burton-on-Trent, Staffordshire, DE14 3SL
Tel: 01283 505000
Fax: 01283 516208

Bury
Humphrey House, Angouleme Way, Bury, Greater Manchester, BL9 0BQ
Tel: 0161 762 2000
Fax: 0161 762 2001

Bury St Edmunds
St Andrews House, St Andrews Street North, Bury St Edmunds, Suffolk, IP33 1TT
Tel: 01284 775500
Fax: 01284 775656

Buxton
The Benefits Agency, Holker Road, Buxton, Derbyshire, SK17 6BA
Tel: 0345 585513
Fax: 01298 306999

Caernarfon
Government Buildings, Penrallt, Caernarfon, Gwynedd, LL55 2HN
Tel: 01286 768000
Fax: 01286 768001

Caerphilly
Crown Buildings, Claude Road, Denscombe, Caerphilly, Monmouthshire, CF8 2XD
Tel: 029 2042 4300
Fax: 029 2042 4303

Cambridge
Henry Giles House, 73-79 Chesterton Road, Cambridge, Cambridgeshire, CB4 3BQ
Tel: 01223 545200
Fax: 01223 545248

Campbeltown
40 Hall Street, Campbeltown, Argyll & Bute, PA28 6BZ
Tel: 01586 559200
Fax: 01586 559230

Canning Town
197 Freemansons, Canning Town, London, E16 3PE
Tel: 020 7599 8899
Fax: 020 7599 8898

Cannock
Government Buildings, Beecroft Road, Cannock, Staffordshire, WS11 1JR
Tel: 01543 461000
Fax: 01543 461001

Canterbury
Nutwood House, Chaucer Road, Canterbury, Kent, CT1 1ZZ
Tel: 01227 596700
Fax: 01227 596707

Cardiff Central
South Gate House, Wood Street, Cardiff, CF10 1JJ
Tel: 029 2042 8000
Fax: 029 2042 8001

Cardiff East
Eastgate House, 35-43 Newport Road, Cardiff, CF24 0YP
Tel: 029 20423 000
Fax: 0292 042 3401

Cardiff West
377 Cowbridge Road East, Canton, Cardiff, CF5 1WU
Tel: 029 2042 3200
Fax: 0292 042 3201

Carlisle
Rufus House, 5 Castle Street, Carlisle, Cumbria, CA3 8TF
Tel: 01228 829700
Fax: 01228 829701

Carmarthen
Ty Myrddin, Dan y Banc Road, Carmarthen, Carmarthenshire, SA31 1GS
Tel: 01267 322100
Fax: 01267 322185

Castleford
Bridge House, 28 Wheldon Road, Castleford, West Yorkshire, WF10 2JG
Tel: 01977 464111
Fax: 01977 464000

Chatham
Crown House, The Brook, Chatham, Kent, ME4 4LQ
Tel: 01634 810200
Fax: 01634 810207

Chelmsford
Government Buildings, Beeches Road, Chelmsford, Essex, CM1 2RT
Tel: 01245 214300
Fax: 01245 214395

Cheltenham
Rivershill House, St Georges Road, Cheltenham, Gloucestershire, GL50 3EX
Tel: 01242 843400
Fax: 01242 843404

Chester
Chantry House, City Road, Chester, Cheshire, CH1 3AQ
Tel: 01244 357500
Fax: 01244 357511

Chesterfield
Beetwell House, Beetwell Street, Chesterfield, Derbyshire, S40 1TF
Tel: 01246 553100
Fax: 01246 553140

Chester-Le-Street
Crown Buildings, Station Road, Chester-le-Street, Co. Durham, DH3 3BT
Tel: 0191 387 0000
Fax: 0191 387 0001

Chichester
Friars House, 52A East Street, Chichester, West Sussex, PO19 1JS
Tel: 01243 812500
Fax: 01243 812561

Chippenham
St Paul's House, 1 Marshfield Road, Chippenham, Wiltshire, SN15 1LA
Tel: 01249 428000
Fax: 01249 428001

Cinderford
32 Market Place, Cinderford, Gloucester, Gloucestershire, GL14 2RX
Tel: 01452 366297
Fax: 01594 820026

Cirencester (Neighbourhood Office)
Forum House, Southway, Cirencester, Gloucester, Gloucestershire, GL7 1LW
Tel: 01285 662950
Fax: 01285 662975

City
60 Commercial Road, London, E1 1LP
Tel: 020 7301 8200
Fax: 020 7301 8300

Clacton-on-Sea
55 Station Rd, Clacton-on-Sea, Essex, CO15 1RS
Tel: 01255 233200
Fax: 01255 233280

Clitheroe (Caller Office)
31 Lowergate, Clitheroe, Lancashire, BB7 1AE
Tel: 01254 355800
Fax: 01254 355801

Clydebank
Radnor House, 245 Kilbowie Road, Clydebank, West Dunbartonshire, G81 2JN
Tel: 0141 951 3100
Fax: 0141 951 3101

Coatbridge District Office
3-5 South Circular Road, Coatbridge, North Lanarkshire, ML5 3AR
Tel: 01236 502800
Fax: 01236 502808

Colchester
Crown Building, 40 Chapel Street South, Colchester, Essex, CO2 7AZ
Tel: 01206 288000
Fax: 01206 288100

Colwyn Bay
4A Coed Pella Road, Colwyn Bay, Conwy, LL29 8LR
Tel: 01492 614800
Fax: 01492 614801

Consett Caller Office
5 Medomsley Road, Consett, Co. Durham, SR8 1PB
Tel: 01207 580753

Corby
52 Elizabeth Street, Corby, Northamptonshire, NN17 1PG
Tel: 01536 343400
Fax: 01536 343404

Coventry
Cofa Court, Cheylesmore, Coventry, West Midlands, CV1 2HJ
Tel: 024 7623 2200
Fax: 024 7623 2534

Cowdenbeath
12 Factory Road, Cowdenbeath, KY4 9SB
Tel: 01383 316000
Fax: 01383 316001

Crawley
5 The Boulevard, Crawley, West Sussex, RH10 1UP
Tel: 01293 655600
Fax: 01293 614907

Crewe
Wellington House, 38-44 Delamere Street, Crewe, Cheshire, CW1 2JY
Tel: 01270 538000
Fax: 01270 538111

Cricklewood (BBC)
249-253 Cricklewood, Broadway, London, NW2 6RR
Tel: 0845 377 1002
Fax: 0845 377 7629

Croydon
Concord House, 454-458 London Road, Croydon, Surrey, CR9 2WZ
Tel: 020 8710 5600
Fax: 020 8710 5881

Crystal Palace (MBC)
9 Cargreen Road, London, SE25 5AE
Tel: 0845 377 6003
Fax: 0845 377 8106

Cumbernauld
Fleming House, 2 Tryst Road, Glasgow, G67 1JW
Tel: 01236 786500
Fax: 01236 786600

Cumnock (Customers only)
51 Glaisnock Street, Cumnock, Ayrshire, KA18 1BY
Tel: 01290 420089
Fax: 01290 425876

Cwmbran
Glyndwr House, The Mall, Cwmbran, NP44 1XR
Tel: 01633 241600
Fax: 01633 208001

Darlington
Bondgate House, 90 Bondgate, Darlington, DL3 7JY
Tel: 01325 385000
Fax: 01325 385001

Dartford (Caller Office)
Crown Building, Home Gardens, Dartford, Kent, DA1 1UQ
Tel: 01322 488800
Fax: 01322 4888801/2

Daventry Caller Office
14 Oxford Street, Daventry, Northamptonshire, NN11 4 AD

Deeside
Flint House, Chapel Street, Flint, CH6 5AY
Tel: 01352 896000
Fax: 01352 896001

Derby Becket Street
Forester House, Becket Street, Derby, DE1 1NW
Tel: 01332 243800
Fax: 01332 243801

Derby London Road
St Andrews House, 201 London Road, Derby, DE1 2TZ
Tel: 01332 254200
Fax: 01332 254321

Dewsbury
Crown Building, Rishworth Road, Dewsbury, West Yorkshire, WF90 1BB
Tel: 01924 436800
Fax: 01924 436899

Diss
6 Mount Street, Diss, Norfolk, IP22 3QF
Tel: 01379 652005
Fax: 01379 643538

Dolgellau
Government Buildings, Arran Road, Dolgellau, LL40 1BP
Tel: 01341 525300
Fax: 01341 525301

Doncaster
Crossgate House, Wood Street, Doncaster, South Yorkshire, DN1 3LL
Tel: 01302 503503
Fax: 01302 503500

Dover
109 London Road, Dover, Kent, CT17 0TH
Tel: 01304 868000
Fax: 01304 868001

Dudley
Trident House, Wolverhampton Street, Dudley, West Midlands, DY8 1ES
Tel: 01384 553000
Fax: 01384 553190

Dulwich (MBC)
29-25 Lordship Lane, East Dulwich, London, SE22 8EN
Tel: 0845 377 6002
Fax: 0845 377 9084

Dumbarton
15 Meadowbank Street, Dumbarton, West Dunbartonshire, G82 1SJ
Tel: 0141 951 3100
Fax: 0141 951 3416

Dumfries
124 Irish Street, Dumfries, Dumfries & Galloway, DG1 2AW
Tel: 01387 223000
Fax: 01387 223091

Dundee
Lindsay House, 30 Ward Road, Dundee, DD1 1QB
Tel: 01382 313400
Fax: 01382 313700

Dunfermline
Merchiston House, Foundry Road, Dunfermline, Fife, KY12 9DF
Tel: 01383 813800
Fax: 01383 813801

Durham
Milburngate House, Durham, Co. Durham, DH1 5TQ
Tel: 0191 382 5000
Fax: 0191 382 5035

Ealing (GBC)
21 The Mall, London, W5 2QZ
Tel: 0845 377 0001

East Kilbride
Murray House, Murray Road, East Kilbride, South Lanarkshire, G75 0JY
Tel: 01355 572200
Fax: 01355 572202

Eastbourne
St Annes House, 2 St Annes Road, Eastbourne, East Sussex, BN21 3XX
Tel: 01323 413000
Fax: 01323 413135

Ebbw Vale
Crown Buildings, Ty Gantre, Civic Centre, Ebbw Vale, Blaenau Gwent, NP23 6XG
Tel: 01495 263000
Fax: 01495 263002

Edgware
Middlesex House, 29-45 High Street, Edgware, Middlesex, HA8 7DX
Tel: 020 8732 6000
Fax: 020 8732 6029

Edinburgh City
38 Castle Terrace, Edinburgh, EH3 9SJ
Tel: 0131 229 4311
Fax: 0131 222 5818

Edinburgh East
Phoenix House, 275 Portobello High Street, Portobello, Edinburgh, EH15 2AQ
Tel: 0131 657 7400
Fax: 0131 657 7500

Edinburgh West
Haymarket House, 8 Clifton Terrace, Edinburgh, EH12 5EX
Tel: 01506 772000
Fax: 0131 456 5500

Edmonton
St Georges Chambers, 23 South Mall, Edmonton, London, N9 0BW
Tel: 020 8535 8000
Fax: 020 8535 8245

Elgin
21 Trinity Road, Elgin, Moray, IV30 1RJ
Tel: 01343 528000
Fax: 01343 528001

Epsom (Caller Office)
Town Hall, The Parade, Epsom, Surrey, KT18 5BY
Tel: 01372 740072
Fax: 01372 740049

Eston
Hadrian House, 81 High Street, Eston, Cleveland, TS26 9EH
Tel: 01642 398300
Fax: 01642 398393

Euston (GBC)
1 Melton Street, London, NW1 2ED
Tel: 0845 377 40002
Fax: 0845 377 2871

Exeter (East Devon)
Clarendon House, Western Way, Exeter, Devon, EX1 2DA
Tel: 01392 474700
Fax: 01392 474708

Exeter City
Clarendon House, Western Way, Exeter, Devon, EX1 2DA
Tel: 01392 474700
Fax: 01392 474708

Failsworth
160 Oldham Road, Failsworth, Manchester, Greater Manchester, M35 0RA
Tel: 0161 683 2000
Fax: 0161 683 2001

Falkirk
Heron House, 10B Wellside Place, Falkirk, Stirlingshire, FK1 5SE
Tel: 01324 505000
Fax: 01324 505100

Fareham
Crown Building, Civic Way, Fareham, Kent, PO16 6HR
Tel: 01329 243700
Fax: 01329 243702

Folkestone
Palting House, Trinity Road, Folkestone, Kent, CT20 2RH
Tel: 01303 713800
Fax: 01303 713801

Fort William
10 Tweeddale High Street, Fort William, Highland, PH33 6QZ
Tel: 01397 708000
Fax: 01397 708040

Fulham (MBC)
Waterford House, Waterford Road, Fulham, London, SW6
Tel: 0845 377 6001
Fax: 0845 377 5461

Galashiels
Government Buildings, 53 Market Street, Galashiels, Scottish Borders, TD1 3AJ
Tel: 01896 612400
Fax: 01896 612500

Gateshead
Bede House, Tynegate Precinct, Sunderland Road, Gateshead, Tyne & Wear, NE8 1JB
Tel: 0191 220 4000
Fax: 0191 220 4001

Glasgow Annielsland
21 Herschell Street, Anniesland, Glasgow, G13 1HT
Tel: 0141 950 5100
Fax: 0141 950 5220

Glasgow Bridgeton
9 Muslin Street, Bridgeton, Glasgow, G40 4AZ
Tel: 0141 551 3000
Fax: 0141 551 3095

Glasgow City
174 Pitt Street, Glasgow, G2 4DZ
Tel: 0141 225 4000
Fax: 0141 225 4003

Glasgow Craigton Customer Service Point
1479 Paisley Road West, Glasgow, G52 1SY
Tel: 0141 636 8100
Fax: 0141 636 8399

Glasgow Cranstonhill
67 Minerva Street, Glasgow, G3 8LD
Tel: 0141 532 8800
Fax: 0141 532 8801

Glasgow Maryhill
1455 Maryhill Road, Glasgow, G20 9JA
Tel: 0141 532 8300
Fax: 0141 532 8301

Glasgow Newlands BO
8 Coustonholm Road, Glasgow, G43 1SS
Tel: 0141 636 8100
Fax: 0141 636 8399

Glasgow Partick
20 Benalder Street, Partick, Glasgow, G11 6QN
Tel: 0141 337 7100
Fax: 0141 337 7195

Glasgow Pollock Customer Service Point
590 Nitshill Road, Pollock, Glasgow, G53 7SS
Tel: 0141 636 8100
Fax: 0141 636 8399

Glasgow Provan
25 Stepps Road, Provan, Glasgow, G33 3NG
Tel: 0141 766 2000
Fax: 0141 766 2001

Glasgow Rutherglen Customer Service Point
35 Mitchell Arcade, Main Street, Rutherglen, G73 2LS
Tel: 0141 420 4100

Glasgow Shettleston
955 Shettleston Road, Shettleston, Glasgow, G32 7NY
Tel: 0141 532 8500
Fax: 0141 532 8502

Glasgow South District Office
159-181 Pollokshaws Road, Glasgow, G41 1PW
Tel: 0141 420 4100
Fax: 0141 420 4342

Glasgow Springburn
200 Atlas Road, Springburn, Glasgow, G21 4DL
Tel: 0141 557 4000
Fax: 0141 557 4298

Glenrothes(Customer Service Point)
North House, North Street, Glenrothes, Fife, KY7 5NA

Gloucester
Cedar House, Spa Road, Gloucester, Gloucestershire, GL1 1XL
Tel: 01452 366000
Fax: 01452 366121

Goldthorpe PCO
High Street, Goldthorpe, Rotherham, South Yorkshire, S63 9LH
Tel: 01709 895462
Fax: 01709 881666

Goole
Burlington House, North Street, Goole, East Riding of Yorkshire, DN14 5QZ
Tel: 01405 752000
Fax: 01405 763198

Grantham
Crown House, 49A Castlegate, Grantham, Lincolnshire, NG31 6SY
Tel: 01476 513100
Fax: 01476 513146

Gravesend
44-46 The Grove, Gravesend, Kent, DA12 1DF
Tel: 01474 592600
Fax: 01474 592685

Grays
Crown House, Crown Road, Grays, Essex, RM17 6JH
Tel: 01375 364200
Fax: 01375 364300

Great Yarmouth
45 Yarmouth Way, Great Yarmouth, Norfolk, NR30 2Q7
Tel: 01493 633400
Fax: 01493 633500

Greenock
2 Cross Shore Street, Greenock, Renfrewshire, PA15 1DU
Tel: 01475 881500
Fax: 01475 881501

Greenwich Park (BBC)
110-114 Norman Road, Catford, London, SE6 4AW
Tel: 0845 377 1000
Fax: 0845 377 4341

Grimsby
Crown House, Nelson Street, Grimsby, North East Lincolnshire, DN32 7DE
Tel: 01472 245300
Fax: 01472 245301

Guildford
Leys House, 86-88 Woodbridge Road, Guildford, Surrey, GU1 4QD
Tel: 01483 442400
Fax: 01483 442438

Hackney
17 Sylvester Road, London, E8 1DZ
Tel: 020 8533 8600
Fax: 020 8533 8662

Halesowen
Maybrook House, Queensway, Halesowen, West Midlands, B63 4AH
Tel: 0121 585 2200
Fax: 0121 585 2350

Halifax
Crossfield House, St James Road, Halifax, West Yorkshire, HX1 1PE
Tel: 01422 305000
Fax: 01422 305100

Hamilton
19 Douglas Street, Hamilton, South Lanarkshire, ML3 0DE
Tel: 01698 456000
Fax: 01698 456156

Hanley
15 Stafford Street, Hanley, Stoke-on-Trent, ST1 1RF
Tel: 01782 216600
Fax: 01782 224539

Harlesden (BBC)
Harlesden House, 161-163 High Street, Harlesden, London, NW10 4TJ
Tel: 0845 377 1002
Fax: 0845 377 7321

Harlow
Beaufort House, Crown Gate, Harlow, Essex, CM20 1NA
Tel: 01279 693000
Fax: 01279 693001

Harrogate
Berkeley House, 35 Victoria Avenue, Harrogate, North Yorkshire, HG1 5PZ
Tel: 01423 832800
Fax: 01423 832885

Harrow
Kings House, Clarendon Road, Harrow, Middlesex, HA1 1YJ
Tel: 020 8426 3000
Fax: 020 8426 3223

Hartlepool
Ward Jackson House, Wesley Square, Hartlepool, TS24 8EY
Tel: 01429 253700
Fax: 01429 253719

Hastings
Heron House, 149 - 159 London Road, St Leonards-on-Sea, East Sussex, TN37 6LJ
Tel: 01424 452000
Fax: 01424 452001

Hatfield (Caller Office)
Gracemead House, Woods Avenue, Hatfield, Hertfordshire, AL10 8NH
Tel: 01707 346000
Fax: 01707 346002

Haverfordwest
1 Cherry Grove, Haverfordwest, Pembs., SA61 2NS
Tel: 01437 823000
Fax: 01437 823001

Haywards Heath
2nd Floor, Kingsley House, Boltro Road, Haywards Heath, West Sussex, RH16 1BP
Tel: 01444 419800
Fax: 01444 338007

Hemel Hempstead (Caller Office)
Government Buildings, 1 Waterhouse Street, Hemel Hempstead, Hertfordshire, HP1 1EQ
Tel: 01923 208200
Fax: 01923 208321

Hemsworth
Low Hall, Market Street, Hemsworth, West Yorkshire, WF9 4LF
Tel: 01977 624000
Fax: 01977 624020

Hendon (Caller Office)
10 Finchley Lane, Hendon, London, NW4 3DA
Tel: 020 8732 3400
Fax: 020 8732 3411

Hereford
St Nicholas House, 6 St Nicholas Street, Hereford, Herefordshire, HR4 0DD
Tel: 01432 363600
Fax: 01432 363605

Hertford
Sovereign House, Hale Road, Hertford, Hertfordshire, SG13 8ED
Tel: 01992 903800
Fax: 01992 903801

Hexham
St Andrews House, Haugh Lane, Hexham, Northumberland, NE46 3RB
Tel: 01434 610700
Fax: 01434 610701

High Wycombe
Newman House, Oxford Road, High Wycombe, Buckinghamshire, HP11 2DW
Tel: 01494 555200
Fax: 01494 555201

Highgate (GBC)
1 Elthorne Road, London, N19 4AF
Tel: 0845 377 0002
Fax: 0845 377 3384

Holyhead
The Old Vicarage, Newry Street, Holyhead, Anglesey, LL65 1DB
Tel: 01407 602500
Fax: 01407 602501

Houghton-le-Spring
Broadway House, Frederick Place, Houghton-le-Spring, Tyne & Wear, DH4 4AH
Tel: 0191 554 6300
Fax: 0191 554 3101

Hounslow
10 Montague Road, Hounslow, Middlesex, TW3 1LE
Tel: 020 8607 1600
Fax: 020 8607 1601

Hove
Boundary House, Boundary Road, Hove, Brighton & Hove, BN3 7HD
Tel: 01273 368100
Fax: 01273 368101

Hoxton
30 Drysdale Street, London, N1 6LT
Tel: 020 7749 7000
Fax: 020 7749 7151

Huddersfield
Crown House, Southgate, Huddersfield, West Yorkshire, HD1 1SW
Tel: 01484 484500
Fax: 01484 484700

Hull East
Oriel House, 49 High Street, Hull, Kingston upon Hull, HU1 1QJ
Tel: 01482 584444
Fax: 01482 584880

Hull West
Britannia House, 2 Ferensway, Hull, Kingston upon Hull, HU2 8NF
Tel: 01482 584444
Fax: 01482 584587

Hyde
Beech House, Clarendon Street, Hyde, Greater Manchester, SK14 2LP
Tel: 0161 253 8200
Fax: 0161 253 8201

Ilford
Wentworth House, 350 Eastern Avenue, Ilford, Essex, IG2 6NN
Tel: 020 8532 4200
Fax: 020 8532 4342

Ilkeston
58 South Street, Ilkeston, Derbyshire, DE7 8TU
Tel: 0115 944 8000
Fax: 0115 944 8001

Inverness
83-97 Church Street, Inverness, Highland, IV1 1ES
Tel: 01463 663500
Fax: 01463 663506

Ipswich
St Felix House, Silent Street, Ipswich, Suffolk, IP1 1TF
Tel: 01473 267700
Fax: 01473 267799

Irvine
44 Bank Street, Irvine, North Ayrshire, KA12 0HL
Tel: 01294 314500
Fax: 01294 314555

Isle of Wight
Broadlands House, Staplers Road, Newport, Isle of Wight, PO30 2HX
Tel: 01983 273000
Fax: 01983 273001

Jarrow Community Benefit Office
23-25 Grange Road, Jarrow, Tyne & Wear, NE32 3JY
Tel: 0191 489 3016
Fax: 0191 489 3019

Keighley
Worth House, Worth Way, Keighley, West Yorkshire, BD21 5AG
Tel: 01535 617400
Fax: 01535 617555

Kendal
Kentmere House, 1 Blackhall Road, Kendal, Cumbria, LA9 4BS
Tel: 01539 795000
Fax: 01539 795001

Kennington Park
206-210 Kennington Park Road, London, SE11 4DE
Tel: 020 7820 5800
Fax: 020 7820 5881

Kensington (MBC)
Charles House, 375 Kensington High Street, London, W14 8QL
Tel: 0845 377 6001
Fax: 0845 377 5650

Kettering Caller Office
Northamton House, Northamton Road, Kettering, Northamptonshire,

Kidderminster
Crown House, Bull Ring, Kidderminster, Worcestershire, DY10 2DH
Tel: 01562 623600
Fax: 01562 623750

Kilmarnock
12 Woodstock Street, Kilmarnock, East Ayrshire, KA1 2BN
Tel: 01563 578500
Fax: 01563 578555

King's Lynn
Priory House, Austin Street, King's Lynn, Norfolk, PE30 1EB
Tel: 01553 695800
Fax: 01553 695840

Kingston
3 Brook Street, Kingston-on-Thames, Surrey, KT1 2EU
Tel: 020 8481 3000
Fax: 020 8481 3003

Kirkcaldy
26 Victoria Road, Kirkcaldy, Fife, KY1 1EA
Tel: 01592 647500
Fax: 01592 647555

Kirkintilloch CSP
76 Townhead, Kirkintilloch, Glasgow, G66 1NN
Tel: 0141 776 2301

Kirkwall
Government Buildings, Tankerness Lane, Kirkwall, Orkney Islands, KW15 1AQ
Tel: 01856 885300
Fax: 01856 885316

Lanark
Atholl House, 55 Bannatyne Street, Lanark, South Lanarkshire, ML11 9HB
Tel: 01555 554652
Fax: 01555 554661

Lancaster
Mitre House, Church Street, Lancaster, Lancashire, LA1 1EQ
Tel: 01524 598000
Fax: 01524 598001

Larkhall
28-30 Union Street, Larkhall, Lanarkshire, ML9 1DR
Tel: 01698 889924
Fax: 01698 456156

Launceston
St John's, Western Road, Launceston, Cornwall, PL15 7AX
Tel: 01566 766000
Fax: 01566 766100

Leamington Spa
Brandon House, Holly Walk, Leamington Spa, Warwickshire, CV32 4JE
Tel: 01926 302600
Fax: 01926 302601

Leeds East
Southern House, 529 York Road, Leeds, West Yorkshire, LS9 6TF
Tel: 0113 214 8000
Fax: 0113 285 0001

Leeds North
Hume House, Tower House Street, Merrion Way, Leeds, West Yorkshire, LS2 8NT
Tel: 0113 214 8000
Fax: 0113 214 8302

Leeds North West
21-22 Park Place, Leeds, West Yorkshire, LS1 2SL
Tel: 0113 214 8000
Fax: 0113 214 8002

Leeds West
Century House, Church Lane, Pudsey, Leeds, West Yorkshire, LS28 7RQ
Tel: 0113 214 8000
Fax: 0113 205 8822

Leicester Wellington Street
60 Wellington Street, Leicester, LE1 6DS
Tel: 0116 252 9000
Fax: 0116 252 9111

Leicester Yeoman Street
Yeoman Street, Leicester, LE1 1UU
Tel: 0116 252 9000
Fax: 0116 248 0526

Leigh
Roydale House, 2-10
Windermere Road, Leigh,
WN7 1UT
Tel: 01942 263700
Fax: 01942 263701

Leith
199 Commercial Street,
Edinburgh, EH6 6QP
Tel: 0131 555 8000
Fax: 0131 555 8100

Lerwick
Charlotte House, Commercial
Road, Lerwick, Shetland
Islands, ZE1 0LQ
Tel: 01595 732000
Fax: 01595 732001

Leven
Walton House, Victoria Road,
Leven, Fife, KY8 4RN
Tel: 01333 593000
Fax: 01333 593001

Lewes
Medwyn House, Mountfield
Road, Lewes, East Sussex,
BN7 2XR
Tel: 01273 368000
Fax: 01273 368001

Lewisham (BBC)
9-19 Rushey Green, Catford,
London, SE6 4AW
Tel: 0845 377 1000
Fax: 0845 377 4026

Leytonstone
1-3 Lemna Road, Leytonstone,
London, E11 1JJ
Tel: 020 8988 5300
Fax: 020 8988 5396

Lichfield
Guardian House, Rotton Row,
Lichfield, Staffordshire, WS13
6JG
Tel: 01543 461000
Fax: 01543 420105

Lincoln Newland
Viking House, 98 Newland,
Lincoln, Lincolnshire, LN1 1XT
Tel: 01522 346000
Fax: 01522 346210

Lincoln Orchard St
Lancaster House, 36 Orchard
Street, Lincoln, Lincolnshire,
LN1 1YZ
Tel: 01522 346000
Fax: 01522 346001

Liverpool Belle Vale
302 Childwall Valley Road,
Liverpool, Merseyside, L25
2UF
Tel: 0151 801 8000
Fax: 0151 801 8001

Liverpool Bootle
Linacre House, Stanley
Precinct, Bootle, Merseyside,
L20 3DJ
Tel: 0151 944 3000
Fax: 0151 944 3001

Liverpool Breckfield
58 Breckfield Road South,
Breckfield, Liverpool,
Merseyside, L6 5JF
Tel: 0151 551 8200
Fax: 0151 551 8201

Liverpool Crosby
Hougoumont House, 29
Hougoumont Avenue,
Waterloo, Liverpool,
Merseyside, L22 0PB
Tel: 0151 949 4000
Fax: 0151 949 4001

Liverpool Edgehill
Kinglake House, Shenstone
Street, Liverpool, Merseyside,
L7 3PF
Tel: 0151 708 4700
Fax: 0151 708 4716

Liverpool Garston
Cressington House, 249 St
Mary's Road, Garston,
Liverpool, Merseyside,
L19 0NF
Tel: 0151 802 2000
Fax: 0151 802 2001

Liverpool Huyton
Edendale House, Lathom
Road, Huyton, Merseyside,
L36 9XS
Tel: 0151 443 6500
Fax: 0151 443 6592

Liverpool Kirkby
Webster House, Cherryfield
Drive, Kirkby, Liverpool,
L32 8RP
Tel: 0151 549 5000
Fax: 0151 549 5200

Liverpool Norris Green Retrieval Centre
Charnock Road, Stopgate
Lane, Liverpool, Merseyside,
L9 8RP
Tel: 0151 524 0782
Fax: 0151 524 0508

Liverpool Toxteth
High Park House, 7 High Park
Street, Toxteth, Liverpool, L8
8DY
Tel: 0151 801 8200
Fax: 0151 801 8201

Liverpool West Derby
Springfield House, 416 Eaton
Road, West Derby, Liverpool,
Merseyside, L12 3HT
Tel: 0151 801 6300
Fax: 0151 801 6301

Livingston
Ochil House, Owen Square,
Livingston, West Lothian,
North Ayrshire, EH54 6PW
Tel: 01506 460531
Fax: 01506 412492

Llanelli
Crown Buildings, Town Hall
Square, Llanelli,
Carmarthenshire, SA15 3TH
Tel: 01554 876000
Fax: 01554 876091

Llangefni
Government Buildings, Bridge
Street, Llangefni, LL77 7YJ
Tel: 01248 283600
Fax: 01248 283601

Longton
83-87 The Strand, Longton,
Stoke-on-Trent, ST3 2PF
Tel: 01782 592300
Fax: 01782 592319

Loughborough
2 Lemyngton Street,
Loughborough, Leicestershire,
LE11 1U7
Tel: 01509 831000
Fax: 01509 831111

Lowestoft
Rishton House, Clapham
Road South, Lowestoft,
Suffolk, NR32 1RW
Tel: 01502 504000
Fax: 01502 504140

Luton
Cheviot House, 55 Guildford
Street, Luton, Bedfordshire,
LU1 2ER
Tel: 01582 744000
Fax: 01582 744111

Macclesfield
Craven House, Churchill Way,
Macclesfield, Cheshire,
SK11 6AA
Tel: 01625 603000
Fax: 01625 603001

Maidstone
Medvale House, Mote Road,
Maidstone, Kent, ME15 6AH
Tel: 01622 402400
Fax: 01622 402402

Manchester Cheetham
31 Cheetham Parade,
Crumpsall, Manchester,
Greater Manchester, M8 6DH
Tel: 0161 720 5000
Fax: 0161 720 5001

Manchester Chorlton
Graeme House, Chorlton
Place, Wilbraham Road,
Chorlton, M21 9RU
Tel: 0161 882 2800
Fax: 0161 882 2915

Manchester Longsight
123 Clarence Road, Longsight,
Manchester, Greater
Manchester, M13 0ZL
Tel: 0161 256 6000
Fax: 0161 256 6094

Manchester Middleton
Othen House, 7 Oldham Road,
Middleton, Greater
Manchester, M24 1BE
Tel: 0161 654 2000
Fax: 0161 654 2018

Manchester Openshaw
135 Old Lane, Openshaw,
Manchester, Greater
Manchester, M11 1EJ
Tel: 0161 371 6500
Fax: 0161 371 6501

Manchester Remote Store
Unit 12, Ringway Trading
Estate, Wythenshawe,
Manchester, M22 5LH
Tel: 0161 437 2902
Fax: ....

Manchester Rusholme
96 Wilmslow Road,
Manchester, Greater
Manchester, M14 5BJ
Tel: 0161 882 2800
Fax: 0161 248 3803

Manchester Wythenshawe
Simon House, Wavell Road,
Wythenshawe, Manchester,
Greater Manchester,
M22 5RA
Tel: 0161 435 2000
Fax: 0161 435 2003

Mansfield
Hill House, Commercial Gate,
Mansfield, Nottinghamshire,
NG18 1LN
Tel: 01623 413400
Fax: 01623 413484

Merthyr Tydfil
Ty Bethesda, Avenue de
Clichy, Merthyr Tydfil, CF1
1ZH
Tel: 01685 306500
Fax: 01685 306503

Mexborough
Crown Buildings, Adwick
Road, Mexborough, South
Yorkshire, S64 0BD
Tel: 01709 343434
Fax: 01709 343435

Middlesbrough
James Cook House, 79
Corporation Road,
Middlesborough, Cleveland,
TS1 2BA
Tel: 01642 398300
Fax: 01642 398393

Millom (Caller Office)
Government Buildings, St
Georges Road, Millom,
Lancashire, LA18 5DN
Tel: 01229 753700

Milsomer Norton (Caller Office)
Pows Orchard, Mid-Norton,
Bath, Bath & North East
Somerset, BA3 2HY

Milton Keynes
Bowback House, 299 Silbury
Boulevard, Milton Keynes,
MK9 1NS
Tel: 01908 208600
Fax: 01908 208601

Mitcham
Boundary House, 317-321
London Road, Mitcham,
Surrey, CR4 4YF
Tel: 020 8687 3000
Fax: 020 8647 3029

Morecambe (Caller Office)
Heron House, Queen Street,
Morecambe, Lancashire, LA4
5HW
Tel: 01524 302100

Morriston
Oldway House, Clase Road,
Morriston, Swansea, SA6 8BT
Tel: 01792 495700
Fax: 01792 495701

Motherwell
Flemington House, 600
Windmillhill Street,
Motherwell, North
Lanarkshire, ML1 2HN
Tel: 01698 483500
Fax: 01698 483725

Neasden
Chancel House, Neasden Lane, London, NW10 2TW
Tel: 0845 377 1002
Fax: 0845 377 7321

Neath
Percival House, 119 London Road, Neath, Neath Port Talbot, SA11 1LG
Tel: 01639 634400
Fax: 01639 634401

New Forest
1 High Street, Totton, Southampton, SO40 9HL
Tel: 023 8066 5200
Fax: 023 8066 5300

Newbury
Hill View House, 21 West Street, Newbury, West Berkshire, RG14 1BE
Tel: 01635 564000
Fax: 01635 564108

Newcastle (Staffs)
Paradise Street, Newcastle-under-Lyme, ST5 1RS
Tel: 01782 382000
Fax: 01782 382200

Newcastle District Information Centre
Unit 17, Brough Park Industrial Estate, Byker,
Tel: 0191 265 2618
Fax: 0191 265 3646

Newcastle East
Saxon House, 50-52 Heaton Road, Newcastle Upon Tyne, Tyne & Wear, NE6 1SL
Tel: 0191 275 2400
Fax: 0191 275 2553

Newcastle St James
St James House, St James Street, Newcastle Upon Tyne, Tyne & Wear, NE1 4QN
Tel: 0191 275 2400
Fax: 0191 226 6222

Newport
Sovereign House, 1 Kingsway, Newport, Isle of Wight, NP20 1WR
Tel: 01633 241600
Fax: 01633 241667

Newton Abbot
Sherborne House, Kingsteignton Road, Newton Abbot, Devon, TQ12 2PG
Tel: 01626 325400
Fax: 01626 325420

Newton-Le-Willows (Caller Office)
DSS Caller Office, Borron Road, Newton-le-Willows, Merseyside, WA12 0ER
Tel: 01925 785605
Fax: 01925 785690

Newtown
Afon House, The Park, Newtown, Powys, SY16 2PZ
Tel: 01686 863000
Fax: 01686 863001

North Shields
Unicorn House, Suez Street, North Shields, Tyne & Wear, NE30 1BG
Tel: 0191 293 0000
Fax: 0191 293 0001

Northallerton
Elder House, East Road, Northallerton, DL6 1NU
Tel: 01609 852200
Fax: 01609 852271

Northampton
Frances House, 21 Lower Mounts, Northampton, Northamptonshire, NN1 3LY
Tel: 01604 446100
Fax: 01604 446222

Northwich
Hartford House, Meadow Street, Northwich, Cheshire, CW9 5AD
Tel: 01606 813700
Fax: 01606 813711

Norwich Mountergate
Baltic House, Mountergate, Norwich, Norfolk, NR1 1QB
Tel: 01603 248248
Fax: 01603 248200

Notting Hill (GBC)
Westbourne House, 14-16 Westbourne Grove, London, W2 5RH
Tel: 0845 377 0001
Fax: 0845 377 2573

Nottingham Castle Gate
70 Castle Gate, Nottingham, NG1 6AP
Tel: 0115 909 3200
Fax: 0115 909 3201

Nottingham David Lane
David Lane, Basford, Nottingham, NG6 0JT
Tel: 0115 980 3400
Fax: 0115 980 3401

Nottingham Station Street
25 Station Street, Nottingham, NG2 3BZ
Tel: 0115 979 3600
Fax: 0115 979 3601

Nottingham Upper Parliament Street
57-59 Upper Parliament Street, Nottingham, NG1 6AX
Tel: 0115 909 3400
Fax: 0115 909 3401

Nuneaton
Mill House, Mill Walk, Nuneaton, Warwickshire, CV11 4DL
Tel: 01203 818000
Fax: 01203 818001

Oban
1 Miller Road, Oban, Argyll, PA34 4AF
Tel: 01631 569300
Fax: 01631 569308

Oldham
Phoenix House, 46 Union Street, Oldham, Greater Manchester, OL1 1BN
Tel: 0161 912 8000
Fax: 0161 912 8001

Orpington (Caller Office)
Crown Buildings, The Walnuts, Orpinton, Kent, BR6 0TH
Tel: 01689 896820
Fax: 01689 303800

Oxfordshire
Floyds Row, St Aldates, Oxford, Oxfordshire, OX1 1SS
Tel: 01865 44 2600
Fax: 01865 443141

Paddington (GBC)
Tresco House, 65 Lisson Grove, London, NW1 6UW
Tel: 0845 377 0002
Fax: 0845 377 3021

Peckham (MBC)
Collyer Court, Collyer Lane, London, SE15 5DL
Tel: 0845 377 6002
Fax: 0845 377 9685

Pembroke Dock
Devonshire Road, Llanion Park, Pembroke Dock, SA72 6XY
Tel: 01646 483300
Fax: 01646 483385

Penrith
Voreda House, Portland Place, Penrith, Cumbria, CA11 7QQ
Tel: 01768 242500
Fax: 01768 242501

Penzance
Branwell House, Clarence Street, Penzance, Cornwall, TR18 2NU
Tel: 01736 334400
Fax: 01736 334444

Perth
21 Mill Street, Perth, Perth & Kinross, PH1 5JQ
Tel: 01738 412000
Fax: 01738 412001

Peterborough
Clifton House, 84 Broadway, Peterborough, PE1 1QZ
Tel: 01733 297600
Fax: 01733 297640

Peterhead
Government Buildings, Constitution Street, Peterhead, Aberdeenshire, AB42 2SE
Tel: 01779 428800
Fax: 01779 428801

Peterlee
Hatfield House, St Cuthberts Road, Peterlee, Co. Durham, SR8 1PB
Tel: 0191 220 2000
Fax: 0191 220 2001

Plaistow
Francis House, 760 Barking Road, Plaistow, London, E13 9PH
Tel: 020 8210 2800
Fax: 020 8210 2801

Plymouth Crownhill
Crownhill Court, Tailyour Road, Crownhill, Plymouth, PL6 5UE
Tel: 01752 761600
Fax: 01752 761718

Plymouth Durley
Durley House, 5-11 Millbay Road, Plymouth, PL1 3LE
Tel: 01752 272000
Fax: 01752 272198

Pontefract
Enterprise House, 22-26 Horsefair, Pontefract, West Yorkshire, WF8 1RG
Tel: 01977 692800
Fax: 01977 692900

Pontypridd
Oldway House, Broadway, Pontypridd, Rhondda Cynon Taff, CF37 4SP
Tel: 01443 484700
Fax: 01443 484701

Poole
Civic Centre, Park Road, Poole, BH15 2RP
Tel: 01202 712600
Fax: 01202 712623

Poplar
13 Dod Street, Poplar, London, E14 7EP
Tel: 020 7510 1300
Fax: 020 7537 9137

Port Glasgow
6 Scarlow Street, Port Glasgow, Renfrewshire, PA14 5EY
Tel: 01475 881500
Fax: 01475 495388

Port Talbot
Cymric House, Bethany Square, Port Talbot, SA13 1PQ
Tel: 01639 875500
Fax: 01639 875501

Porth
Oldway House, Porth Street, Porth, Mid Glamorgan, CF39 9ST
Tel: 01443 680400
Fax: 01443 680414

Porthmadog
Thedford House, High Street, Porthmadog, Gwynedd, LL49 9LS
Tel: 01766 465000
Fax: 01766 465001

Portsmouth District Office
Roebuck House, Roebuck Close, Cosham, Hampshire, PO6 2TA
Tel: 023 9230 8000
Fax: 023 9230 8001

Preston Barry House
Barry House, 67-69 London Road, Preston, Lancashire, PR1 4DE
Tel: 01772 841000
Fax: 01772 841100

Reading
Princes House, 73A London Road, Reading, RG1 5BS
Tel: 0118 9524400
Fax: 0118 952 4571

Redcar
Dawson House, 11 Ridley Street, Redcar, Redcar & Cleveland, TS10 1RG
Tel: 01642 394037
Fax: 01642 394039

Redditch
St Stephen's House, Prospect Hill, Redditch, Worcestershire, B97 4DP
Tel: 01527 590000
Fax: 01527 590005

Redhill
73 London Road, Redhill, Surrey, RH1 1LP
Tel: 01737 775800
Fax: 01737 775844

Renfrew
2 Lonend, Paisley, Renfrewshire, PA1 1SS
Tel: 0141 847 4000
Fax: 0141 847 4250

Rhyl
64 Brighton Road, Rhyl, Denbighshire, LL18 3HP
Tel: 01745 352400
Fax: 01745 352401

Rochdale
Newgate House, 1 Newgate, Rochdale, Greater Manchester, OL16 1XA
Tel: 01706 714000
Fax: 01706 714001

Romford
30 Main Road, Romford, Essex, RM1 3HH
Tel: 01708 774000
Fax: 01708 774349

Rossendale
Unit 21, The Centre, Rawtenstall, Rossendale, Lancashire, BB4 7QQ
Tel: 01282 473200
Fax: 01726 228465

Rotherham South
Portland House, Mansfield Road, Rotherham, South Yorkshire, S60 2EA
Tel: 01709 722222
Fax: 01709 722122

Rugby
Kingsforth House, Albert Street, Rugby, Warwickshire, CV21 2JD
Tel: 01788 534000
Fax: 01788 534005

Runcorn (Caller Office)
Hilden House, 103 Sankey Street, Warrington, Cheshire, WA1 1LA
Tel: 01925 246000
Fax: 01925 246237

Sale
Portakabin, 83 High Street, Bridgewater, Runcorn, Cheshire WA7 1AX
Tel: 0151 422 2424

Salford
Baskerville House, Browncross Street, New Bailey Street, Salford, M60 9HP
Tel: 0161 837 1000
Fax: 0161 837 1234

Salisbury
Summerlock House, Summerlock Approach, Salisbury, Wiltshire, SP2 7RW
Tel: 01722 315200
Fax: 01722 315201

Saltash
27 Fore Street, Saltash, Cornwall, PL12 6AF
Tel: 01752 850000
Fax: 01752 850001

Scarborough
19 Market Street, Scarborough, North Yorkshire, YO11 1EZ
Tel: 01723 504000
Fax: 01723 504002

Scunthorpe
Crown Building, Laneham Street, Scunthorpe, North Lincolnshire, DN15 6JT
Tel: 01724 274444
Fax: 01724 274440

Seaham
Caroline House, St Johns Square, Seaham, Co Durham, SR7 7JE
Tel: 0191 554 6300
Fax: 0191 513 0231

Sheffield North East
Sorby House, 44-62 Spital Hill, Sheffield, South Yorkshire, S4 7LE
Tel: 0114 260 6162
Fax: 0114 260 6163

Sheffield North West
Bents Green House, 40-50 West Street, Sheffield, South Yorkshire, S1 3TL
Tel: 0114 260 8260
Fax: 0114 260 8261

Sheffield South East
19 Eastern Avenue, Sheffield, South Yorkshire, S2 2FZ
Tel: 0114 260 8000
Fax: 0114 260 8002

Sheffield South West
Chesham House, 15 Charter Row, Sheffield, South Yorkshire, S1 3EE
Tel: 0114 260 8400
Fax: 0114 260 8401

Shotts (Caller Office)
Dyfrig Street, Shotts, North Lanarkshire, ML7 4DL
Tel: 01698 483500
Fax: 01698 483725

Shrewsbury
Whitehall, Monkmoor Road, Shrewsbury, Shropshire, SY2 5AL
Tel: 01743 266000
Fax: 01743 266201

Sittingbourne
Roman House, 9 Roman Square, High Street, Sittingbourne, ME10 4BP
Tel: 01795 562500
Fax: 01795 562600

Skegness
1A Wainfleet Road, Skegness, Lincolnshire, PE25 3PA
Tel: 01754 613000
Fax: 01754 613020

Skelmersdale
Whelmar House, Southway, Skelmersdale, Lancashire, WN8 6NS
Tel: 01695 714000
Fax: 01695 714111

Skipton
Cavendish House, Newmarket Street, Skipton, North Yorkshire, BD23 2PA
Tel: 01535 617400
Fax: 01535 617555

Slough
Upton Lodge, 2A Yew Tree Road, Slough, SL1 2AQ
Tel: 01753 615600
Fax: 01753 615682

Smethwick
Church Hill Street, Smethwick, Warley, West Midlands, B67 7AF
Tel: 0121 555 4000
Fax: 0121 555 4005

South Circular (BBC)
9-19 Rushey Green, Catford, London, SE6 4AW
Tel: 0845 377 1000
Fax: 0845 377 4026

South Shields
Wouldhave House, Market Place, South Shields, Tyne & Wear, NE33 1JN
Tel: 0191 201 2727
Fax: 0191 201 2728

Southall (GBC)
Merrick House, Middlesex Business Centre, Bridge Road, Southall, Middlesex, UB2 4AB
Tel: 0845 377 40001
Fax: 013990 42013

Southampton
St Cross House, 18 Bernard Street, Southampton, SO14 3PJ
Tel: 023 8071 3600
Fax: 023 8071 3700

Southend
Victoria House, 47 Victoria Avenue, Southend-on-Sea, Essex, SS2 6DR
Tel: 01702 222300
Fax: 01702 222435

Southport
Eastbank House, 68B Eastbank Street, Southport, Merseyside, PR8 1HE
Tel: 01704 306200
Fax: 01704 306201

Southwark (London Bankside)
Wedge House, 36-40 Blackfriars Road, London, SE1 8PB
Tel: 020 7902 8600
Fax: 020 7902 8763

St Albans (Caller Office)
Beauver House, 6 Bricket Road, St Albans, Hertfordshire, AL1 3JU
Tel: 01923 208200
Fax: 01923 208321

St Austell
Carlyon House, 20 Carlyon Road, St Austell, Cornwall, PL25 4BX
Tel: 01726 293293
Fax: 01726 293287

St Helens
Gregson House, 2 Central Street, St Helens, Merseyside, WA10 1UF
Tel: 01744 698000
Fax: 01744 698036

Stafford (Caller Office)
Kemley House, Victoria Road, Stafford, Staffordshire, ST16 2AB
Tel: 01543 461000
Fax: 01785 222505

Stanley
Townley House, Stanley, Co. Durham, DH9 0AQ
Tel: 01207 291000
Fax: 01207 291062

Stevenage
Brickdale House, Danestrete, Stevenage, Hertfordshire, SG1 1XQ
Tel: 01438 206200
Fax: 01438 206202

Stirling
2 St Ninians Road, Stirling, FK8 2HF
Tel: 01786 432600
Fax: 01786 432770

Stockport
Heron House, Wellington Street, Stockport, Greater Manchester, SK1 3BE
Tel: 0161 429 2000
Fax: 0161 429 2001

Stockport Apsley House (BA Fraud Only)
Apsley House, Wellington Road North, Stockport, Greater Manchester, SK4 1LW
Tel: 0161 475 1000
Fax: 0161 475 1021

Stockton
Tees Buildings, 10-16 Bridge Road, Stockton-on-Tees, TS18 3BU
Tel: 01642 636000
Fax: 01642 636200

Stoke Newington
52-58 Arcola Street, London, G8 2DL
Tel: 020 8533 8600
Fax: 020 7275 2257

Stornoway
2 Castle Street, Stornoway, Western Isles, HS1 2BA
Tel: 01851 763000
Fax: 01851 763001

Stourbridge (Caller Office)
Scotland House, Lower High Street, Stourbridge, West Midlands, DY8 1ES
Tel: 0121 585 2200

Stranraer
80 Ashwood Drive, Stanraer, Wigtownshire, DG9 7PF
Tel: 01776 802900
Fax: 01776 802902

Stratford
Jubilee House Farthingale Walk, Station Street, Stratford, London, E15 1AN
Tel: 020 8532 3000
Fax: 020 8532 3327

Streatham (Caller Office)
Crown House, Station Approach, Streatham, London, SW16 6HW
Tel: 020 8682 8000
Fax: 020 8682 8695

Stroud
Unicorn House, Cornhill Shopping Centre, Stroud, Gloucestershire, GL5 2JT
Tel: 01453 438000
Fax: 01453 438033

Sunderland
Wear View House, Eden Street West, Sunderland, Tyne & Wear, SR1 3EY
Tel: 0191 5546300
Fax: 0191 5546315

Sutton
Helena House, 348 High Street, Sutton, Surrey, SM1 1PX
Tel: 020 8652 5000
Fax: 020 8652 5100

Sutton-in-Ashfield
70-78 High Pavement, Sutton in Ashfield, NG17 4FT
Tel: 01623 492300
Fax: 01623 492420

Swansea
Oldway House, Rutland Place, Swansea, SA1 1JA
Tel: 01792 450200
Fax: 01792 450206

Swindon
Spring Gardens House, Princes Street, Swindon, SN1 2HY
Tel: 01793 489600
Fax: 01793 489601

Taunton
Brendon House, 35-36 High Street, Taunton, Somerset, TA1 3NY
Tel: 01823 349100
Fax: 01823 349101

Telford
New Town House, Telford Square, Town Centre, Telford, Shropshire, TF3 4HB
Tel: 01952 207400
Fax: 01952 207579/80

Thames Park (London Bankside) 'Thames South'
Keyworth House, Keyworth Street, London, SE1 6LS
Tel: 020 7302 8000
Fax: 020 7302 8003

Thanet
Queens House, Queens Street, Ramsgate, Kent, CT11 9EW
Tel: 01843 258000
Fax: 01843 258006

Tonypandy
Thistle House, Llwynypia Road, Tonypandy, Rhondda Cynon Taff, CF40 2EP
Tel: 01443 616000
Fax: 01443 616001

Torbay
Cotswold, Warren Road, Torbay, Devon, TQ2 5UX
Tel: 01803 210600
Fax: 01803 290237

Tottenham
640-659 High Road, London, N17 0AA
Tel: 020 8365 5200
Fax: 020 8365 5208

Trowbridge
Homefield House, Polebarn Road, Trowbridge, Wiltshire, BA14 7EJ
Tel: 01225 498000
Fax: 01225 498007

Truro Lemon Quay House
Lemon Quay House, Lemon Quay, Truro, Cornwall, TR1 2PU
Tel: 01872 355000
Fax: 01872 355018

Tunbridge Wells
Vale House, Clarence Road, Tunbridge Wells, Kent, TN1 1HH
Tel: 01892 507300
Fax: 01892 507444

Twickenham
121-125 Heath Road, Twickenham, Middlesex, TW1 4BE
Tel: 020 8258 8200
Fax: 020 8258 8204

Uxbridge
Colham House, Bakers Road, Uxbridge, Middlesex, UB8 1SF
Tel: 020 8426 3000
Fax: 01895 454151

Wakefield
Crown House, 127 Kirkgate, Wakefield, West Yorkshire, WF1 1ST
Tel: 01924 433600
Fax: 01924 433800

Wallasey
Dominick House, St Albans Road, Wallasey, Merseyside, CH44 5XS
Tel: 0151 649 1000
Fax: 0151 691 4701

Wallsend
Hadrian House, Station Road, Wallsend, Tyne & Wear, NE28 6HW
Tel: 0191 295 2300
Fax: 0191 295 2301

Walsall Glebe Street
Government Buildings, Glebe House, Glebe Street, Walsall, West Midlands, WS1 3LT
Tel: 01922 852000
Fax: 01922 636512

Walsall Lower Hall Lane
Government Buildings, Lower Hall Lane, Walsall, West Midlands, WS1 1RP
Tel: 01922 852000
Fax: 01922 852297

Walthamstow
Dansom House, 656A Forest Road, Walthamstow, London, E17 3SH
Tel: 020 8535 6100
Fax: 0181535 6198

Wandsworth (Caller Office)
Arndale House, Arndale Walk, Wandsworth, London, SW18 4BU
Tel: 020 8682 8000
Fax: 020 8682 8500

Warrington
Hilden House, 103 Sankey Street, Warrington, Cheshire, WA1 1LA
Tel: 01925 246000
Fax: 01925 246237

Watford
Exchange House, 60 Exchange Road, Watford, Hertfordshire, WD18 0JJ
Tel: 01923 208200
Fax: 01923 208321

Wearside District Information Retrieval Centre
Unit 5, Sunprise Enterprise Park, Sunderland, Tyne & Wear, SR5 3RX
Tel: 0191 5543300
Fax: 0191 5543301

Wellingborough
Lothersdale House, West Villa Road, Wellingborough, Northamptonshire, NN8 4NE
Tel: 01933 221200
Fax: 01933 221345

West Bromwich
Parham House, 416 High Street, West Bromwich, West Midlands, B70 9JR
Tel: 0121 331 8200
Fax: 0121 331 8205

Wester Hailes
Murrayburn House, 1 Westerhailes Centre, Edinburgh, EH14 2SP
Tel: 01506 772000
Fax: 0131 456 4379

Weston-super-Mare
Carlton House, Carlton Street, Weston-super-Mare, North Somerset, BS23 1TQ
Tel: 01934 634000
Fax: 01934 634007

Weymouth
Westwey House, Westwey Road, Weymouth, Dorset, DT4 8TG
Tel: 01305 328000
Fax: 01305 328001

Whitehaven
Mark House, Strand Street, Whitehaven, CA28 7LQ
Tel: 01946 514400
Fax: 01946 514450

Wick
Government Buildings, Girnigoe Street, Wick, Highland, KW1 4HL
Tel: 01955 673100
Fax: 01955 673101

Widnes
2 Kingsway House, Caldwell Road, Widnes, Cheshire, WA8 7EA
Tel: 0151 422 2300
Fax: 0151 422 2385

Wigan
Brocol House, 73 King Street, Wigan, Greater Manchester, WN7 1YX
Tel: 01942 758000
Fax: 01942 758001

Wilmslow
Venture House, 46-52 Water Lane, Wilmslow, Cheshire, WN1 1EB
Tel: 01625 608100
Fax: 01625 608101

Wimbledon
Ravensbury House, 3 Palmerston Road, London, SW19 1PG
Tel: 020 8784 4900
Fax: 020 8784 4901

Winchester
City Gate, 8 City Road, Winchester, Hampshire, SO23 8GB
Tel: 01962 848848
Fax: 01962 848800

Wishaw
156-160 Main Street, Wishaw, Lanarkshire, ML2 7PJ
Tel: 01698 361705
Fax: 01698 483725

Woking
Lynton House, Station Approach, Woking, Surrey, GU22 7PT
Tel: 01483 736000
Fax: 01483 736006

Wolverhampton Temple Street
Molineux House, Temple Street, Wolverhampton, West Midlands, WV2 4AU
Tel: 01902 482000
Fax: 01902 482001

Wood Green
Granta House, 1 Western Road, London, N22 6UH
Tel: 020 8899 3200
Fax: 020 8899 3307

Woolwich (Thameside)
Crown Building, 48 Woolwich New Road, London, SE18 6HF
Tel: 020 8301 8300
Fax: 020 8301 8380

Worcester
Vine House, Farrier Street, Worcester, Worcestershire, WR1 3EL
Tel: 01905 720300
Fax: 01905 720305

Workington
Simon House, 197-199 Vulcans Lane, Workington, Cumbria, CA14 2BW
Tel: 01900 608800
Fax: 01900 608860

Worksop
Crown House, Newcastle Avenue, Worksop, Nottinghamshire, S80 1NX
Tel: 01909 537200
Fax: 01909 537226

Worthing
Crown House, High Street, Worthing, West Sussex, BN11 1NG
Tel: 01903 286000
Fax: 01903 236984

Wrexham
15-17 Grosvenor Road, Wrexham, LL1 1BW
Tel: 01978 316500
Fax: 01978 316506

Yeovil
Federated House, 29/31
Hendford, Yeovil, Somerset,
BA20 1UU
Tel: 01935 463100
Fax: 01935 463101

York
11-17 Monkgate, York,
YO31 7JZ
Tel: 01904 682100
Fax: 01904 682314

CHAPTER FOUR

Housing

Housing

CHAPTER FOUR

Housing

INTRODUCTION

The Office of the Deputy Prime Minister is the central government department responsible for formulating and co-ordinating policies on housing and the environment and so provides the legislative framework for the provision and management of housing.

Local authorities act as enablers in the provision of housing and are expected to take a strategic approach encompassing all the housing issues in their area. They publish Housing Strategy Statements, setting out their policies and programmes and the contributions of other organisations in the housing field, including the private sector, for meeting the housing needs of their area. They also have powers to help private householders improve their own houses, to assist landlords to provide new housing for rent and to regulate standards of building in their area. They have responsibilities for rehousing certain families displaced by slum clearance or development schemes, for the control of houses in multiple-occupation and for assisting homeless people. They are also responsible for the improvement, repair and management of their own housing and have powers to build new and demolish existing houses. Outside London, the local authorities mainly responsible for housing are the metropolitan and non-metropolitan district councils. In London, the housing authorities are the London boroughs set up under the London Government Act 1963 and the common council of the City of London.

MAIN LEGISLATION

Extensive legislation gives central government and local authorities powers and duties for a variety of housing functions, ranging from provision of housing and financial assistance to encourage the purchase and improvement of houses, through the control and regulation of rents, to the enforcement of regulations concerning multi-occupied and unfit housing, eviction and harassment. The main trends of recent legislation has been to widen and diversify the provision of housing; meet the needs of individuals and groups who have been disadvantaged in the housing market; and improve and rehabilitate existing housing rather than attempt large clearances which break up communities. The following brief list of legislation illustrates these trends.

Housing Act 1988

was intended to encourage more investment in the private rented sector by deregulating rents on new lettings, thenceforth generally to be assured or assured shorthold tenancies. New tenancies granted by registered housing associations would normally be assured tenancies rather than secure tenancies. The system of finance for housing associations was revised to allow the maximum use of private money to supplement public funds. Local authority tenants were given the right to choose a new landlord. The Act also gave the power to create Housing Action Trusts to take over, renovate and then dispose of areas of run-down local authority housing.

Leasehold Reform, Housing and Urban Development Act 1993

gives most long leaseholders of flats the collective right to buy their freehold and the individual right to extend their leases. The Act also introduced a rent to mortgage scheme and a right to compensation for repairs for tenants in public sector housing. It also introduced a tenants' right to management audit and powers for the Secretary of State to approve codes of management practice. The Act established the Urban Regeneration Agency to secure the reclamation and re-use of vacant, derelict and underused buildings throughout England, particularly in urban areas.

The Housing Act 1996

enables the Housing Corporation to register a wider range of social landlords including local housing companies (housing associations are now known as registered social landlords (RSLs)); extends to certain RSL tenants the right to buy their homes at a discount; extends the rights of leaseholds to buy the freehold of their building; made it easier for leaseholders to challenge unreasonable service charges; strengthened right of first refusal; allowed more effective action to be taken against anti-social tenants; revised existing homelessness legislation to allow fairer treatment to all those waiting for social housing; introduced changes to the assured shorthold tenancy regime, strengthened local authority powers to control houses in multiple occupation (see Multiple occupation section), and created an introductory tenancy regime for local authority tenants.

The Housing Grants, Construction and Regeneration Act 1996 is intended to give local authorities freedom to decide their own priorities for tackling unfitness and disrepair in private housing and to provide disabled facilities grants for people who need to adapt their homes.

THE MAIN TYPES OF HOUSING

The following sections are a general guide to financial and legal provisions relating to housing in the private and public sectors. Specialised free advice and information for all housing enquiries and problems is available to consumers and social work agencies from housing aid and advice centres, provided either by local authorities or by voluntary organisations, such as Shelter, which have been established throughout the country. There is also an independent, Government-funded organisation called the Leasehold Advisory Service (LEASE) which specialises in providing advice on the residential leasehold system (call 020 7490 9580). Citizens advice bureaux are also well equipped to deal with housing queries and problems.

Home ownership

Mortgage loans for home purchase and improvement are offered mainly by building societies, banks and, to a lesser extent, insurance companies. Local authority mortgages are now very seldom arranged. Authorities can indemnify building society and some other mortgages which may help buyers in areas which are otherwise unattractive to mortgage lenders.

Everyone who buys a home has an obligation to make a realistic appraisal of their capacity to meet mortgage payments, and to consider how they would meet payments if they lost their income through ill health or unemployment. Private insurance is one way borrowers can protect themselves against such eventualities. A DWP leaflet (IS800) "Protecting Your Mortgage Planning for a Rainy Day" gives guidance on this.

Homesteading scheme

A handful of local authorities have tried 'homesteading' schemes, selling at a discount homes which the buyer agrees to improve within a certain period. Homesteading schemes have declined since the 1980s due to a shortage of suitable properties, although the Empty Homes Agency have been looking into the viability of reviving the idea particularly in areas of declining demand.

Low cost home ownership (LCHO)

Local authorities and registered social landlords can also offer shared ownership as an alternative to outright sale. Under this scheme, people part-own and part-rent a property with the option to buy into full home-ownership later if their income increases. Details of registered social landlord schemes are available from the Housing Corporation, 149 Tottenham Court Road, London W1P 0BN and its regional offices.

Homebuy and Cash Incentive Schemes

Registered social landlords may offer interest free equity loans to their tenants and local authority tenants under the Homebuy Scheme to meet 25% of the cost of buying their own home to help them move into owner occupation, and release their tenancies for others in housing need. Section 129 of the 1988 Housing Act provides powers for local authorities to make available cash grants to tenants for the purchase of properties on the open market or to carry out works on a house to provide additional accommodation (which is rarely used). The main aim of CIS is to free up existing council housing for households in housing need. It has also been seen as a way of encouraging owner occupation.

Starter Homes Initiative

The Starter Home Initiative (SHI) helps key workers, particularly teachers, police, nurses and other essential health staff, to purchase homes in areas where the high cost of housing may otherwise price them out of the communities they serve. SHI assistance is being provided through local scheme managers to help key workers in London, the South East and high cost areas in the South West, Eastern and West Midlands regions. Most of the schemes are being run by registered social landlords. The contact details for local scheme managers can be found on the following websites: www.housing.odpm.gov.uk and www.housingcorp.gov.uk.

New house building warranties

Most new homes built privately are protected by a warranty against defects. Two separate schemes exist.

The National House-Building Council (NHBC) provides a ten year warranty (Buildmark). For the first two years, the housebuilder must put right any defects caused by breach of

NHBC's technical requirements. NHBC itself will deal with cases where the builder fails to put right faults either by default or through bankruptcy. From the third to tenth year, NHBC provides direct insurance cover. For properties registered up to 31 March 1999, the insurance is for major damage caused by a defect in the loadbearing structure. In addition, cover is included for defects in underground drainage systems, and, subject to an excess, damage caused by defects in roof tiles and slates, floor decking and screeds and external render and tile hanging. **For properties registered from 1 April 1999,** in addition to the above, Buildmark also covers contaminated land, and failure of double-glazing. Also, instead of major damage, the validity of a claim is determined by whether the value of the remedial work is more than £500 (indexed). Further information can be obtained from **NHBC,** Buildmark House, Chiltern Avenue, Amersham, Bucks, HP6 5AP. Customer Service Help Line 0845 845 6422, website address: www.nhbc.co.uk

Zurich Insurance Building Guarantees has a ten year latent defects warranty. It covers newly built homes for sale or rent by the private or social housing sector, it also covers conversions. Where elements of the home are factory built, a manufacturers warranty is available. For the first two years either the developer or manufacturer are responsible for rectifying defects that do not meet Zurich's published technical requirements, but if they do not deal with them Zurich will act for the policy holder and arrange for remedial action themselves. The remainder of the ten years is insured by Zurich. The policy provides a range of options to widen the cover and the warranty can be extended by five years at the end of the ten year term, subject to claims experience and the payment of an additional premium. Warranty cover can also be provided for self builders and commercial buildings. Further information can be obtained from Zurich Insurance Building Guarantees, Southwood Crescent, Farnborough, Hampshire GU14 0NL. Tel: 01252 522000. Fax: 01252 372989.

Local authority housing

Local authorities are expected to maintain their existing stock in a sound condition and ensure that older housing is brought up to modern standards as resources permit. The allocation of local authority tenancies is the responsibility of the local housing authority which owns it. Local housing authorities may also have rights to nominate applicants for social housing to housing association tenancies. Local housing authorities are required to allocate all such tenancies through a single housing register.

Local authorities are subject to the Housing Act 1985, which requires that they set reasonable rents and review them from time to time. Under the Local Government and Housing Act 1989, a local authority, when determining rents, shall have regard, in particular, to the principle that rents should vary between different kinds of property in broadly the same way that they would vary in the private market.

The voluntary housing movement

Registered Social Landlords (RSLs) also known as Housing Associations have a continuing role as the main new providers of social housing. Large charitable trusts such as Peabody and Guinness Trusts have long owned large housing estates. Other voluntary bodies have, with government assistance, formed housing associations and developed much new housing from the 1960s. The housing association movement entered a period of rapid expansion from the late 1980s and is now the main provider of additional subsidised accommodation for around 1.7 million people in housing need. RSLs are registered with the Housing Corporation, a non-departmental public body sponsored by the Office of the Deputy Prime Minister, which is responsible for all matters relating to the regulation and inspection of RSLs. RSLs' main objectives include ensuring that their stock is managed efficiently and used effectively, and continuing to bring in private finance to complement public resources. They work closely with local authorities to deliver local housing strategies. Many registered social landlords specialise in providing accommodation to meet the special needs of vulnerable sections of the community, such as Black and Minority Ethnic communities, older people and people with disabilities with the aid of revenue funding from the Housing Corporation. RSLs have become increasingly involved in housing homeless people. They are also involved in providing low-cost accommodation for people in rural communities and developing low-cost home ownership schemes, as well as providing rented accommodation for those on low incomes. In April 2002 the Housing Corporation's new Regulatory Code came into effect. The code aims to regulate and promote a viable, properly governed and managed housing association sector, encourage RSLs to provide decent homes and to deliver high quality, value for money services through a process of continuous improvement leading to safer, inclusive and sustainable communities. Inspection is a new feature of the regulatory regime aimed at continuous improvement in the provision of services to tenants.

Since the House Act 1974, RSLs have been able to apply for Housing Association Grant (HAG), now known as Social Housing Grant (SHG). The Housing Act 1988 introduced a number of changes to the grant regime. SHG now meets a proportion of the capital costs of developing or acquiring new housing or renovating existing housing. The remaining costs are met directly by RSLs through private sector loans.

The Housing Corporation can be contacted at 149 Tottenham Court Road, London W1P 0BN Tel: 020 7393 2000 Email: enquiries@housingcorp.gsx.gov.uk
The National Housing Federation (NHF) represents nearly 2,000 registered social landlords in England. It negotiates on behalf of RSLs with government and other agencies, as well as offering advice, training and publications. 175 Gray's Inn Road, London WC1X 8UP Tel: 020 7955 5696 Email: info@housing.org.uk

National Disability Housing Network

was launched in October 1999. The NDHN is co-ordinated by RADAR (The Royal Association for Disability and Rehabilitation) and supported by the Office of the Deputy Prime Minister (ODPM). NDHN meets twice a year to discuss those issues involved in providing accessible housing for the disabled. This initiative follows the extension of Part M of the Building Regulations to Housing which states that all new housing meets the access needs of disabled people: wider entrances, corridors and internal doors; entrance-level lavatories; accessible electric light switches and sockets. Government departments and national organisations involved include: the Housing Corporation; Local Government Association; organisations representing estate agents, landlords and the building industry; national charities representing the disabled; Housing Departments; local disability organisations; colleges, schools and universities. To find out more about the NDHN, please contact RADAR at 12 City Forum, 250 City Road, London EC1V 8AF, Tel: 020 7250 3222, Minicom: 020 7250 4119, Fax: 020 7250 0212, Web:www.radar.org.uk

Almshouses

have provided sheltered accommodation for the past thousand years and information about them can be obtained from the **Almshouse Association,** Billingbear Lodge, Wokingham, Berkshire RG40 5RU Tel: 01344 52922 Fax: 01344 862062, E-mail: naa@almshouses.org
Older people are offered a unique form of tenure. At present, there is a total stock of almshouses in excess of 300,000 units, whilst old dwellings are undergoing modernisation, charity land is being developed to provide additional housing. The Association gives advice, promotes research and makes grants and loans to members, whilst keeping under review existing and proposed legislation affecting almshouses, taking appropriate action when necessary.

Privately rented housing

Although private housing for rent declined sharply in the post-war years, this decline has been reversed and it provides for nearly 10% of all households. With the exception of those where the landlord lives in the same building, most tenancies granted by private landlords are assured and assured shorthole tenancies and an outline of the statutory provisions on rents and security of tenure is given in the following sections. As in the public and voluntary sectors, tenants of private landlords are eligible for housing benefit.

THE RIGHTS OF TENANTS

The field of rent protection and security of tenure is still complex and only a summary can be given here. The Office of the Deputy Prime Minister produces a series of explanatory booklets about the rights of both landlord and tenant, but it is advisable to consult a solicitor, a citizens advice bureau, law centre or local authority about individual problems.

Tenancies with a non-resident landlord

Tenancies which commenced before 15 January 1989 will usually be regulated tenancies under the Rent Act 1977 or protected shorthold tenancies under the Housing Act 1980. Regulated tenants have long term security and such tenancies can only be ended on certain grounds set out in the Rent Act 1977. Tenancies which started on or after that date can be assured or assured shorthold tenancies under the Housing Act 1988. Under provisions in the Housing Act 1996 all future tenancies are assured shorthold unless the parties agree otherwise. Only the courts can order such tenants to leave, even when a notice to seeking possession has expired or a fixed term tenancy has ended. The court can make such an order only on one or more grounds laid down in the Acts mentioned above. These grounds include:

- non-payment of rent, or breach of the tenancy agreement;
- conduct which has damaged the property, or is a nuisance or annoyance to the neighbours;

- the property is needed by the landlord for himself or herself and notice of this was given before the tenancy started;
- the letting is a shorthold tenancy and the landlord wishes to recover possession after the end of the fixed term.

Rents

For a regulated tenancy under the Rent Act 1977, either the tenant or the landlord or both may ask the Rent Officer to determine a fair rent for the tenancy. Both landlord and tenant normally have the right of objection to the rent officer's assessment and objections are dealt with by the Rent Assessment Committee. A rent will be registered based on the state of repair of the dwelling, its age, character and locality, not on the personal circumstances of the landlord or tenant, A tenant cannot legally be required to pay more than the registered rent apart from increases in water rates. A registered rent cannot be raised except by a new registration. A further registration cannot come into effect within two years unless there is some relevant change of circumstances, e.g., alterations to the dwelling. The Maximum Fair Rent Order limits the amount that the rent can be increased by a new registration to inflation plus five or seven percent. But this cap does not apply if there is no existing rent registration for the property, or if the new fair rent determined for the property is at least 15% more than the existing registered rent due to repairs or improvements carried out by the landlord.

Under the Rent Act 1977, landlords and tenants of dwellings for which no rents have been registered may, if they wish, agree rent increases between themselves and without going to the Rent Officer. Even if there is an agreement, the landlord or tenant may still apply to the Rent Officer for a rent to be registered.

For assured and assured shorthold tenancies under the Housing Act 1988, the landlord and tenant can agree a market rent without statutory interference. They may do this at any time, either with a tenancy agreement or simply by agreeing on a figure. If this is not done the landlord can formally propose a rent increase to the tenant, who can refer to the Rent Assessment Committee which will determine a market rent. The Landlord will not be able to force the tenant to pay above the assessed rent. The Housing Act 1996 amended the rights of assured shorthold tenants to apply to the assessment committee if they believe that the initial rent is excessive. Assured shorthold tenants whose tenancies were entered into on or after 28th February 1997 can now only apply to the Rent Assessment Committee during the initial fixed term of the tenancy: the committee will set a market rent if there is evidence that the rent is significantly higher than rents for similar tenancies in the locality.

Tenancies with a resident landlord

A tenant occupying unfurnished accommodation in the landlord's house, having done so from before 14 August 1974, is usually subject to the same 'protection' outlined above. Otherwise, whether the accommodation is furnished or unfurnished, if the landlord and tenant have lived in the same house since the start of letting, the tenant does not normally have full security of tenure. A further distinction was introduced by the Housing Act 1980 so that, where a letting began before 28 November 1980, the tenant can, on receipt of a notice to quit, apply to the local Rent Tribunal to suspend the operation of the notice. Rent Tribunals can give up to six months' security at a time. Such a tenant may also consult the Rent Tribunal if s/he considers the rent to be too high and ask the Tribunal to reduce it. Rents fixed by the Tribunal are registered and can only be changed by a fresh determination by the Tribunal, either after two years or at any time when circumstances have changed. A landlord who charges more than the registered rent for the accommodation is liable to prosecution.

Where a letting started on or after 28 November 1980, the Rent Tribunal no longer has the power to suspend the operation of a notice to quit. Instead, if the landlord applies to the county court for a possession order, the court has power to suspend the order for a period of up to three months. The Rent Tribunal can still fix the rent. If the letting commenced on or after 15 January 1989, the tenant has no means to object to the rent the landlord wants to charge. If the landlord and tenant do not share living accomodation (such as a bathroom or living room), the landlord must still give notice in prescribed form and apply to the county court for possession if the tenant does not leave at the end of it. Where there is sharing of accomodation the notice the landlord gives doesn't have to be in a prescribed form, and s/he doesn't have to get a possession order.

Local authority tenants - Right to Buy

Since 1980, local authority tenants have had the right to buy the home in which they live at a discount. Tenants of housing associations whose homes have been transferred from local authorities under large-scale voluntary transfer schemes have a similar preserved right to buy.

The amount of discount depends on the area in which their home is located and on the length of time they have spent in public sector tenancies.
Some properties can be excluded from the right to buy. These include:

- properties suitable for occupation by elderly persons - i.e. which were first let before January 1990, meet certain criteria in terms of location, size and design, and are occupied by a person who took up the tenancy after the age of 60
- properties suitable for occupation by physically disabled people - i.e, if they are part of a group of similar properties, meet certain criteria in terms of location, size and design, are served by a warden service, and have a nearby common room.

Such properties can be kept by landlords for future letting. More detailed information on the Right to Buy scheme is given in the Government's booklets 'Your right to buy your council home' and 'Thinking of buying a council flat?' These are avaiable from: Free Literature, PO Box 236, Wetherby, West Yorkshire LS23 7NB.

As part of the Citizen's Charter scheme, a Right to Repair scheme and a Right to Compensation scheme were introduced for council tenants from 1 April 1994. The Right to Repair scheme was introduced with the intention of giving council tenants a simple and reliable way of ensuring that urgent repairs are carried out by the local authority. It will make sure that certain small urgent repairs which might affect your health, safety or security, are done quickly and easily. Under the Right to Compensation scheme, council tenants have a new right to compensation for improvements they have made to their homes. Compensation is paid at the end of a tenancy, usually when a tenant moves. Two leaflets, "A better deal for tenants - your Right to Repair" and "A better deal for tenants - your new Right to Compensation" give details on how each scheme works and are available free of charge from DTLR Free Literature, PO Box 236, Wetherby, West Yorkshire LS23 7NB.

A ODPM (Housing Directorate) Action Plan

An Action Plan for addressing the housing needs of black and minority ethnic (BME) people was published by the Department in November 2001.
The Plan brings together in a single document the full range of DTLR housing policies and initiatives in play and planned to help meet the housing needs of BME people. The Plan contains a strong commitment to race proof the Department's housing policies and provides an important baseline from which the Department and others can monitor performance in delivering this commitment and the range of actions set out in the plan.

Copies of the Action Plan are accessible from the Department's housing website at www.housing.dtlr.gov.uk/information/bme/index.htm. Alternatively additional copies can be obtained free of charge from DTLR Free Literature, PO Box 236, Wetherby, West Yorkshire LS23 7NB.

Tenants who wish to move to another area have the right to exchange their homes. Further information about this right, and about two schemes for helping people to move, the Tenants Exchange Scheme and the National Mobility Scheme, may be found in the booklet 'Home Mobility Scheme', available from the HOMES, 242 Vauxhall Bridge Road, London SW1V 1AV.

The Rent Service

The Rent Service (TRS) was established as an Executive Agency of the then Department of the Environment, Transport and the Regions on 1 October 1999, and took over the responsibilities of the former Rent Officer Service (which operated through 77 separate units based in local authorities). TRS is now an Agency of the Office of the Deputy Prime Minister.
TRS makes fair rent evaluations for regulated and secure tenancies. Appeals against the Rent Officer's decision are made to Rent Assessment Committees. Proceedings before the Committee are informal and any party may appear in person, or be represented by either a solicitor or counsel or some other authorised person.

TRS also carry out rental valuations for housing benefit purposes, i.e. to determine whether housing benefit claimants (and prospective claimants) are being asked to pay more rent than their landlords might reasonably be expected to obtain in open market conditions. The amount determined by the Rent Officer will be the maximum eligible for housing benefit purposes, although local authorities will have a limited fund to 'top-up' benefit in cases of exceptional hardship.

Chartered Surveyors' Voluntary Service

This is a service sponsored by the Royal Institution of Chartered Surveyors. Its aim is to provide free advice to people who could not otherwise afford a surveyor's help. Referrals at present may be made through a Citizens Advice Bureau. Common subjects for referral are repair problems, disputes with builders and fair rents. CABx can contact the Secretary of the Service for the nearest surveyor in the scheme on Tel: 020 7222 7000 or Tel: 020 7669 4757

Notice to quit

If a landlord wishes to terminate a tenancy, then, unless the tenancy is for a fixed period, s/he must usually serve on the tenant a notice to quit or a notice of intention to seek possession in the prescribed form. To bring an assured shorthold tenancy to an end after six months (or longer if a longer fixed term was agreed) the landlord must give at least two months' notice in writing. To bring an assured shorthold tenancy to an end during the initial six months or fixed term, or to end an assured tenancy, the landlord must rely on one of the grounds for possession set out in The Housing Act 1988. Different lengths of notice apply to different grounds and the notice must be in the prescribed form. Notices to quit must, in most cases, be in writing and give a minimum of four weeks' notice. Tenants of local authorities and other public bodies who are 'secure tenants' would need to have a 'Notice of Seeking Possession' served on them.

If the tenant does not leave the dwelling, the landlord must, in most cases, get an order for possession from the court before the tenant can lawfully be evicted. The landlord cannot apply for such an order before the notice to quit has run out. There is an accelerated possession procedure introduced in 1993 which means that the court can issue an order for possession without a hearing for assured shorthold tenancies in some cases.

A tenant who does not know if s/he has any right to remain in occupation after a notice to quit or notice seeking possession runs out, or is otherwise unsure of his or her rights, can obtain advice from a solicitor. Help with all or part of the cost of legal advice and assistance may be available. The tenant should also be able to obtain information from a citizens advice bureau, a solicitor or a housing aid centre.

Protection against harassment and eviction

Under the Protection from Eviction Act 1977, the landlord must in most cases go to court to get a possession order if the former tenant remains after the tenancy has lawfully come to an end. For such tenancies it is also a legal requirement for the landlord to get court bailiffs to carry out an eviction if the ex-tenant refuses to leave: it is illegal for a landlord to evict an ex-tenant him/her self. This applies to tenancies in both the public and private sector. The Housing Act 1988 has, however, excluded certain types of tenancy from the requirement of a court order to evict, including those where landlord and tenant share accommodation, holiday lets and in cases where certain public bodies give a licence to occupy to someone living in a hostel.

Illegal eviction is a criminal offence, as is harassing any tenant knowing or having reasonable cause to believe that this will make the tenant leave his or her home. Prosecutions may be brought by any person but are, in practice, normally brought by the local authority, which has specific powers to prosecute for those offences; therefore, any complaints should be made to the local authority concerned. Maximum penalties are currently a fine of £5,000, six months' imprisonment, or both, on summary conviction; and unlimited fines, or two years' imprisonment, or both, on indictment.

Rent books

The provision and content of rent books are governed by the Landlord and Tenant Act (1985). Any landlord who lets residential accommodation where rent is payable weekly must provide a rent book or other similar document, unless board is provided as well as lodging and the value of the board forms a substantial element of the rent. This provision applies whether furnished or unfurnished. The Landlord must include his/her name in the rent book. In addition, if the letting is an assured tenancy under the Housing Act 1988 or a regulated tenancy or restricted contract (under the Rent Act 1977, or Housing Act 1980) certain further information is prescribed by law. These items are what rent is payable; the Tenant's Rights under the Acts for his/her particular type of tenancy; claiming Housing Benefit. Whether a rent book is actually required by law or not, a landlord who provides one must also include - again in standard form - certain information about overcrowding offences. Local Authorities are empowered to prosecute any landlord who fails to provide a rent book where one is legally required, or who does not include in it the information prescribed.

Landlord's identity

The landlord must, on the written request of a tenant, furnish the tenant in writing with particulars of his or her name and address. If the landlord is a company, the tenant can ask for the name and address of every director or the secretary of the company which owns the property. It is the duty of the agent or rent collector to pass such a request to the landlord. If a tenanted dwelling is sold or passed on, or if a part-owner sells an interest or passes it on, then the new landlord must notify the tenant in writing of his or her name and address not later than the next date, or if the next rent date is within two months of the assignment, then the end of that period of three months. In the case of landlords who are companies, the address to be given is the registered office. There are special rules for the information to be given by trustee landlords. These requirements are laid down in sections 1, 2 and 3 of the Landlord and Tenant Act 1985 and carry a maximum penalty on summary conviction of £2,500 for non-compliance.

Complaints

The 1996 Housing Act introduced an independent housing ombudsman service for investigating complaints against social landlords. Tenants, leaseholders, and others who receive a service from a social landlord can ask the ombudsman to consider complaints of maladministration once the landlords' formal complaints procedure has been exhausted. Landlords are expected to comply with the ombudsman's findings and recommendations. Local authority tenants will continue to have access to the Local Government Ombudsman, although the first point of call should be the local authority internal complaints procedure.

FINANCIAL ASSISTANCE

Housing benefit

The Social Security Act 1986 provided the framework for major changes to earlier rent and rate rebate schemes with effect from 1988 and it has since been superseded by the Social Security Contributions and Benefits Act 1992 and the Social Security Administration Act 1992. Housing benefit can be claimed by those who pay rent whether working or not.

The amount of housing benefit is based on a comparison of income and capital including earnings calculated on a net basis and an amount intended to cover day-to-day living expenses. The aim is to ensure that tenants are left with at least the basic income support levels for day-to-day living expenses after paying their reasonable housing costs.

The applicable amount is assessed as follows:

- personal allowance: each claimant is entitled to a personal allowance depending on their age and marital status;
- dependants' allowances: an amount is added to the claimant's personal allowance for each dependent child or young person living with them. No addition is made if the child has capital in excess of £3,000;
- premiums: a premium is added to the personal and dependants' allowances for certain categories of claimant. This is in line with the premiums related to income

support. If a person qualifies for more than one premium, they will normally get the premium which gives the most money. Family premium, disabled child's premium, severe disability premium, enhanced disability premium and carer premium, however, can be paid in addition to any other premiums. Details of these rates are shown in the table below.

Housing Benefit Provisions 2002/2003

Description	***£ per week***
PERSONAL ALLOWANCES	
Single person aged 16-24 and lone parent under 18	£42.70
Single person 25 or over and lone parent 18 or over	£53.95
Couple both aged under 18	£64.45
Couple *at least one aged 18 or over*	£84.65
Dependent children:	
from birth to the September following the 16th birthday	£33.50
from the September following the 16th Birthday to the 19th Birthday	£34.30
PREMIUMS	
Family	£14.75
Family (Lone parent)	£22.20
Pensioner *65-75*	
single person	£44.20
couple	£65.15
Pensioner *enhanced, 75-79*	
single person	£44.20
couple	£65.15
Pensioner *higher premium, 80+ or 60+ and disabled*	
single person	£44.20
couple	£65.15
Disability	
single person under 60	£23.00
couple, if one partner under 60	£32.80
Severe disability	
single person	£42.25
couple, one person qualifying	£42.25
couple, both qualifying	£84.50
Disabled child	£35.50
Carer	£24.80
Enhanced Disability Premium	
couple	£16.25
single home parent	£11.25
child	£11.25
Bereavement Premium	£21.55

The following items are deducted from gross earnings to arrive at the net earnings for housing benefit purposes:

- income tax;
- national insurance contributions;
- 50% of contributions towards an occupational or personal pension scheme made by an employed or self-employed person.

Earnings are ignored or 'disregarded' in part; the disregard varies according to individual circumstances. The earnings disregards are £25 for lone parents; £20 if the carer premium, disability premium, the severe disability premium or, in certain circumstances, the higher pensioner premium is included in the applicable amount; £10 for couples and £5 for single people. An earnings disregard of £20 a week also applies where people are in special jobs, such as part-time firefighters and auxiliary coastguards. In addition, people with children or who are disabled and who work at least 30 hours a week on average can get a further £11.65 disregarded.

Certain childcare charges (up to £94.50 per week per family where there is one child and up to £140 per week where there are two or more children) can also be offset against earnings. This disregard, which is in addition to the other earnings disregards, applies in respect of children up until the September following their 15th birthday (or 16th birthday if the child is disabled) and is available to lone parents who are working 16 hours or more a week, couples where both partners are working 16 hours or more a week and couples where one member is working 16 hours or more a week and the disability premium or, in certain circumstances, the higher pensioner premium is included in the applicable amount on account of the other member's incapacity.

Claimants whose assessed income for housing benefit purposes is less than, or equal to, their "applicable amount" and whose rent is considered "reasonable" are entitled to the maximum benefit. The maximum housing benefit payable is 100% of the eligible rent (if the rent is regarded as "reasonable"). Changes introduced in January 1996 are designed to give new claimants an incentive to negotiate lower rents or choose less expensive accommodation. Benefit will continue to meet in full rents which are at or below the general level of rent for similar accommodation in the same locality.

The new rules affect most new claims. Tenants in the private sector who claimed housing benefit before 6th October 1997 and were subject to the Local Reference Rent (LRR) rules were able to receive 50% of the difference between the LRR and the appropriate rent, subject to a limit of two times the LRR where the appropriate rent was higher than the LRR. Claimants receiving this top-up on 5th October 1997 retain the right to the top-up. The top-up will continue as long as the claimant continues to occupy the same dwelling, remains entitled to and in receipt of housing benefit and the appropriate rent is more than the LRR. Once lost, the top-up cannot be regained. Anyone whose claim dates from before January 1996 will not be affected by the change unless they move house or have a break in claim of more than four weeks. Council tenants and people living in certain types of special needs accommodation will also be unaffected. Where income is greater than the applicable amount, the housing benefit payable is reduced by 65% of income in excess of the applicable amount.

A claimant with capital of more than £16,000 will not be eligible for housing benefit or council tax benefit. Capital of less than £3,000 or £6,000 if the claimant (or partner) is aged 60 or over, will not be taken into account. If a claimant has capital between these two amounts, each £250 of this amount is deemed to earn an income of £1 per week. Holdings of national savings certificates and premium bonds will be regarded as capital.

Housing benefit is paid in two main ways:

- where a person pays rent to the local authority, the amount that has to be paid will be reduced accordingly;

- where a person pays rent to a private landlord or housing association, housing benefit will be paid to the person concerned by cheque or cash, directly into an account or any other way that the council decides, taking into account the person's needs and convenience. In some circumstances, the local authority may pay housing benefit direct to the landlord.

Council tax benefit

Council tax benefit is available to people on low incomes to help them meet some or all of their council tax liability. Council tax benefit is administered by local authorities on behalf of the Department of Social Security which has responsibility for the policy. The calculation of how much help a person needs to pay their council tax follows much the same rules as housing benefit assessment.

For further information about housing benefit and council tax benefit, leaflets RR 1 and CTB 1 are available from local council offices, benefit agency offices and post offices. There is also a more detailed leaflet, RR 2, which covers both housing benefit and council tax benefit. Advice or help can also be obtained from the local council.

Rent or mortgage arrears

Council tenants who are in receipt of income support and who have arrears of rent, accrued other than by non-payment of an amount equal to the expected contribution of any non-dependant living in the household, may, at the discretion of the DSS, have £2.70 per week deducted from their benefit and paid direct to the housing authority in order to reduce the arrears. Where the tenant pays a fixed charge for heating, hot water, lighting or cooking, this may also be paid direct. Enquiries should be made of the local DSS office. If they are wage-earners, the tenants may enter into a voluntary agreement with their employers to have their rent paid direct to the housing authority.

Owner-occupiers who are unable to meet their mortgage commitments should discuss their situation with their lender and should consider seeking independent advice from their local Citizens Advice Bureau. Under the Council of Mortgage Lender's Mortgage Code lenders are committed to considering cases of financial difficulty and mortgage arrears sympathetically and positively. Mortgage lenders have sought to help their borrowers through a variety of ways, most of them accepting reduced payments, deferring or capitalising interest or extending the term of the loan or changing the type of mortgage. Also, where an owner-occupier is in receipt of Income Support or income based JobSeekers Allowance, this may include help with the interest on a mortgage or loan on the property. In most cases, there is a waiting period before this help begins. There are provisions for this mortgage interest to be paid direct to lenders in most cases. A DWP leaflet (IS8) gives details of benefit entitlement and sets out borrowers' rights and responsibilities.

Lenders who are members of the Council of Mortgage Lenders, and this includes most of the large building societies and banks, have undertaken not to take possession action in cases where the full interest payments are covered by income support, or in cases where borrowers have suffered a significant reduction in their income and therefore cannot fully meet their present interest costs but are making a reasonable and regular repayment toward them.

If borrowers fail to meet their mortgage payments and are unable to agree with their lender arrangements to deal with the situation, it is open to lenders to take steps to repossess the property. But they must first obtain an order from a county court. No-one can evict borrowers from the property unless the court has agreed. To do this a lender must issue a claim form summons which will tell the court and the borrower why they are seeking repossession. This will include details of any arrears of mortgage payments or any other breach of the mortgage agreement. They will also have to provide the court with information about the composition of the arrears, how the account has been conducted, and about the borrower's personal and financial circumstances, if these are known. The borrower is sent copies of all the information provided with the claim form response pack. The response pack allows the borrower to tell the court if any information given by the lender is incorrect. It also provides an opportunity to give details which will support an offer to pay off the arrears by instalments. The decision about whether the lender should be entitled to have the property back is made at a private court hearing which both the lender and the borrower can attend.

At the hearing, the court has a statutory duty to consider whether, even if it makes an order for possession, the operation of the order should be postponed to give the borrower an opportunity to pay off the arrears over a reasonable period (a suspended possession). Where a suspended order is made, so long as the borrower makes the payments under the order, they cannot be evicted.

HOUSING CONDITIONS

House renovation grants

The present system of home improvement grants came into operation in England and Wales in December 1996 under the provisions of the Housing Grants, Construction and Regeneration Act 1996. The grants are designed to help the poorest people, living in houses in the worst condition, to bring them back up to an acceptable standard. All grants, except disabled facilities grant, are discretionary.

There are special grants for house adaptations for disabled people, for houses in multiple occupation and for works to the common parts of buildings containing flats. Furthermore, smaller sums of money are also available under home repair assistance for minor repairs, improvements and adaptations needed to help older people, people who are disabled or infirm, or those in receipt of income related benefits.

With the exception of Home Repairs Assistance, all these grants are subject to a test of the applicant's financial resources. Further information is available from the local authority's renovation grants officer, or from one of the booklets covering this area. These are entitled 'House Renovation Grants', 'Disabled Facilities Grant' and 'Home Repair Assistance' and are obtainable from local Council offices, housing advice centres or citizens advice bureaux. From summer 2003 the grant giving powers in the 1996 Act (except for those relating to DFGs) will be replaced by a new general power to give assistance for housing renewal.

Regulatory Reform Order 2002

In March 2001, the Government published a consultation paper on proposals to reform private sector housing renewal by local authorities in England and Wales. The Regulatory Reform (Housing Assistance)(England and Wales) Order 2002 became law in July 2002. The Order gives local authorities greater discretionary powers to award grants, loans and other forms of assistance to private homeowners to help them to renovate, repair or adapt their home. The Order also extends local authorities powers to help someone move to more suitable accommodation where this is a better option than repairing or adapting their existing home.

Local authorities will have the flexibility to determine eligibility criteria, whether to perform a means test and the type of assistance available (e.g. grant, loan advice, works). Use of the new power to give housing renewal assistance is subject to authorities producing a published policy. Mandatory Disabled Facilities Grants are outside the scope of the new reforms, but the Order does extend eligibility to those living in park homes and houseboats. Information on what housing renewal assistance may be available in your local area can be obtained from the local council.

Home Improvement Agencies (HIAs)

These are local schemes which provide independent advice and help to assist older people, people with disabilities and those on low incomes to carry out repairs and improvements to their properties. There are over 230 HIAs operating in England, many of which are known as 'Care and Repair' or 'Staying Put' schemes. 227 agencies covering 284 local authority areas are supported by the government under a grant programme introduced in 1991. Further information can be obtained from **Foundations,** the national co-ordinating body for HIAs, at Bleaklow House, Howard Town Mills, Glossop SK13 8HT Tel: 01457 891909 Fax: 01457 869361.

Housing defects

Certain types of dwelling have been designated as inherently defective, either by the Secretary of State or by individual local authorities. Owners of such designated dwellings may be eligible for assistance from their local authority if their homes were previously owned by the public sector, they bought the property before the inherent defects became generally known, and they applied to their local authority for assistance by specified deadlines; 30 November 1994 for owners of 22 of the 24 nationally designated types; 30 April 1996 for owners of Smith (BSC) houses; and 7 April1997 for owners of Boswell houses. The main form of assistance is a grant of 90% or, in cases of financial hardship, 100% towards the cost of reinstating a house to mortgageable standard, subject to certain limits that vary according to the type of house. If, however, the local authority is not satisfied that reinstatementwill be cost effective or feasible, it has to offer to repurchase the house at 95% of the defect-free value. Repurchase is the only form of assistance available for those who own flats. The scheme is in its concluding stages, with 99% of eligible owners having received assistance.

Multiple occupation

Part XI of the Housing Act 1985 as amended by the Local Government and Housing Act 1989 and Part II of the Housing Act 1996 provides local housing authorities in England and Wales with powers to deal with unsatisfactory conditions in houses in multiple occupation (HMOs). Authorities usually take action through their environmental health departments. HMOs are defined in the 1985 Act as those 'occupied by persons who do not form a single household'. Such premises can include large houses or flats divided into bedsitters, shared houses or flats not constituting a single household and 'hotels' and guest houses providing accommodation for those people who otherwise have no home.

If a local authority consider an HMO is unfit for the number of occupants they may serve a notice under Section 352 of the 1985 Act, specifying the works required to make the premises fit e.g. additional kitchen or bathroom facilities, means of escape from fire or other fire precautions. In certain high risk categories of HMO, local authorities are under a mandatory duty to ensure that fire safety standards are adequate. This duty was recently expanded to include an additional number of HMOs and is being phased in over a three year period.

Instead of, or in addition to, the service of a notice under section 352, a limit may be placed on the number of occupants of an HMO. A local authority may also take action under section 189 if they consider an HMO unfit for human habitation (see the section on Repairs below).

Regulations require the manager of an HMO and to keep existing facilities in good repair. If this duty is not complied with, the authority may carry out the works instead and can also prosecute.

The local authority must inform all the occupants of an HMO when a notice is served and must also keep a register of notices served, which must be made available for public inspection at all reasonable hours. If the requirements of a notice are not complied with, the authority may carry out the works instead and can also prosecute.

In extreme cases, where living conditions in the house are likely to affect the health, safety or welfare of the residents, the local authority can place a control order on the premises. While this is in force, the local authority has wide powers, including the right to carry out works and to receive rents from residents in place of the owner.

The 1996 Act enabled local authorities to adopt stronger registration schemes for HMOs. These allow registration to be refused or revoked in certain circumstances, for instance if the house is incapable of being made suitable for the number of people it is registered for, or, if it could be made suitable, if works are not carried out to make it so. Certain categories of HMO are exempt from registration.

If a local authority decide to adopt a model registration scheme they are required to publish advance notice in a local paper and make a copy of the scheme, and the register, available for public inspection at all reasonable hours. Anyone wishing to know whether an HMO registration scheme exists in their area, and if so whether or not a particular property is registered, should contact the environmental health department of their local authority.

Any resident of an HMO who considers that action needs to be taken in respect of the property they occupy should contact the environmental health department of their local authority.

The Government is committed to introducing a national licensing system for HMOs and published a consultation paper on proposals in March 1999. Primary legislation will be required to implement these proposals.

Repairs

It is difficult to generalise about the respective responsibilities of landlords and tenants for repairs. The Landlord and Tenant Act 1985 (Section 11), as amended by the Housing Act 1988 (Section 116), sets out the statutory repairs obligations placed on landlords where the tenancy or lease is for less than seven years. The main source of information for a particular case is the terms of the individual tenancy. Legal advice should be sought in case of difficulty. There are, however, two types of claim open to tenants whose homes are in a state of disrepair: damages for inconvenience suffered from disrepair, coupled with an order to repair; and damages for personal injuries and loss caused by the disrepair. A local authority can, and in some cases must, serve a notice on the landlord under the Environmental Protection Act 1990 or Housing Acts, requiring works to be carried out to remove danger to the health of the occupiers and to make the house fit for habitation. In extreme cases, the local authority can require the closure or demolition of the house. When this occurs, the local authority must ensure that the occupiers are offered suitable alternative accommodation and, in certain circumstances, financial compensation. The local authority also has many individual powers and duties relating to specific items and services, especially drainage and sanitary services. In such cases, the local authority can act quickly to remove any danger to health and recover costs from the owner or occupier afterwards.

Since April 1994, council tenants have had a right to repair. It covers small urgent repairs costing up to £250 which, if not carried out within a specified period, will jeopardise the health, safety or security of the tenant. A leaflet on this is available from local authorities or from the Office of the Deputy Prime Minister.

Vermin

Under the Prevention of Damage by Pests Act 1949, local authorities are responsible for ensuring that their districts are kept, as far as is practicable, free of rodents. In addition, the Act requires that occupiers of non-agricultural land must notify the local authority if "substantial numbers" of rodents are living on or resorting to the land. The Act gives local authorities the power to require landowners and occupiers to control rodent infestations on their land. Local authorities can also, where necessary, carry out the control work in default and recover the cost of such action from the landowner or occupier. The Department for Environment, Food and Rural Affairs has certain default powers to initiate action, should local authorities fail to discharge their responsibilities under the 1949 Act. DEFRA monitors the level of rodent presence through the annual English House Condition Survey undertaken by the Office of the Deputy Prime Minister. Householders having a rat problem that they do not wish to deal with themselves are advised to contact the Environmental Health Department of the local authority or call in a pest control company.

Noise

Most nuisance caused by noise can be dealt with either under the Control of Pollution Act 1974, the Environmental Protection Act 1990, the Noise and Statutory Nuisance Act 1993 or the Noise Act 1996. Action will usually be taken by the local authority. Environmental noise nuisance that can be dealt with in this way includes neighbour noise such as that from parties, and commercial and construction noise, but not aircraft, road or rail traffic noise.

In cases of environmental noise nuisance, where an informal approach fails or is not appropriate, the environmental health department of the local authority should be contacted. It has a duty to investigate complaints from people living within its area, and, if it decides that a statutory nuisance exists, must serve an abatement notice on the person responsible or on the owner or occupier of the premises. The Noise Act 1996 provides local authorities with powers to enter premises and confiscate noise-making equipment. Also included in the 1996 Act is the Night Noise Offence which is available for local authorities to adopt and applies to night noise from domestic premises. The local authority will then have the power to serve a warning notice on the person responsible for the noise and may take further action if necessary. In the case of noise from vehicles, machinery or equipment in the street, the notice will be served on the person responsible.

The notice can specify the steps to be taken to abate the nuisance, or can set conditions such as maximum noise levels. Non-compliance with the terms of a notice can result in the local authority bringing a prosecution against the person responsible. Alternatively, individuals can take their own independent action. Details on the procedure involved are available from the Clerk to the local magistrates' court.

The Land Compensation Act 1973, the Noise Insulation Regulations 1975 (Statutory Instrument No. 1763) and the Noise Insulation (Railways and other Guided Transport Systems) Regulations 1996 (Statutory Instrument No.428) provide for grants to be made available towards the cost of providing insulation where traffic noise over and above a specified level has increased, owing to alterations to or construction of new roads and railways.

The **Department of the Environment, Food and Rural Affairs** produces a free booklet, 'Bothered by Noise? There's no need to suffer', available from local council offices, Citizens Advice Bureaux or the Department of the Environment, Food and Rural Affairs by telephoning 08459 556 000 or online at http://www.defra.gov.uk.

Anti-Social Behaviour

The Home Office have recently introduced anti-social behaviour orders (ASBOs) which enable local authorities and the police to apply to the magistrates court for an order prohibiting a person aged 10 or over behaving in an anti-social manner. If this order is breached, the individual may be fined or imprisoned. The orders are preventative in nature and intended to be used to put an end to persistent and serious anti-social behaviour which can make life a misery for a community. The prohibitions in the order must be such as are necessary to protect people from further anti-social acts by the defendant in the locality.

HOMELESSNESS

Part 7 of the Housing Act 1996, often referred to simply as "the homelessness legislation", places a general duty on housing authorities to ensure that advice and information about homelessness, and preventing homelessness, is available to everyone in their district free of charge. It also requires authorities to assist individuals and families who are homeless and apply for help. Part 7 is amended by the Homelessness Act 2002.

The main homelessness duty

Under the legislation, certain categories of household, for example, families with children and households that include someone who is vulnerable, for example because of pregnancy, old age, or physical or mental disability, have a priority need for accommodation. Housing authorities must ensure that suitable accommodation is available for people who have priority need, if they are homeless through no fault of their own. This is known as the "main homelessness duty". The housing authority can provide accommodation in their own stock or arrange for it to be provided by another landlord, for example, a housing association or a landlord in the private rented sector.

Accommodation must be made available in the short term until the applicant can find a settled home, or until some other circumstance brings the duty to an end, for example, where the household voluntarily leaves the temporary accommodation provided by the housing authority. In many cases, the allocation of a suitable secure or introductory tenancy in an authority's housing stock (or nomination for a housing association assured tenancy) under Part 6 of the 1996 Act will bring the homelessness duty to an end. It would also end if the applicant made their own arrangements for accommodation or accepted the offer of a tenancy with a private landlord.

Interim duty to accommodate

When first considering an application, the housing authority needs to decide if they have reason to believe that the applicant may be eligible, homeless and have a priority need, even before they have completed their inquiries. If the applicant meets these criteria, the housing authority have an immediate duty to ensure that suitable accommodation is available until they make their decision on the homelessness case. This is an important part of the safety net for people who have priority need and are unintentionally homeless.

When is someone homeless?

Broadly speaking, somebody is statutorily homeless if they do not have accommodation that they have a legal right to occupy, which is accessible and physically available to them (and their household) and which it would be reasonable for them to continue to live in. It would not be reasonable for someone to continue to live in their home, for example, if that was likely to lead to violence against them (or a member of their family).

Intentional homelessness

People make themselves homeless intentionally where homelessness is the consequence of a deliberate action or omission by them (unless this was made in good faith in ignorance of a relevant fact). A deliberate act might be a decision to leave their previous accommodation even though it would have been reasonable for them to stay there. A deliberate omission might be non-payment of rent that led to rent arrears and eviction.

Other homelessness duties

If people are homeless but do not have priority need or if they have brought homelessness on themselves, the housing authority must ensure they get advice and assistance to help them find accommodation for themselves - but they do not have to ensure that accommodation becomes available for them. The housing authority can provide advice and assistance itself or arrange for another agency to do this. The housing authority must ensure that this includes a proper assessment of their housing needs and information about where they are likely to find suitable accommodation.

Applications and inquiries

Housing authorities must give proper consideration to all applications for housing assistance, and make inquiries to see whether they owe them any duty under Part 7. This assessment process is important in enabling housing authorities to identify the assistance which an applicant may need either to prevent them from becoming homeless or to help them to find another home. In each case, they will need to decide whether they are eligible for assistance, actually homeless, have a priority need, and whether the homelessness was intentional. If they wish, housing authorities can also consider whether applicants have a local connection with the local district, or with another district. Certain applicants who are persons from abroad (i.e. most persons subject to immigration control and others who are not habitually resident in the UK, Channel Islands, Isle of Man or the Republic of Ireland) are not eligible for any assistance under Part 7 except free advice on homelessness and the prevention of homelessness.

Allocation of Social Housing

The allocation of social housing is governed by Part 6 of the Housing Act 1996. This will be amended by the Homelessness Act 2002 which comes into effect in January 2003.

Local housing authorities are required to allocate housing through a single housing register. All applicants for local authority housing, or nomination to housing association tenancies must be considered in accordance with the authority's published allocation scheme. In framing their allocation schemes, councils are required to give reasonable preference to:

- people occupying insanitary or overcrowded housing or otherwise living in unsatisfactory housing conditions;
- people occupying housing accommodation which is temporary or occupied on insecure terms;
- families with dependent children;
- households consisting of or including someone who is expecting a child;
- households consisting of or including someone with a particular need for settled accommodation on medical or welfare grounds;
- households whose social or economic circumstances are such that they have difficulty in securing settled accommodation.

Authorities have to give weight to the factors listed above when deciding their allocations policies, but they are not restricted to only taking only those factors into account. Authorities could add other factors of their own, such as housing key workers coming into the area, whose presence is essential for economic growth. But the authorities' own secondary criteria must not dominate their allocations scheme at the expense of factors in the statutory list. Authorities have some discretion in determining other groups who may or may not be qualifying persons but these groups cannot override the reasonable preference category.

The authority is free to decide the structure of their allocations scheme, for example, whether it is points-based, date order or quota based, or any combination of these, what indicators to use, and what weighting to give to the reasonable preference categories provided, of course, that reasonable preference is still given to those categories when allocating housing. The allocation scheme will be decided by local councillors.

The housing register

The housing register will be managed either by the authority or may be contracted out the management of the allocation scheme. The authority may contract out this function to another body such as a local housing association. Officers will make enquiries about each application and decide whether the applicant is a qualifying person within the terms of the allocation scheme. The council may contract out this function as well, so it could be done by either council officials or others.

A person on the housing register of a local authority is entitled to see his/her own entry on the register and to receive a copy of it free of charge. An applicant is also entitled to be given general information to enable him/her to assess how much time is likely to elapse before accommodation appropriate to his/her needs becomes available. Applicants should be able to receive sufficient information to enable them to form a view of when they are likely to be made an offer. Although authorities are not required to give their own estimate, there is nothing to prevent them from doing so. What counts as sufficient information will depend on local housing conditions and the authority's own allocation scheme. At a minimum, the authority should give an applicant an indication of his/her position in the queue and of the likely supply of appropriate properties over the coming year.

Each authority must publish a summary of its allocation rules and provide these on request, free of charge to any member of the public who requests one. The authority must also make the scheme available for inspection at its principle office and provide a copy of the full scheme on payment of a reasonable fee.

Disagreements

If the authority decides not to put someone on their housing register who has applied to be put on it, or to remove someone from their register other than at his/her own request, the authority is required to notify the person of their decision and the reasons for it. The notice must, also inform the person of his/her right to request a review of the decision and of the time within which such a request must be made. Once such a request has been made the authority is required to review their decision. Complaints must be made in writing.

Allocation of Social Housing from January 2003

The Homelessness Act 2002 amends part 6 of the Housing Act 1996. Under the amended provisions, housing authorities must consider all applications for social housing that are made except if the applicant is a person from abroad subject to immigration control. The allocation of housing accommodation must be seen as part of the district-wide housing strategy, which includes:

- a lettings plan, which estimates supply and demand for different types of dwelling, analyses how demand can be met and sets general objectives and priorities;
- formal or informal arrangements with RSLs and other providers of housing in the area to meet the objectives in the lettings plan; and
- the provision of advice and assistance for those wishing to make housing applications.

Each housing authority must have and publish an allocation scheme, that scheme must contain a statement as to the housing authority's policy on choice of accommodation or the opportunity for applicants to express preferences about housing accommodation.

Housing authorities must ensure that reasonable preference is given to the following categories of people:

- people who are homeless (within the meaning of Part 7 of the 1996 Housing Act);
- people who are owed a duty by any housing authority under section 190 (2), 193 (2) or 195 (2) of the 1996 Housing Act (or under section 65 (2) or 68 (2) of the Housing Act 1985) or who are occupying accommodation secured by any housing authority under section 192 (3);

- people occupying insanitory or overcrowded housing or otherwise living in unsatisfactory housing conditions;
- people who need to move on medical or welfare grounds; and
- people who need to move to a particular locality in the district of the housing authority, where failure to meet that need would cause hardship (to themselves or to others).

People who would normally qualify under the above categories can be treated as ineligible by local authorities on the basis of unacceptable behaviour, where the local authority is satisfied that an applicant or member of their household is guilty of unacceptable behaviour serious enough to make them unsuitable tenants.

An allocations scheme must give applicants rights under the scheme to request certain information, to request to be informed of certain decisions and in some cases to request reviews of decisions.

Hostels

A large proportion of hostel accommodation is supplied by voluntary bodies and nearly half of it is in London. The 'London Hostels Directory', published by the Resource Information Service, gives details of accommodation and is available from them at The Basement, 38 Great Pulteney Street, London W1R 3DE Tel: 020 7494 2408. The Service also publishes the 'London Day Centres Directory', giving detailed information on day centres for homeless people in the capital. Emergency information about the availability of hostel spaces can be obtained from **Shelter Nightline**, Tel: 0800 446441 and Tel: 0800 622410 for the hard of hearing.

Night shelters

A number of voluntary organisations such as **Centrepoint**, **The Depaul Trust** and **The Passage** have established projects for single homeless and rootless people. Night shelters have been set up in various cities to provide overnight accommodation for those unable to find it elsewhere.

Rough Sleeping

In December 1999, the Prime Minister launched Coming in from the Cold – the Government's Strategy on Rough Sleeping, which set out its approach to meeting its target of reducing rough sleeping in England by at least two-thirds by 2002.

This document marked a step-change in approach to tackling and preventing rough sleeping both inside and outside London. The strategy sets out proposals covering all areas of rough sleeper provision from the street to a permanent home, and focuses particularly on those who are most vulnerable: those who are alcoholics, drugs addicts or who have mental health problems. In addition, the strategy sets out the Government's plans to prevent new people becoming tomorrow's rough sleepers. In particular, it details how better support will be given to children leaving care, ex-offenders and those who have served in the armed forces.

The Prime Minister announced on 3 December 2001 that the Government had met, ahead of time, its target of reducing rough sleeping in England by two thirds by 2002. In determining ways to sustain the reduction, the Government has taken into account the views of local authorities, voluntary organisations and others, an evaluation of the rough sleepers strategy, and the current extent and nature of rough sleeping. In consultation with local voluntary agencies and other partner organisations, key local authorities have been asked to draw up strategies for their own areas for the period up to 31 March 2004. These strategies will outline clearly how they will sustain the reductions in rough sleeping and also indicate how they will integrate into the new homelessness strategies under the Homelessness Act. They will also have to be linked in with future arrangements of Supporting People. Once these strategies have been agreed, in some areas, funding will be allocated to local authorities to commission these services. Where this is the case, local authorities will enter into arrangements similar to local Public Service Agreement targets.

Squatting

This is a term used to describe the action taken when an individual or group occupies empty property belonging to someone else. Squatting as a means of obtaining accommodation is not a new phenomenon, but has grown rapidly since its re-emergence in London and other large conurbations in the late 1960s. Surveys have suggested that in 1990 there were some 30,000 squatters in London and about 50,000 in the UK as a whole. Some local authorities have made agreements with groups squatting in their property and will allow the groups limited tenure in return for payment of maintenance and water rates and an agreement to move to another nominated property when required. This is sometimes known as 'licensed' or 'legalised' squatting. If the local authority does not wish to make such an agreement, they may take proceedings to regain possession of the propery in the civil courts. People attempting to occupy a property also run the risk of prosecution under the laws relating to forcible entry, burglary and criminal damage. The Criminal Law Act 1977 section 7, contains provisions under which it is possible for a person who is squatting to be prosecuted for refusing to leave when requested to do so by a displaced resident or by certain intending occupiers, or for obstructing a bailiff in the execution of duty. Most private owners of property are protected by the 1977 Act, since they fall within the definition of either a displaced resident or an intending occupier.

Sections 72-76 of the Criminal Justice and Public Order 1994 sets out a new procedure which enables property owners to regain possession of their premises more quickly and easily. Under the scheme, a property owner is able to apply to a civil court for an 'interim possession order'. If the judge is satisfied that the owner is entitled to possession, s/he will grant the order, which will then require the squatters to leave the premises within 24 hours of the order being served. Failure to comply with an interim possession order will be a criminal offence. The owner can then approach the police, supplying them with a copy of the order to show that the relevant period has expired. It is a matter for the police to evict the squatters and decide whether or not to bring a criminal prosecution. The squatters are also forbidden to return to the premises, without the permission of the landlord or tenant, for up to 12 months. There are also safeguards against misuse of the procedure by landlords seeking to evict legitimate tenants: any landlord trying to obtain an interim possession order against anyone other than a trespasser will be guilty of an offence. The criminal aspects of the procedure are contained in Part V of the Criminal Justice and Public Order Act 1994.

Information and advice may be obtained from: **Advisory Service for Squatters,** 2 St Paul's Road, Islington, London N1 2QN Tel: 020 7359 8814, who also publish the 'Squatters' Handbook'; **Shelter London**, Kingsbourne House, 229-231 High Holborn, London WC1V 7DA Tel: 020 7404 7447, **ShelterLine** Tel: 020 7404 6929; or from any legal advice or law centre.

Gypsies

Gypsies are defined in law as "persons of nomadic habit of life, whatever their race or origin...". Until 3 November 1994, local authorities in England and Wales had a duty to provide adequate accommodation for gypsies, and were able to apply for Exchequer grant aid to provide and equip Gypsy caravan sites in their areas. As at January 2002, 325 sites had been provided in England, providing 5,005 pitches. The duty to provide sites has now been repealed, but local authorities retain their discretionary powers to provide further caravan sites in their areas if they consider it necessary. The Office of the Deputy Prime Minister publishes an annual list of local authority gypsy sites and this is available free of charge from the website www.housing.odpm.gov.uk.

Local authorities have powers, under section 77 to 79 of the Criminal Justice and Public Order Act 1994, to direct all unauthorised campers (not just Gypsies) to leave land where they are camped without permission. The powers can be used in respect of highway land, unoccupied land, and occupied land where the occupier has not given his consent to the camping. Failure to comply as soon as possible with a direction to leave, or returning to the land with a vehicle within 3 months of the direction, are offences attracting a maximum fine of £1,000.

The police also have powers under Section 61 of the Criminal Justice and Public Order Act 1994 to deal with unauthorised camping. If reasonable efforts have been made to ask Travellers to leave an unauthorised site and they have refused, the senior police officer present may direct them to leave if certain statutory conditions are fulfilled. These conditions are that the Travellers must have been abusive to the landowner or his or her agent, have caused damage or brought six or more vehicles on the land. The powers do not apply to land forming part of a highway.

The Department of the Environment's Circular 18/94, "Gypsy Sites Policy and Unauthorised Camping" gives advice to local authorities on the scope and use of the powers, and makes it clear that they should be used in a humane and compassionate fashion, primarily to reduce nuisance and to protect private landowners from unauthorised camping. The Circular reiterates long-standing government advice that local authorities should consider providing emergency stopping places for Gypsies who visit their area on a regular basis and should make suitable arrangements for the management and maintenance of their existing sites. Such sites with basic facilities such as a skip, water supply and temporary toilets may deter Gypsies from camping on less suitable land.

The Circular goes on to remind local authorities that their Social Service Departments have a duty under Section 17 of the Children's Act 1989, to safeguard and promote the welfare of all children in their area who are 'in need'. The Social Service Departments are expected to work with education, housing and health authorities to provide an appropriate package for Traveller children who have been assessed as being 'in need'.

In October 1998, the Department of the Environment, Transport and the Regions and the Home Office produced joint practice advice to local authorities and the police for managing unauthorised camping. The good practice is based largely on case study research carried for DETR by the School of Public Policy at the University of Birmingham. Copies of the good practice and the asociated research project are available (at £10 and £12 respectively) from ODPM's Publications Sales Centre (address below). Complementary copies of the Social Services in local authoritiesin England and Wales and to other Chief Officers and relevant bodies.

The Office of The Deputy Prime Minister (previously the DETR and DTLR) are in the process of issuing new Good Practice Guidance on Managing Unauthorised Camping jointly with the Home Office later this year.

The Government is keen to encourage more gypsies to provide sites for themselves within the planning system. The Department's Circular 1/94, "Gypsy Sites and Planning", makes it clear that local authorities should include policies in their development plans which meet the accommodation needs of gypsies, and should offer practical advice and help to gypsies with planning procedures. Copies of Circulars 1/94 and 18/94 are available from The Stationery Office Publications Centre, PO Box 276, London SW8 5DT Tel: 020 7873 9090.

The Office of the Deputy Prime Minister's Gypsy Site Refurbishment Programme aims to keep the existing network of 325 local authority authorised sites in good repair and available for use. The programme is making £17 million available over a 3 year period 2001-02 to 2003-04. The grant profile for the 3 years is £3 million/£6 million and £8 million. The Gypsy Site Refurbishment Grant meets 75% of these costs and those local authorities who submit successful bids fund the remaining 25%.

Further information can be obtained from the Office of the Deputy Prime Minister Gypsy Sites Branch, Zone 1/J4, Eland House, Bressenden Place, London SW1E 5DU Tel: 020 7890 3673, including copies of the annual list of local authority gypsy sites and contact list of local authority Gypsy liaison officers (GLOs), and general advice on Circulars 1/94 and 18/94. Copies of the good practice document managing unauthorised camping; and the associated research 'Local Authority Powers for Managing Unauthorised Camping' are available from the ODPM Publication Sales Centre, Unit 21 Goldthorpe Industrial Estate, Rotherham S63 9BL Tel: 01709 891318 Fax: 01709 881673.

FURTHER INFORMATION AND SPECIALIST ADVICE

Advice can be obtained from local authority offices, rent officers, rent tribunals, citizens advice bureaux, housing aid centres, day centres for homeless people and racial equality councils. Many leaflets are published in languages other than English. The ODPM also publishes booklets covering most of the areas mentioned in this chapter. Copies may be obtained free of charge from the DETR Free Literature, PO Box 236, Wetherby, West Yorkshire LS23 7NB Tel: 0870 1236 236 Fax: 0870 1236 237. Bulk orders can be made for many leaflets. A list of current leaflets is available on request.

There are also many voluntary organisations, some of which are listed here.

Centrepoint, Bewlay House, 2 Swallow Place, London W1R 7AA Tel: 020 7629 2229 runs emergency shelters in the West End and five hostels across London.

Children Act Housing Group (The), a co-ordinating body for organisations working with young people, advice projects, homeless and child care organisations, has been set up to monitor the implementation of the Children Act 1989 and make sure that it meets the needs of homeless 16 to 17 year olds. The Group is based at **CHAR,** 5-15 Cromer Street, London WC1H 8LS Tel: 020 7833 2071. CHAR also publishes 'In on the Act', an advisers' guide to homelessness legislation and single people, and a guide to means tested benefits for single people without a permanent home.

Homes for Homeless People, 6 Union Street, Luton, Bedfordshire LU1 3AN Tel: / Fax: 01582 481426.

Irish Women's Housing Action Group, c/o Box 85, London Irish Women's Centre, 59 Stoke Newington Church Street, London N16 0AR Tel: 020 7249 7318, was set up to campaign on all housing issues relevant to Irish women and has produced the booklets 'What to do if you are homeless' and 'Information for the single homeless and private tenants'.

The Resource Information Service, The Basement, 38 Great Pulteney Street, London W1R 3DE, Tel: 020 7494 2408, produces practical information for homeless people and those advising them on the full range of options available to them, including the London Hostels Directory, the London Day Centres Directory, the London Benefit Agency Offices Users' Guide, and the National Telephone Helpline Directory.

Shelter, 88 Old Street, London EC1V 9JU Tel: 020 7253 0202. The Shelterline Tel: 0800 800 446441, a 24-hour free helpline.

HOUSING

AARONSON & CO
308 Earls Court Road, London SW5 9BA
Tel: **020 7373 9516** *Fax:* **020 7835 1014**
Docx: **400750 EARLS COURT 1**

Legal Aid franchise adn block contracts in immigration family law, housing and welfare benefits. Members of Law Society Family Law Panel, Immigration Law Practitioners Association adn Personal Injury Panel.

ANTHONY GOLD
43 Streatham Hill, Streatham, London SW2 4TP
Tel: 020 8678 5500 ***Fax:*** 020 8674 8004
Docx: 58604 STREATHAM
Email: mail@anthonygold.co.uk
Web: www.anthonygold.co.uk

ASTON CLARK
225-227 High Street, Acton, London W3 9BY
Tel: 020 8752 1122 ***Fax:*** 020 8752 1128
Docx: 80267 ACTON
Email: aston@clark1996.fsnet.co.uk

CARVERS (PART OF THE WILKES PARTNERSHIP)
10 Coleshill Road, Hodge Hill, Birmingham, West Midlands B36 8AA
Tel: 0121 784 8484 ***Fax:*** 0121 783 4935
Docx: 27434 HODGE HILL
Email: legal@carverslaw.co.uk
Web: www.carverslaw.co.uk

DREW JONES
17 Queens Road, Coventry, West Midlands CV1 3EG
Tel: 024 7655 5511 ***Fax:*** 024 7655 5577
Docx: 706791 COVENTRY 9
Email: law@drewjones.co.uk

GLAISYERS
628 StockportRoad, Longsight, Manchester• M13 0SH
Tel: 0161 224 3311 ***Fax:*** 0161 257 3239
Email: rnc@glaisyers.com
A specialist franchised firm offering expert advice on community care law, public law, housing law, welfare benefits.

GLAZER DELMAR
223/229 Rye Lane, Peckham, London SE15 4TZ
Tel: **020 7639 8801** *Fax:* **020 7358 0581**
Docx: **34258 PECKHAM**
Web: **www.glazerdelmar.com**

HARRY BOODHOO & CO
21 Copson Street, Withington, Greater Manchester M20 3HE
Tel: 0161 445 0588 ***Fax:*** 0161 445 4949
Docx: 28608 WITHINGTON
Email: harryboodhoo@harryboodhoo.co.uk
Criminal Defence Specialists, Housing Problems, Famliy Law.

HENRY Y SMITH & CO
152-154 Essex Road, London N1 8LY
Tel: 020 7704 2881 ***Fax:*** 020 7704 2436
Docx: 58279 ISLINGTON

HODGE JONES & ALLEN
31-39 Camden Road, London NW1 9LR
Tel: 020 7482 1974 ***Fax:*** 020 7267 3476/02
Docx: 57050 CAMDEN TOWN
Email: hja@hodgejonesallen.co.uk
Web: www.hodgejonesallen.co.uk
We specialise in possession cases, disrepair, homelessness applications, assistance to asylum seekers and community care.

HOPKIN MURRAY BESKINE
Tower House, 149 Fonthill Road, London N4 3HF
Tel: **020 7272 1234** *Fax:* **020 7272 4050**
Docx: **57474 FINSBURY PARK**

HOWARD & OVER
114 & 116 Albert Road, Devonport, Devon PL2 1AF
Tel: 01752 556606 ***Fax:*** 01752 607101
Docx: 120027 PLYMOUTH 12
Email: howard-over.co.uk
Web: www.howard-over.co.uk

KTP SOLICITORS
KTP Chambers, Dinas Isaf Industrial Estate, Williamstown, Pontypridd, Rhondda Cynon Taff CF40 1NY
Tel: 01443 424800 ***Fax:*** 01443 441194
Email: ktpsolicitors@aol.com

OLIVER & CO
Booth Mansion, 30 Watergate Street, Chester, Cheshire CH1 2LA
Tel: 01244 312306 ***Fax:*** 01244 350261
Docx: 19977 CHESTER
Email: oliverlaw@aol.com

SMITH LLEWELYN PARTNERSHIP
18 Princess Way, Swansea SA1 3LW
Tel: 01792 464444 ***Fax:*** 01792 464726
Docx: 92051 SWANSEA 3
Email: mainofficeslp@virgin.net

T V EDWARDS
Park House, 29 Mile End Road, Tower Hamlets, London E1 4TP
Tel: 020 7791 1050 ***Fax:*** 020 7790 5101
Docx: 300700 TOWER HAMLETS
Email: enquiries@tvedwards.com

CHAPTER FIVE

Employment

CHAPTER 5

Employment

INTRODUCTION

Since the last General Election in 2001 the main organisation responsible for employment is the Department for Work and Pensions (DWP). It was created together with the Department for Education and Skills (DfES) in a merger of the former Department of Education and Employment and parts of the former Department of Social Security. The DWP has taken over the running of employment, benefits, pensions and child support, with exception of War pension which have been transferred to the Ministry of Defence, while the DfES handles education training and life long learning.

From the beginning of April 2002, the Benefits Agency and the Employment Service has been replaced by two new businesses-Jobcentre Plus and The Pension Service. The Jobcentre Plus network will take over buildings previously run by both the Employment Service and the Benefits Agency such as Jobcentres and Social Security offices. There are also currently 56 Jobcentre Plus offices that offer a fully integrated work and benefit service with a further 225 due to open between October 2002 and April 2003. It will be several years before the entire office network is successfully combined but local Social Security offices and Jobcentres will continue to operate normally during this period. The Pension Service is now run from regional centres that offer a telephone-based service for enquiries supported by local branches for personal consultation. This organisation will be extended over the next two years until there are 26 centres covering the whole of England, Scotland and Wales.

EMPLOYMENT AND TRAINING SERVICES

Jobcentre Plus - www.jobcentreplus.gov.uk

Jobcentre Plus has now replaced the Employment Service in providing opportunities for people to get jobs and helping employers to fill their vacancies. It also gives advice on training and benefits for those seeking work and arranges the right financial assistance for those who cannot find any. When someone first goes to a Jobcentre Plus office they are given a new claims interview where their details are taken and they are asked whether they are ready to look for work and if they want to claim benefits. The interior of the Jobcentres has been modernised with cards detailing vacancies being replaced by computers (Jobpoints) that can be searched to find the most suitable type of job. A meeting with a client adviser is also arranged and if the person is seeking work they will be given information on any suitable local vacancies. In the meeting a Jobseekers Agreement is drawn up, under the conditions of which Jobseekers Allowance can be claimed. After 13 weeks, if they are still unemployed, then the adviser will review the Agreement with them and see if any assistance can be given such as basic skills training or an ESOL (English for Speakers of Other Languages) course. After six months unemployment, all clients are screened for basic skills needs and may then be referred for an Independent Basic Skills Assessment. The outcome of the Independent Assessment determines the most appropriate provision to meet the basic skills needs. At the six months of unemployment stage, clients aged 25 and over will be eligible for Work Basic Learning for Adults (WBLA). WBLA provision comprises of Short Job-Focused Training, Basic Employability Training, Self Employment Provision and on reaching 12 months unemployment, Longer Occupational Training. Some clients may be allowed early entry if they fall into the early entry groups. WBLA aims to get people, predominantly the long-term unemployed, into jobs, through occupational training, improving employability and/or work experience. If aged 18-24 they will be put on the New Deal 18-24 at this stage. If older than 24 they will not be put on the New Deal until they have been out of work for 18 months. A person must be actively seeking full time work in order to qualify for Jobseekers Allowance and they are not allowed to refuse suitable employment if it is offered to them. If they are suspected of working while claiming benefit their case will be investigated. If found to be working and claiming, their benefits may be stopped and they may also face criminal prosecution.

Jobseeker Direct - 0845 6060 234

This is the new name for Employment Service Direct, a service that keeps people in touch with the latest job vacancies. By phoning this number the jobseeker is given access to thousands of vacancies from which they can find the right one for them. The textphone number for Jobseeker Direct is 0845 6055 255 and there is also a Welsh language service available on 0845 601 4441.

Programme Centres

These are centres that offer training tailored specifically to the needs of individual jobseekers. They are run by external organisations under contract to Jobcentre Plus. Each Programme Centre gives the participants access to useful resources such as telephones, word processors, fax machines, the internet, stamps and stationery that they can use to apply for jobs and other training opportunities. Priority is given to long-term unemployed although referral is possible after just 13 weeks of unemployment.

New Deal - www.newdeal.gov.uk

As part of their welfare to work strategy, the current government has introduced the New Deal to help unemployed people get back to work. They aim to do this by closing the gap between the skills that employers want and the skills that people can offer. This is done by offering new training and opportunities to the people who join the scheme so that employers get new talent for their business.

- **New Deal for Young People:** Unemployed people aged between 18 and 24 who have been claiming Jobseekers Allowance for at least six months will join the New Deal for Young People. Upon joining the scheme the first thing they will do is meet a New Deal Personal Adviser who will work with them to find the best path back into work. Once this is done they enter the "Gateway" where up to four months of intensive, personalised help and support is given in the hopes of finding an unsubsidised job. If this is unsuccessful the Adviser will help them to decide which of the other New Deal options is the best. They can either go into subsidised work that includes training, voluntary sector work, assisting the environmental task force, full-time education or training, or maybe self-employment. During time on the New Deal they may be given access to a mentor who will offer independent opinions on how to make the best of the opportunities the New Deal provides.

- **New Deal 25 plus:** If someone has been claiming Jobseekers Allowance for 18 months out of the last 21 and is aged 25 or over they are eligible to join the New Deal 25 plus. After the initial meeting with a Personal Adviser they have repeated further meetings during the four-month Gateway period in which a plan for getting a job is discussed and agreed before being put into action. In addition the Adviser will help them to address any barriers to work that may exist and identify any additional help that is needed. The Gateway is followed by an Intensive Activity Period (IAP) that normally lasts between 13 and 26 weeks. People aged 25-49 are expected to participate in the IAP and could face benefit sanctions if they fail to do so. People aged 50 and over are free to choose if they want to take part in the IAP or not. During the period jobseekers should gain the skills and experience they need to move into work by putting together a package of help that is uniquely designed for them. Provision available to choose from includes self-employment support (and possibly access to the New Deal for Musicians), Basic Employability Training, Education and Training Opportunities, work experience, work placements, Work Trials and work-focused training. A period of six or more weeks of focussed jobsearching using the skills gained during the IAP normally follows. A Personal Adviser can give assistance throughout this period to ensure that they are better off upon moving into a job by recommending in-work benefits such as jobgrants, help with housing costs or working families' tax credit.

- **New Deal 50 plus:** If a jobseeker is aged 50 or over and has been claiming one of the following benefits; Jobseekers Allowance, Income Support, Incapacity Benefit, Severe Disablement Allowance or National Insurance Credits for at least six months then they are eligible to join the New Deal 50 plus programme. Also, any time spent claiming the following also counts towards eligibility - Invalid Care Allowance, Bereavement Allowance or Widowed Parent Allowance. The New Deal 50 plus programme is entirely voluntary so they will not lose any other benefits by declining to take part. It gives people access to specialised help on finding a job from a Personal Adviser and by joining the scheme they will also be entitled to tax-free financial incentives once they find work. Once in employment or self-employment, there is a tax-free Employment Credit payable for up to 52 weeks for employment which is expected to last for at least five weeks and which complies with employment legislation. There is also an in-work Training Grant available for clients wishing to update their skills and increase their employability.

- **New Deal for Disabled People:** Most people receiving health-related or disability benefits are eligible to join the New Deal for Disabled People. A number of different organisations run this scheme on behalf of the Government by setting up Job Brokers who are tasked with helping the sick and disabled find work if they wish to do so. Job Brokers work with people to help them understand and compete in the labour market and support them in finding and keeping employment. They agree with each person what is the most appropriate route into work for them and work closely with providers of training where this is needed.

- **New Deal for Lone Parents:** This part of the New Deal is voluntary and intended to help single parents who want to work. Getting a job gives lone parents the chance to learn new skills to improve their employability and an opportunity to build confidence, earn money and increase financial security for themselves and their family. As with other sectors of the New Deal they are given their own Personal Adviser who will help them take the necessary steps towards finding a job (for example skills training or finding childcare) and make sure that they are better off in work than on benefits.

- **New Deal for Partners:** A person may be eligible to join the New Deal for Partners if their partner has been claiming benefits for six months. A partner is considered to be someone who is either married to, living with, or being financially supported by someone else. They are given their own personal adviser who will help andencourage them to find work and demonstrate how much better off they and their family could be by working.

- **New Deal for Musicians:** People serious about seeking a career as either an instrumentalist, vocalist, composer, songwriter or performing DJ can join the New Deal for Musicians which helps them progress into careers in all types of music. A Personal Adviser will work with them during the four month Gateway period to identify practical solutions to any problems they are having getting started. The Adviser will not judge their musical ability but will refer them to someone in the music industry that will serve as a consultant. They can also access the services of a music open learning provider on a weekly basis. At the end of the Gateway period they have the same opportunities available to them as you would if they were on the New Deal 18-24 or 25 plus as well as the continued support of a music industry consultant

- **Self Employment Provision (SEP):** SEP provides participants with access to good quality advice and support and also, where appropriate, the opportunity to undertake a period of test trading to help clients move into unsupported self-employment. This allows participants to experience the realities of self-employment while continuing to receive help and support from the provider. SEP also offers support to those participants who decide during their time on provision, that they would rather seek employment with an employer than be self-employed. SEP is available to 18-24 year olds and New Deal 25 plus clients.

Travel to Interview Scheme

The Travel to Interview Scheme (TIS) helps people to get back to work by allowing them to widen their jobsearching area. It provides them with the financial assistance needed to travel further than they could in one day. The TIS is available to anyone claiming benefit (directly or indirectly) or signing for National Insurance credits. Interviews must be for specific jobs that are expected to last at least three months and offer 16 or more hours work per week.

Worktrain - www.worktrain.gov.uk

Worktrain is a national jobs and learning site provided by the DWP that can be used to search for jobs in the UK and abroad, training courses, voluntary work, local childcare provision and careers information.

Learn Direct - www.learndirect.co.uk or 0800 101 901

Offers over 600 online courses that are available to people to use to gain the skills needed to get the job they want. It also gives advice on over 500,000 courses offered by various institutions nationwide as well as help for running small businesses and recommendations for large employers.

Career Development Loan (CDL) - www.lifelonglearning.co.uk/cdl/

A CDL can help pay for up to two years of vocational education or training (or three years including work experience). A CDL is a deferred repayment bank loan for between £300 and £8000 to cover up to 80% of course fees plus the cost of books, materials and other related expenses. Borrowing money to cover living costs may also be possible if other grants or state benefits do not already cover this and the course is considered to be full time. Also, working more than 30 hours a week while studying is not permitted. CDLs are available because of a partnership between the DfES and four major banks, Barclays, Clydesdale Bank, Co-Operative Bank and Royal Bank of Scotland. The DfES pays the interest on the loan during the study/training period until one month after the course is finished (or five months if you are registered unemployed and claiming benefit). The loan must then be repaid within the specified period agreed with the bank concerned.

Career Transition Partnership (CTP) - www.ctp.org.uk

The Career Transition Partnership (CTP) brings together the Ministry of Defence and Coutts Consulting Group, providing resettlement support for individuals leaving the Armed Services. Through ten Regional Resettlement Centres (RRCs) in the UK and Germany, a Resettlement Training Centre (RTC), and the offices of our Employment Consultants in the Officers' Association (OA) and the Regular Forces Employment Association (RFEA), CTP provides an extensive network of resettlement and jobfinding support.

EMPLOYMENT AND TRAINING FOR YOUNG PEOPLE

Arrangements for Further Education (FE)

Further education institutions and sixth form colleges deliver a substantial proportion of Britain's vocational education and training. This arrangement is used to identify priorities for FE and to influence colleges to meet labour market needs. Two funds, the FE Competitiveness and Development Funds are available to support capital purchases and infrastructure improvements related to this. Regional and sub-regional groupings of the Training and Enterprise Council (TEC), Government Office and Further Education Funding Council representatives determine criteria for and consider bids against the Competitiveness Fund. TECs are directly responsible for channeling the Development Fund to colleges in addition to approving colleges' strategic plans.

Connexions - www.connexions.gov.uk

This is a new service for young people aged 13-19 to help them make the transition to adult working life by providing advice, guidance and access to personal development opportunities. Connexions joins up the work of six government Departments and their agencies and organisations on the ground, together with private and voluntary sector groups and youth and careers services. It brings together all the services and support young people need during their teenage years. It offers practical help with choosing the right courses and careers, including access to broader personal development through activities like sport, performing arts and volunteering activities. It will also provide help and advice on issues like drug abuse, sexual health and homelessness.

Connexions is being delivered through local Partnerships working to national planning guidance. The Partnerships will cover the same geographical areas as the Learning and Skills Councils. They will have flexibility to meet local needs using the design that works best. Delivery of the service will be managed and monitored by local management committees, which usually cover the same areas as local authorities.

Connexions offers differentiated and integrated support to young people. All young people will have access to a personal adviser. For some young people this may be just for careers advice, for others it may involve more in-depth support to help identify barriers to learning and find solutions brokering access to more specialist support. The personal advisers will work in a range of settings, schools, colleges, one-stop shops community centres and on an out-reach basis. There are now 28 areas in England that provide the service. All the rest are planning to go live later in 2002/03. Connexions will not be available in Scotland, Wales or Northern Ireland

Compacts

These are arrangements between employers, young people, schools, colleges and training providers in inner city areas that seek to motivate people to achieve more at school and continue into further education and training after they reach the age of 16. They must work towards personally agreed goals in return for employment related incentives such as a job with training or a guaranteed job in the future. There is a network of 62 compacts in inner cities (plus 52 in other areas) covering 10,000 employers, 800 schools and over 180,000 young people.

Education Business Partnerships

By arranging a number of activities aimed at encouraging young people to reach their highest potential Education Business Partnerships help them to be better prepared for the world of work. They seek to do this by co-ordinating education-business collaboration and assisting TECs in delivering their education strategy objectives. There are 120 formal partnerships with at least one in every TEC area.

Modern Apprenticeships

Modern Apprentices learn on the job, building up knowledge and skills, achieving qualifications and earning money at the same time. The competences are linked to the skills identified by employers as necessary for the job.

There are two levels of Modern Apprenticeship: Foundation (FMA) and Advanced (AMA). Both of them include National Vocational Qualifications (NVQs), Key Skills, technical certificates and other qualifications required by the framework.

The FMA leads to an NVQ Level 2 and the AMA leads to an NVQ Level 3. The qualifications gained as a Modern Apprentice can help young people to enter higher education. There are five levels of NVQ:

Level 1 equivalent to 5 GCSEs at grades D-G

Level 2 equivalent to 5 GCSEs at grades A-C

Level 3 equivalent to 2 A levels/1 Vocational A level

Level 4/5 equivalent to HNC, HND and Degree level MAs are completed at the apprentice's own pace, but usually last around 12 months for a FMA and 24 months for an AMA. The actual length of time depends on the MA framework completed.

EMPLOYMENT AND TRAINING FOR PEOPLE WITH A DISABILITY

Remploy - www.remploy.co.uk

This is a company that provides training and employment opportunities for disabled people. Remploy currently employs around 6,000 disabled people in a network of 81 factory sites across England, Scotland and Wales. In addition to internal employment, Remploy's Interwork programme also places around 4,000 disabled people into mainstream employment.

A growing number of sites also have Learning Centres, where employees have access to on site training. Learning Centres offer individuals access to the Internet, Open Learning packages and interactive CD-ROMs. In addition, many sites operate Jobclubs to help participants with job searching and the application process: for example, completion of CVs, interview techniques and general confidence building.

Remploy is the largest single provider of WORKSTEP (formally supported employment programme) and is also a provider of New Deal for disabled people.

Disability Employment Advisers

Disability Employment Advisers (DEA's) are located at Jobcentres and Jobcentre Plus offices and provide specialist support to disabled jobseekers, or disabled people already in work. This might take the form of recommending what type of jobs to look for or assessing their skills and abilities and directing to the best sources of employment and training.

New Deal for Disabled People

Most people receiving health-related or disability benefits are eligible to join the New Deal for Disabled People. A number of different organisations run this scheme on behalf of the Government by setting up Job Brokers who are tasked with helping the sick and disabled find work if they wish to do so. Job Brokers work with people to help them understand and compete in the labour market and support them in finding and keeping employment. They agree with each person what is the most appropriate route into work for them and work closely with providers of training and other provision where this is needed.

PENSIONS

The Pension Service - www.thepensionservice.gov.uk

The government has created a new organisation (the Pension Service-part of the DWP) to improve the way it handles pensions. The Pension Service will:

- Work out the amount of State Retirement Pension and Minimum Income Guarantee people are entitled to.
- Pay entitlements and answer questions over the phone, by post or email.
- Tell people how they can access other pension-related entitlements and services.

- Work in partnership with other local organisations to deliver pension related services. Anyone who is already a pensioner does not need to do anything as the payments you receive and the way they are collected will not change. There is no need to apply for your payments again and you should get a letter informing you of these changes.

Stakeholder Pensions

The Government estimates that by 2040 there will only be two working people supporting each pensioner compared to four as there is now. They therefore believe that everyone who can save for their retirement has a responsibility to do so. They have introduced stakeholder pensions to give those people who did not previously have access to an occupational pension scheme or a good value personal pension the opportunity to save for their retirement. People can have a Stakeholder Pension in addition to the Basic State Retirement Pension. The provision of access to a Stakeholder Pension scheme for their workforce is now a legal obligation for all employers who employ five or more staff and do not provide a satisfactory alternative scheme. If a company does not designate a stakeholder pension scheme for employees when required to do so, this may result in them being fined £50,000. Stakeholder Pensions are a new type of pension launched in April 2001 by the Government to target people on moderate to higher incomes who do not have any private pension provision. The Government has set certain minimum standards that the pension must meet with regards to payment levels, costs and conditions. Holders of stakeholder pensions pay yearly management charges of no more than 1% of the total fund and are free to stop, start or vary their pensions, or transfer them from one provider to another at any time without penalty. Employers are not required to provide access to a stakeholder pension scheme for certain employees; for example those who have been employed for less than three months or whose earnings do not equal or exceed the National Insurance Lower Earnings Limit for at least three consecutive months. Payments made to stakeholder pensions attract tax relief, so the Government is, in effect, paying money in to your pension scheme. Often the pension money will be invested in a variety of stocks and shares managed by stakeholder mangers from banks or insurance companies.

Service Pensions

These are administered by the Armed Forces Personnel Administration Agency (AFPAA). In all three branches of the armed forces 22 years service from the age of 18 (or 16 years service from the age of 21 for officers) is required to qualify for a service pension. Years served in addition to this and any promotions gained increase the rate of the pension.

War Pensions

A person who has been injured or disabled serving in the armed forces during time of war may be entitled to a War Disablement Pension. The amount received depends on how disabled the person is and the pension cannot be claimed while still serving in HM Armed Forces. Also, the widow/widower or dependent of someone who died during their time in the service may be eligible for a War Widow's/Widower's Pension. This may affect entitlement to Social Security Bereavement Benefit although the War Widow/Widowers Pension is normally paid at a higher rate. If a person claiming this remarried, they may be unable to claim the pension although any children they had should still be able to do so.

EMPLOYER SCHEMES

The Single Regeneration Budget (SRB)

This provides the necessary resources to assist regeneration initiative in England being undertaken by local regeneration partnerships. Its main aims are to improve employment prospects, address social exclusion, create more opportunities, promote sustainable regeneration, protect the environment and infrastructure, support growth in local business and reduce crime. SRB partnerships involve a diverse range of organisations in the management of their scheme. Since the scheme began in December 1994 over 900 projects have been approved, worth over £5.5 billion in SRB support over their lifetime of up to seven years. It is estimated that these will attract around £10 billion of private sector investment and attract European funding as well.

Small Firms Training Loans (SFTL)

Businesses employing less than 50 people can borrow between £500 and £125,000 to fund training and up to £5,000 for consultancy needs. The bigger the loan the business takes out, the longer it is permitted to defer repayment. The loan can cover up to 90% of the firms' training and consultancy costs and the Training and Enterprise Council (TEC) or Chamber of Commerce Training and Enterprise (CCTE) may be able to provide grants to cover the remaining 10%. The training covered by the loan does not have to lead to a formal qualification although the TEC or CCTE will provide assistance if one is used as a framework.

The Loan Guarantee Scheme

Some small firms are unable to get a conventional loan due to lack of security even if they have perfectly viable business proposals. The small firm's loans guarantee scheme run by the Small Business Service (SBS) guarantees loans to these businesses. Any company with a turnover of less than £1.5 million (or £5 million if they are a manufacturer) can borrow between £5000 and £100,000 (or up to £250,000 if the business has already been trading for more than two years) for periods of two to ten years. The SBS guarantees 70% of the loan (85% if they have been trading for more than two years) and in return the firm pays the SBS a premium of 1.5% per year on the outstanding loan amount.

New Deal for Employers

Employers can benefit financially by getting involved in the Government's New Deal scheme. Taking on a jobseeker aged between 18 and 24 may gain a business a subsidy of £60 a week (full time) or £40 a week (part time) towards wages plus £750 towards training for the first six months of the employment. If the New Deal jobseeker is 25 or over the subsidies rise to £75 and £50 respectively. This subsidy scheme does not apply to potential employees who are already on the New Deal for Disabled People. All potential recruits are pre-screened in the "Gateway" process to ensure that they are employable, motivated and committed and right for the job. The New Deal scheme gives employers the opportunity to recruit employees that have a wealth of experience and interpersonal skills to offer. If a significant amount of training (15 or more days within the first eight weeks) needs to be carried out the Upfront Skills Shortage Subsidy provides financial assistance so long as the training is towards a recognised qualification. Employers can be paid 75% of the funding straight away with the remaining 25% to follow after 26 weeks. For example, a person aged 18-24 is employed and trained full time under the New Deal's subsidised employment option, the employer will receive £1,730 at the start of the job to cover up front training costs. The remaining £580 will be paid upon achievement of the objectives in the employees' Individual Training Plan. When employing someone where the number of hours worked are reduced by disability, the full time rate of subsidy will apply.

Jobcentre Plus for Employers - 0845 601 2001

Jobcentre Plus is committed to helping fill employer vacancies quickly with the best personnel available. Vacancies are immediately accessible via around 9,000 touch screen Jobpoints located in over 1,000 Jocentre Plus offices and Jobcentres across Great Britain as well as being advertised on the Job Bank, the largest online vacancy database in the world. A Vacancy Service Manager will manage the recruitment process until the vacancy is filled and offer a range of additional services and help where appropriate.

CONDITIONS OF EMPLOYMENT

The Advisory, Conciliation and Arbitration Service (ACAS) - www.acas.org.uk

ACAS is an independent statutory body, established in 1975. It is directed by a Council consisting of the ACAS Chairman and employer, trade union and independent members. ACAS has a general duty to promote the improvement of industrial relations. Its services are impartial and confidential. ACAS provides conciliation and mediation as a means of avoiding and resolving disputes and makes facilities available for arbitration. It provides advisory and information services on industrial relations and related matters to employers, employees and their representatives in every sector of industry and commerce. It provides conciliation in disputes between individual employees and their employers on issues such as unfair dismissal equal pay and sec, disability and race discrimination. ACAS publishes a number of advisory publications and issues codes of practice on various aspects of employment relations. It has five regional offices in England and offices in Scotland and Wales. The Head Office is at:

Brandon House
180 Borough High Street
London SE1 1LW
Tel: 020 7210 3613
www.acas.org.uk

Employment Tribunals - www.employment-tribunal.org.uk

Created as part of the Industrial Training Act 1964 these hear complaints and appeals concerning matters to do with employment such as unfair dismissal, redundancy payments, sex, race and disability discrimination together with certain issues relating to wages, terms and conditions of employment. Claims normally need to be brought within three months of the event. Employment Tribunals are less formal than courts but are run in a similar independent manner and cannot give legal advice. Cases are usually held in permanent tribunal offices that are open to the public and press except for when the case involves allegations of sexual misconduct. The tribunal is obliged to deal with each case as quickly and fairly as possible but if the result is felt to be unjust by either of the parties involved, they may be able to appeal against the final decision.

The Sex Discrimination Act 1975

Makes it generally unlawful to discriminate on the grounds of sex in employment and in the provision of goods, facilities, services, premises and education. The employment provisions of the Act, as amended by the Sex Discrimination Act 1986 and 1989 make it illegal in Great Britain to treat a woman less favourably than a man, and vice versa. Discriminating against married in favour of single people when recruiting, training, promoting, dismissing or retiring staff is outlawed as well. Indirect sex discrimination, when an unjustifiable requirement or condition is applied equally to both sexes but has a disproportionately adverse affect on one, is dealt with by the Act. Discrimination in recruitment, with very few exceptions, is always unlawful. The Sex Discrimination Act 1975 protects against victimisation and sexual harassment and permits training organisations and employers to provide single sex training courses to help people enter jobs in which their sex is disproportionately represented. Anyone who feels they are being discriminated against in employment because of their sex and marital status can complain to an Employment Tribunal within three months of the action complained about. There is no qualifying period of employment before complaints can be made against an employer and since November 1994, the Employment Tribunal now has the power to award unlimited compensation in sex discrimination cases.

The Equal Pay Act 1970

The Equal Pay Act 1970 with extensions in 1984 was implemented to prevent discrimination and encourage equality between men and women in the same employment with regards to their pay and other contractual benefits such as holiday entitlement, childcare or sickness benefits, and car allowances. If a man or woman is involved in work they believes is like, equivalent to, or of equal value to someone of the opposite sex they can claim they are deserving of equal pay. However, they may not be entitled to it if the employer can prove that the difference in treatment is due to another material factor other than gender. It is the responsibility of the employer to justify the reasons for their discrimination. The Act provides for application to an Employment Tribunal to settle any dispute if necessary. Claims can be made at any time up to six months after leaving the job to which it relates. The legal advice and assistance scheme is available to assist people who consider that they have a claim for equal treatment under the Equal Pay Act, but not for tribunal proceedings.

Welfare and Pensions Act 1999

Supplements the Pensions Act 1995 with sections dealing with the provision of Stakeholder Pensions as well as changes to the framework of existing pension schemes. It also covers changes to maternity allowance, bereavement benefit, incapacity benefit, attendance allowance, sever disablement allowance, disability living allowance and changes to National Insurance contributions.

The Race Relations Act (Amendment) 2000

This Act is an amendment to the Race Relations Act 1976 that made it unlawful to discriminate on racial grounds in relation to employment, training and education, the provision of goods, facilities and services, and certain other specified activities only. The Commission for Racial Equality (CRE) was established at this time as well. It also allowed any person or local authority to train members of a particular racial group if it is felt they are under-represented in any area of work so long a selection is still carried out on merit. In addition to this the 1976 Act made employers liable for acts of race discrimination committed by their employees whilst they were working for them, subject to a defence that the employer took reasonable steps to prevent it. Complaints under the Race Relations Act may be taken to an Employment Tribunal so long as this happens within three months of the date of the act complained of. The Race Relations (Remedies) Act 1994 removed the limit on compensation that could be awarded by these Tribunals in cases of racial discrimination. The 2000 Act's main purposes were to extend further the 1976 Act in relation to public authorities, outlawing race discrimination in functions not previously covered and to make it their duty to work towards the elimination of unlawful discrimination and promote equal opportunities and better race relations. It also made chief officers of the Police liable for acts of discrimination by their officers and amended the exemption in the 1976 Act for actions in the interests of safeguarding national security.

The Disability Discrimination Act 1995

This includes a new right of non-discrimination in employment that replaced the outdated quota provisions of the Disabled Persons (Employment) Act 1944. Under the legislation, it is unlawful for an employer to treat a person with a disability less favourably than anyone else because of their disability without justifiable reason. Employers are also required to make reasonable adjustments to working conditions or the workplace where this would overcome the practical effect of an individual's disability. People with a disability who feel they have been discriminated against can take their case to an Employment Tribunal.

Trade Union Reform and Employment Rights Act 1993

Established a more balanced legal framework for industrial relations and restrict employment practices such as union labour only agreements ("closed shops").

Employment Protection Act 1975

Put in place machinery for promoting the improvement of industrial relations and amended the law relating to workers, employers, trades unions and employers' associations.

Employment Relations Act 1999

Extended the "ordinary maternity leave" period form 14 to 18 weeks, brining maternity leave into line with the statutory maternity pay leave period. "Maternity absence" is now known as "additional maternity leave" and the employment qualification for this has been reduced form two years to one year. The Employment Relations Act 1999 implements the EU Parental Leave Directive (EOR 66) providing for regulations entitling a parent to a minimum of three months leave to care for a child under eight years old (including adoptive parents). Employers are not expected to accommodate this as paid leave although an employee can bring a complaint to an employment tribunal if they feel they have been unreasonably delayed or denied parental leave. The Act also covers unpaid leave to cover domestic incidents such as fire, flood, burglary and emergency childcare arrangements due to incapacity or death of a family member. Part time workers now have the same rights to annual leave and maternity/parental leave as full time colleagues on a pro-rata basis. The Employment Relations Act also sets out new statutory procedures for the recognition and derecognition of trade unions for collective bargaining when unions and employers are unable to reach an agreement voluntarily. Changes were made to the law on trade union membership to prevent discrimination by omission and blacklisting of people. Another provision of the Act was to change the law on industrial action to enable dismissed strikers to complain of unfair dismissal in certain circumstances. Making it easier for workers to balance demands of work and their family was another provision made by the Act.

Redundancy

The Employment Protection Act 1975 (Part IV) gives many employees additional warning of possible redundancy by requiring employers to consult appropriate recognised trade unions and, under another EC directive, other workers' representatives so that workers not in unions or in unions not recognised by employers are also involved whenever employers propose to make even a single employee redundant. The Act also requires employers to notify the Secretary of State if they plan to make ten or more employees redundant at one establishment within a specified period. If the employer and trade union fail to reach agreement, then a conciliation officer from the Advisory Conciliation and Arbitration Service (ACAS) may be asked to help the parties reach agreement without recourse to an Employment Tribunal. Where conciliation is not possible or fails, then the tribunal will hear the complaint. If an employer does not consult the unions concerned, they can apply to an Employment Tribunal for a protective award. This requires the employer to continue to pay the employees affected by the redundancies for a specified period.

In very general terms, the redundancy payments provisions contained in the Employment Protection (Consolidation) Act 1978 (Section VI) require an employer to make a lump-sum compensation payment, called a 'redundancy payment', to an employee under the age of 65 who is dismissed because of redundancy after at least two years continuous reckonable service since the age of 18. If there is an earlier, non-discriminatory retiring age for the job, this earlier limit will apply. The amount of payment depends on age, years of service and weekly benefits. A redundancy payment may also be claimed in certain circumstances by an employee who has been laid off or kept on short time for a specified period. Any entitled employee who is unable to secure the due redundancy payment from the employer may apply for payment from the Redundancy Fund, which is financed by an allocation from employers' and employees' National Insurance contributions. Disputes about entitlement to a redundancy payment may be referred to an Employment Tribunal. Under the Employment Protection (Consolidation) Act 1978, an employee who is given notice of dismissal because of redundancy is entitled to reasonable time off with pay during working hours to look for another job or make arrangements for training for future employment.

Selection for redundancy on certain grounds, for example because the individual was a trade union member or because she/he raised a health and safety concern in certain circumstances will be deemed automatically unfair by an Employment Tribunal to which a complaint is made.

Dismissal

Under the Employment Protection (Consolidation) Act 1978, as amended by the Employment Act 1980 and the Employment Act 1982, most employees are entitled to a minimum period of notice of dismissal, which is one week after one month's service and two weeks are two years' service. An employee is entitled to an additional week's notice for each year of service, up to a maximum of 12 weeks after 12 years. Provided they ask their employer for one, employees who have been continuously employed for two continuous years are entitled to a written statement of the reasons for dismissal, which must be provided within 14 days of the request. An employee dismissed during pregnancy or the statutory maternity leave period, however, is entitled to a written statement of the reasons without having to request it. If an employee believes he or she has been unfairly dismissed, then he or she may complain to an Employment Tribunal. No claim for unfair dismissal can be made if the period of employment was less than two years, except in certain circumstances, e.g., where the reason for dismissal was membership or non-membership of a trade union where there is no qualifying period of service, for taking specified types of action on health and safety ground, for seeking to enforce statutory employment rights and for maternity related reasons. Where a complaint is upheld by an Employment Tribunal, it will either make an order for reinstatement or re-engagement, or, if this is not practicable or is refused, it will make a monetary award. Dismissed employees, regardless of length or service who believe their dismissal was wrongful – for example, if any contractual company disciplinary or grievance procedure was not followed, or if they did not receive the notice to which they were entitled – can also seek a remedy for breach of contract through the Employment Tribunals or civil courts.

Action short of dismissal

It is unlawful for an employer to take 'action short of dismissal' against employees i.e., penalise them at work for being, or not being, trade union members, or for taking certain types of action on health and safety grounds. No qualifying periods of service apply to these rights. If an employee believes they have been penalised on these grounds, they may complain to an Employment Tribunal.

Part-time Workers Regulations 2000 and the EC Part-time Work Directive 2000

All workers, no matter how many hours they work are entitled to protection after two years. This includes the right to redundancy pay, the right to claim unfair dismissal, the right to itemised pay statements, the right to time off for public and trade union duties, the right to extended maternity leave and the right to a written statement of terms and conditions of their employment. The rights to part time employees concerning pay, pensions, training and holidays were extended in May 2000 to include those working at home or through an agency. Regulations introduced in July 2000 mean that part time workers should now receive the same levels of pay as comparable full time workers, the same overtime rates, the same access to training opportunities and the same quantity of annual and maternity or parental leave.

Health and Safety at Work

The Health and Safety at Work Act 1974 makes provision for the protection of people at work and the public from risks to their health and safety arising from work activity, including major industrial accidents. Duties are placed on all persons connected with health and safety at work, whether as employers, employees, the self-employed, or as manufacturers and suppliers of articles or substances. The Act set up the Health and Safety Commission and the Health and Safety Executive (HSE).

The Commission is appointed by the Secretary of State for the Environment, who can give statutory directions to it, and it includes representatives of employers, trade unions, local authorities and the public interest. It is required to consult widely in the exercise of its functions. It can appoint agents and it works in conjunction with local authorities, who enforce the Act in such premises as offices and warehouses. It is independent from government, which is seen as necessary to enable it to fulfil its functions and command public confidence. The Commission's basic aims are to stimulate and guide the efforts of employers to achieve higher standards of health and safety at a cost that is realistic; and, in doing so, to protect both people at work and the public, who may be affected by risks arising from the way any undertaking is conducted, and keep them properly informed about the dangers and the protective measures adopted. One of its major functions is the preparation of health and safety legislation, resulting either from its own remit under the Health and Safety at Work Act to reform and update safety law or from European directives. In this and in other matters, the Commission or Executive may act with or on behalf of any of a number of Secretaries of State or their Departments.

The Commission's major instrument is the Health and Safety Executive, which, through its inspectorate, enforces health and safety law in the majority of industrial premises to protect both workers and the public. The Executive advises the Commission in its major task of laying down safety standards through regulations and practical guidance for very large numbers of industrial processes, liaising as necessary with government departments and other institutions. The Executive is also the licensing authority for nuclear installations and the body designated to administer with the UK the European Community's notification scheme for new chemical substances. This latter function entails receiving data on the properties of new chemicals and the environment. The HSE also issues guidelines on how to assess and avoid risks to pregnant workers under the EC's Pregnant Workers directive. In carrying out its statutory functions, the Executive acts independently of government, guided by the Commission as to general health and safety policy. The Commission is also assisted by a number of expert advisory bodies concerned with different industries and different hazards, as, for example, toxic substances, genetic manipulation, nuclear installations, etc. These bodies are serviced by the Executive.

A list of publications and leaflets are available from the HSE website www.hse.gov.uk.

Reinstatement in Civil Employment

Members of the services who are called out for a period of full time service in the armed forces may have a legal right for reinstatement in their civil employment on completion of that service. The relevant legislation is contained in the Reserve Forces Act 1980 and the Reserve Forces (Safeguard of Employment) Act 1985. A person covered by this legislation has a right to reinstatement, subject to certain conditions, on application to the former employer within a specified time. Any disputes between the employers and those seeking reinstatement are determined by Reinstatement Committees composed of employers' and workers' representatives and an independent chair. If any ex-serviceman or woman has doubts about their entitlement to reinstatement they can inquire at their local Jobcentre or Jobcentre Plus office.

EMPLOYMENT

CARVERS (PART OF THE WILKES PARTNERSHIP)
10 Coleshill Road, Hodge Hill, Birmingham, West Midlands B36 8AA
Tel: 0121 784 8484 ***Fax:*** 0121 783 4935
Docx: 27434 HODGE HILL
Email: legal@carverslaw.co.uk
Web: www.carverslaw.co.uk

CHANCELLORS LEA BREWER
246 Broadway, Bexleyheath, Kent DA6 8BB
Tel: 020 8303 0077 ***Fax:*** 020 8304 4023
Docx: 31800 BEXLEYHEATH
Email: athomas@chancellors.com

DREW JONES
17 Queens Road, Coventry, West Midlands CV1 3EG
Tel: 024 7655 5511 ***Fax:*** 024 7655 5577
Docx: 706791 COVENTRY 9
Email: law@drewjones.co.uk

HENRY Y SMITH & CO
152-154 Essex Road, London N1 8LY
Tel: 020 7704 2881 ***Fax:*** 020 7704 2436
Docx: 58279 ISLINGTON

MAIDMENTS
St Johns Court, 74 Gartside Street, Manchester, Greater Manchester M3 3EL
Tel: 0161 834 0008 ***Fax:*** 0161 832 4140/01
Docx: 14307 MANCHESTER 1
Email: info@maidments.co.uk
Web: www.maidments.com

MASON & MOORE DUTTON
Kirkton Hse, Hunter Street, Chester, Cheshire CH1 2AS
Tel: 01244 348881 ***Fax:*** 01244 351513
Docx: 22151 CHESTER NORTHGATE
Email: law@masonmooredutton.co.uk

NAUNTON LYNCH HALL
Oakley Lodge, 20 Liverpool Gardens, Worthing, West Sussex BN11 1RY
Tel: 01903 234556 ***Fax:*** 01903 212162
Docx: 3746 WORTHING 1
Email: nlh@dial.pipex.com

T V EDWARDS
Park House, 29 Mile End Road, Tower Hamlets, London E1 4TP
Tel: 020 7791 1050 ***Fax:*** 020 7790 5101
Docx: 300700 TOWER HAMLETS

Community
Legal Service

THOMPSON SMITH & PUXON
4-5 North Hill, Colchester, Essex CO1 1EB
Tel: **01206 574431** *Fax:* **01206 563174**
Docx: **3617 COLCHESTER**
Email: **info@tsplegal.com**
Web: **www.tsplegal.com**

CHAPTER SIX

Equality and Citizenship

Equality and Citizenship

CHAPTER SIX

Equality and Citizenship

INTRODUCTION

This chapter gives a brief outline of the law relating to nationality, citizenship, immigration and race relations. It is not intended to be definitive or authoritative and, as these are complex subjects, it is advisable to seek advice on any problems from the statutory and voluntary agencies mentioned in the text. At the time of writing (June 2002), the Government's latest proposals regarding citizenship and immigration were still being discussed in Parliament. The Nationality, Immmigration and Asylum Bill is a radical overhaul of legislation in this area. A summary of the main points of the Bill is presented below, though this of may be subject to change before the Act is passed. The rest of this chapter detailed the legislation that is in place but it will undoubtedly be superseded by the new Act at some point in late 2002 / early 2003.

THE NATIONALITY, IMMIGRATION AND ASYLUM BILL

The Nationality, Immigration and Asylum Bill was introduced in the House of Commons on the 12th April 2002. It is a package of measures to reform nationality, immigration and asylum law that were detailed in the Government's White Paper, *Secure Borders Safe Haven: Integration with Diversity in Modern Britain*, published in February 2002. The Bill is in eight parts:

Part 1 - This section of the Bill will amend current legislation on nationality and includes changes to the requirements for naturalisation.

Part 2

This section details the Government's plans to house and asylum seekers in purpose built accommodation centres. The idea is that these self-contained centres will meet asylum seekers needs for financial support and will also provide educational and other facilites. The Bill propses that there be a number of different types of centre - induction, reception, accommodation, reporting and removal. Accommodation centres are to house 3,000 people.

Part 3

This section aims to make further changes to the system of support for asylum seekers. These changes are outside of the accommodation centre system, they are more concerned with regulating the provision of financial support. It will enable reporting and residence requirements to be imposed on all asylum seekers. It redefines "destitution" as a criterion for the provision of cash support for people not in the accommodation centres, and also details a voluntary assisted return scheme.

Part 4

This section contains provisions for the detention, temporary release and removal of asylum seekers. It proposes an extension of the Secretary of State's powers to detain as well as an extension of the powers of detainee custody officers. The Bill also proposes to rename detention centres as "removal centres".

Part 5

This section details proposed reforms to the current system for immigration and asylum appeals. The aim is to speed up and simplify the process by reforming the "one stop procedure" in which any grounds of appeal available to an appellant must all be raised at a single appeal. It also defines the grounds of appeal in relation to the Human Rights Act 1988, the Race Relations Act 1976, EU law and the Refugee Convention.

Part 6

This section is concerned with immigration procedure, in particular border control. The Bill will introduce various schemes for the provision of data for the purposes of effective border control, including a voluntary scheme for the collection of physical data. It provides for the introduction of an authority to carry schemes where by carriers will be required to check the details of passengers against a Home Office database to ensure they do not pose an 'immigration risk'. Finally the Bill allows for a fee to be charged for work permit applications.

Part 7

This section introduces new immigration offences in the following areas: Assisting unlawful immigration, traffic in prostitution, illegal working, offences relating to registration cards and immigration stamp offences.

Part 8 - This section contains general provisions that deal with the commencement, extent and interpretation of the Bill.

The passage of the Nationality, Immigation and Asylum Bill through Parliament has come up against some controversy. Whilst welcoming the Government's committment to dealing with the issue of asylum and immigration, some organisations as well as a number of the Government's bankbenchers have voiced concerns over a number of aspects of the proposed legislation. These organisations include Oxfam, the Refugee Council, the Immigration Law Practitioner's Association, the Local Government Association, the Immigration Advisory Service and the Scottish Asylum Seekers Consortium. The criticism has focused on the size of the proposed centres and the plan to keep them housed entirely separately from the community. At the time of writing the Home Secretary, David Blunkett, had just committed to more flexibility in the size of accommodation centres, to capping the length of stay at centres to nine months and for education officials to review the provision of education, ensuring that mainstream education is available if deemed to be more suitable.

BRITISH NATIONALITY

The law on nationality was altered by the British Nationality Act 1981, which came into force in 1983. The Act replaced citizenship of the United Kingdom and Colonies with three separate citizenships:

- British citizenship, for people closely connected with the UK, the Channel Islands and the Isle of Man;
- British Dependent Territories citizenship, for people connected with the dependencies;
- British Overseas citizenship, for those citizens of the UK and Colonies who did not acquire either of the other citizenships at commencement.

The Act provides for the acquisition and renunciation of these citizenships and makes amendments to the Immigration Act 1971 so as to express the right of abode in terms of the new British citizenship.

General points

No one who was a citizen of the UK and Colonies on 31 December 1982 was left without citizenship and the Act contains provisions which more than comply with the UK's obligations under the United Nations Convention on the Reduction of Statelessness. The Act does not adversely affect the position under immigration law of anyone who was lawfully settled in the UK before 1 January 1983. The special voucher scheme, under which certain UK passport holders, originally from East Africa, may be admitted to the UK for settlement, continues. The Act provides that, where the Home Secretary is required to exercise discretion, this shall be done without regard to the race, colour or religion of the person concerned. Women transmit citizenship to their children born abroad after 1 January 1983 on equal terms with men. Children who are still minors, born abroad before 1983 to women born in the UK, continue to be able to be registered as British citizens under the Home Secretary's general discretion to register minor children. There is no general restriction on dual nationality in the Act.

British citizenship

All citizens of the UK and Colonies who had the right of abode in the UK immediately before 1 January 1983 acquired British citizenship automatically on that date. The exception to this was the case of stateless persons who had been registered as citizens of the UK and Colonies by virtue of their mother's citizenship of the UK and Colonies; they acquired whichever of the three new citizenships their mother acquired. So those people who had the right of abode only through their registration, but whose mothers became British Dependent Territories citizens or British Overseas citizens, did not become British citizens.

Acquisition of citizenship by birth

A child born in the UK after 1 January 1983 is a British citizen automatically at birth if either the father or mother is a British citizen or is settled in the UK. A child adopted by a British citizen by court order made in the UK is a British citizen, as is a foundling. A child born in the UK who does not acquire British citizenship at birth has an entitlement to be registered as a British citizen if either parent later becomes a British citizen or becomes settled. The child will also have an entitlement to registration if s/he spends the first ten years of life in the UK.

Acquisition of citizenship by descent

A child born abroad after 1 January 1983 is a British citizen by descent if either the father or mother is a British citizen otherwise than by descent, eg, if s/he was born, adopted, or naturalised in the UK or was registered on the basis of previous residence in the UK. A child born abroad to a British citizen by descent is entitled to be registered as a British citizen by descent if application is made within 12 months of the birth and the parent is:

- born to a British citizen who was born, adopted, naturalised or generally speaking registered in the UK; and
- has spent three years in the UK at any time prior to the birth, this requirement does not apply if the child is stateless.

In addition, male British citizens by descent who were married and resident in foreign countries on 1 January 1983 could have any of their children who were born in a foreign country between 1 January 1983 and 31 December 1987 registered as British citizens by descent, provided there was a specified parental or grandparental link with the UK. Application had to be made within 12 months of the birth. A child born overseas to a British citizen by descent who is not registered as such a citizen within 12 months of birth will have an entitlement to registration if s/he subsequently comes to the UK to live with both parents for three years. If registered, the child would be a British citizen otherwise than by descent. A child born abroad to a British citizen who is in Crown service, the service of a European Community institution, or other service designated as closely associated with the activities abroad of the UK government, is a British citizen whether or not the parent was born in the UK and the child will be able to transmit citizenship to his or her own children on the same terms as a British citizen born in the UK.

Acquisition of citizenship by naturalisation or registration

British Dependent Territories citizens, British Overseas citizens, British subjects under the Act, British protected persons and British Nationals *Overseas* are normally entitled to be registered as British citizens after spending five years in the UK. British Dependent Territories citizens connected with Gibraltar have an absolute right to be registered as British citizens without the need to be resident in the UK. Certificates of naturalisation may be granted, at the Home Secretary's discretion, to other Commonwealth citizens and foreign nationals. The qualifications for naturalisation are related to good character, time spent in the UK or Crown service, knowledge of English, Welsh or Scottish Gaelic and future intentions. The husband or wife of a British citizen can apply after spending three years in the UK instead of the normal five. S/he must meet the requirement to be of good character, but not the requirement to have a sufficient knowledge of English or Welsh or Scottish Gaelic. The Home Secretary also has discretion to register any minor as a British citizen.

Preserved entitlements to registration

Certain rights to register as a British citizen came to an end on 31 December 1987. Among others, the rights applied to Commonwealth or Irish citizens who had lived in the UK, without immigration restrictions on their stay, since before 1 January 1973 and to the wives of men who were citizens of the UK and Colonies on 31 December 1982 and who became British citizens on 1 January 1983. For those who were minors on 1 January 1983, the right to registration continues for five years after reaching the age of 18.

Renunciation and resumption

Provision is made for British citizens to renounce their British citizenship and to resume it subsequently; and for certain people who have renounced citizenship of the UK and Colonies to be registered as British citizens.

British Dependent Territories citizenship

The provisions of the Act dealing with the acquisition and renunciation of British Dependent Territories citizenship follow a similar pattern to those for the acquisition and renunciation of British citizenship. British Dependent Territories citizens are normally entitled to registration as British citizens after they have spent five years in the UK.

British Overseas citizenship

This citizenship is essentially transitional in its nature. It was acquired on 1 January 1983 by any citizen of the UK and Colonies who did not become either a British citizen or a British Dependent Territories citizen. British Overseas citizenship cannot normally be transmitted automatically to children born after the commencement date. There are provisions for a minor to be registered at discretion as a British Overseas citizen, but this is rarely done. There is also provision for British Overseas citizens to renounce this status.

British subjects and British protected persons

The use of the term 'British subject' as a common description for all Commonwealth citizens ceased under the Act and the term 'Commonwealth citizen' is now used. The scope of the meaning of the term 'British subject', as used in legislation passed before 1 January 1983 for example, that dealing with the right to vote, is, however, preserved. British subjects without citizenship, and British subjects who had that status by reason of a connection with the Republic of Ireland before 1949 and who claimed their right to remain British subjects under the British Nationality Act 1948 (Section 2), continue to be known as British subjects. Those citizens of the Irish Republic who were British subjects before 1949 are still able to make a claim that they have remained British subjects. The Home Secretary has discretion to register any minor as a British subject. There is provision for renunciation of British subject status and a former British subject without citizenship automatically loses that status on acquiring any other citizenship or nationality. The status of British protected person is continued by the Act. British protected persons and British subjects are normally entitled to registration as British citizens after they have spent five years in the UK.

British Nationals (Overseas)

This status was created on 1 July 1987 by the Hong Kong (British Nationality) Order 1986 made under the Hong Kong Act 1985. The status is applicable only to British Dependent Territories citizens by connection with Hong Kong. It can be acquired by registration at any time before 1 July 1997. The status is not transmissible.

In addition to the 1986 legislation, the British Nationality (Hong Kong) Act 1990 makes provision for the registration as British citizens of up to 50,000 heads of households, together with their dependants, on the recommendation of the Governor of Hong Kong. The purpose of the 1990 Act was to discourage the emigration of Hong Kong's most talented residents in the run-up to the transfer of sovereignty over the territory to China in 1997.

The Falkland Islands. The British Nationality (Falkland Islands) Act 1983 provided for the acquisition of British citizenship by people connected with the Falkland Islands. The Act was passed on 28 March 1983 and deemed to have come into force on 1 January 1983.

Enquiries

The section above gives only an outline of the law and more detailed advice may be obtained by writing to the Immigration and Nationality Division, Lunar House, 40 Wellesley Road, Croydon CR9 2BY Tel: 0820 606 7766. Questions about passports should be addressed to the UKPA - Passport Office, 89 Eccleston Square, London SW1V 1PN Tel: 0870 521 0410 (24hr). A voluntary organisation, International Social Service of the United Kingdom, can help with welfare problems arising when nationality or citizenship are in question. Its address is 3rd Floor, Cranmer House, 39 Brixton Road, London SW9 6DD Tel: 020 7735 8941. A reference to inter-country adoption is contained in ChapterOne, Section One.

IMMIGRATION

This section deals with the categories of people allowed to enter the UK and the rules concerning such immigration. The main law covering this is the Immigration Act 1971 as amended and supplemented by the Immigration Act 1988 ("the 1988 Act"), particularly the Asylum and Immigration Appeals Act ("the 1993 Act") and the Asylum and Immigartion Act 1996 ("the 1996 Act") (applying also to Scotland and Northern Ireland) and under which Immigration Rules are made. The Act came fully into force on 1 January 1973. Under it, a distinction is drawn between those who have a right of abode in the UK and all other people who are subject to immigration control, whatever their citizenship or ethnic origin.

Right of abode

All British citizens have the right of abode in the UK. In the long term, only British citizens will have it, but Commonwealth citizens retain the right as do British citizens who, immediately before 1 January 1983, had the right of abode because they had a parent born in the UK or who, if women, were or had been married to a man who had or would have had the right of abode. The only way a BDTC or BOC could acquire the right of abode is by acquiring British Citizenship itself.

Admission for settlement

Certain people who do not have the right of abode are eligible under the Immigration Rules to be admitted for settlement. These include:

- UK passport holders, who have been given a special voucher, and their dependants. This scheme is for heads of households, mainly from East Africa, who have no other citizenship. Certain East African countries and India are allocated a set number of vouchers per annum.

- *The dependants of those already settled in the UK, or of those accepted for settlement at the same time. This is subject to the ability and willingness of the sponsors to support and accommodate their dependants without recourse to public funds in accommodation of their own or which they occupy themselves. In these terms 'dependants' include:

- wives and children under 18;

- older people, such as parents and grandparents aged 65 or over, widows and widowers aged 65 or over and parents or grandparents travelling together, at least one of whom is 65 or over, who are mainly dependent on their children or grandchildren settled in the UK and have no close relatives in their own countries on whom they can rely;

- other parents and grand-parents, including those below 65, as well as sons, daughters, sisters, brothers, aunts and uncles of any age who are living alone in the most exceptional compassionate circumstances and who are mainly dependent on relatives settled in the UK and are without other close relatives to turn to in their own country.

- *Spouses and fiancé(e)s of people who are present and settled in the UK, subject to certain tests designed to show that the marriage is not entered into primarily to obtain admission. They must have met and must show that there is adequate accommodation and maintenance until the marriage and thereafter without recourse to public funds. Admission is subject to a time limit which may subsequently be removed.

** An entry clearance is mandatory.*

Others who may be eligible for settlement

Certain other categories of people already in the UK also have certain rights of settlement. These include:

- Commonwealth citizens who have been continually resident since before 1 January 1973;

- those who complete four years in approved employment, mainly through the work permit scheme.

Visitors

from overseas, whether on holiday or visiting for social, family, cultural or business reasons, will be required before being admitted to show that there are sufficient funds available for their maintenance and accommodation for the duration of their visit, that they have no intention of seeking employment and that they intend to remain only for a limited period. The duration of the visit may not exceed six months.

Students

are admitted if they can show that arrangements have been made for them to study at a university, polytechnic or further education establishment, an independent school or bona fide private educational establishment and that they will spend not less than 15 hours a week in organised daytime study, or that the course will occupy the whole or a substantial part of their time. The student must also be able to show that the cost of the course can be met, along with the student's own maintenance and accommodation and that of any dependants, without working or recourse to public funds. The student must also intend to leave the UK on completion of the studies. Students are not allowed to take full-time employment, but they are normally allowed to work in their spare time and during vacations if they first obtain the approval of the Department for Work and Pensions. Their spouses and any children under 18 who may be admitted with them will not be restricted in their freedom to take employment, unless the student is prohibited from doing so, provided they will be here for at least one year.

Au pairs

Young people aged 17-27 inclusive, who are unmarried and without dependants, may be admitted to the UK as au pairs in order to learn the English language and to live for a time as members of English speaking families. In return for their keep and pocket money, au pairs are expected to help with light household duties, including the care of any children. This should not be confused with domestic employment, for which a work permit is required. Only young women who are nationals of the following states are eligible and they will be permitted to spend no more than a total of two years in the UK as au pairs: Andorra, Austria, Cyprus, Czechoslovakia, The Faeroes, Finland, Greenland, Hungary, Iceland, Liechtenstein, Malta, Monaco, Norway, San Marino, Sweden, Switzerland and Turkey.

Holders of work permits

Work permits are issued by the DWP for a specific job with a particular employer; the employer must apply to the DWP. In general, a person may be admitted for employment only if s/he holds a current permit. Visa nationals also require a visa. There are some exceptions, eg, ministers of religion, representatives of foreign newspapers, self employed writers and artists, but anyone seeking to come for employment should first make enquiries of the British representative in his or her own country. In general, nationals of member states of the EC are admitted, regardless of their purpose in coming to the UK, for an initial period of six months, without employment restrictions, upon presentation of a valid passport or national identity card. After entering employment, an EC national will be issued with a residence permit normally valid for five years. After four years in employment, the time limit on the stay may be removed.

A Commonwealth citizen who has a grandparent born in the UK and who wishes to take or seek employment here may be granted entry clearance or leave to remain for that purpose. Anyone who qualifies in this category does not need a work permit. Upon arrival, s/he will normally be admitted for four years and may apply for settlement on completion of that period, but does not qualify for the right of abode.

DOCUMENTS NEEDED FOR ENTRY

Passports

Everyone coming to this country, including people who have the right of abode, needs a passport or other document establishing identity and nationality. In addition, certain people may require the following:

- Visa: nationals of some foreign countries mainly in Eastern Europe, the Near and Middle East and Africa must hold a current visa if they wish to enter or re-enter the UK for any purpose. Unless they are visa exempt, people who do not hold a national passport issued by a government recognised by the UK Government also require a visa on their travel document, although this requirement is waived for certain holders of refugee travel documents if coming for visits of three months or less.

- Certificate of entitlement: this is required by anyone arriving in the UK who claims to have the right of abode, but who is not a British citizen by birth, adoption or grant in the UK or by descent from a parent or grandparent who was a citizen in one of these ways. A woman who is a British Dependent Territories Citizen or a British Overseas Citizen, and who has the right of abode by marriage to a man who is *or would have been* a British citizen in one of the above ways, does not require a certificate of entitlement.

- Entry certificates: these are only issued to Commonwealth citizens. Anyone seeking to enter the UK for settlement, as the dependant of a person settled in the UK or being admitted for settlement, requires an entry certificate issued by a British Representative overseas. So do people of independent means, business and self employed people and those entering for some categories of employment that do not require a work permit, together with dependants of all such people and dependants of work permit holders; also husbands and wives seeking to join their spouses and fiancé(e)s seeking entry for marriage settlement. Commonwealth citizens for whom an entry certificate is not mandatory may also, if they wish to ascertain in advance whether they qualify for admission, obtain an entry certificate before setting out for this country.

With effect from 16 May 1991, the facility for acquiring UK re-entry visas was withdrawn. Visa nationals wishing to re-enter the UK normally need to obtain a fresh visa from a UK diplomatic post. This is not necessary where a person is visa exempt or holds a valid multiple entry visa. Since May 1991, people granted leave to stay in the UK for more than six months benefit from an extended visa exemption scheme, under which they are not required to present a visa if they depart from the UK and return within the terms of their original leave. They will, however, be liable to examination at the port of entry to confirm that they qualify for re-admission. The visa exemption scheme will also apply to people granted indefinite leave to remain in the UK who return for settlement after an absence of two years or less.

Leave to enter will be refused to anyone who does not have the right of abode if the person does not qualify to enter the UK, does not hold a required entry document or if there is a deportation order in force against him or her. Leave to enter can also be refused on such grounds as criminal record, danger to public health or danger to national security. These powers cannot be used against dependent wives or children under 18 of a person settled in the UK, nor can they be used against returning residents who are Commonwealth citizens and were settled in the UK before 1 January 1973, unless they are subject to a deportation order. In addition, provisions for refusal on medical grounds may not be used against any other returning resident.

Registration with the police

A foreign national whose stay is subject to a time limit may be required to register with the police and to report any subsequent changes in address, occupation, etc. Two passport-size photographs are required and a fee is payable. Commonwealth citizens and EC nationals are not normally required to register with the police.

Deportation

With certain limited exceptions, people subject to immigration control are liable to deportation if they remain beyond the time limit of their stay, or breach a condition attached to it for example, by taking unauthorised employment, or if they engage in criminal or other activity against the public interest. In almost all circumstances where deportation action is taken, the subject of it has a right of appeal exercisable prior to removal.

Illegal entry

A person subject to immigration control is liable to removal as an illegal entrant if entry to this country was gained unlawfully, eg, by clandestine means or by deceiving the immigration officer on arrival as to the individual's true purpose in coming to the UK. Illegal entrants have a right of appeal which is normally only exercisable from abroad after removal.

Rights of appeal

Commonwealth citizens and foreign nationals may appeal from abroad to an independent adjudicator against refusal of a certificate of entitlement or an entry clearance ie, an entry certificate or visa. A person arriving at a port who is required to obtain leave to enter, but who claims to have a right of abode, may appeal to an adjudicator if s/he has a UK passport or certificate of entitlement to a right of abode. Similarly, a person who is refused leave to enter may appeal to an adjudicator, but must do so from abroad unless s/he holds a current entry clearance or work permit.

All appeals are heard in the UK, but the appellant may be represented by relatives, solicitors or other agents eg, the Immigration Advisory Service (IAS), listed under voluntary organisations below. Either party to an appeal may also appeal, usually with leave, to the Immigration Appeal Tribunal against the decision of an adjudicator.

A person in the UK may also appeal to an adjudicator and thereafter, with leave, to the Tribunal against any refusal to vary a leave to enter or remain, or any variations of the leave, provided that the application for variation is made before the expiry of the leave in question. There is no requirement to notify an applicant of his or her appeal rights if the decision is taken at his or her request and is not less favourable than that requested.

Other rights of appeal include that against any curtailment or restriction of leave and against a decision to deport a person for being in breach of leave to enter or remain; a person can also object to directions given for his or her removal to a particular country on deportation by specifying another country or territory to which s/he ought to be removed if at all. Where the person has been in the UK for less than seven years, the right of appeal against a deportation decision is, with certain exemptions, restricted to the facts that is, whether he or she has overstayed or broken the conditions of stay and does not extend to the merits of the case. A person is normally deported to the country of which s/he is a national unless s/he can show that another country will receive him or her, notwithstanding deportation. Where a court recommends deportation following a conviction, an appeal against deportation may be made to a higher court only, but there is a right of appeal to an adjudicator against removal directions. A person may also appeal against deportation if s/he is being deported on the grounds that it is conducive to the public good, or if s/he is the spouse or child under 18 of someone to be deported. Appeals in these cases go to the Tribunal in the first instance instead of to the adjudicator. There is also an appeal against removal directions.

In all cases, the person concerned will be given a written notice of the decision to deport, or it will be sent through the post to his or her last known address. Information about how to exercise the right of appeal, the time limit for appealing and the appropriate appeal forms will also be given or sent with the written notice. In certain cases, where the Secretary of State in person, and not someone acting under the Secretary's authority, decides that a person should be refused entry, required to depart or be deported because it is felt to be conducive to the public good for certain special reasons eg, national security, there is no right of appeal. In certain circumstances, however, a deportee may be given the opportunity to make representations before a panel of advisers appointed for that purpose on a non-statutory basis, who will tender advice to the Secretary of State.

Financial help in returning home

International Social Service, listed under Voluntary Organisations below, administers a scheme under the Immigration Act 1971 (Section 29) which enables financial assistance to be given towards the travel costs of people who have no right of abode, who wish to leave this country permanently and in whose interests this would be. Assistance is discretionary and is subject to means-testing and employment prospects. In order to safeguard the voluntary nature of this scheme, only direct personal applications will be considered.

European Community nationals

Nationals of member states of the EC have the right under EC law to seek employment in the UK for a limited period, to take paid employment, to engage in self employment or to provide or receive services for remuneration. They do not need to obtain permission to do any of these things, although they may obtain residence permits from the Home Office in confirmation of their rights if they want them. These rights extend to their spouses and adult or child dependent relatives, even if the spouse or dependants are not themselves nationals of EC member states. Where such people are visa nationals or would need other forms of pre-entry clearance, they should obtain 'family permits' from a British diplomatic port abroad or, if already in the UK, obtain a 'residence document' from the Home Office. From 1992, EC nationals who are in the UK as vocational students, as retired people, or as other non-economically active people not covered by other aspects of Community law, have also had a right of residence here and that right will again extend to their spouses and dependants. These rights will lapse, however, if the EC national or dependants become a charge on public funds.

Refugees

People recognised as refugees by the UK under the 1951 convention relating to the status of refugees and the 1967 Protocol are eligible for all appropriate central and local government services. If in doubt or difficulty, they can generally find assistance from one of the many refugee organisations and their own national committees.

Further information

Enquiries about the Immigration Act 1971 and the 1994 Immigration Rules (HC395) as amended should be addressed to the Under Secretary of State, Immigration and Nationality Department, Home Office, Lunar House, 40 Wellesley Road, Croydon, Surrey CR9 2BY Tel: 020 8686 0688. Copies of the 1994 Immigration Rules (HC395) as amended may be obtained from The Stationery Office. For information on Legal Aid contact The Legal Services Commission on 0845 608 1122 for England and Wales, the Scottish Legal Aid Board on 0131 226 7061for Scotland and the Law Society for Northern Ireland on 028 9024 6441 for Northern Ireland.

USEFUL ADDRESSES AND VOLUNTARY ORGANISATIONS

There are many voluntary and non-statutory organisations which offer advice and help to people with problems arising from all aspects of nationality and immigration. These include the following:

Asylum Aid, 28 Commercial Street, London E1 6LS. Tel: 020 7377 5123.

Free Representation Unit dealing with refugee problems. 4th Floor, Peer House, 8-14 Verulam Street London WC1X 8LZ. Tel: 020 7831 0692. The Unit normally accepts only referrals through advice centres and solicitors.

The Immigration Advisory Service (IAS), Head Office, County House, 190 Great Dover Street, London SE1 4YB Tel: 020 7357 7511

International Social Service of the United Kingdom, 3rd Floor, Cranmer House, 39 Brixton Road, London SW9 6DD Tel: 020 7735 8941 offers a casework service to help those British, Commonwealth, foreign, refugee or stateless people whose personal and family problems extend across national frontiers. One of the many services offered is a foreign marriage advisory service.

Joint Council for the Welfare of Immigrants, 115 Old Street, London EC1V 9JR *advice line* Tel: 020 7251 8706 advises and represents people with problems in connection with the immigration and nationality laws. It also campaigns for justice in connection with these laws.

Law Centres Federation, Duchess House, 18-19 Warren Street, London W1P 5DB. Tel: 020 7387 8570

Law Centre NI, 124 DDonegall Street, Belfast BT1 2GY. Tel: 028 9024 4401

Liberty (National Council for Civil Liberties), 21 Tabard Street, London SE1 4LA Tel: 020 7403 3888 Fax: 020 7407 5354 campaigns to protect the rights and liberties of all private citizens, particularly those of minority groups, publishes factsheets and guides to civil rights and provides limited advice on specific civil rights issues.

London Gypsy and Traveller Unit, 6 Westgate Street, London E8 3RN Tel: 020 8533 2002 Fax 020 8533 7110 helps gypsy and traveller families in London to gain access to adequate caravan sites, health, education and social services.

National Asylum Support Service, Tel: 0845 602 1739 Fax: 0845 601 1143

Northern Ireland Association of Independent Advice Centres, 303 Ormeau Road, Belfast BT7 3GG. Tel: 028 9064 5919

Refugee Arrivals Projects are based at Gatwick and Heathrow for asylum seekers in need of housing assistance. The Project worker will talk to asylum seekers to assess their housing needs.

The Refugee Council, Bondway House, 3-9 Bondway, London SW8 1SJ Tel: 020 7582 6922 is the recognised co-ordinating body for voluntary agencies working for refugee relief in the UK and abroad.

The Refugee Legal Centre, (formerly UKIAS Refugee Unit) Sussex House, 39-45 Bermondsey Street, London SE1 3XF Tel: 020 7827 9090.

Scottish Association of Law Centres, c/o Paisley Law Centre, 65 George Street, Paisley PA1 2JY Tel: 0141 561 7266.

The Scottish Council for Civil Liberties, 146 Holland Street, Glasgow G2 4NG Tel: 0141 332 5960.

The Telephone Legal Advice Service for Travellers, offering free legal advice and information to gypsies and travellers under threat of eviction or facing problems including site provision, licensing and children's schooling Tel: 020 2087 4580.

Youth Access, 1a Taylors Yard, 67 Alderbrook Road, London SW12 8AD. Tel: 020 8772 9900.

UKCOSA: The Council for International Education, 9-17 St Albans Place, London N1 0NX. Tel: 020 7354 5210.

RACE EQUALITY

Commission for Racial Equality

The Race Relations Act 1976 which applies to England, Wales and Scotland, but not to Northern Ireland provides for a statutory body appointed by the Home Secretary, the **Commission for Racial Equality (CRE).** The functions of the CRE are to work towards the elimination of discrimination, to promote equality of opportunity and good relations between people of different racial groups and to keep the operation of the 1976 Act under review. It has wide powers to undertake investigations for any purpose concerned with its duties. Where it finds discrimination occurring, it may take steps to bring the discrimination to an end.

The CRE also undertakes advisory and education work and supports the work of local racial equality councils, which have been established in most areas with substantial numbers of people from ethnic minorities. The CRE is empowered to give financial assistance to local racial equality councils and to other organisations working for good race relations. A complete list of these local councils is available free from the CRE, or along with other information and publications is available on its website at www.cre.gov.uk. The CRE is run by a commission, consisting of a Chair and not more than 14 other members, appointed by the Home Secretary. It is based at Elliot House, 10-12 Allington Street, London SW1E 5E Tel: 020 7828 7022. There are regional offices in Leeds, Birmingham, Manchester and offices for Scotland and Wales in Edinburgh and Cardiff.

The Race Relations (Northern Ireland) Act 1997 established a parallel commission for Racial Equality in Northern Ireland, which has now been merged into the new Northern Ireland Equalities Commission.

Race Relations Act 1976

The Act repealed previous Race Relations Acts. It was amended by the Race Relations (amendment) Act 2000. It makes racial discrimination generally unlawful in the provision to the public of goods, facilities and services, and in education, employment and in the disposal and management of premises. It defines 'discrimination' as

- direct: treating a person less favourably on racial grounds than others in the same circumstances; and

- indirect: applying a rule or requirement which adversely affects one racial group more than another and cannot be justified on non-racial grounds.

Complaints under the Act can be taken to an Employment Tribunal for employment cases, or to a county court or Sheriff Court in Scotland for other matters. For court cases, legal aid may be granted under the legal aid scheme. Other local bodies, including legal advice centres, citizens advice bureaux and racial equality councils, may be in a position to give advice. For employment cases members of trade unions can get assistance with their case from their union. Although the CRE is not required to support individual complaints, it can advise individuals who wish to bring legal proceedings and may give legal assistance in presenting a case at no charge. The law on incitement to racial hatred remains unchanged. For this, a prosecution made under the Public Order Act 1986 may only be brought in England and Wales by, or with the consent of, the Attorney General.

The Crime and Disorder Act 1998 introduced the concept of racially aggravated offences and some 1500 such cases are being handled each year in England and Wales. All such cases are matters for the criminal law and not the CRE.

The Amendment Act 2000 extended the coverage of the Race Relations Act to bring within its scope all activities of public authorities, with the exception of actions by the Immigration Service and decisions of courts. The Act now covers the use of policing and other regulatory powers such as decisions to compulsorily detain individuals under mental mental health legislation or decisions taken in relation to children in care.

The new legislation also requires public bodies to promote race equality and prevent discrimination by the start of 2002. As part of their work in fulfilling these duties public bodies had to publish race equality schemes by 31 May 2002. These should be available for employees and members of the public to inspect. The CRE has published Codes of Practice and guidance documnents to assist in the fulfillment of the duties and texts of these are available from the CRE website at www.cre.gov.uk.

EQUALITY AND CITIZENSHIP

SMITH LLEWELYN PARTNERSHIP
18 Princess Way, Swansea SA1 3LW
Tel: 01792 464444 ***Fax:*** 01792 464726
Docx: 92051 SWANSEA 3
Email: mainofficeslp@virgin.net

CHAPTER SEVEN

Taxation

Taxation

CHAPTER SEVEN

Taxation

INTRODUCTION

Although taxation may seem far removed from the social services, direct taxation may be regarded as part of the welfare benefits system insofar as tax allowances provide relief from income tax on the basis of assumed needs. Such allowances determine the amount people have to spend and, to this extent, may be regarded as equivalent to cash benefits. The criteria on which such 'fiscal welfare' is based are not, however, identical with those in other areas of welfare provision and discrepancies may arise between the different systems of benefit. Above all, the now well-known phenomenon of the 'poverty trap' is a consequence of the interaction of the tax and benefit systems which would be remedied by closer links between them.

This chapter is intended to assist those working in any field relating to the social services who need some basic knowledge of the taxation system in order to help their clients. It is not concerned with indirect taxation such as VAT nor with the taxation of companies. The government department responsible for direct taxation is the Inland Revenue: income tax and capital gains tax are dealt with by local tax offices. The relevant tax legislation is set out in the Income and Corporation Taxes Act 1988, the Taxation of Chargeable Gains Act 1992 and in a series of annual Finance Acts. The tax year runs from 6 April one year to 5 April the following year and proposals for the coming year are made by the Chancellor of the Exchequer in the Budget. In 1993, the Chancellor delivered the first unified Budget covering both taxation and Government expenditure. Previously, spending plans for the coming financial year were announced in the autumn and revenue measures the following spring in the Budget.

While employed people pay tax on the actual amount they are currently earning, for the self-employed taxes will broadly be charged by reference to the profits of the 12-month accounting period ending in the tax year.

Although this chapter gives a broad outline of the law concerning taxation, it cannot deal with every variation which may occur in specific cases and the relevant tax office; that is, either the local one or the one relating to an employee's place of work, should be consulted on specific matters. There is some degree of flexibility in the British system and local tax inspectors have some powers of discretion: for instance, they may decide to waive tax due if it is a very small amount.

Please note that details in this chapter refer to the tax position for the tax year 2002-2003 with references to the previous year where these may be helpful. The general principles of taxation remain relatively static although details can change. Information on changes can be obtained from any tax office and by reference to the publications recommended in the Further Reading section at the end of the book.

INCOME TAX

Income from earnings, pensions, investments and savings is taxed, but, since various allowances are made, taxable income is normally less than gross income. From 1996/97 the responsibility of assessing liability to tax has fallen on the individual and therefore all tax documents such as P60s, certificates of tax deducted from interest payments etc. should be retained. Self-assessment forms are required to be completed by anyone who is self-employed, a business partner, a company director, an employee (or pensioner) with more complex tax affairs, a trustee or a personal representative. If the form is completed by 30th September the Inland Revenue will calculate the amount of tax payable on the basis of the information given. If it is returned after that date the taxpayer must also calculate the tax. Any delay or error incurs fixed penalties. Such forms ask for information concerning income and outgoings during the preceding year and for information concerning allowances for the coming year. On the basis of the assessment made, the taxpayer will be sent a code number *on form P2* which indicates his or her allowances.

The code number shows the allowances to which each person is entitled according to their particular circumstances and not according to gross income. If the taxpayer has any reason to think the notice of coding is inaccurate, the tax office should be contacted straight away.

Pay As You Earn (PAYE)

Those who are not self-employed normally pay their taxes under PAYE. This method of collecting tax on wages, salaries and occupational pensions avoids the difficulties for the taxpayer of paying tax in a lump sum. Under this system, employers are responsible for the deduction of tax from an employee's income and for handing this amount over to the Inland Revenue. From the notice of coding sent to a taxpayer, the employer can compute the amount of income which is taxable after relief has been given on outgoings and allowances. Where a taxpayer has more than one employer, the code is adjusted by the Revenue to ensure the correct amount of total tax is paid. Employers are given tax tables which enable them to calculate the amount of tax they must deduct in equal instalments over the year, on either a weekly or a monthly basis, depending on how the employee is normally paid. The tables are in effect self adjusting if the rate of pay varies during the year. They are based on the current rates of taxation. If these are changed, the employer is issued with new tables which automatically correct any 'wrong' deductions prior to the change.

The tax rates for the year 2001-2002 and 2002-2003 are as follows:

Rate of taxation	***Band of taxable income 2001-2002***	***Rate of taxation***	***Band of taxable income 2002-2003***
Starting 10%	0 - £1,880	Starting 10%	0 - £1,920
Basic 22%	£1,881 - £29,400	Basic 22%	£1,921 - £29,900
Higher 40%	over £29,400	Higher 40%	over £29,900

On changing employment, the taxpayer must obtain a leaving certificate, form P45, from the previous employer so that the new employer is aware of the code number and tax paid in the current year. If this is not obtained, the new employer will deduct tax at the emergency rate, which allows relief based on the personal allowance only; the taxpayer will receive any rebate which may be due when the code number is known. A taxpayer out of employment for more than a month may apply for repayment of tax unles he or she is claiming the Jobseekers Allowance or other benefit during that time.

It is the taxpayer's responsibility to inform the tax office of any changes such as new outgoings or allowances which could affect his or her coding during the tax year. If, on checking tax paid, a taxpayer discovers an error or realises that s/he has not claimed a relief or allowance to which there might have been entitlement, it is possible to reclaim excess tax paid up to six years previously. Interest at the current rate is payable to a taxpayer due for a refund more than one year after the end of the year for which the tax was paid (provided the tax was paid on time). Alternatively, if a taxpayer fails to pay a bill, and this does not normally happen under PAYE, it should be remembered that the Inland Revenue charges interest from the date on which it should have been paid.

The taxpayer's own earnings from employment and the amount of tax and other deductions, such as pensions contributions should be stated on the tax return, form P60, received annually from the employer. Most taxpayers (whose income is wholly or mainly dealt with through PAYE) do not need to complete a tax return. However, some people (for example those paying higher rate tax) will receive a tax return. If a taxpayer receives profits from any business carried on by that taxpayer (however small or part-time the employment) or profits or income from any other source from which tax has not been deducted at source (including maintenance or alimony), then he/she must complete a tax return. Each person is responsible for his or her own tax affairs and for claiming individual tax allowances and exemptions. All other earnings, such as tips, insurance commission and payments received for casual work, should be listed in a tax return. When giving such amounts, it is customary to round down each total to the nearest pound. Any benefits and expense allowances received from an employer must be declared. These might include a company car, accommodation or a paid holiday. State pensions should be listed, but some social security benefits, such as the mobility allowance and the maternity allowance, are not taxable. Payments of short-term statutory sick pay, made by the recipient's employer, are taxable through PAYE. Social security benefits paid to people who are unemployed or on strike are taxable. Details of any other pensions, for example from a former employer, should be given.

Strikes

Where a taxpayer is involved in an industrial dispute, any benefit received for themselves or their spouse will be treated as taxable income. However, the benefit will be paid gross and the tax due on that income will need to be recovered by the Inland Revenue. When the strike is over, or at the end of the tax year if the strike is still continuing at that time, the benefit office will send a statement showing how much taxable benefit has been paid. A copy of this will also be sent to the Inland Revenue. Any tax due will be recovered by adjusting the tax code in a later year. If the taxpayer is entitled to a tax refund, this will not be made until after the strike ends.

Redundancy and other leaving payments

Any statutory redundancy payments which an employee or director receives on leaving employment are tax free. The current statutory redundancy compensation limit is £7,500. Earnings owed by an employer, such as normal wages, commission, or pay in lieu of a holiday, are taxed in the normal way. In addition, other terminal payments, sometimes described as a 'golden handshake', may be given by a former employer. If such a payment represents provision made under the original contract of service to cater for premature termination of employment, it may be liable to taxation under Schedule E. If the payment is regarded by the Inland Revenue as being genuinely made to compensate for loss of employment, however, the first £30,000 of the payment is not taxable. Anything above this is fully taxable. Any exempt statutory redundancy payment made to the leaving employee will be counted in calculating the £30,000 exempt amount. Other leaving payments may be tax free: these include compensation for an injury or disability, death gratuities from the armed forces, payments made under approved superannuation or retirement benefit schemes and compensation relating to a job done entirely outside the UK.

Employers' (occupational) pension scheme

An employee obtains tax relief on his or her contributions to an Inland Revenue approved employer's scheme. The maximum contribution on which an employee can get tax relief is 15% of earnings (benefits in kind which are assessed for tax as emoluments under Schedule E can normally be included). The maximum pension which can be approved by the Inland Revenue on retirement is two-thirds of final earnings, being calculated as one-sixtieth for each year of service, with a maximum of 40 years. Generally, the maximum lump sum payable on retirement is 1½ times final earnings, again dependent on the number of years of service.

For new schemes starting on or after 14 March 1989, and new members joining existing schemes on or after 1 June 1989, benefits and employee contributions on which tax relief is granted are restricted by reference to a maximum final salary of £97,200. Thus the maximum approvable pension will be £64,800 and the maximum tax-free lump sum £145,800. These limits will be increased each year in line with inflation. Employers can establish 'top-up' schemes for employees earning higher salaries, but these will not qualify for tax relief. Anyone who is a member of an employer's occupational pension scheme can make additional voluntary contributions (AVCs) to it. Tax relief is given on AVCs, but they are limited to 15% of earnings. The amount and timing of AVCs can now be varied. Alternatively, instead of making AVCs to the employer's scheme, an employee can contribute to a separate scheme and these payments are called free-standing AVCs; tax relief is available on these up to the same limit. This limit applies to the employee's total contributions to all schemes relating to the same employment.

Stakeholders Pension Scheme

The New Stakeholder Pension Scheme are dealt with in Chapter five. However, for tax purposes they are classed as Personal Pensions Schemes.

Personal pension scheme

For the self-employed or those who are not members of an employer's pension scheme, one or more personal pension schemes can be taken out. The total maximum approvable contribution is 17.5% of earnings or profits for those under 35. This maximum is gradually increased to 40% at the age of 61 or over. There is a limit on maximum net relevant earnings by reference to which relief is available; for the tax year 2002-2003, the limit is £97,200. This is increased in line with inflation annually.

Whilst pension schemes still represent very tax efficient investment, their tax advantages were reduced in the 1997 budget. Pension funds can no longer claim back the tax credit, paid by a company distributing their profits, from the Exchequer.

Investment income

Although in general all income an individual receives is taxable, the proceeds from certain types of investment are tax free. These include the following:

- premium bond prizes;
- National Savings Certificate bonuses;
- the first £70 interest from a National Savings Bank Ordinary Account;
- proceeds from life insurance (see below)

Certain other investment income is paid to the investor after deduction of tax. Starting and basic rate taxpayers are not liable to any further tax on interest on bank and building society accounts, and income from authorised unit trusts. In both cases, the tax deducted is at the rate of 20% and this gives the taxpayer a tax credit for both starting and basic rate tax due. In the case of bank and building society accounts, non-taxpayers are able to avoid deductions altogether. It is worth remembering, that with the advent of independent taxation, married women whose income is less than their allowances no longer have to pay tax on their savings. For this reason, it is sometimes worthwhile ensuring that savings are in the name of the non-taxpayer. Form R85 is able to be completed for a joint account where only one party is a non-taxpayer, but in this case only 50% of the interest will be paid gross. The certificate contains an undertaking by the person completing it that, if they become liable to pay any amount by way of income tax for the year in which the payment of interest is made, he/she will notify the bank or building society accordingly. Similarly, bank and building society accounts opened for children should also have a Form R85 completed in order that their interest is paid gross unless their income is above the personal allowance level. When a company pays a dividend, it carries a tax credit which satisfies the tax liability for starting and basic rate tax payers. Higher rate tax payers will have additional tax to pay on the dividend. Individuals whose income is below their personal allowance will not be able to reclaim the tax credit unless the shares, in respect of which the dividend is paid, are held in an ISA or PEP.

Investment income also includes income from the letting of any property such as a flat or a house. In this case, tax is payable on the amount of rent obtained less, for instance, expenses incurred in the maintenance of the property. However, there is a tax incentive to encourage owners/occupiers and tenants with a spare room in their house to let it out. Since 6 April 1997 where gross annual rents exceed £4,250, the individual has a choice whether to pay tax in the normal way or alternatively on the amount of rent received less £4,250 with no relief for expenses.

Individual Savings Accounts (ISAs)

Individuals over 18 who are resident and ordinarily resident in the UK may invest in ISAs, which are to be exempt from both income tax and capital gains tax for a minimum of 10 years. In addition, until 5 April 2004, the 10% tax credit can be reclaimed from the Revenue where it is paid to a non-taxpayer in respect of dividends from UK equities held in ISAs. An ISA must be managed by an appropriate manager. The annual subscription limit is £7,000 for the years 1999-2000 to 2005-2006 but is reduced to £5,000 from 6 April 2006. There will be no statutory lock-in period and withdrawals do not cause a clawback of tax relief, but once a limit has been reached for the tax year the investor may make no further subscriptions, regardless of withdrawals.

The annual limit may be invested totally in stocks and shares or alternatively up to £3,000 in years 1999-2000 to 2005-2006 and £1,000 from 6 April 2006 onwards may be invested in cash and up to £1,000 in life insurance. If different managers are desired for each element, mini-ISAs may be opened although this is likely to incur greater costs. No further subscriptions to PEPs or new TESSAs may now be made. Subscriptions to existing TESSAs may be made until the end of the 5 year period of the TESSA without affecting contributions to the ISA. The full value of existing PEPs and TESSAs may continue to be held tax free after 5th April 1999. In the case of TESSAs on maturity the capital (but not accumulated interest) may be transferred (without affecting the other limitations) into a new savings account and in the case of PEPs held at 5th April 1999, they may continue, outside the new savings account, with the same tax advantages as the new account.

Outgoings

These are the amounts of expenditure which taxpayers may deduct from income before calculating tax. Details should be stated on the tax return. Certain outgoings, such as contributions to an employer's pension scheme, receive automatic tax relief and need not be specifically claimed.

Expenses

Expenses incurred wholly, exclusively and necessarily as part of the taxpayer's employment may be claimed and these should be listed in the income section of the tax return. Examples of such expenses are protective clothing, tools and other equipment, professional fees and subscriptions and travelling expenses incurred on business and not refunded by the employer. It may be useful to obtain an employer's letter authorising such expenditure and stating that it has not been reimbursed.

Interest on loans

Bridging loans, bank loans and mortgages to secure money borrowed for certain purposes qualify for relief on the payment of interest incurred, but interest on overdrafts is, generally speaking, only allowable where the loan is for business purposes.

Tax relief may also be claimed on the interest paid in respect of a loan used for the purchase of plant or machinery in connection with employment eg, a car or a typewriter, for up to three years after the end of the tax year when the loan was granted. A share in a partnership may be bought with the aid of a loan and the interest on this could qualify for tax relief.

Perks

Tax may have to be paid on fringe benefits or 'perks' paid for by an employer, such as a car, holiday or insurance policy. Other expenses may be tax free unless the person concerned is a director or earns over £8,500 per year including expenses and benefits. Despite the necessity of paying tax on some fringe benefits, they are frequently at least as valuable as extra pay, if not more so, and are sometimes used in this way by an employer. This is because the tax may be calculated on a smaller sum than the true cost of providing the benefit.

Child care

Since April 1990, the provision of a place at a workplace nursery has not been treated as a taxable benefit. There is presently no tax relief on payments to childminders or private nurseries which are not provided by the employer.

However, for low-income working families, the Working Families Tax Credit (WFTC), which has been payable since October 1999, will meet 70% of eligible child-care costs up to a maximum of £135 a week for one child families, or £200 a week for families with more than one child.

The WFTC offers the following:

Working Families Tax Credit

Basic tax credit (one per family)		£62.50
Tax credits for each child aged	0-15	£26.45
	16-18	£27.20
Extra tax credit for working 30+ hours a week		£11.65

Life insurance

Tax relief in relation to insurance premiums can no longer be claimed other than in relation to policies issued before 14 March 1984 which have been varied after that date.

The proceeds of most life insurance policies, whether taken out before or after 14 March 1984, are free of income tax unless a taxpayer supplements his or her income by cashing a policy before the minimum period has elapsed or by paying up the policy. In that case, income tax will be charged on the gain if one of the following conditions also applies:

- the policy was one with a term of not less than ten years but cashed or paid up within three quarters of that term, or within the first ten years, whichever was the shorter. Such policies if issued before 14 March 1984 would normally have qualified for tax relief on the premiums; or

- the policy was one which, whether issued before 14 March 1984 or not, could not have qualified for relief in any event, for example a single premium bond. Other factors can give rise to a change in respect of such a policy and further advice should be taken.

Friendly Societies

If contributions are made more frequently than annually small savers may invest up to £270 a year with a friendly society in respect of policies paying benefits in the event of sickness and on death. This type of policy is now unusual and the majority of friendly society policies do not meet the conditions for the relief.

Personal allowances

Allowances mean that a part of personal income is not taxed, or that the tax a person would otherwise pay on their total income is reduced by a fixed amount. Since the introduction of independent taxation of husbands and wives on 6 April 1990, all taxpayers are taxed as separate individuals, each entitled to a personal allowance according to age. Additional allowances depend on circumstances. The amount of such allowances can vary from tax year to tax year. Table VIII gives the current allowances for 2002-2003. A taxpayer in any doubt about qualifying for an allowance should consult his or her tax office. All allowances can be claimed on the tax return although some, such as the personal allowance, are given automatically.

The married couple's allowance was abolished with effect from 5 April 2000, except where either husband of wife is aged 65 or over, on or before 5 April 2000 or where a person getting married was born on or before 5 April 1935. This should be borne in mind in relation to advice below. The relief given by the married couple's allowance is restricted to 10%.

Tax Allowances

Allowance		***Who can claim it***
Personal		
age under 65	£4,615	Every taxpayer is entitled, according to age
age 65-74	£6,100	
age 75 and over	£6,370	There are income limits for elderly people
Married couple's		
born before 6 April 1935	£5,465	Available where either spouse is aged 65
age 75 and over	£5,535	
Blind person's	£1,480	Anyone registered with a local authority as a blind person. Husband and wife may each claim if both are blind. The allowance is transferable between husband and wife even if he or she is not blind

PENSIONERS

Those who continue to work after the official retirement, age 65 (for men) or 60 (for women), may still claim the retirement pension, although national insurance contributions are no longer due. They continue to be given a code number indicating the level of tax on their earnings, whether working full or part time. Tax is not deducted from the national insurance retirement pension or a widow's pension before it is paid, so it may have to be collected later, according to the pensioner's total income. Former employers paying a pension deduct tax from the pension under the PAYE system. In such cases, any tax due on the national insurance retirement pension can be paid by adjusting the PAYE code. Pensioners who do not pay tax in this way will be given a special code known as an F code to enable tax to be collected. This will normally be paid in four instalments over the tax year. Married pensioners are taxed separately. Husband and wife are responsible for their own tax affairs and each receives a personal allowance according to age as set out in the Table above.

SELF-EMPLOYMENT

This section applies not only to someone who owns a business or is in partnership with someone else, but also to those who do spare time or freelance work on their own account. Self-employed people do not pay tax through the PAYE system, which is strictly for employees. Instead, they pay tax on their profits or freelance earnings under a Schedule D tax assessment. This tax is collected in two instalments each year on 1 January and 1 July. There is a system of 'self-assessment' whereby the annual tax returns filed by individuals and trustees should include a self-assessment of the taxpayer's liability for income tax and capital gains tax. Payment of taxes then due is automatically based on the self-assessment. Interest on overdue payments will run from the due date to the date of payment. There is also a 5% surcharge on any tax unpaid by 28 February following the year of assessment and a further 5% surcharge on any tax unpaid by the following 31 July. Those who have a job apart from their freelance earnings, and already pay tax under the PAYE system, can either have the extra tax collected by their employer or can pay the tax under a separate assessment. If a statement of extra earnings is not sent to the tax office, an estimate of the tax due will be made. Similarly, during the first year of a business, when tax becomes due before the final total of profits is known, an estimated assessment will be made. In either case, an appeal can be made against the estimate within 30 days. Alternatively, if it is later discovered that too much has been paid, the tax can be reclaimed.

The details of accountancy and taxation in relation to a business, particularly on a large scale, are outside the scope of this chapter. Tax under Schedule D depends on both accurate written accounts and detailed tax returns and those involved in such matters either need the necessary knowledge themselves or should employ a qualified accountant. For the benefit of those reading this chapter who may have some extra earnings which should be taxed in this way, a few further points are given.

Expenditure

The main advantage of paying tax under a Schedule D assessment is that additional allowances and expenses can be claimed. Normally, tax relief is only given for expenditure which is incurred 'wholly and exclusively' for the business; this does not in practice completely rule out expenditure which covers both business and private life. For instance, if a car is used for both business and private purposes, a proportion of its cost may qualify for tax relief. In all such matters, agreement has to be reached with the appropriate tax office and there is scope for negotiation.

It should be noted that individuals who provide their services through a service company and withdraw the company's dividend (or otherwise) may be deemed to have been paid a salary by the service company, which will be liable to account for PAYE and National Insurance Contributions accordingly. This is under the rule usually known as 'IR35'

Business expenses

As far as businesses are concerned, a considerable range of expenditure may normally be allowed. A complete list can be obtained from various publications or from a tax office, but the following examples give some indication of the range:

- all basic costs, eg wages, salaries, employers' national insurance contributions, postage, tools and specified bad debts
- business subscriptions and magazines
- fees paid, e.g. to register a trade mark, design or patent.

Where the business or freelance work takes place wholly or in part in one's own home, a proportion of the expenditure on such costs as rent, rates, telephone, lighting and heating can be claimed. This is important as such allowances are not given under the PAYE system. It is, however, worth noting that the use of a part of the home exclusively for business purposes can reduce the value of the usual exemption for capital gains tax purposes.

Capital allowances

Relief can be claimed on expenditure involved in the purchase of capital equipment used 'wholly and exclusively' for the business. Examples of such purchases are machinery, vehicles, typewriters and other office equipment. If these are used for private purposes as well, the tax relief available will be reduced accordingly.

CHILDREN'S INCOME

For the purposes of the Inland Revenue, the term 'child' applies to anyone under the age of 18 and unmarried at the end of the tax year. A child with an income, whatever his or her age, is taxed in the same way as an adult, must complete a tax return and can claim the usual allowances. However, any of the child's income which is the result of parental investment on his or her behalf normally counts for tax purposes as the parent's and must be declared by the parent (subject to £100 limit for small amounts of income).

An exception to this is income arising from funds invested in a trust which existed before 5th April 1999 and in which the child has a right to income. In this case the income is treated as the child's. However, any income arising either from funds added after 5th April 1999 to existing trusts or from a trust created since 5th April 1999 will now be taxed as that of the parent, subject to £100 limit.

The mother usually receives tax-free child benefit for each child who is under 16, or under 19 and receiving full time education at a recognised educational establishment.

STUDENTS

Although, of course, students at university are subject to the same tax rules as everyone else, and therefore receive the same allowances, student grants, scholarships and research awards are all not taxable. However, for a student on a placement scheme the situation is more complicated. Money paid over the period while he or she is working is taxable while the money paid to the student during the period of study may not be taxable. Further details should be obtained from the National Union of Students Welfare Office or the local tax office. Where a student starts a holiday job but the total taxable income in the whole of the tax year (including any unemployment benefit) is likely to be less than the basic personal allowance, the student should request a form P38(S). This should then be completed and returned to the employer to enable the student to be paid without tax being deducted. Any tax deducted before the completion of the form will be refunded. However, it should be remembered that, should the student's earnings amount to more than the basic personal allowance, tax will be payable on the difference.

GIFTS TO CHARITIES

Tax relief is available on payments made within the Gift Aid scheme.

Payroll giving scheme

Employees whose employer is prepared to operate a scheme are entitled to tax relief on donations (GAYE) made to any charity or charities of their choice. The government will add a supplement of 10% to any such donations until April 2003. The designated amount is taken by the employer from the pay of donors before deduction of income tax. There used to be a minimum amount which could be donated but this has been abolished. Higher rate tax payers can claim higher rate tax relief against their donations.

Single gifts – Gift Aid

All donations may now be given under the Gift Aid scheme. This enables charities to reclaim the basic tax already paid in respect of a donation or subscription. There is neither a maximum nor a minimum donation required.

CAPITAL GAINS TAX

Capital Gains Tax is the tax levied on any capital gain or profit which is made when an asset or possession is sold or transferred. The charge to tax may arise even if the asset is given away rather than sold. If the asset is sold at a loss or is lost, destroyed or stolen, this is regarded as a capital loss which may be offset against any capital gains made in the same tax year or carried forward to future years. Though this gives a very broad tax base, certain provisions reduce or extinguish most people's liability. The most important of these provisions are set out below.

The amount of a capital gain is arrived at by deducting the value of the asset at the time when it was bought or acquired from the actual or notional proceeds of sale. Expenses such as the cost of advertising the asset for sale may also be deducted.

Taper Relief

Taper relief is available to individuals. This reduces the amount of the chargeable gain the longer the asset has been held, thereby effectively reducing the rate of tax for longer-held assets, particularly business assets.

Where an individual disposes of an asset, the gain will be calculated by deducting the price paid on acquisition from the sale proceeds, as described above. If the asset was acquired before 5 April 1998, then the acquisition price will be increased by reference to the rate of indexation which applied from acquisition until 6th April 1998, thereby linking the cost assumed for tax purposes to the retail price index on the date of purchase, or if later, March 1982. Any losses realised in the same or prior tax years will then be set off against the gain. If there is a resulting net gain, taper relief will apply. For business assets the percentage of the gain which is chargeable reduces by a certain amount for each complete year after 5 April 1998 for which the asset has been held. For non-business assets the percentage of the gain chargeable reduces for each complete year after 6 April 1998 for which the asset is held after the asset has already been held for three complete years. The percentage of the gain which is chargeable is reduced at a greater rate for business assets. In either case, if the asset was owned on 17 March 1998, an extra year of ownership would automatically be deemed to be added for the purposes of calculating the appropriate rate of taper relief. The holding period for business assets to be eligible the holding period tax relief is a maximum of 4 years (for the assets disposed of on or after 6 April 2000). The annual exemption described below will continue to be available.

The net capital gains for a taxpayer are treated as if they were the "top slice" of the taxpayer's income. They are therefore liable to the same rates of tax as income for the period in which the disposal is made. Full details of all profits and losses made on assets or possessions must be entered on the self-assessment form and it may be worth taking professional advice about the planning of sales over several years, so that net taxable gains are minimised and the maximum use is made of allowable losses, reliefs and allowances over a period of time. It is possible in certain circumstances, for example in disposing of business assets, to defer the payment of capital gains by exchanging an asset for another of the same type, eg a property. This is known as "roll over relief". The entire capital gain is then taxed on the later disposal.

BUSINESS ASSETS

Number of complete years after 5/4/98 for which asset held	*% of gain chargeable*	*EQUIVALENT TAX RATES: Higher rate taxp'r %*	*20% rate taxp'r %*
Disposals after 5 April 2002			
0	100	40	20
1	50	20	10
2 or more	25	10	5
Disposals after 5 April 2000 but before 5 April 2002			
0	100	40	20
1	50	35	17.5
2	75	30	15
3	50	20	10
4 or more	25	10	2
Disposals before 6 April 2000			
0	100	40	20
1	92.5	37	18.5
2	85	34	17.0
3	77.5	31	15.5

NON BUSINESS ASSETS

Number of complete years after 5/4/98 for which asset held	*% of gain chargeable*	*EQUIVALENT TAX RATES: Higher rate taxp'r %*	*20% rate taxp'r %*
0	100	40	20
1	100	40	20
2	100	40	20
3	95	38	19
4	90	36	18
5	85	34	17
6	80	32	16
7	75	30	15
8	70	28	14
9	65	26	13
10 or more	60	24	12

Tax free assets

Certain possessions or assets may be sold or transferred without being taxed. Typical examples of these are as follows:

- cars;
- only or main residence, including grounds;
- personal belongings such as jewellery, antiques, furniture, pictures, provided the value of each object at the time of disposal was less than £6,000;
- life insurance policies unless the person making the disposal obtained the interest for consideration;
- national savings certificates, defence bonds, premium bonds, national development bonds, save as you earn deposits;
- certain gilt edged stock and qualifying corporate bonds;
- winnings from gambling including pools and the National Lottery;
- investments in a personal equity plan (PEP) or ISA.

Annual exemption

If, having taken account of any capital losses incurred during the tax year, total capital gains amount to less than £7,700 for an individual, those gains are tax free and a statement that capital gains are below this figure should be made on the tax return.

Transfers of assets between husbands and wives who are not separated do not give rise to a capital gains tax charge. The recipient spouse takes over the asset at the same base value as applied to the donor spouse. This can be used to allow disposals generating gains to £15,000 to be made tax-free by a couple in any year.

Disposal on death

When a person dies, no capital gains tax charge arises. When a person inherits from another, the base value for the beneficiary is generally the value of the asset at the death of the deceased person. Hence, gains which have accrued during the deceased's lifetime are in effect exempt from capital gains tax. This provision, should however be read in conjunction with the later section on Inheritance Tax.

On death, any PETs made within the previous seven years are converted into chargeable transfers (CTs) and are treated as part of the deceased's estate. Where a PET was made more than three years before death, the inheritance tax rate applicable to that transfer on death would be reduced as shown in Table X.

INHERITANCE TAX

Inheritance tax is a tax on transfers of capital by way of gift or legacy which operates primarily on transfers which occur on death. Tax is payable when the total value of the estate, together with chargeable lifetime gifts, exceeds £250,000, for the tax year 2002-2003. Lifetime gifts which fulfil certain conditions are free from inheritance tax provided that the donor survives seven years after making the gift. Such transfers are known as 'potentially exempt transfers' (PETs). The donor must not reserve a benefit out of the gift for him/herself. Most lifetime gifts will qualify as PETs; those which do not *e.g., a transfer into a discretionary trust* are chargeable at half the death rates, i.e. currently at 20%. There is a further 20% IHT payable on the death of the settler of the trust. The rates at which inheritance tax is charged on death are shown in the table below.

Years before death	*% of IHT rate on death*
More than 3 but less than 4	80%
More than 4 but less than 5	60%
More than 5 but less than 6	40%
More than 6 but less than 7	20%

There are a number of reliefs which provide either 100% or 50% exemption for transfers of businesses or unquoted shareholdings subject to certain conditions being met.

Certain transfers are exempt from inheritance tax, including the following:

- transfers between spouses, whether during their lifetimes or on death;
- transfers up to £3,000 in each tax year;
- small gifts of up to £250 per annum to any one person;
- commercial transfers not intended to confer a gratuitous benefit on the other party.

Generally, it is the person transferring who is liable for the payment of inheritance tax on lifetime transfers, although it can be claimed from the recipient if the Inland Revenue cannot claim it from the donor. On death, it is the deceased's personal representatives who are primarily liable for the payment of any tax, although this is limited to assets which they receive or might have received but for their negligence or default in their capacity as personal representatives. If they fail to pay, beneficiaries entitled under the will or intestacy, they are liable but only to the extent of the property which they receive.

POVERTY TRAP OR POVERTY PLATEAU?

The existence of a fiscal welfare system, based on yet another set of criteria, adds to the inconsistencies of the different welfare systems to the point where not only are various means-tested benefits withdrawn as earnings increase but tax may also have to be paid. This situation has been referred to as a 'poverty plateau', since there is a range of earnings relevant to this problem depending on the size of family involved. This can cause those at the lowest level of earning to suffer the highest effective margin rate of tax.

Some attempts have been made by successive governments to avoid the poverty trap. In particular, the recipients of some means-tested benefits for people in employment are no longer obliged to report changes in their situation. As a result, it should in practice be unlikely that there will be a sudden drop in disposable resources and a wage earner may slip in and out of eligibility as s/he becomes due for reassessment for the various benefits or has a wage increase. Family credit and housing benefit are now based on net income, that is the amount people are left with after paying tax and national insurance contributions. However, the 'poverty trap' still affects a significant number of people and it falls especially hard on part time workers.

FURTHER INFORMATION

Clear and detailed leaflets are issued by the Inland Revenue (www.inlandrevenue.gov.uk) on all the major regulations in the tax system. For detailed personal queries, it is advisable to consult the appropriate tax office, preferably by appointment.

For titles of books written on tax law and designed to be accessible to the lay person, please refer to the Further Reading section at the end of this book. Factsheets on income tax, savings and investment, etc, are available from the **Money Management Council**.

TAXATION

HENRY Y SMITH & CO
152-154 Essex Road, London N1 8LY
Tel: 020 7704 2881 ***Fax:*** 020 7704 2436
Docx: 58279 ISLINGTON

CHAPTER EIGHT

Education

Education

CHAPTER EIGHT

Education

INTRODUCTION

The education agenda in the UK is based on giving everyone the chance to achieve their full potential by raising educational standards, reducing the effect of social exclusion and opening up opportunities for lifelong learning:

- every child should get the basics of literacy and numeracy early on, through good teaching in early years education and primary schools;
- all schools will be challenged to improve and must take responsibility for raising standards, using proven best practice, with the right balance of pressure and support from the Government;
- children learn at different speeds and have different abilities;
- the quality of teaching is vital, with pressure matched by support for good teaching and leadership;
- parents and local communities are fully and effectively involved in the education of their children;
- there must be effective partnerships at local level to help schools work together towards the common goal of higher standards;
- standard-raising policies should apply to all children including those with special educational needs and/or with disabilities. The white paper *Excellence in Schools* commits the Government to exacting targets and proposed a challenging programme to achieve them;
- children should be included in mainstream education where this meets parental wishes, is appropriate to their and other children's needs and does not incur unreasonable public expenditure.

The UK further and higher education sectors have seen dramatic expansion, with the number of both younger and mature students more than doubling since 1979. *Higher Education in the Learning Society,* a fundamental review of higher education in the UK, was published in July 1997. It presents many opportunities and challenges which are being taken forward.

In today's world, the education people receive in their youth is no longer enough. With the advance of technology and the growth of global competition, businesses need highly motivated and flexible people with a range of modern skills. Real security of employment lies in people updating their skills and qualifications throughout life and in employers investing in their human resources as much as in their plant or R & D. Lifelong learning is key to personal prosperity, to business success and to national competitiveness.

A package of employment and training programmes has been introduced for various groups of unemployed people to help them move from welfare to work. The New Deal programmes help the young unemployed (age 18–24), long term unemployed people aged 25 plus, the partners of unemployed people, lone parents, and disabled people.

Education provision in England, Wales and Scotland is part of the local government structure. In Northern Ireland, education is a central government responsibility with local authorities having a consultative role through local Education and Library Boards.

The Government helps set the framework for the education and training system and works in partnership with other central and local bodies to implement those policies. It also provides funds for many of the public bodies involved in education and training. The Government aims:

- to support economic growth and improve the nation's competitiveness and quality of life by raising standards of educational achievement and skills;
- to promote an efficient and flexible labour market by enhancing choice, diversity and excellence in education and training, and by encouraging lifelong learning.

Structure

The Department for Education and Skills (DfES) is the Government Department responsible for policy on education and training in England. The Secretary of State for Education and Skills is a Cabinet Minister in Her Majesty's Government. With the help of seven other ministers, he (or she) is responsible to Parliament for developing and administering policies on education and training. The newly formed Department for Work and Pensions is responsible for policies on employment in England.

The Secretaries of State for Wales and Northern Ireland are also Cabinet Ministers who look after the interests of their respective countries in Parliament. However, responsibility for education and training policy has been devolved to the National Assembly for Wales and the Northern Ireland Assembly.

The Department of Education for Northern Ireland has a strategic role in developing and implementing education policies. It is concerned with education from nursery through to further and higher education as well as sport and recreation, youth services, the arts and culture (including libraries) and the development of community relations within and between schools.

The Scottish Executive Education Department is responsible for policy on education in Scotland; training is the responsibility of the Scottish Executive Enterprise and Lifelong Learning Department. The Minister for Education, and the Minister for Enterprise and Lifelong Learning are part of the ministerial team working with the First Minister in the Scottish Parliament, who has overall responsibility for Scottish affairs.

THE LEGISLATIVE FRAMEWORK

The education systems in the UK are governed by a series of Acts of Parliament and Statutory Instruments.

The legislation sets out the rights, obligations and powers of individuals and institutions, controls the spending of public money, and lays down penalties for failure to comply with legal obligations.

Participation in full-time education is compulsory for children from the term after their fifth birthday (fourth birthday in Northern Ireland) to the term after their fifteenth birthday.

A national curriculum has been introduced in schools in England, Wales and Northern Ireland, to give all young people access to a broad and balanced education. Established under the Education Reform Act 1988, this sets out the subjects pupils should study, what they should be taught and the standards they should achieve.

In Scotland, there is no prescribed national curriculum; guidelines on the curriculum provide the framework within which schools work. These guidelines were introduced after consultation and reflect the consensual, pragmatic approach taken towards education in Scotland.

Equality of Opportunity

The Government is committed to equality of opportunity and is determined that its policies, programmes and services allow all those pursuing employment, education and training to develop to their full potential, free from unjustified discrimination.

The Equal Pay Act 1970 introduced equal pay for work of equal value for women and men. The Sex Discrimination Act 1975 makes sex discrimination in education, employment and training generally illegal. The Race Relations Act 1976 covers the same areas and makes it generally illegal to discriminate on grounds of colour, race, nationality or ethnic or national origins

The Disability Discrimination Act 1995 (DDA) protects disabled people against discrimination in employment and in accessing goods, services and facilities, including access to transport. The introduction of the Disability Rights Commission (DRC) in April 2000 remedied one of the major flaws in the DDA. The DRC has specific functions and powers to assist disabled people.

The Special Educational Needs and Disability Act 2001 was passed in May 2001 to protect the rights of disabled people to access education and improve the standard of education for all children with special educational needs. The Act makes it unlawful for schools, Local Education Authorities and those institutions providing Post-16 education to discriminate against disabled pupils and students because of their disability.

Northern Ireland

The Northern Ireland Act 1998 places a duty on all public authorities to promote equality of opportunity and have regard to the desirability to promote good relations between persons of different religious belief, political opinion or racial group. Specifically, authorities must promote equality of opportunity between:

- persons of different religious belief, political opinion, racial group, age, marital status or sexual orientation;
- men and women generally;
- persons with a disability and persons without; and
- persons with dependants and persons without

EARLY, PRIMARY AND SECONDARY EDUCATION

Early (or Nursery) education

Compulsory schooling begins at the age of five, but the vast majority of children begin their education before that age. Early education for three and four year olds is mainly provided by LEAs, through maintained nursery schools, nursery or reception classes in primary schools, but also by the private and community and voluntary sectors, including through independent and pre preparatory schools, pre schools and playgroups. Though parents may pay for their children's early education, all four year olds, and a steadily increasing number of three year olds, are guaranteed a free, part time place if their parents want it. The entitlement will be extended to all three year olds by September 2004.

All providers of early education, whatever their sector, can receive Government funding to provide free places, if it can be shown through OFSTED inspection that curricular goals are being met. Early education places are typically part time and available during the regular school terms. But the distinction between early education and childcare is becoming less significant with the growth of extended or full day, integrated services. An increasing number of settings, including Early Excellence Centres, will now offer education and care from the same site as well as providing other family support, including training, help with parenting skills and health services. Early Years Development and Childcare Partnerships in each LEA area bring together interested parties and responsible for supporting, developing, monitoring and advising on provision locally.

The Pre-school Learning Alliance is the main voluntary organisation concerned with early education and childcare provision and playgroups and can be contacted at 69 King's Cross Road, London WC1X 9LL - Tel: 020 7833 0991.

Primary education

Primary schools may be infant schools for children aged five to seven, junior schools for those aged seven to 11 or combined infant and junior schools for the whole range from five to 11. Many primary schools admit children during their fifth year, although this is not compulsory. The dividing line between primary and secondary education is not a fixed age and lies between ten and 12 years so as to allow transfer to be made at the beginning of the school year. Many infant schools contain nursery classes for children under the age of five, but attendance at school is not compulsory until the term after that in which a child reaches the age of five; in practice, many schools admit children to reception classes in primary schools before they reach compulsory school age.

Secondary education

At about the age of 11, most children pass on to a secondary school. County or voluntary schools, however, may provide for age ranges which avoid the necessity for a transfer from primary to secondary school at the age of 11 plus. Some authorities have therefore established 'middle schools', providing for children between the ages of eight and 12 or nine and 13. Before they can introduce such a change, they must publish proposals in accordance with the requirements of the Education Act 1980 and, where necessary, obtain approval from the Secretary of State for Education. Most LEAs have moved towards a form of comprehensive secondary education, although the Education Act 1979 removed the compulsion on LEAs to submit plans for reorganising secondary schools along comprehensive lines.

The Education Act 1980 gave parents the right to express a preference for the school they would like their child or children to attend. In general, admission authorities - that is the governing bodies of grant maintained and voluntary aided schools and the LEA for county schools - must comply with that preference if places are available. The only exceptions are for church schools and selective schools which may keep places open in order to preserve their distinctive character. Under the provisions of the Education Reform Act 1988, schools must admit up to their standard number, or their published admissions limit, if this is higher. The standard number is an indicator of the school's physical capacity. Parents also have a right of appeal against non-admission to an independent appeal committee. The decision of the appeal committee is binding on the admission authority concerned.

It is obligatory for LEAs and schools to publish information to help parents make their choice, including such matters as the way a school is organised, the policy on discipline and the most recent external examination results. Information on LEAs' general policy and admissions is available, for reference, at LEA offices, public libraries and schools and is sent free of charge to parents of children moving from one stage of education to the next: for example, from primary schools to middle or secondary schools. Information about individual schools is available free on request from the school itself. Information on the achievements of all secondary schools and FE sector colleges in England is provided in the School and College Performance Tables, published yearly by the DfES. Tables for each LEA area are available free of charge from the DfES.

The compulsory school-leaving age has been 16 since 1972. In practice, a child who reaches the age of 16 during the months of September to January inclusive must stay at school until the end of the spring term and a child whose sixteenth birthday falls during the months of February to August inclusive may leave school on the Friday before the last Monday in May of the same year. However, the government's policy is to encourage more young people to continue in full-time education after 16.

Early Education Curriculum

The Foundation Stage was introduced by the Government in September 2000. For the first time, this period of children's development has been explicitly recognized as a distinct curriculum phase with its own identity and language. It covers the ages of three to the end of the Reception Year, when children will be aged five to rising six, and is complemented by a set of Early Learning Goals formulated by the Qualifications and Curriculum Authority (QCA) and the early years community. The Goals set out what the majority of children should achieve by the end of their Reception Year which immediately precedes Key Stage 1 and 2. They aim to make learning a fun and challenging experience with an explicit recognition of the value of play. They will enable children to develop key skills such as speaking, listening, concentration, persistence, learning to work with others and early literacy and numeracy.

NATIONAL CURRICULUM

The School Curriculum

All state schools must ensure that the school curriculum is broad and balanced, and promotes the spiritual, moral, physical and mental development of pupils.

England

All state schools in England must teach the National Curriculum. This sets out the subjects pupils should study, what they should be taught and the standards they should achieve. Through the National Curriculum pupils cover a broad range of subjects that helps them to develop the qualities and skills needed in adult and working life as citizens in a democracy.

The period of compulsory education is divided into four key stages, depending on pupil age:

Key Stages	**1**	**2**	**3**	**4**
Ages	5-7	7-11	11-14	14-16
English	•	•	•	•
Mathematics	•	•	•	•
Science	•	•	•	•
Physical science	•	•	•	•
Design & technology	•	•	•	•
Information & communication tech	•	•	•	•
Modern foreign language			•	•
History	•	•	•	
Geography	•	•	•	
Music	•	•	•	
Art and design	•	•	•	
Citizenship (from September 2002)				•

Source: Department for Education and Skills

The smaller range of subjects at Key Stage 4 gives pupils flexibility to study vocational options if they wish. In addition, schools have the flexibility to let pupils drop one or two subjects out of science, design and technology or a modern foreign language, if a programme of structured work-related learning is put in its place. For each subject, at each key stage, programmes of study set out what pupils should be taught with attainment targets and level descriptions setting out the expected standards of pupils' performance.

Wales

All state schools must incorporate the National Curriculum for Wales into their school curriculum. This consists of the same subjects as in England at Key Stages 1, 2 and 3, but includes the teaching of Welsh. At Key Stage 4, Welsh, English, mathematics, science and physical education are the only compulsory subjects.

Northern Ireland

Here the curriculum is made up of religious education and six broad areas of study: English, mathematics, science and technology, the environment and society, creative and expressive studies and, in Irish-medium and secondary schools only, language studies. It also includes six cross-curricular themes that are woven into the curriculum: education for mutual understanding, cultural heritage, health education, information technology and, at secondary level only, economic awareness and careers education.

Scotland

In Scotland the curriculum in state schools is not prescribed by law. Instead, the First Minister issues national advice and guidance to schools and Scottish Local Authorities. Under the 5–14 Development Programme pupils aged between five and 14 study a broad and balanced curriculum based on national guidelines which set out the aims of study, the ground to be covered, and the way that pupils' learning should be assessed and reported.

The programme aims to achieve breadth, balance, coherence, continuity and progression for all pupils. Pupils aged between 14 and 16 in Scotland generally study for Standard Grade examinations and may also take National Certificates in vocational subjects.

TYPES OF SCHOOL

The duties imposed jointly on parents, LEAs and the Funding Agency for Schools (FAS) by the Education Act 1993, to ensure that children receive primary and secondary education according to their ages, abilities and aptitudes, may be met in one of the following schools.

County schools

are primary or secondary schools, other than nursery and special schools, wholly provided and maintained by an LEA. Primary schools may be infant or junior, or include both; secondary schools may be comprehensive, modern or grammar. Some LEAs maintain middle schools which provide for pupils of both primary and secondary ages.

Voluntary schools

are usually denominational and fall into one of three categories:

- controlled schools, whose premises remain the property of the voluntary body but with the LEA meeting all the costs of maintenance. Denominational religious education may be given for two periods a week where parents so request.

- aided schools, where the governors of the school are responsible for repair to and maintenance of the exterior of the school building and for improvements, enlargements or alterations. The LEA bears the cost of internal repairs and maintenance, pays the teachers and meets the cost of generally running the school; up to 85% of the expenditure incurred by the governors may be reimbursed by the appropriate Secretary of State. Religious education is under the control of the governors.

- special agreement schools, voluntary schools for which a special agreement including special provisions as to grants has been made with the LEA. Religious education is under the control of the governors.

Grant-maintained schools

are county or voluntary schools which have voted to become grant-maintained by grant from the Secretary of State, not the authority. Funding is provided through the FAS. The schools are run by their governing body and provide free education just like LEA maintained schools.

City Technology Colleges (CTCs) and City Colleges for the Technology of the Arts (CCTAs)

A network of some 15 CTCs/CCTAs has been established. They are independent schools offering a free education to pupils of all abilities aged from 11 to 18. The subjects of the national curriculum are taught and national arrangements for assessment and testing apply. In addition to this broad curriculum, an extra emphasis is given to science and technology in the case of CTCs and to the application of technology to the creative and performing arts in the case of CCTAs. Industrial and commercial sponsors have contributed significantly to the capital costs of the colleges; they continue to be involved with the running of the colleges on a day-to-day basis through their representation on governing bodies. The government has committed itself to expanding the CTC programme by making the legislative changes necessary to allow other schools to take on the characteristics of CTCs.

City Academies

City Academies are publicly funded independent schools. They replace schools in challenging circumstances or are set up as part of a wider school reorganisation or where there is an unmet demand for school places. The Academies are owned and run by sponsors, who provide significant capital funds to the school, with the Government providing the balance of capital costs and recurrent funding. They provide free education to secondary age pupils of all abilities, including provision for children with special educational needs. City Academies have state of the art facilities and offer a broad and balanced curriculum, with specialisms in areas such as business, science, technology, modern foreign languages, arts or sport. Plans to open 13 City Academies in major urban areas have been announced to date. The Government is committed to expanding the programme and to allow Academies to be established in rural areas and which cater for pupils aged 5-18 years.

Specialist Schools Programme

There are currently four types of specialist school – Arts, Language, Sports and Technology Colleges. The opportunity to apply for specialist school designation is available to all maintained secondary schools in England. The Green Paper published on 12 February 2001 set out the Governments plans to increase the number of specialist schools to 1,000 by 2003 and 1,500 by 2006 and proposed to extend the range of specialisms to include: engineering, science and business and enterprise. The specialist schools programme helps schools, in partnership with private sector sponsors and supported by additional Government funding, to develop particular strengths, establish distinctive identities through their chosen specialisms, and achieve their targets to raise standards. In addition these schools are expected to share facilities and good practice with other schools and their local communities.

An important feature of specialist schools is the close involvement of one or more sponsors in the life of the school. Raising money is only one part of this. All schools wishing to apply must first raise £50,000 in sponsorship from business, charitable or other private sector sponsors to support a capital project to help the school deliver its development plan. This sponsorship, together with a Government grant of £100,000, funds a capital project to enhance the school's facilities for teaching its specialist subject. Designated schools also receive an annual grant based on pupil numbers (typically £130,000) for a period of four years. Applications are judged against the published criteria and only those schools which best meet the criteria are designated.

Non-maintained special schools

are non-profit-making schools which cater for pupils with special educational needs. They are not provided or maintained by an LEA, but any authority may make a grant or payments for educational facilities provided.

Independent schools

are outside the state system. They range from the large public schools to local ones catering for a few children. Fees are charged at nearly all these schools, but many of the larger ones have private endowments and scholarship funds. All independent schools have to register with the DfES or the Welsh Office (National Assembly for Wales), and are subject to inspection arrangements which obtain evidence about whether satisfactory standards of premises, accommodation, staffing and instruction are met. Independent boarding schools must also safeguard and promote the welfare of their pupils. Where the school does not maintain these standards enforcement action is taken.

Music & Ballet Scheme

Central Government support for children of outstanding potential who wish to train for a career in dance or music is concentrated on the awards to Aided Pupils under the Music & Ballet Scheme (MBS). At the present time, the Scheme is limited to three independent specialist ballet schools - the Royal Ballet School, London, the Arts Educational School, Tring and Elmhurst Ballet School, Surrey, and four independent specialist music schools - Chethams School of Music, Manchester, The Yehudi Menuhin School, Surrey, The Purcell School, Bushey and Wells Cathedral School, Somerset. MBS schools have been selected to participate in the scheme because they are both pre-eminent in their specialist field - providing the best available specialist training - and offer high standards of teaching and learning across a broad curriculum, including a good range of A-levels. Parents contribute on a sliding scale linked to their gross income. The scheme makes up the difference between the parental contribution and the schools aided pupil fee. This ensures that parents pay the same regardless of the MBS school their child attends. Ministers are committed to maintaining the MBS, which receives all-Party support

Sixth form and further education colleges

Provision for the 16 to 19 age group is made in sixth form colleges and tertiary colleges. These colleges normally provide both academic and vocational courses. Sixth form and further education colleges receive their principal funding from the Further Education Funding Council (FEFC).

SCHOOL GOVERNMENT

The Education (No 2) Act 1986 specifies that the composition of school governing bodies shall be according to the size and type of school. County, controlled and maintained special schools must have equal numbers of elected parent governors and LEA-appointed governors, one or two elected teacher governors plus the head unless s/he chooses not to be a governor and governors from the local community who are co-opted by the elected and appointed governors. The Act provides for foundation governors at voluntary controlled schools, and representative governors in certain primary schools and special schools, to take the place of one or more co-opted governors. At voluntary aided and special agreement schools, there must be at least one elected parent governor; there do not have to be any co-opted governors; and the foundation governors must outnumber the other members of the governing body. The Act establishes a framework of responsibilities for the governing body, the LEA and the head teacher in relation to the main matters concerned with the running of a school.

Fair Funding

The School Standards and Framework Act (1998) established a new framework of community, voluntary and foundation schools. Since 1999, **Fair Funding** has complemented the new framework by establishing a single, unified, system of funding which builds on Local Management of Schools (LMS) by allowing schools to develop further their capacity for self-government by increased delegation of responsibility through funding. As previously under LMS, the key aspects of Fair Funding is the formula funding of schools and the delegation of financial responsibility to governing bodies. Formula funding is designed to bring about an equitable allocation of resources between schools, based on objectively-measured needs rather than historical spending patterns. Within each LEA, therefore, schools with the same characteristics and the same number of pupils receive the same level of financial resources under the LEA's formula. "Delegation" concerns the proportion of the Local Education Authority's total expenditure on schools, which is allocated to the schools in the form of budget shares through the Authority's formula, as distinct from being retained and managed centrally by the LEA. Special schools continue to be funded on the basis of place-led rather than pupil-led funding. In most cases, the LEA funds pupil referral units centrally; nursery schools are funded separately under arrangements outside of the Local Schools Budget (LSB).

To ensure that more resources are delegated to schools, the Government has set LEAs delegation targets. In 2001-02, LEAs are expected to delegate 85% of the Local Schools Budget (LSB) to schools. In 2002-03, the target is 87%, with the aim of achieving a national average of 90% by 2003-04.

SPECIAL EDUCATION

Part IV of the Education Act 1996, which incorporates the provisions originally contained in Part III of the Education Act 1993, updates the law for the education of children with special needs. The 1996 Act carries forward the main provisions of the Education Act 1981 but clarifies the responsibilities of schools and LEAs in the light of recent changes in the broader education field.

Special Educational Needs (SEN) and Disability Act 2001

The Special Educational Needs (SEN) and Disability Act 2001 builds on the existing SEN framework in the Education Act 1996 as well as giving new rights to disabled pupils, students and adult learners. For children with SEN in England and Wales, the Act strengthens their right to attend a mainstream school, if that is what their parents want and it is compatible with the education of other children. From September 2001, Local Education Authorities (LEAs) will also be required to make arrangements for the provision of information to parents of children with SEN and to make arrangements for resolving disagreements between parents and the LEA and/or schools. The Act also refines the workings of the SEN Tribunal and the Code of Practice to better support parents and children.

The disability provisions in the Act will make it unlawful for education providers in England, Scotland and Wales to discriminate against disabled pupils, students and adult learners in the provision of education because of their disability. Reasonable adjustments will have to be made for them so that they are not substantially disadvantaged compared to pupils, students and adult learners who are not disabled. LEAs and schools in England and Wales will also have to plan, over time, to increase accessibility to schools for disabled pupils. This will involve planning to increase access to school buildings, planning to increase access to schools' curriculums and planning to improve the delivery of written information in an accessible way to disabled pupils. The majority of the disability provisions will come into force in September 2002.

The Disability Rights Commission will produce two Codes of Practice - one for schools and one for Post-16 - to explain and illustrate the legislation to help those affected by it understand their rights and responsibilities.

Inclusion

The Special Educational Needs and Disability Act 2001 strengthens the right to a mainstream place for children who have a statement of SEN. Part 1 of the Act replaces the existing section 316 of the Education Act 1996 with two new sections (sections 316 and 316A). These transform the statutory framework for inclusion into a positive endorsement of inclusion that will enable more pupils who have additional needs or disabilities to be included successfully within mainstream schools and settings.

In the future children who have statements can only be refused a mainstream place, against their parents' wishes, where local education authorities and maintained schools can demonstrate that there are no reasonable steps they could take to prevent the child's inclusion being incompatible with the efficient education of other children. The SEN and Disability Act requires the Government to produce guidance on the practical operation of the new inclusion framework.

The Act defines educational needs as covering all learning difficulties except those arising solely because of a difference of language between a child's home and his school. Under the Act, governing bodies of all maintained schools are under a duty to use their best endeavours to secure that appropriate provision is made to meet a child's special educational needs. LEAs in turn have a duty to identify those children in their area whose special needs cannot be met within the facilities and resources normally available to mainstream schools in the area, and to conduct a multi-professional assessment of the child, taking medical, educational, psychological and other relevant factors into account.

If, following assessment, a child's special educational needs are such that the authority consider that they themselves should determine the special educational provision to meet these needs, then they are required to make a statement of special educational needs for that child. Should the authority and parents fail to reach agreement about the proposed educational provision to meet the child's needs, the parents have the right to appeal to an independent Special Educational Needs Tribunal.

As required by the Act, the Secretary of State for Education has published a Code of Practice on the Identification and Assessment of Special Educational Needs giving guidance on how these duties should be carried out. All maintained schools and LEAs are required to have regard to the Code. It recommends a staged approach which matches provision to need, emphasising the importance of early identification of special needs and, at each stage, a close working partnership with parents.

Special Education for children with learning difficulties is provided in a variety of ways: in ordinary schools, special schools, units attached to ordinary schools or in hospitals. Special schools and their classes are more generously staffed than ordinary schools and provide, where possible, physiotherapy, speech therapy and other such services as are required. The government's policy, embodied in the Education Act 1996, is that where it is appropriate, practicable and consistent with the wishes of their parents, children with special educational needs should be educated in ordinary schools. The Act gives parents of children with statements for the first time the right to express a preference for the school - ordinary or special - which they would like their child to attend. Subject to conditions of suitability and efficient use of resources, the authority is obliged to comply with that preference.

Under the Education Act 1996, the LEA has a duty to provide for children with statements of special educational need who are over the age of two. As long as pupils remain registered at a school the authority may maintain their statements up to the age of nineteen. Many colleges are seeking to reduce the difficulties for students with special educational needs in obtaining further and higher educational and numbers of such students have increased.

Section 1

Funding is available for projects concerned with minority ethnic groups in the community and in the education system for instance, bilingual children, refugees etc. There is a budget of £30 million reduced from £100 million for the UK.

LEA USE OF BOARDING EDUCATION

Local authorities are under a duty to consider the expediency of providing boarding education, either in boarding schools or otherwise, for pupils for whom education as boarders is considered by their parents and by the authorities to be desirable. Local Education Authorities have a discretionary power to assist parents with the costs of boarding fees if they consider there is a boarding need. It is for individual authorities to decide whether to exercise this power and to decide the criteria against which applications for assistance will be considered.
The kinds of circumstances which might lead to a decision to send a child to boarding school may be as follows:

- where the child is an orphan;
- where the family circumstances are such that it is impractical for the child to be looked after at home and attend a day school;
- where the parents are temporarily living abroad;
- where the child requires placement on educational and social grounds;
- where the child has a disability.

SOCIAL WORK IN THE EDUCATION SERVICE

The education service is concerned with broad areas of the health and welfare of pupils attending school. Within the primary and secondary education system, provision should be made for ensuring that services are available to meet the health and welfare needs of all schoolchildren and their families. Education social work is currently the responsibility of the education welfare service, which in most local authorities is part of the LEA.

Education Welfare Officers (EWOs)

The primary function of EWOs, in some areas known as Education Social Workers, is to enforce the statutory responsibilities of LEAs with regard to school attendance, but they also perform important functions in the area of child protection and child employment. They establish contact with schools and families to identify and assist children in social distress and to help foster close relationships between all parents and their children's schools. To this end, the education welfare service usually works closely with other statutory and voluntary bodies.

Children with problems

EWOs are increasingly working with children over a wide range of social and emotional problems which can include disability, behavioural difficulty and pregnancy. They are involved in the assessment of children for special education, in preparing reports on home circumstances for other agencies such as child guidance clinics and social services departments and in helping parents cope with difficult and disturbed children.

Non-attendance

When a child is absent from school, the parent is normally required to give a reason. The legally acceptable reasons for absence include:

- sickness or unavoidable emergency;
- a day of religious observance for the child and his or her family;
- participation in an entertainment;
- a family holiday with leave granted by the school. Schools have discretion to agree such requests but leave of absence must not normally exceed 10 school days in any one school year.

Where a child is persistently absent from school without good reason, the EWO and the school should liaise closely to resolve any problems in the family. They can, however, use legal action as a last resort after warnings and a full investigation of the case. If it appears to an LEA that a parent is failing in his or her duty to ensure that a child receives appropriate education, then the authority has to serve a notice on the parent requiring him or her to satisfy the authority, within a period of not less than 14 days, that the child concerned is being properly educated. If the parent fails to satisfy this requirement, and if the authority considers it expedient that the child should attend school, then it must serve on the parent a school attendance order. The parent must be given a fortnight's notice of the intention to serve the order. If the parent fails to comply with the attendance order, or otherwise fails to secure the education of a child of compulsory school age by regular attendance at school or otherwise, then s/he is guilty of an offence under the Education Act 1993. Proceedings under this legislation can only be instituted by an LEA.

Pastoral care

Schools in England and Wales should be concerned with their pupils' general well-being. In recent years, new approaches to pastoral care have been tried in many schools. For example, in larger schools it is now usual for each pupil to receive advice on personal matters, as well as educational matters, from a nominated member of staff, usually a teacher. Sometimes a school counsellor is appointed specifically to undertake responsibility for pastoral care.

SCHOOL RECORDS

The Education (School Records) Regulations 1989 require schools to disclose to parents of pupils aged under 18 and to pupils aged 16 or over, upon written request, material held on pupils' records, with the exception of certain specified categories of information. Inspection is free of charge but a charge not exceeding the cost of supply may be made for copies of material. The regulations cover manual records only: personal data held on computer is subject to the provisions of the Data Protection Act 1984. The regulations also require schools to provide an opportunity for the correction of inaccurate records and to make arrangements for appeals against refusals to disclose, transfer, copy or correct the educational record. Access to statements of special educational needs is governed by the Education (Special Educational Needs) Regulations 1983, as subsequently amended.

Information exempted from the disclosure requirement includes:

- material placed on the record before 1 September 1989;
- material supplied by persons other than employees of the LEA, teachers and education welfare officers;
- material whose disclosure might cause serious harm to the pupil or someone else;
- material concerning actual or suspected child abuse;
- material concerning other pupils;
- references supplied to employers or bodies such as UCCAS;
- reports by schools to juvenile courts.

Schools and colleges will not be able to require the disclosure of ethnically-based data. Schools and colleges considering pupils for admission will not be able to require disclosure of their individual assessment results.

EMPLOYMENT OF CHILDREN

The employment of children below the age of 13 is prohibited under the Children Act 1972. Under the Children and Young Persons Act 1933, children who are of an age to be employed may not, generally, be employed for more than two hours on school days or Sundays; or before 7 am or after 7 pm or until after school hours on school days; nor may they be employed to lift, carry or move anything heavy enough to be likely to cause them injury. Under the Education Act 1944 (Section 59), LEAs may prohibit an employer from employing a child or impose restrictions on him or her if it appears that the health or education of the child is suffering. LEAs are empowered to make bye-laws to give greater protection to children in their areas and they are responsible (usually through education welfare services) for enforcing the law concerning children in employment.

Children in entertainment
Children under school leaving age cannot be employed as entertainers unless a licence is obtained from the LEA. This also includes children performing in film, radio or television advertisements.

EDUCATION WELFARE BENEFITS
There are a number of ways in which parents can obtain financial and other material help for their children at school. These include the following:

School meals and milk
Section 512 of The Education Act 1996, amended by The School Standards and Framework Act 1998 and The Immigration and Asylum Act 1999, allow Local Education Authorities (LEAs) to provide pupils with meals milk and other refreshment. LEAs have a duty to provide a lunch, free of charge, to those children whose parents are in receipt of income support, income based jobseekers allowance, children in receipt of these benefits in their own right and in certain circumstances, children of asylum seekers. All other meals must be charged for at the same price for the same quantity of the same item of food.

Legislation introduced in April 2001 sets minimum nutritional standards for school lunches and also places a duty on LEAs to provide a paid meal when requested to do so. LEAs are responsible for ensuring that the standards are met. LEAs must also provide facilities they consider appropriate for the consumption of meals or other refreshment brought into the school by registered pupils. Governors at schools with delegated budgets for school lunches are under similar duties to those of LEAs as described above - Statutory Instrument no 2164.

Clothing and uniform
The Education (Miscellaneous Provisions) Act 1948 (Section 5) allows clothing and footwear to be provided where a child is unable to take full advantage of his or her education because of the inadequacy or unsuitability of his or her clothing and footwear. A grant may be given under the Education Act 1944 (Section 81) towards the cost of providing distinctive school uniform. In practice, cash limits mean that few LEAs can offer much help.

School transport
Children who attend their nearest suitable school, and whose journey there necessarily exceeds the statutory walking distances, will be provided with free transport for the journey between home and school. LEAs may also help other pupils by paying all or part of the pupil's travelling expenses. Under the Public Passenger Vehicles Act 1981, a school bus may carry, as fare-paying passengers, both pupils who do not qualify for free transport and members of the public.

Maintenance and other grants
For children who remain at school over the compulsory school leaving age, discretionary maintenance allowances may be paid where family income is low. The amount of grant depends on the family income from whatever source. Children of low income families may also receive help with the cost of school journeys and visits, but such assistance is entirely discretionary. Local EWOs can give advice and help in obtaining the above benefits.

HEALTH CARE IN THE EDUCATION SERVICE
School Health Service
It is the duty of the Secretary of State for Health, under Section 5 of the National Health Service Act 1977, to provide for the medical and dental inspection at appropriate intervals of pupils in attendance at schools maintained by local education authorities, and for the medical and dental treatment of such pupils.

Schedule 1 to the Act provides that the Secretary of State may, by arrangement with the proprietor of any educational establishment which is not maintained by a local education authority, make any such provision in respect of junior or senior pupils in attendance at the establishment. Such an arrangement may provide for payments by the proprietor in question.

Child guidance service
Child guidance clinics are normally the joint responsibility of the LEA and the local health authority. The clinics are staffed by a team which usually includes psychiatrists, educational psychologists and psychiatric social workers. Children may be referred to the clinics through various agencies, e.g., the school, the GP or the social services department, when they show signs of difficulties, particularly in their personal relationships. The team of specialists makes a

study of the child and the family, including their history and the child's school record. Recommendations for treatment may include therapeutic work with the child and his or her family at the clinic, or placement in a residential setting, e.g., boarding school or hostel. Although most children receiving help from child guidance clinics are of school age, the service can help children under five. Many clinics are now paying special attention to work with this group of young children as a preventive measure.

Health education

Section 241 of the Education Act 1993 requires all maintained secondary schools to provide sex education in addition to the requirements of national curriculum science. Sex education must include teaching about HIV/AIDS and other sexually transmitted diseases. Governing bodies are required to keep an up-to-date written statement of the content and organisation of the sex education. The statement must be available to all parents. The governing bodies of maintained primary schools should consider whether or at what stage they will offer sex education and keep a written statement of the policy they choose to adopt. The policy must be available to all parents. Parents have the right to withdraw their children from sex education other than those elements required by national curriculum science. These new arrangements for sex education came into force in September 1994 The DfEE published Sex and Relationship Education Guidance in July 2000. This replaced Circular 5/94. The guidance takes account of the revised National Curriculum, published in September 1999, the need for guidance arising out of the new Personal, Social and Health Education framework and the Social Exclusion Unit's report on teenage pregnancy.

The Learning and Skills Act 2000 amended certain sections of the Education Act 1996. It particularly strengthens section 403 (the manner of provision of SRE) of the 1996 Act. Pupils must now learn about the nature of marriage and its importance for family life and the bringing up of children and should be protected from teaching and materials which are inappropriate with regard to their age and religious and cultural background.

Personal, Social and Health Education (PSHE)

Section 351 of the Education Act 1996 requires that the school curriculum should promote the spiritual, moral, cultural, mental and physical development of pupils and of society; and that pupils should be prepared for the opportunities, responsibilities and experiences of adult life. Schools meet this requirement through the PSHE framework. Introduced in September 2000, following a review of the National Curriculum in 1999, the framework sets out through all the four key stages a structured programme of learning opportunities through which pupils can be taught the knowledge, skills and understanding to take responsibility for themselves, show respect for others and to develop the self-awareness and confidence needed for life. The framework covers a wide range of learning opportunities ranging from the basic emergency aid procedures, becoming competent in managing personal money through to managing risk and making safer choices about healthy lifestyles, including drug misuse.

Certain aspects of drug education are a statutory requirement as part of the national curriculum science order at all key stages. This includes education about tobacco, alcohol, solvents and other drugs. The DfES issued Circular 4/95 in May 1995 to all schools, offering guidance on delivery of drug education and in dealing with drug-related incidents on school premises.

Physical education

Local authorities are required by the Education Act 1944 to ensure that their facilities for primary, secondary and further education include provision for recreation and social and physical training. In addition, the LEA may establish or support camps, holiday classes, etc, and organise games and expeditions for the pupils in its area. The LEA can, in certain circumstances, provide free clothing suitable for the physical training provided in its schools.

CAREERS SERVICE

In 1994, the statutory duty of securing the provision of careers guidance was transferred from LEAs to the Secretary of State for Employment. Free independent and impartial advice is available to young people attending school or college full time, or college on part-time vocational courses, and to people under 21 who left education, or full-time training, up to two years earlier.

Careers advisers liaise with schools and colleges to provide a range of information and guidance which is well informed, independent and impartial. They work with teachers and college staff to offer guidance on the full range of options available in vocational training, employment and further and higher education. The services offered are provided in ways which ensure that they are equally accessible to all clients, regardless of background, gender, religion, stage of development, ability or disability and sexual orientation. Careers services need to be pro-active in providing particular help to people who are disadvantaged in securing access to the full range of careers opportunities available.

The **Connexions Service** will take over from the careers service to comply with the Secretary of State's duty to provide careers information, education and guidance to young people.

Connexions Service

The Government's Connexions Service brings together a wide range of existing agencies in the public, private and voluntary sectors to provide an integrated and modernised advice, support and personal development service to all 13-19 year olds. The Service is being introduced across England with 12 local Connexions Partnerships now in operation, followed by four more Partnerships in September 2001, and the remaining 31 intended for 2002.

The Connexions Service Partnerships will draw together community and voluntary organisations, young person's advisers for 16 and 17 year olds in and leaving care (under the Children (Leaving Care) Act 2000), existing careers services, local authorities (social services, youth service), schools, youth offending teams, and further education colleges' student support staff. Other bodies will also be involved such as community drugs teams and local drug projects; Jobcentre Plus; health services (including mental health, drugs treatment and advice, contraceptive and sexual health services); housing services and specialist housing providers; informal youth, community, arts and sports activities; and specialist voluntary sector organisations.

FURTHER AND HIGHER EDUCATION

The Further and Higher Education Act 1992 provides that the Further Education Funding Council (FEFC) for England and Wales have a duty to secure the provision of sufficient facilities for the full-time education of 16 to 18 year olds, for certain types of part-time education for those over 16 and full-time education for those over 18. This is done mainly through courses offered at further education colleges in the FE sector, but courses are also provided at other institutions. Local education authorities are responsible for securing the provision of the type of further education for adults which does not fall within the remit of the FEFCs, generally the less formal leisure and recreational courses. The main providers of higher education that is, education of a standard above A level or its equivalent are universities and other HE institutions, which receive public funds from the Higher Education Funding Councils (HEFCs). Courses may be full-time, sandwich or part-time, day or evening. Information about courses in further and higher education and their entry requirements may be obtained throughout the year from the Educational Counselling and Credit Transfer Information Service (ECCTIS). Information about this service can be obtained from ECCTIS 2000 Ltd, Fulton House, Jessop Avenue, Cheltenham, Gloucestershire Tel: 01242 518724.

Centres of Vocational Excellence in Further Education

This initiative will address these key operational objectives:

- To ensure half of all general education colleges in England have at least one Centre of Vocational Excellence by 2004-05.
- To develop and strengthen innovative approaches to meeting the nation's current and future skills needs.
- To enhance the standing of colleges with employers.
- To encourage collaboration amongst providers and promote the concept of provider excellence in economically relevant vocational specialisms.

Context

The pace of economic change and the need for skilled people is increasing. In his statement, 'Colleges for Excellence and Innovation' (November 2000), the former Secretary of State for Education and Employment set out his vision to modernise the Further Education sector in England to enable it to play a key role in addressing the nation's skills gap. This will be achieved by creating a network of quality, specialist provision tightly focused on the skills needs of business and industry across a range of occupations, both new and traditional.

The Learning and Skills Council (LSC) will be responsible for implementing the policy. The consultation period has ended and responses on key issues will be set out in a Prospectus to be issued in July. At the same time, a small number of Pathfinder Centres (10 to 15) will be announced by the LSC. These colleges will be able to demonstrate excellent vocational provision. The LSC will publish more detail planning guidance in September setting out how all Further Education colleges can bid for support to develop Centres. Applications will be due back for assessment in January, and will start to come on stream from April 2002 onwards.

Further Education for Adults

The Learning and Skills Council is a radical, new organisation established to plan and fund all post-16 learning up to Higher Education level in England. It became fully operational on 2 April 2001. It will provide a real focus on skills and employment needs, and has a statutory duty to encourage participation in learning.

Key objectives include encouraging more young people to stay on in learning until at least age 19, and achieve a level 2 qualification; increasing demand for learning amongst adults; promoting equality of opportunity; and raising the skill levels of the workforce as a whole, including tackling basic skill needs. It will also drive up standards, and ensure excellence in teaching and training. Specifically, the LSC is responsible for funding and advocacy of provision through:

- further education sector colleges
- school sixth forms (from April 2002)
- work-based training for young people
- workforce development
- adult and community learning
- information, advice and guidance for adults
- education business links

The LSC has a budget of £5.5 billion in 2001/2 and each local Learning and Skills Council will be responsible for an average budget in excess of £100 million, to fund the learning provision of 100,000 learners. Local Learning and Skills Councils can be contacted via the LSC Helpline on 0870 900 6800.

Adult literacy

In recent years, statutory and voluntary organisations have co-operated in an intensive programme aimed at helping adults who have serious difficulties in reading and writing. There are very few adults in the UK who are completely illiterate, but there is a substantial number unable to cope with the demands of everyday life. They cannot, for example, fill in forms, check pay slips or give the correct change. Responsibility for the provision of basic skills courses for adults rests with the FEFCs. The Councils work largely through the FE colleges, but courses put on by other providers, including LEAs and voluntary bodies, can also be funded by the FEFC via a 'sponsoring college' in the FE sector.

The Basic Skills Agency *formerly ALBSU* acts as the central focus in England and Wales for programmes in adult literacy, numeracy and related basic skills. It provides a range of consultancy and advisory services, funds development projects, including research, publishes materials for teachers and students and organises and sponsors staff training. Central government initiatives to tackle the adult literacy problem include support for a new Family Literacy Initiative. Research has shown that children whose parents have literacy difficulties and no school qualifications are likely to have poor literacy skills themselves. Family literacy programmes seek to raise both children's and parents' attainments by educating them in tandem, both separately and together. The initiative involves various elements: intensive pilot programmes, grants to establish family literacy work through local partnerships and technical support through publications, training and promotion.

Further information or help with basic skills is available from LEAs, FE colleges and libraries, or from the **Basic Skills Agency's** national referral service *freephone* Tel: 0800 700987. Further information about its work can be obtained from 7th Floor, Commonwealth House, 1-19 New Oxford Street, London WC1A 1NU Tel: 020 7405 4017.

Financial Support for Students in Higher Education

The Government changed the student support arrangements for students starting in higher education in the 1998/99 academic year or later. Support for students ordinarily resident in England and Wales is now in the form of a grant for tuition fees and a loan for living costs. There are also supplementary grants for living costs for students in particular circumstances.

To be eligible for student support under the new arrangements, students must be undertaking a designated course. As a general rule courses are designated if

- they are full-time or sandwich courses or certain part-time initial teacher training courses; and

- they are of at least one academic year's duration; and
- they take place in a UK university, another publicly funded college or a specified private college; and they lead to
    - a first degree (e.g. BA, BSc or BEd); or
    - a Diploma of Higher Education; or
    - a higher national diploma of higher national certificate; or
    - a postgraduate certificate of education; or
    - a course for the further training of teachers or youth and community workers; or certain courses which provide education higher than that of "A" levels or their equivalent.
- they are settled in the United Kingdom within the meaning of the Immigration Act 1971, and they are ordinarily resident in England and Wales on the first day of the first academic year of the course and they were ordinarily resident in the United Kingdom and Islands for three years before the start of the course or would have been so resident if the student or either parent had not been temporarily employed outside the United Kingdom and Islands, or if is an EEA migrant worker or the spouse or child of an EEA migrant worker, who satisfies certain conditions in the regulations with special arrangements for those recognised as refugees; and
- they are not eligible to receive a non-income assessed bursary while undertaking a diploma course in nursing or midwifery; and
- they are not in default on repayment of a previous student loan.

The grant for tuition fees, about 25% of the student loan and some supplementary grants for living costs can be reduced by factors such as the student's income; a parental contribution, the amount of which is based on the parents' income and certain outgoings; or a contribution from the student's spouse, also fixed at a level that takes account of income.

Students from EU countries are eligible for the grant for tuition fees provided they satisfy eligibility conditions similar to those which have to be met by students ordinarily resident in England and Wales who qualify for the grant.

Students should apply to the appropriate LEA. This will usually be the LEA in whose area the student has been ordinarily resident. EU students should apply to the European Team, Department for Education and Skills, Student Support Division 1, Mowden Hall, Staindrop Road, Darlington Co Durham, DL3 9BG.

THE STUDENT SUPPORT SYSTEM FOR HIGHER EDUCATION

The Education (Student Support) Regulations make provision for eligible, full-time students whose homes are in England or Wales to receive financial support towards the costs involved in studying towards a higher education qualification. The support available comprises of help towards tuition fee costs, and a student loan which is repayable only after the applicant completes or ceases their course, and only when they reach a specific level of income. The loan is available up to a maximum amount which is set each year (£3,815 in 2001/02 for students living away from home and studying outside London). Some applicants may receive full entitlement to support and may not need to contribute towards either their fees or upkeep, but only LEAs are able to determine this once the applicant has been assessed. Although this is a broad guide to what is available, it is not exhaustive and detailed information should always be obtained from the applicant's LEA. Support is also available for part-time students on low incomes, either through their university or college (help with tuition fees) or through their LEA (a loan to help with other course costs).

Who is eligible?

Generally, to be eligible students must have been resident in England or Wales for the past three years (although there are some exceptions to this rule), and studying towards a course of higher education. However, detailed advice on eligibility should always be obtained from the applicant's LEA.

What help is available?

If applicants are eligible, help is available towards the costs of tuition fees for full time study and, through a student loan, the general living costs associated with study. Eligible applicants who wish to pursue a course of part time study can obtain help towards the cost of tuition fees, and also a one off loan payment (£500 in 2001/02) per academic year.

For both full time and part time study, extra financial help may be available for applicants in specific circumstances, for example people who are disabled. Again, LEAs can provide specific advice on further help available to applicants and their advice should always be sought before advising prospective applicants. Access funds and bursaries are sometimes available from institutions to help students who would otherwise be prevented from undertaking their course.

How is an application made?

Full time study

Applications are made through LEAs in a two part process. The applicant must initially complete an eligibility application form and return this to their LEA. This enables the LEA to determine whether the applicant is entitled to receive support. If the applicant is eligible, the LEA will ask them to complete a financial assessment form which will enable the LEA to calculate the level of support the applicant is entitled to. Once the applicant is notified of the level of support to which they are entitled, they can then decide the level of student loan they wish to apply for and complete a loan request form to arrange for payment of this amount.

Part time study

Part time students on low incomes can apply to their university or college for help with their tuition fees. They can obtain a loan application form from their LEA, the institution at which they intend to study, or from the Department for Education and Skills. When completed, the applicant must obtain verification from their institution before sending the form to their LEA. If they are entitled to support, the LEA will arrange for payment of support to be made direct into the applicant's bank account.

How are student loans and fees paid?

Full time students

Students who are assessed by their LEA to pay a fee contribution do so directly to their university or college. The Student Loans Company (SLC) pays the public fee contribution directly to the institution. The SLC arranges for the amount that an applicant requests as a loan to be split into three instalments. These are then paid at the beginning of each term of study (i.e. usually October, January and May).

Part time students

For students who are eligible, their tuition fees are paid for them. The SLC arranges for the full amount of the loan to be paid directly into the applicant's bank account. This is paid in one amount, usually in the January following the start of the course.

When should applications be made?

Applications for support for full time courses should be made from the January of the year in which the course starts. For part time courses, applications for fee support should be made before the course starts. Loan applications by part-time students should be made once the course has started.

Further information

More information can be found in the annual guide, Financial Support for Higher Education Students, produced by the Department and available free from LEAs, by calling 0800 731 9133 or from our website http://www.dfee.gov.uk/studentsupport

Loans

Loans are available to eligible students, undertaking designated full-time courses of higher education below postgraduate level, a postgraduate certificate in education, which last at least one academic year. The student must be aged less than 55 when the course begins. S/he must also hold a bank or building society account capable of handling direct debits and credits. Students can apply for a loan for each academic year of their course.

There is a strict maximum amount set for the loan in each academic year and different rates apply to students living at home or away from home, students studying in London and students in their final year. Repayments start in the April following completion of the course. The rate of interest for the loan is linked to inflation in line with the Retail Price Index. This means the value of the amount students pay back is broadly the same, in real terms, as the value of the amount borrowed. Repayments are through the Inland Revenue and repayments are linked to income. Repayment is at 9% of income each year over £10,000. Repayment is not required while income is below the threshold of £10,000. The loans scheme is administered by the Student Loans Company Ltd, 100 Bothwell Street, Glasgow G2 7JD Tel: 0800 405010.

Supplementary grants for living costs are available to students in certain circumstances.

- Disabled students allowances (DSAs) are available to students who incur additional costs in undertaking a course of higher education as a result of their disability. There is no age limit for eligibility for the allowances which, subject to certain limits, provide assistance with the costs of non-medical helpers, specialist equipment and travel.

- Care leavers grant is available to students who have entered higher education on leaving local authority care to help with the costs of accommodation during the long vacation.

- Students with dependants may be eligible for additional grants for their living costs, help with the costs of registered or approved childcare and help with the cost of school meals.

- Medical and dental students undertaking clinical training and students attending an overseas institution as a necessary part of their course may be eligible for a grant to assist with travel costs.

Support for students undertaking part-time courses

Part-time students who meet the residence conditions set-out above and whose courses are designated for part-time support are eligible for a part-time loan of £500 and for DSAs. Certain students may also have their tuition fees waived. To be designated for part-time support, a part-time course must exceed one academic year's duration but not exceed twice the period normally required to complete a full-time equivalent. Entitlement to the part-time loan depends on the student's income but no parental contribution or contribution from a spouse or partner is assessed.

Support for students undertaking postraguate courses

Support for full-time postgraduate courses is provided through the British Academy and the five Research Councils, depending on the subject of the course. Such support is usually selective and competitive. The conditions for eligibility for postgraduate awards are subject to much greater variation and advice should be sought from the relevant award-making body. Further details can be obtained from the **Educational Grants Advisory Service** (see details below). Postgraduate students can apply to their LEA for a postgraduate DSA. The eligibility criteria for the allowance are similar to those for undergraduate DSAs.

Further information

The Departement for Education and Skills has produced the following booklets which give advice about the student support system and what help is available;

- Financial support for higher education students in 2001/2002 – A Guide

- Childcare grant and other financial help for higher education students in 2001/02

- Bridging the Gap – A guide to the disabled students' allowances in higher education in 2001/2002

- Student loans: A guide to terms and conditions

- All four booklets are issued free and available from LEAs or the DfES information line on: 0800 731 9133. These and other student support guides can also be downloaded from the DfES website at: www.dfes.gov.uk/studentsupport/.

Educational Grants Advisory Service

EGAS provides up-to-date advice, information and guidance on potential sources of student funding. The service is open to both individual students and educational organisations. Students wishing to use the service must send a stamped addressed envelope to: EGAS, Family Welfare Association, 501-505 Kingsland Road, London E8 4AU.

YOUTH SERVICE

Overview

Youth Services provide informal personal and social education for young people. They help them prepare for adult life by

- acquiring social skills,
- helping them to become responsible citizens and
- preparing them for the world of work.

Local Education Authorities (the statutory sector) and a range of voluntary organisations provide the Youth Service. The priority age group for the service is 13-19 year olds but the target age group may extend to 11-25 year olds in some cases. Provision is usually in the form of youth clubs and centres, or through "detached" or outreach work aimed at young people at risk from alcohol or drug misuse, or of drifting into crime. There is an increasing emphasis on youth workers working with disaffected, and socially excluded young people.

The Role of Local Education Authorities

The Learning and Skills Act 2000 gives powers to LEAs in England to provide a Youth Service. They are required to provide adequate facilities for further education including social, physical and recreational training and organised leisure-time. Individual authorities decide how they discharge this requirement, taking into account the often-substantial contribution from the voluntary sector.

National Voluntary Youth Organisations

Through its three-year cycle of funding to NVYOs, the Department aims to promote the personal and social education of young people. The grant for the current scheme is £12m and runs from April 1999-March 2002. This scheme has been focused on two broad Ministerial objectives: tackling social exclusion through targeting priority groups and raising the standard and quality of youth work. DfES's National Voluntary Youth Organisation Grant Scheme is the only source of direct Government support for the voluntary youth sector.

The current cycle of grants, to the headquarters of 81 national voluntary youth organisations, supports a total of 84 projects. This includes nine joint projects involving two or more organisations. OFSTED consider that the Scheme provides good value for money and has already involved many thousands of young people in youth service activities for the first time.

Current Consultations

On 27 March 2001, Ministers launched a consultation document "Transforming Youth Work". The Department will run consultations on this document up to the end of July 2001. DfES will include consultations on the future of the voluntary sector grant fund. Another aim of the review is to see how funded organisations can become integrated into Connexions.
On 8 May 2001 the DFES announced a new Youth Service Standards Fund worth £20 million over 2002-04. The consultations on the "Transforming Youth Work" document will include consultations on the use of this fund. It will be designed to help the sector address some of the issues highlighted in "Transforming Youth Work".

How Will Youth Services be a part of Connexions

Youth Services will bring expertise and a wide-ranging network to the Connexions Partnerships. They will contribute in a number of ways including the Personal Adviser role, high quality youth work, volunteering, community activities, organised sport, out of school and summer activities. Their access to a wider network, through the Connexions Partnerships, will also allow youth workers to take their services to other young people, particularly those who have not traditionally used Youth Services.

Amongst the organisations supporting youth work are:

- National Council for Voluntary Youth Services, 11 St Bride Street, London EC4A 4AS Tel: 0207 353 6909, the co-ordinating body for voluntary organisations.
- National Youth Agency, 17-23 Albion Street, Leicester LE1 6GD Tel: 0116 285 3700 Fax: 0116 285 3777, is funded by councils for local education authorities and provides a detailed information and advice service for all those working in or interested in the youth service, both statutory and voluntary.

Other functions of the Agency include curriculum development, training development including accreditation and endorsement of youth and community work training courses and support for organisations within the youth service, with special emphasis on bringing together local authorities and the voluntary sector.

EDUCATION

BAILEY WIGHT & CO
Guildhall Buildings, Navigation Street, Birmingham, West Midlands B2 4BT
Tel: 0121 244 6600 ***Fax:*** 0121 244 6611
Email: solicitors@baileywright.com

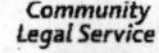

CARVERS (PART OF THE WILKES PARTNERSHIP)
10 Coleshill Road, Hodge Hill, Birmingham, West Midlands B36 8AA
Tel: 0121 784 8484 ***Fax:*** 0121 783 4935
Docx: 27434 HODGE HILL ***E***
mail: legal@carverslaw.co.uk
Web: www.carverslaw.co.uk

HENRY Y SMITH & CO
152-154 Essex Road, London N1 8LY
Tel: 020 7704 2881 ***Fax:*** 020 7704 2436
Docx: 58279 ISLINGTON

LEVENES SOLICITORS
Ashley House, 235-239 High Road, Wood Green, London N22 8HF
Tel: **0800 118899** *Fax:* **020 8889 63**
Docx: **135576 WOOD GREEN 4**
Email: **info@levenes.co.uk**
Web: **www.levenes.co.uk**

NAUNTON LYNCH HALL
Oakley Lodge, 20 Liverpool Gardens, Worthing, West Sussex BN11 1RY
Tel: 01903 234556 ***Fax:*** 01903 212162
Docx: 3746 WORTHING 1
Email: nlh@dial.pipex.com

SYMONS & GAY
91A South Street, Romford, Essex RM1 1PA
Tel: 01708 744211 ***Fax:*** 01708 727614
Docx: 138127 ROMFORD 4
Email: symons-gay@lineone.net

T V EDWARDS
Park House, 29 Mile End Road, Tower Hamlets, London E1 4TP
Tel: 020 7791 1050 ***Fax:*** 020 7790 5101
Docx: 300700 TOWER HAMLETS

CHAPTER NINE

Law and Legal Services

Law and legal services

CHAPTER NINE

Law and Legal Services

INTRODUCTION

This chapter is about those aspects of the law and legal services which are particularly relevant to the services outlined in the rest of the book. The information provides an outline of the following: the system of courts and tribunals; legal advice and assistance and legal aid schemes; criminal law; family law; consumer protection; complaints and compensation.

CIVIL AND CRIMINAL JURISDICTION

Cases before the courts are either civil or criminal. Civil cases are concerned with disputes between one person or organisation and another, whilst criminal cases involve proceedings against individuals with the object of imposing penalties for breaches of the law. Some courts deal with both civil and criminal cases, whilst others are confined either to one category of case or the other. In addition to these two main forms of jurisdiction, there are a large number of administrative tribunals and other courts which deal with matters specifically referred to them.

Magistrates' Courts

The majority of criminal cases begin in the magistrates' court, even if they are afterwards passed on to and dealt with by a higher court. The vast majority of criminal prosecutions are, however, dealt with in these courts, which are fundamental to the legal system of England and Wales. Lay magistrates, Justices of the Peace or JPs, are unpaid and appointed by the Lord Chancellor on the recommendation of local advisory committees. These magistrates can normally only exercise their jurisdiction when two or more of them are present, although single justices have substantial powers now for managing cases prior to trial or other conclusion. In London and other large urban areas, there are paid magistrates, known as District Judges (Magistrates' Court), who are professional lawyers, and who, when sitting alone, exercise the jurisdiction of a bench of justices. There are no juries in magistrates' courts. In general, a magistrates' court is limited to passing a sentence of six months' imprisonment and to imposing fines and other minor punishments. Provisions exist, however, whereby the justices can send a person who is convicted before them to the higher court if they consider that their sentencing power is inadequate in his or her case. Similarly, after a preliminary hearing, more serious criminal offences are also sent on to the higher court.

Magistrates' courts also have a civil jurisdiction which includes 'domestic proceedings' (adoption and care proceedings, separation, maintenance, affiliation and guardianship); the granting of liquor, betting and gaming licences; the settlement of certain disputes between employers and employees; and the enforcement of the payment of local rates and of income tax. Cases involving children can be transferred to the high courts where they are of sufficient complexity or importance or there is need to avoid delay or link up related proceedings.

Youth Courts

In dealing with cases concerning children between the ages of 10 and 14 inclusive and young people of 15 to 17 brought before the court in criminal proceedings, magistrates sit as youth courts. Magistrates who sit in the youth court must be members of a panel appointed from amongst those in the division who are considered specially qualified for dealing with cases involving young people. Up to three magistrates may sit as a youth court and must include a man and a woman. If a child or young person is charged jointly with an adult, the matter comes before an ordinary magistrates' court. If the young person is found guilty, that court may remit the case to the youth court, unless it makes a minor order. The change of title from juvenile court to youth court was brought about by the Criminal Justice Act 1991, which also raised the upper age limit of young people to be brought before the youth court from 16 to 17.

For young people aged 10 to 15 the youth justice system aims to encourage parents to take responsibility for their children in the prevention of offending. Parents are required to attend any criminal proceedings where the child or young person is under 16. For children and young people aged 10 to 15 parents will be ordered to pay monetary orders; for those aged 16 to 17 they may be ordered to do so. The Court must consider imposing a Parenting Order to any offender under 16. Parenting orders can consist of two elements: First for the parent or guardian to attend counselling or guidance sessions, and second, a requirement to encourage the parent or guardian to exercise control over the child. The Court will usually consider a report on the Offender from the Youth Offending Team before deciding what sentence to pass. More detail is given later in this chapter in the section on Criminal Law.

NACRO Youth Crime, 169 Clapham Road, London SW9 0PU Tel: 020 7582 6500 works with local authorities, probation services and other agencies, at both local and national level, to develop more effective responses to youth crime and young offenders, aiming to reduce levels of crime committed by young people and to promote community-based approaches to dealing with young offenders which have the confidence of the public and the courts. Current work includes developing and promoting local authority family support services, bail support schemes, partnerships dealing with repeated offending by juveniles and community sentence options for young adult offenders.

Crown Court

is presided over by a High Court judge or by a circuit judge or recorder, depending on the seriousness of the case. It sits at any place and any time determined by the Lord Chancellor. When the Crown Court sits in the City of London it is properly called the Central Criminal Court, though it is more commonly known as the Old Bailey. In contested trials, judges sit with a jury. In other cases eg, appeals from magistrates' courts the judge or recorder usually sits with between two and four JPs. Circuit judges must be barristers of at least ten years' standing or recorders who have held that office for at least three years. A recorder, who acts as a part-time judge, can either be a barrister or a solicitor of at least ten years' standing. Appeals from the Crown Court may be made to the Court of Appeal Criminal Division. In addition to criminal cases, the Crown Court also hears certain appeals in civil cases which originated in the magistrates' court or elsewhere.

County Courts

Most civil cases which are brought in England and Wales are dealt with by the county courts. These courts, of which there are 220, are constituted under the County Courts Act 1984. Under the High Court and County Courts Jurisdiction Order 1991, all personal injury cases worth up to £50,000 must start in a county court. Other claims involving debt or damages may generally start in a county court, whatever their value. The county courts also deal with landlord and tenant disputes; undefended and most defended matrimonial cases such as divorce, nullity and disputes about children (adoption and care proceedings) whether or not the parents are married; maintenance in divorce proceedings; and disputes over consumer credit agreements. Cases started in a county court may be transferred up to the High Court for trial, providing they are of sufficient substance, importance or complexity. Similarly, cases started in the High Court may be transferred down to a county court if they do not meet the criterion for High Court trial. Cases involving children can be transferred up or down where they are of sufficient complexity, importance, or there is a need to avoid delay or link up related proceedings. There is a simplified procedure for bringing small claims up to £5000 before the court. This makes it easier for a person to bring a claim before a county court without any legal knowledge or professional assistance. This procedure is slightly different in Scotland. Each county court has one or more circuit judges assigned to it by the Lord Chancellor. In addition, each county court has one or more district judges appointed by the Lord Chancellor. Amongst other duties, they judge small claims and hear ancillary applications. They may also hear trials of claims up to £15,000. A circuit judge or district judge has power to commit a person to prison for up to two years or to fine him or her up to £5000 for contempt or misbehaviour in court. Appeals on points of law or upon the admission or rejection of any evidence, and sometimes on questions of fact, may be made to the Court of Appeal.

The High Court of Justice

is one of the three branches of the Supreme Court, the others being the Court of Appeal and the Crown Court. The High Court has three divisions:

- Queen's Bench Division, which deals mainly with claims for damages, breach of contracts, actions arising out of civil wrongs such as defamation and wrongful arrest and administrative law;
- Chancery Division, which is principally concerned with matters of trust, injunctions, property, company and bankruptcy matters;
- Family Division, which has jurisdiction for matrimonial matters, wardship and guardianship, adoption and care proceedings, international matters such as child abduction and proceedings relating to maintenance and matrimonial property.

The Court of Appeal

has two divisions, civil and criminal. The court hears appeals from any of the three divisions of the High Court as well as from the lower courts. The court has 28 judges called 'Lords Justices'. The Lord Chancellor, the Lord Chief Justice, the Master of the Rolls, the President of the Family Division and the Vice-Chancellor are ex officio judges of this court.

House of Lords

The ultimate domestic court of appeal for all the courts is the House of Lords. The permission of the Court of Appeal or the House of Lords itself is necessary before an appeal can be taken to the House.

The Crown Prosecution Service

is responsible for all prosecutions arising from police investigations. Nearly 1½ million cases are handled each year. In the magistrates' courts, lawyers for the Crown Prosecution Service conduct the daily list of prosecutions. In the Crown Courts, cases are presented by practising private barristers who appear on behalf of the service. The organisation is divided into four regions, comprising 31 areas. Each area is handled by a Chief Crown Prosecutor. Certain cases which require specialist attention are retained by the Headquarters in London eg, breaches of the Official Secrets Act and terrorism and race relations cases. **CPS HQ**, 50 Ludgate Hill, London EC4M 7EX Tel: 020 7796 8000.

Coroners' Courts

A coroner is an independent judicial officer of the law, whose main responsibility is to enquire into all cases in which there is reasonable cause to suspect that a person has died either a violent or an unnatural death, or has died a sudden death of which the cause is unknown, or has died in prison, or has died in certain other prescribed circumstances. The coroner's function is to establish who the deceased person was, and how, when and where s/he died. It is not part of the coroner's duty to apportion blame or determine questions of civil liability.

Cases may be brought to the coroner's notice by the registrar of deaths, by the police, by hospital authorities, by medical practitioners, by relatives of the deceased or by members of the public. The coroner takes full responsibility for the conduct of any enquiries into any death reported to him or her. There is a coroner's court for every part of England and Wales.

Administrative tribunals

The Tribunals and Inquiries Act 1971 consolidated and repealed previous legislation on tribunals. Tribunals deal mostly with matters about which a citizen is in conflict with a government department or other public body. They are a means by which a decision may be taken or reviewed outside and independently of the department or body concerned. Some tribunals have a detailed code of procedure, others operate in a less formal way. In most cases, there is provision for appeal, whether to an appellate tribunal, a minister or the courts. Legal representation is usually allowed to a person appearing before a tribunal, but not legal aid.

Legal aid is available for proceedings in The Lands Tribunal, Employment Appeal Tribunal and before The Commons Commissioners. It may be available for the preparation of Employment Tribunal cases. Legal advice and assistance by way of representation is available for proceedings before Mental Health Review Tribunals.

The legislation provides for a Council on Tribunals which supervises the work of tribunals and certain other inquiries. Tribunals have increased in number and importance in recent years and are concerned with, amongst other things, mental health, employment rights, national insurance, taxation, land and property.

PUBLICLY FUNDED LEGAL SERVICES

Public funding is assistance given in conducting or defending proceedings, whether civil or criminal, in the courts. The legislation relating to the provision of public funding for legal services is intended, in both civil and criminal cases, to make legal services available to people who might otherwise be unable to obtain the services of a solicitor or a barrister on account of their means.

In England and Wales, the Lord Chancellor sets the overall policy framework for public funding, within which the Legal Services Commission operates. The Lord Chancellor expects the Commission to ensure that legal advice, assistance and representation are made available to those who need it, in ways that are effective and give the best possible value for money. The cost of the scheme is met by the Community Legal Services Fund, which is financed by central government.

The scheme is administered by 12 Regional Offices, assisted by Funding Review Committees of independent solicitors and barristers. The committes hear appeals against decisions made by Regional Office staff, and decide whether certificates should be granted, refused, limited, discharged, or revoked. The Funding Review Committees' role is to assess whether those granting funding have acted within the scope of the scheme in refusing an application,

More information about funding in civil and criminal cases can be obtained from the Legal Services Commission, 85 Gray's Inn Road, London WC1X 8AA. Tel: 020 7759 0000.

Special Investigation Unit

The Commission's Special Investigation Unit (SIU) examines the means of applicants in both civil and criminal cases who have complex finances and an aura of wealth. Its role was extended to include providing assistance to criminal courts in assessing the means of applicants for legal aid orders where the applicant has a complex financial profile. It aims to ensure that any non-disclosure of assets is detected, and to provide accurate means assessment in accordance with public funding regulations.

PUBLICLY FUNDED CIVIL WORK

On 1st April 2000, the Access to Justice Act came into force, effectively replacing the Legal Aid Board with the Legal Services Commission and launching the new Community Legal Service. The Community Legal Sevice fund replaced legal aid funding for all cases from this date. The Legal Services Commission is responsible for both the administration of the Community Legal Service fund and the development of the wider Community Legal Service network.

Through the Community Legal Service, the Commission will work in partnership with local authorities and other funders to create a network of co-ordinated services and funding to increase access to quality assured legal services for members of the public through England and Wales.

The majority of personal injury cases (except clinical negligence) have now been removed from the scope of publicly funded legal work. Personal injury cases will now largely be funded through conditional (or "no win no fee") agreements. Since February 1999, publicly funded clinical negligence cases have been restricted to contracted service providers. From April 2001, funding in any civil case has been restricted to contracted firms.

The old concepts of advice, assistance and representation have been replaced by a more flexible system of "Levels of Service" (see below), access to which is defined in the new Funding Code. The code contains a standard set of criteria, called the General Funding Code, which apply to all cases except where there are specific criteria that provide otherwise. This criteria is then applied to each service, in a way that tailors the funding assessment to the importance of the service and the nature of funding being provided.

Levels of Service

Legal Help - Legal help provides initial advice and assistance with any legal problem. This level of service covers work previously carried out under the 'green form' or advice and assistance scheme, and does not cover representation. The maximum help that can be given is normally £500 worth.

Help at Court - This allows a solicitor or advisor to speak on a client's behalf at certain court hearings, without formally acting in the whole proceedings. As with Legal Help, Help at Court is available in England and Wales and applies only to questions of English Law.

Family Mediation - This provides funding for mediation of a family dispute for couples and family members who qualify financially. Mediation can help with disputes relating to children, money and property and encourages parties to reach their own decisions in a neutral environment with the help of a specialist mediator. This service is an alternative to resolving issues through solicitors or the courts, and does not replace other legal advice or assistance.

Approved Family Help - This provides help in relation to a family dispute, including assistance in resolving that dispute through negotiation or otherwise. This includes the services covered by legal help, but also includes issuing proceedings and representation where necessary to obtain disclosure of information from another party, or to obtain a consent order following an agreement of matters in dispute. It is available in two forms; **Help with Mediation,** which is legal advice and assistance if attending family mediation, and **General Family Help,** which is legal advice and assistance on family matters when not attending family mediation.

Legal Representation - This level of service provides legal representation in court if a client is taking or defending court proceedings. This is the same level of service previously known as civil legal aid and assistance by way of representation (ABWOR). It is available in two forms: Investigative Help, where funding is limited to the investigation of the strength of a claim; and Full Representation, where funding is provided to represent the client in legal proceedings. It is possible to grant emergency help at both these levels of service.

Financial Eligibility

When calculating eligibility, account is taken of all income that applicants may receive in the calendar month up to and including the date of application. If an applicant's gross monthly income exceeds £2,034 they will not qualify for funding automatically. An applicant's gross income includes all earnings or profits from business; maintenance payments received; pensions; all welfare benefits, except housing benefit, attendance allowance, disability living allowance and constant attendance allowance; income from savings and investments; dividends from shares; money received from friends and relatives; and student grants. An applicant's income includes the income of the applicant's husband, wife, or partner, unless there is a conflict of interest between them. Where a couple are living together they will normally share the accommodation and other resources available to them. The extent of sharing will vary from couple to couple, but where the couple live together in a single household, it is not unusual for their resources to be combined for assessment in other areas such as applying for a mortgage or assessment of resources for social security benefits.

To calculate disposable income, certain allowances are offset against this gross income. These include income tax; national insurance contributions; pension scheme contributions; maintenance payments to an ex-spouse; fares to and from work; child-care expenses incurred because of work; rent or mortgage repayments (limited to £545 per month); the council tax; and water rates. There are also fixed allowances for dependants. Other allowances may also be made at the discretion of the assessment officer taking into account all the circumstances of the case - for example, for arrears of tax, mortgage, gas or electricity.

Account is also taken of an applicant's disposable capital. This includes all capital assets, such as land and buildings (other than their principal homes); all money held in a bank, building society or Post Office account; any investments, stocks and shares; the money value of valuable items such as a boat, caravan, antiques or jewellery; and money that can be borrowed against business assets. The only items specifically excluded from the calculation are any equity in their homes, up to a limit of £100,000; the contents of their homes, personal clothing, personal tools and equipment of a trade; any loans or grants from the social fund; and any savings, valuable items or property whose ownership is the specific subject of the case.

There are set limits for disposable income and capital for each level of service.

Eligibility Limits

It must be remembered that in all cases, an applicant whose gross monthly income is in excess of £2,034 will not receive funding at any level.

Legal Help, Help at Court and Legal Representation before Immigration Adjudicators and the Immigration Appeal Tribunal share qualifying criteria. An applicant will automatically qualify on income if in receipt of Income Support or income based JobSeeker's Allowance but may still be ineligible on capital. An applicant who is not in receipt of either of these benefits must have their disposable income assessed. If this figure does not exceed £611 per month, they qualify on income.

There is no automatic qualification on capital. Therefore disposable capital must be assessed in all applications. The capital limit for these levels of service is £3,000.

Family Mediation, Help with Mediation, General Family Help, Support Funding and all other Legal Representation share different eligibility limits to those levels listed above. Again, an applicant will qualify automatically on income if in receipt of Income Support or income based JobSeeker's Allowance. An applicant who is not in receipt of either of these benefits must have their disposable income assessed. If this figure does not exceed £695 per month, they qualify on income but may still be ineligible on capital.

For these levels of service, the applicant will also qualify automatically on capital if in receipt of Income Support or income based JobSeeker's Allowance. Otherwise, the capital limit is £8,000.

Depending on the applicant's level of income and capital, a single contribution from capital or a monthly contribution from income may be payable by the applicant towards the cost of General Family Help and Legal Representation (see below).

Contributions

For legal representation before the Immigration Adjudicator or the Immigration Appeal Tribunal, no contributions are payable from either income or capital. For all other types of Legal Representation, and for General Family Help, an applicant's disposable income and capital determine what, if any, contribution is payable.

If an applicant's monthly disposable income is £263 or less, they will pay no contribution. However, if disposable income is assessed to be between £263 and £695 per month, the applicant will be required to pay towards the cost of their case from their income. A monthly contribution will be paid to the Legal Services Commission as follows.

Monthly disposable income	Monthly contribution
£264 to £386	One quarter of income in excess of £259
£387 to £513	£31.37 + one third of income in excess of £386
£514 to £695	£74.08 + one half of income in excess of £513

If an applicant's disposable capital is assessed at £3,000 or less, or if they are receiving Income Support or income-based JobSeeker's Allowance, they will not have to pay a contribution. If an applicant's capital is between £3,000 and £8,000, they will be required to pay a contribution. This contribution is payable immediately and amounts to either all of the applicant's disposable capital in excess of £3,000 or the likely maximum cost of the funded service, whichever is less.

Exceptional Funding

Some types of cases fall outside of the scope of public funding, and so funding is not normally available for these. Funding is not generally available for advocacy before a coronoer's court, nor in most tribunals and certain magistrates' court proceedings, but Legal Help is available for preparation work. The reason for these exclusions is that these are specifically designed to enable individuals to represent themselves. No funding *at all is* available for these types of work: defamation, boundary disputes, conveyancing, making wills, trust law, negligently-caused personal injury or damage to property (except clinical negligence), and cases arising out of company or partnership law or the carrying on of a business. These cases have either been deemed by the Government as having insufficient priority to command funding, or can be the subjects of alternative sources of funding (such as a conditional -or no win, no fee- agreement).

However, it is recognised that there will always be exceptions in which cases that are outside the scope of funding by the Legal Services Commission do in fact deserve assistance. Under section 6(8)(b) of the Access to Justice Act, the Lord Chancellor can approve one off grants of funding to excluded cases. As with normal public funding, there are stringent criteria as outlined in the Funding Code. In addition to qualifying financially, an applicant must prove that their case satisfies one of three conditions: overwhelming importance to the client; significant wider public interest; or that it would be practically impossible for the applicant to pursue the case in person. Each of these conditions is very narrowly defined by the Lord Chancellor's Guidance. A solicitor acting for the individual or party must make applications for exceptional funding to the Commission's Head Office (address below).

How to Get Help

A solicitor, or a member of a law centre or Citizen's Advice Bureau, will be able to advise an individual about whether they have a reasonable cause for action and whether they will be eligible for funding. If a solicitor is willing to act he or she will apply for funding on the applicant's behalf. Information about which solicitors and advisors undertake publicly funded work can be found in the Community Legal Service Directory, which can be found in most reference libraries and Citizen's Advice Bureaux, or by telephoning the Community Legal Service (CLS) on lo-call 0845 608 1122 (Minicom 0845 609 6677). Alternatively, the CLS has a website containing information on its contracted advisors. The address is www.justask.org.uk.
The Legal Services Commission Head Office is located at 85 Gray's Inn Road, London WC1X 8TX; Telephone: 020 7759 0000; Website: www.legalservices.gov.uk.

Contributions

The way in which contributions are calculated for Legal Representation will change. Three bands will be introduced to calculate contributions. The first £1,500 of annual disposable income (above the lower limit) will be subject to a contribution of one quarter of disposable income. Where an applicant has between £1501 and £3000 disposable income the contribution will be one quarter of the first £1500 above the lower limit and one third of the remainder. An applicant with over £3000 disposable income will be required to pay a contribution of one quarter of the first £1500 over the lower limit and one half of any remaining annual disposable income. This will better reflect ability to pay and so will help target resources in the CLS on the most deserving cases.

Where To Find Help

Lists of suitable contracted firms or advisors undertaking publicly funded legal work are available at any Citizen's Advice Bureau, library or advice centre. They are also listed in the Community Legal Service Directory, and on the Community Legal Service Website. The

Community Legal Service Directory telephone service can be reached on lo-call 0845 608 1122 (minicom 0845 609 6677). The Legal Services Commission Head Office is located at 85 Grays Inn Road, London, WC1X 8TX. Tel, 0207 759 0000. Website address: 'www.legalservices.gov.uk'.

There are separate schemes in Scotland and Northern Ireland. To receive details of these schemes write to The Scottish Legal Aid Board, Drumsheugh Gardens, Edinburgh EH3 7SW. Tel: 0131 226 7061. Fax: 0131 220 4878. Website address: www.slab.org. For Northern Ireland, write to the Incorporated Law Society of Northern Ireland, Law Society House, 98 Victoria Street, Belfast BT1 3JZ. Tel: 02890 231614. Fax: 02890 232 606.

Community Legal Service

On 3 April 2000, the Government launched the Community Legal Service throughout England and Wales in order to improve access to good quality legal information and advice. The launch marked the replacement of the existing civil and family legal aid budget with the Community Legal Service Fund, and the launch of three separate, but interlinked initiatives:

Community Legal Service Partnerships, the Community Legal Service Quality Mark and the Community Legal Service website

In the past the provision of legal and advice services has been patchy and fragmented, and as a result too many people suffered because they could not get access to the appropriate type of advice. The Community Legal Service will make a difference to the lives of many people as it will provide local networks of good quality services based for the first time on local needs and priorities. The networks will provide a seamless service to the public through an active referral system, so that a person will receive the right service of the right quality at the right price to allow them to resolve disputes, enforce their rights or seek the protection of the courts.

Community Legal Service Partnerships are at the heart of the Community Legal Service. These bring together the two principal funders, the Legal Services Commission and local authorities, together with the other funders and providers of legal and advice services, in order to co-ordinate the planning and delivery of these services, and to create and support the local advice networks. The introduction of the Community Legal Service Quality Mark will ensure that the services provided are to a high standard. The launch of the Community Legal Service website, called "JustAsk!" (www.justask.org.uk) will also assist the public, and provides information in English as well as six community languages. The website carries the Community Legal Service Directory of Legal Services so that people can find out where best to go for advice. The hard copy of the Directory, comprising 13 regional volumes has also been published, and is available in a number of public locations, including public libraries. The public can also call a helpline number (0845 608 1122) for guidance on where they can find the advice and information they need.

PUBLICLY FUNDED LEGAL SERVICES IN CRIMINAL PROCEEDINGS

On 2 April 2001, the Government replaced the criminal legal aid scheme with a new Criminal Defence Service (CDS) run by the Legal Services Commission which has replaced the Legal Aid Board. Only firms which meet quality standards are able to do publicly funded criminal legal aid work for advice and assistance and representation in the Magistrates' Court under the General Criminal Contract from this date. There are over 2,900 contracted solicitors' firms in England and Wales providing comprehensive coverage.

All work in the Crown Courts is provided by solicitors with a criminal franchise. Subject to the Government's response to the recommendations made by Sir Robin Auld's Criminal Court's Review, the Commission will introduce contracts for Crown Court work, including advocacy, in 2003.

As from April 2001, the most complex and expensive cases (where the trial is expected to last at least 25 days or where the total cost for any one defendant, or group of defendants represented by the same firm of solicitors amount to £150,000 or more) are covered by individual case contracts on a case by case basis. Only Serious Fraud Panel members who have demonstrated their ability to handle these specialist cases will be able to undertake very high cost cases involving serious fraud.

The Access to Justice Act 1999 made provision for the Commission to employ lawyers as public (i.e. salaried) defenders. Following consultation about establishing a Public Defender Service as part of the CDS in England and Wales, the Government confirmed that it would place safeguards in order to protect, for instance, the interests of the client. With this in mind, the Government published a Code of Conduct for public defenders which was approved by parliament. The Code also provides for a duty to act with integrity and independence and a duty of confidentiality.

On 2nd April 2001, the Government established the Public Defender Service which is being piloted over a four year period. During the first phase of the four year pilot, the Commission plan to open six public defender offices. In May 2001 three offices were opened in Liverpool, Middlesborough and Swansea; a fourth opened in Birmingham in July 2001. The fifth office will open in Cheltenham and the sixth will open in Pontypridd, as a sub-office of the Swansea PDS, later in 2002.

- Liverpool PDS Office: 14 North Street, Liverpool L2 4SH. Tel: 0151 243 5100
- Middlesbrough PDS Office: 121-123 Albert Road, Middlesbrough TS1 2PQ Tel: 01642 499790
- Swansea PDS Office: 4 & 6 Orchard Street, Swansea SA1 5AG. Tel: 01792 633280
- Birmingham PDS Office: 32 Colmore Circus,Queensway, Birmingham B4 6BN. Tel: 0121 237 6909

Advice and Assistance in the Police Station

Suspects can choose from the following sources of free advice assistance: the duty solicitor; another contracted solicitor or the Public Defender Service if they have an office in the area. The chosen solicitor may give initial advice over the telephone before attending at the police station in person. It may not be necessary for the solicitor to attend, where the defendant is not being interviewed about an arrestable offence or there is not to be an identification parade or similar procedure.

Magistrates' Court Duty Solicitor Service

The Duty Solicitor (there is one in each court) is available to give free advice and assistance and representation in cases where the defendant is remanded in custody, or pleads guilty, is at risk of imprisonment for failure to pay a fine or comply with another court order, or where duty solicitor considers advice is required.

Representation Order

The applicant must apply to the court for a right to representation where he wishes to be represented at public expense. It is of course still open for anybody to pay for his or her own defence. All applicants for publicly funded representation need to satisfy the interests of justice test before the right to representation is granted. The Access to Justice Act specifies five factors that must be taken into account when determining whether it is in the interests of justice that representation be granted; they include matters such as whether the charge against the defendant is so serious that they may be imprisoned or lose their job if convicted, or if there is a substantial point of law to be considered in judging the case. The court will also take into account whether the defendant is unable to state his or her own case, either becuase he or she does not speak English well, or is mentally ill, or suffers from some form of disablilty which will make it difficult for him or her to understand the proceedings. The court may also decide that it is in the interests of justice that the defendant be represented if the nature of the defence involves the tracing and interviewing of witnesses or expert cross-examination of a witness for the prosecution, or if it is in the interests of someone other than the accused that the accused be represented.

There are statutory restrictions on a court passing certain sentences on a person who is not legally represented unless he was granted a right to representation and the right was withdrawn because of his conduct, or unless he refuses or fails to apply for a right to representation. These are set out in Section 83 of the Powers of the Criminal Courts (Sentencing) Act 2000. Accordingly, an applicant should be granted a right to representation before the court passes or makes any of the following sentences or orders.

- A sentence of imprisonment on a person who has not been previously sentenced to imprisonment by a court in any part of the United Kingdom
- A sentence of detention under section 90 or 91 of the Powers of the Criminal Courts (Sentencing) Act 2000
- A sentence of Custody for life under section 93 or 94 of the Powers of the Criminal Courts (Sentencing) Act 2000
- A sentence of detention in a young offender institution
- A detention and training order

A right to representation should normally be granted when a defendant is commited for sentence to the Crown Court, where the court is considering making a recommendation for deportation or where the court is considering making a hospital order.

Where the defendant applies for publicly funded representation to cover or be extended to cover proceedings in the Crown Court, he or she is required to furnish the court with details of their means on a form supplied by the court. At the conclusion of their case in the Crown Court or above, the judge has the duty to consider making a Recovery of Defence Costs Order (RDCO) in all cases, taking into account all the circumstances of the case. An order can be made up to the full cost of the representation incurred under the representation order. An RDCO cannot be made against an individual who only appears in the Magistrates' Court, has been commited for sentence to the Crown Court, is appealing against sentence in the Crown Court, or has been acquitted in the Crown Court other than in exceptional circumstances. A defendant is required to provide details of their partner's finances, as it is all the resources that are available to the defendant that the court will need to consider and that the judge will have to take into account when deciding whether to make an Order and for what amount. Courts can refer cases to the Special Investigations Unit at the Legal Services Commission or conduct a short assessment of the defendant's means based on the information supplied to the court. Where a defendant indicates that he or his partner receive Income based Job-Seeker's allowance, Income support, Working Families' Tax Credit or Disabled Person's Tax Credit they are not required to provide full details of their income or capital, because such defendants are unlikely to have income or capital of a level that would make them liable to pay an RDCO. These benefits are not 'passports' to publicly funded representation and it is open to courts to ask for further details of means if appropriate. Supporting documentary evidence is not required with the applicant's statement of means but courts can request the applicant to provide documentary evidence at any stage before an RDCO is made.

Law centres

exist in some areas. They employ full-time staff, including lawyers, and will handle a client's case from beginning to end, including representation in court or at a tribunal. These services are free unless the centre explains otherwise. Law centres restrict the type of case which they are prepared to accept and there may be restrictions on their services, eg, geographical limitations. Most, however, will be prepared to give preliminary advice. The Law Centres Federation represents law centres and can provide information on them; its address is Duchess House, 18-19 Warren Street, London W1P 5DB, Tel: 020 7387 8570. Regional Office 3rd Floor,

Arundel Court, 177 Arundel Street, Sheffield S1 2NU, Tel: 0114 278 7088. A list of law centres is also given in *Charities Digest* published by Waterlow Professional Publishing, Paulton House, 8 Shepherdess Walk, London N1 7LB Tel: 020 7490 0049.

Legal advice centres

have been established in many places. Staffed mainly by volunteer lawyers, they are essentially for advice and usually offer only a limited amount of further assistance. They make no charge for the service given. These advice centres have limited opening hours. Solicitors attending are allowed to continue to act in suitable cases from their offices in the usual way. Details of local facilities are available from Citizens Advice Bureaux and local authority information centres.

CRIMINAL LAW

Sentencing of offenders

There is a range of sentences available to the courts, including a number of sentences which may be imposed as alternatives to imprisonment. Criminal law in regard to the treatment of offenders was consolidated in the Powers of Criminal Courts (Sentencing) Act 2000. Most of the consolidated law applies to England and Wales, but certain sections extend to Scotland and Northern Ireland. Examples of the type of sentences available to the courts include:

Deferment of sentence

The Crown Court or magistrates' court may defer passing sentence on an offender, with his or her consent, on one occasion only and for a period not exceeding six months. This period enables the court to have regard in determining sentence to the convicted person's conduct during the period of deferment or to any change of circumstances.

Probation

The Act empowers a court to make a probation order instead of sentencing an offender aged 16 and over. The order places the offender under the supervision of a probation officer to advise, assist and befriend the offender. The court may also lay down certain requirements for the offender to comply with during the probation period, eg, to reside in a probation hostel or to attend a day training centre on not more than 60 days. Failure to comply with the requirements renders the probationer liable to be sentenced for the original offence, or to pay a fine if probation is to continue, or, if s/he is over 16 but under 21, to attend an attendance centre or be subject to a community service order.

Community Service Orders

provide a means of dealing with offenders who would otherwise be liable to imprisonment. In those areas where arrangements have been made for the performance of work suitable for the purpose, a court may make a community service order requiring a person aged 17 or over convicted of an offence punishable with imprisonment to perform unpaid work for not less than 40 nor more than 240 hours, as an alternative to any other penalty. The offender must consent to the order and be a suitable person for this kind of treatment. The work is arranged by a probation officer. Failure to comply with the requirements of a community service order renders the offender liable to a fine or to be subject to other penalties.

Absolute and conditional discharge

Where a court considers that neither punishment nor a probation order is appropriate, it may discharge the offender either absolutely or conditionally, ie, subject to the condition that s/he commits no offence during the period specified in the order.

Suspended sentences

A court may suspend for a period of from one to two years any sentence of imprisonment of not more than two years. If the offender commits a further imprisonable offence during a period of suspension, s/he is liable to serve the original sentence in addition to any penalty the court may impose for the new offence.

Imprisonment

A sentence of imprisonment cannot be imposed on a person who has not previously been sentenced to imprisonment and who has not been legally represented in court unless s/he had been refused legal aid because of having adequate means, or had refused or failed to apply for legal aid.

Parole

The parole scheme, established under the Criminal Justice Act 1967, provides for the early release of selected prisoners to serve the balance of their sentence in the community under the supervision of the probation and after-care service. Prisoners serving sentences of more than 18 months are eligible for parole and may be released after having served one third of their sentence *time spent remanded in custody counts towards this period* or one year from the date they were sentenced, whichever expires the later. The initial assessment of a prisoner's suitability begins about four months before the date s/he is eligible for release on parole. The independent local review committee at the prison reports to the Home Secretary, who will either refer the case to the Parole Board for advice or, in certain types of cases, act on the committee's recommendation. A prisoner who is not granted parole will have his or her case reviewed again at annual intervals if the sentence is long enough. A prisoner granted parole has to report to a probation officer and keep in touch until, in most cases, the date on which the prisoner would normally have been released from prison. During this period, s/he may be recalled to prison if any of the conditions of parole are broken.

Compensation orders

may be made against a convicted person, requiring him or her to pay compensation for any personal injury, loss or damage resulting from the offence of which s/he was convicted or any other offence taken into consideration. The court must have regard to the means of the offender in determining the amount to be paid. The amount must not exceed £5,000 when ordered by a magistrates' court.

Confiscation orders

The Criminal Justice Act 1988 extends the power of the Crown Court to impose a confiscation order on a person convicted of any offence, other than those already covered by the Drug Trafficking Offences Act 1986. Magistrates' courts may order confiscation in certain cases only.

Rehabilitation of offenders

The Rehabilitation of Offenders Act 1974 provides that a rehabilitated person is an offender who has been convicted of an offence for which rehabilitation is available under the Act and who has served or complied with the sentence imposed and has throughout the period of rehabilitation appropriate to that sentence not been convicted of an offence which is itself excluded from rehabilitation. The rehabilitation period applicable to a conviction varies from two and a half to ten years, according to the nature of the sentence and the age of the offender. An offender who has become a rehabilitated person is treated for all purposes in law as a person who has not committed or been convicted of any offence. Once a conviction becomes spent, it remains spent, even if a person is convicted of other offences later and, under the terms of the Act, a spent conviction shall not be proper grounds for not employing - or for sacking - anyone. Certain exceptions are made to the Act, however, in the public interest. These relate to activities which carry an above average standard of responsibility. They include admission to certain professions and occupations which have legal protection, eg, medical practitioner, barrister, dentist, teacher, accountant, etc, for which spent convictions may be taken into account in judging an applicant's suitability; admission to certain regulated occupations (firearms dealers, casino operators, directors and managers of insurance companies and unit trusts, nursing home proprietors); appointment to jobs where national security may be at risk eg, certain posts in the civil service, defence contractors; and the granting of certain licences, eg, firearms, shotguns or explosives certificates. It should be noted that the Act only covers Great Britain; other countries have their own rules about those to whom they will give visas and work permits and embassies or overseas employment agencies should have information about this.

NACRO (see After-care of offenders below) publishes two practical, free leaflets on the Act, 'Declaring Convictions' and a summary of the Act and subsequent amending orders.

Remand to custody

Young adults not less than 17 but under 21 years of age, whilst on remand or awaiting sentence, and juveniles, aged not less than 14 but under 17 years of age, who have been certified as being of so unruly a character that they cannot safely be committed to the care of a local authority, may be detained in a prison department establishment. It has been the policy of successive governments to phase out making Certificates of Unruliness as the resources available to local authorities allow.

Young Offenders Institution

This whole section has been overtaken by a new order for under 18s at conviction, the **Detention and Training Order** - which came into effect on the 1st April 2000. Detention in a young offender institution for this age group is no longer a valid sentence.

Attendance centres

At these centres, offenders not less than ten, but under 21, may be required to attend for suitable instruction under supervision. Offenders up to and including the age of 24 may also be subject to this order if they are convicted of non-payment of fines. The hours of attendance are usually on Saturdays so as not to conflict with school and employment. The Criminal Justice Act 1988 also gives courts a specific power to attach a school attendance requirement to supervision orders made in criminal proceedings following consultation with the appropriate education authority.

The probation and after-care service

The Home Office is the central government department responsible for the probation and after-care service. There is an inspectorate which visits and advises probation officers and reviews the service at local level. Local administration is the responsibility of the probation committee of each of the 56 probation areas. The committee is composed of local magistrates, judges and co-opted members. The local committee is responsible for the appointment of probation officers. Each magistrates' court must have at least one man and one woman probation officer and a probation officer must be available to the Crown Court. Probation orders have been described above. Under the Powers of the Criminal Courts Act 1973, probation orders may be made only in respect of people of 17 and over. A young person aged over 14, however, who is the subject of a supervision order, may become the responsibility of a probation officer if the family is already known to the service.

Probation officers may be required to provide a social inquiry report to any court to assist the court to determine the most suitable method of dealing with an offender. The report covers, among any other relevant areas, the home surroundings, education, the health and social conditions of the offender. A copy of the report must be made available to the offender.

The duties of the probation and after-care service also include:

- the after-care of offenders released from custodial establishments;
- the supervision of offenders released on licence parole;
- the introduction and staffing of schemes for community service orders;
- matrimonial conciliation;

- acting as Children's Guardian, 'guardian ad litem', in some adoption proceedings and various other social enquiries in domestic proceedings; and
- the provision of probation hostels.

Prison welfare

Probation officers on secondment are attached to all prisons, remand centres and detention centres to help prisoners with personal and family problems and to assist planning after-care on release. There are also probation officers in certain borstals to improve liaison with the probation services outside.

After-care of offenders

Many people released from prison or young offender institutions will be on licence. This means that they will be supervised by the probation service until their licence expires. If a person does not comply with the terms of the licence, s/he may be recalled to the institution.

People released from custody who are not on licence may apply for voluntary after-care from the probation service for up to a year after their release.

Broadly, the probation service provides a general social work and casework service. There are, in addition, a number of voluntary organisations providing aftercare facilities, mainly housing and employment training. Sometimes probation officers will refer clients to these organisations, but they can also be referred by other agencies and can usually refer themselves.

Voluntary organisations

NACRO (National Association for the Care and Resettlement of Offenders), Information Department, 169 Clapham Road, London SW9 0PU Tel: 020 7582 6500, which runs housing, employment, youth training, education and advice projects for ex-offenders and people at risk. It publishes a range of material on the criminal justice system and practical advice for ex-offenders, their families and people working with them. Its Youth Crime Section also runs consultancy services designed to meet specific local or agency needs, to monitor and evaluate local systems and services and design and deliver training.

Prison Reform Trust, whose work includes research and education. The Trust publishes a Prisoners' Information Pack detailing rights and entitlements. Their address is 2nd Floor, The Old Trading House, 15 Northburgh Street, London EC1V 0AH Tel: 020 7251 5070 Fax: 020 7251 5076.

There are also many voluntary organisations which are concerned with specific groups of prisoners and ex-prisoners, campaigning groups and support groups for prisoners' families. These include:

Bourne Trust, Lincoln House, 1-3 Brixton Road, Kennington Park, London SW9 6DE Tel: 020 7582 1313, Counselling Services Tel: 020 7582 6699 which provides practical help, counselling and support to prisoners, ex-prisoners and their families. There are groups of volunteers operating in Yorkshire and North London as well as other areas.

Women Prisoners' Resource Centre, Room 1, 1 Thorpe Close, Ladbroke Grove, London W10 5XL Tel: 020 8968 3121, whose workers regularly visit all women's prisons to give advice and information about housing and other facilities open to women returning to the London area. They also offer advice and support for women imprisoned in the North of England. The Centre is part of NACRO Community Enterprises Ltd.

FAMILY LAW

The following sections give a brief and generalised account of the law as it relates to family life. It is advisable to seek professional legal advice for any problems.

Marriage

The minimum age for marriage is 16 for both parties; people under the age of 18 who have not previously been married must obtain the consent of each parent with parental responsibility and each guardian if any. There must be no legal impediment of relationship by blood or marriage. Except with a special licence, marriages must be solemnised between 8 am and 6 pm and within three months after the complete publication of the banns or the issue of a common licence, or the entry of notice at the register office.

Marital and Relationship problems

There are various services which provide help for people with personal difficulties in marriage. Copies of a directory of marriage support services published by the Lord Chancellor's Department can be obtained by writing to: Family Policy Division, Lord Chancellor's Department, 3rd Floor, Southside, 105 Victoria Street, London SW1E 3QT. The Directory is also available on the Internet: http://www.lcd.gov.uk. Most of the services are organised by voluntary organisations and some addresses are given below.

The main voluntary organisations

Jewish Marriage Council, 23 Ravenshurst Avenue, London NW4 4EE Tel: 020 8203 6311 provides premarital and marital counselling for those of the Jewish faith.

Marriage Care, Clitherow House, 1 Blythe Mews, Blythe Road, London W14 0NW Tel: 020 7371 1341 has local centres which provide services to couples, including remedial counselling, education for marriage and family life and instruction on natural family planning.

Marriage Counselling Scotland, 105 Hanover Street, Edinburgh EH2 1DJ Tel: 0131 225 5006, Helpline Tel: 0131 220 1207, Monday 6-8 pm & Thursday 2-4 pm provides a confidential counselling service to those in marriage and other intimate personal relationships and has 15 local services throughout Scotland.

RELATE, Herbert Gray College, Little Church Street, Rugby, Warwickshire CV21 3AP, Tel: 01788 573241, Fax: 01788 535007, co-ordinates the work of about 100 local marriage and relationship support centres and selects and trains counsellors. A counsellor's main aim is to help individuals or couples clarify their marital problems, but help is also given in preparing people for marriage and parenthood. A charge may be made to cover the running costs of the service.

Tavistock Marital Studies Institute, The Tavistock Centre, Belsize Lane, London NW3 5BA Tel: 020 7435 7111, a unit of the Tavistock Institute of Medical Psychology, undertakes casework into marital problems, offers training and consultation to allied professional groups and engages in research into marital and related family problems.

Family Mediation is offered to separating or divorcing couples by the following organisations.

National Family Mediation 9 Tavistock Place, London WC1H 9SN Tel: 020 7383 5993 Fax: 020 7383 5994 Web: www.nfm.u-net.com, has 68 charitable services providing mediation for couples, married or unmarried, who are in the process of separation or divorce, principally on issues involving children but also expanding to include finance and property.

UK College of Family Mediators 24-32 Stephenson Way, London NW1 2HX. Tel: 0207931 9162. Fax: 020 7391 9165 Web: www.ukcfm.co.uk. The UK College is a representative body for for family mediators and has approximately 1000 members, drawn from all main family mediation bodies.

Solicitors' Family Law Association P.O. Box 302, Orpington, Kent BR6 8QX Tel: 01689 830227 Web: www.sfla.org.uk. Provides information about solicitor mediators.

The Law Society of England and Wales Tel: 020 7242 1222 Web: lawsociety.org.uk. Provides information about solicitor mediators.

Financial provision for spouses

A party to a marriage may apply, to a magistrates' court under the Domestic Proceedings and Magistrates' Courts Act 1978, or to a county court of the High Court under the Matrimonial Causes Act 1973, for financial support from his or her spouse outside divorce proceedings. The normal ground is that the spouse has failed to provide reasonable maintenance for the applicant. The court may make an order for the payment of periodical payments or of a lump sump (limited to £1,000 in magistrates' courts). The court must adjourn the proceedings if it appears that the parties may be reconciled.

From 5th June 2000 a revised procedure was introduced to courts dealing with ancillary relief proceedings. The reforms are designed to control the cost and length of proceedings under the principles of judicial case management, strict timetabling and controlled disclosure. The new procedure encourages couples to settle their financial disputes at a Financial Dispute Resolution appointment (FDR), with cases proceeding to a full court hearing only if agreement cannot be reached. Provision remains for judges to adjourn cases for the parties to go to mediation if appropriate.

On 1 December 2000, pension sharing was implemented as a further option for couples divorcing on or after that date (it is not retrospective). Unlike attachment (commonly referred to as "earmarking"), a pension sharing order will provide a separate pension provision for the ex-spouse. It will allow pension rights to be treated in a way which ensures the fairest overall settlement for couples and provides greater scope for a clean break settlement.

It is for the Courts to decide what use they make of this option. The option remains to the court to offset pension rights against other assets, or to make an attachment order for a lump sum or to pay maintenance from a member's pension directly to the former spouse.

From April 1993, the Child Support Agency assumed jurisdiction in the UK for child support and the periodic payment of child maintenance. The Child Support Acts 1991 and 1995 took away the courts' jurisdiction in many instances. The courts will, however, continue to have jurisdiction over related matters which arise when the parents separate and divorce. Child support maintenance is an amount of money that absent parents pay as a contribution to the upkeep of their children. CSA jurisdiction applies only if all parties are habitually resident in the UK and where the child is a qualifying child under the Child Support Acts. Where the Child Support Acts do not apply, an application may be made for financial provision for a child of the family (which includes a child who has been treated as such as well as a child of the parties) under the Domestic Proceedings and Magistrates' Courts Act 1978, the Matrimonial Causes Act 1973 or Schedule 1 to the Children Act 1989.

Schedule 1 to the Children Act 1989 provides comprehensive powers to make orders for financial assistance for children, including periodical payments, lump sums and the transfer of property, and makes provision for the alteration of maintenance agreements and the variation of orders for periodical payments. The main features of the new powers are that they may be exercised by a court on the application of a parent, guardian or person in whose favour a residence order is in force; that they may be exercised at any time; that they may require payment to be made by a parent; and that they apply equally to the children of married and unmarried parents. Existing powers to make orders for the benefit of children remain available in proceedings related to marriage.

The Maintenance Enforcement Act 1991 makes provision for a number of methods by which the courts can attempt to enforce maintenance and other orders and at the same time provides for the tightening up of the existing methods. Provisions exist for the reciprocal enforcement of maintenance orders made in various parts of the UK and in many foreign countries.

Divorce

Under the Matrimonial Causes Act 1973, the only ground upon which a petition for divorce may be presented is that the marriage has irretrievably broken down. A petition for divorce, however, may not be presented during the first year of marriage. To establish breakdown, the petitioner must satisfy the court of one or more of five 'facts': these are the same as those which may be used to apply for judicial separation and are listed in the paragraph on this. Upon proof of any one of these, the court must, unless it is satisfied that the marriage has not broken down irretrievably, grant a *decree nisi*. Subject to the provisions of the Matrimonial Causes Act 1973 concerning the welfare of the children and the financial protection of the respondent when the petition is based on two or five years' separation, the petitioner may apply for the decree to be made absolute at any time after the expiration of six weeks from the granting of the decree nisi, unless the court fixes a shorter time in a particular case. If no application is made, the other party may apply when three months have expired from the earliest date on which the party granted the decree could have applied. The parties are not free to marry again until the divorce has been made absolute.

Provision is made in the rules of court for requiring the solicitor acting for a petitioner for divorce to certify whether s/he has discussed with the petitioner the possibility of a reconciliation and has given him or her the names and addresses of persons qualified to help effect a reconciliation. A judge at any stage of proceedings for a divorce has the power to adjourn the proceedings for such a period as s/he thinks fit to enable attempts to be made to effect a reconciliation.

A petition for divorce must be filed in a divorce county court, which includes the Principal Registry of the Family Division. In some cases the divorce may be dealt with on the papers only and evidence is given by affidavit. A decree is pronounced by a judge or district judge.

In all divorce cases where there is a child or children of the family, the court considers the arrangements proposed for the children so that it may decide what order, if any, to make under Section 41 of the MCA 1973 as amended. Where there is no dispute regarding the children on divorce if, for example, the parents are able to make satisfactory arrangements as to which of them the child should live with and what contact there should be with the absent parent, the court need not make an order. Orders for residence and contact are described in chapter one.

Under the Matrimonial Causes Act 1973, in deciding what financial provision should be made for the spouse, the court must have regard, first consideration being given to the welfare of any child of the family who has not attained the age of 18, to all the circumstances including in particular the following:

- the present or foreseeable income, earning capacity and property of each of the parties;
- present or foreseeable financial needs, obligations and responsibilities of each of the parties;
- the family's standard of living before the occurrence of the conduct which is the ground of the application;
- the age of each party;
- the length of the marriage;
- any physical or mental disability of either party;
- the parties' contributions to the family's welfare in the present or forseeable future;
- the conduct of each of the parties, if that conduct is such that, in the opinion of the court, it would be inequitable to disregard it.

Separation

Separation of married people may be brought about either by a mutual agreement to separate or by an order of the court. It is advisable before taking action in a court to consult a solicitor. Financial help for matrimonial proceedings is available, where appropriate, under the Community Legal Service. A couple may separate through one of the following ways:

Separation agreement

The effect of which is that each partner is released from his or her duty to cohabit with the other. Separation agreements can vary from simple oral agreements to live apart to more detailed deeds which contain provisions about maintenance, property and children, etc. Where such an agreement is entered into, neither side can subsequently allege desertion for the purposes of obtaining a divorce, nor exclude the jurisdiction of the court in the future in respect of children and finance.

Decree of judicial separation

relieves the petitioner from the duty of cohabiting with the respondent. The decree is used principally by people who wish to separate but who have religious or other objections to divorce, or who wish to preserve rights to an occupational pension should the other spouse die first, or for whom divorce is unobtainable because they have not been married for one year. It can also be used where one or both parties are not certain that the marriage has irretrievably broken down. A decree may be granted by a county court. The following are the five facts, one of which the petitioner will need to allege:

- the partner has committed adultery and the petitioner finds it intolerable to live with him or her;
- the partner's behaviour is such that the petitioner cannot reasonably be expected to live with him or her;
- the partner has deserted for a continuous period of two years;
- the couple have lived apart for a continuous period of at least two years and the partner consents to the making of the decree;
- the couple have lived apart for at least five years.
- The court has the same powers to make orders relating to children and financial provision on judicial separation as it has on divorce.

"Do it yourself" divorce

A range of leaflets is available in all county court offices which set out court procedures in simple terms to enable individuals to handle their own divorce, where possible, and thus avoid incurring substantial legal costs. These leaflets are primarily designed to assist where the divorce is undefended.

Maintenance orders

Either parent may apply to the magistrates' court, county court or High Court for orders for non-periodic financial provision for children. Schedule 1 of the Children Act 1989 provides comprehensive powers to make orders for financial assistance for children, replaces the powers conferred by the Guardianship Acts 1971-73, the Children Act 1975 and the Family Law Reform Act 1987 and makes provision for the alteration of maintenance agreements. The main features of the new powers are that they may be exercised by a court on the application of a parent, guardian or person in whose favour a residence order is in force; that they may be exercised at any time; that they require payment to be made by a parent; and that they apply equally to the children of married and unmarried parents. Existing powers to make orders for the benefit of children remain available in proceedings relating to marriage. The Maintenance Enforcement Act 1991 makes provision for a number of new methods by which the courts can attempt to enforce maintenance and other orders and at the same time provides for the tightening up of the existing methods. A new system for child maintenance was introduced in England, Wales, Scotland and Northern Ireland from 5 April 1993. Under the Child Support Act 1991, child support maintenance is an amount of money that absent parents pay as a contribution to the upkeep of their children. The Child Support Agency was set up as a 'Next Steps Agency' to administer the Act.

Provisions exist for the reciprocal enforcement of maintenance orders made in various parts of the United Kingdom and in many foreign countries.

Orders Relating to Children

The High Court, County and Magistrates' courts (Family Proceedings Courts) are empowered to make orders in any 'family proceedings'. In exercising these powers, the welfare of the child is the first and paramount consideration. The Children Act 1989 is based on principles of parental responsibility, rather than parental rights and authority. The orders, under the Children Act 1989, are:

- contact orders, which define the contact a child is to have with another person;
- residence orders, which make arrangements regarding the person with whom the child is to live;
- prohibited steps orders, which prevent a person from taking a specified step or steps in relation to a child;
- specific issues orders, which give directions concerning a particular question in the child's upbringing.

Parents, guardians or persons in whose favour a residence order is already in force, or who are entitled because, for example, the child has lived with them for three years or they have the consent of the parents to apply for a residence order, can apply for any of the above orders; other people, including the child concerned, may apply if granted leave to do so by the court. The court is required to refrain from making an order unless it is satisfied that doing so would be better for the child than making no order, but in any family proceedings it may also make an order if it considers that one should be made, even if no application has been made.

Matrimonial Home Rights

Where a husband or wife has a right to occupy a dwelling house which is or was intended to be the matrimonial home, by virtue of owning it or being a statutory or contractual tenancy of it, and the other spouse does not have such a right, the Family Law Act 1996 gives matrimonial right to that other spouse. The rights are 1) not to be evicted, where he or she is in occupation, and, 2) a right to enter and occupy, if the court so orders, where he or she is not in occupation.

Occupation Orders

The Act also gives county courts, the High Court and (provided there is no dispute at to ownership of property) magistrates' courts powers to make occupation orders, to protect the interests of spouses, former spouses, cohabitants and former cohabitants where a relationship breaks down. There are different provisions according to whether the applicant and the respondent are 'entitled', ie. they own the property or have a tenancy of it, or they have matrimonial rights under the Act, or 'non-entitled', and according to whether they are spouses, former spouses, cohabitants or former cohabitants. Occupation orders may contain orders excluding the respondent from the house, requiring the respondent to allow the applicant to enter and remain in it, and regulating the parties' occupation rights. In considering what order to make, the court will consider the likely effect of any decision on the health and well-being of the parties and any relevant child; the parties' housing needs and resources, their financil resources and their conduct. It may also make orders declaring what the parties' rights are. In the event of a breakdown of a relationship, it is advisable to seek advice immediately to protect occupation rights in the home. Citizens Advice Bureaux, listed at the end of this book, can help on such matters.

Domestic violence

Part IV of the Family Law Act 1996 introduces a single, consistent set of remedies which will be available in all courts having jurisdiction in family matters. The two principal orders which the court can make under Part IV are occupation orders which regulate the occupation of the family home, and can exclude one party from the home or an area around it, and non-molestation orders which protect family members from molestation.

These orders are available to any applicant who falls within a series of "associated persons" within a domestic or family relationship. These include people who are or have been married to each other; cohabitants and former cohabitants; people who live or have lived in the same household (other than merely by reason of one of them being the other's employee, tenant, lodger or boarder); certain relatives (including parents, step-parents, children, stepchildren, grandparents, grandchildren, brothers, sisters, uncles, aunts, nephews and nieces); people who have agreed to marry one another (provided the agreement has not been terminated for over three years); those who are parents of a child or have had parental responsibility for the child; parties to the same family proceedings; and, where a child is adopted or freed for adoption, the adoptive parents, the natural parents and grandparents, and the adopted child himself.

Non-molestation orders are available to all the above categories of associated person. Occupation orders are available to spouses, former spouses, cohabitants and former cohabitants, and to the other categories of associated person where they have a pre-existing right to occupy the property or are married or have been married. Where the applicant is a child under the age of 16, the leave of the court to apply must be obtained.

Part IV provides that, if it appears to the court that the respondent has used or threatened violence against the applicant or a relevant child, then the court must attach a power of arrest to one or more provisions of the order unless it is satisfied that in all the circumstances the applicant or child will be adequately protected without it. If an application is made ex-parte (i.e. without notice to the respondent), the court may attach a power of arrest if it is satisfied that the respondent has used or threatened violence against the applicant or a relevant child, and there is a risk of significant harm to the applicant or child, attributable to conduct of the respondent, if the power of arrest is not attached immediately.

The police may arrest without a warrant a person who is in breach of any provision to which a power of arrest has been attached. They must bring that person before the court within 24 hours of the arrest disregarding Sundays, Christmas Day and Good Friday, and must not release the person within that time except on the court's direction.

If the respondent breaches any provision of an order to which a power of arrest has not been attached, the applicant can apply to the court for a warrant of arrest to be issued. The courts have power to remand the respondent on bail or in custody where appropriate.

The Select Committee on Violence in Marriage recommended that family refuges should be established throughout the country by voluntary organisations with adequate financial support from local authorities. Organisations providing such help at the moment include the following:

Women's Aid Federation of England Ltd (WAFE), which co-ordinates and promotes the work of refuges which offer safe temporary accommodation for women and their children who have suffered physical violence, mental or sexual abuse. It also offers advice and support to any woman in determining her future. WAFE acts as a pressure group to educate and inform the public, the media, police, social services and other authorities about the problems and needs of battered women and their children. The Federation publishes reports and leaflets and has produced a video, 'It Doesn't Happen Round Here', which discusses the problem. A full publications list is available from WAFE. The Federation has over 100 affiliated groups; a few groups receive local authority grants, but most are dependent on donations and on the rent allowances paid by social security to the women living in refuges. Their address is PO Box 391, Bristol BS99 7WS Tel: 0117 963 3494. There is a national emergency helpline Tel: 0117 963 3542, which is open from 10.30 am to 4 pm and from 7.30 pm to 10.30 pm on weekdays.

London Women's Aid, who fulfil the same function in the London region, can be found at 52-54 Featherstone Street, London EC1Y 8RT Tel: 020 7251 6537.

Welsh Women's Aid co-ordinates services in Wales. They have three regional offices: 12 Cambrian Place, Aberystwyth, Dyfed SY23 1NT Tel: 01970 612748; 38-48 Crwys Road, Cardiff CF2 4NN Tel: 020 2039 0874; and 2nd Floor, 26 Wellington Road, Rhyl, Clwyd LL18 1BN Tel: 01745 334767.

Scotland has a different financial and legal system relating to matrimonial problems and a separate women's aid organisation: **Scottish Women's Aid,** 12 Torphichen Street, Edinburgh EH3 8JQ Tel: 0131 221 0401, Fax: 0131 221 0402.

Nullity

Decrees of nullity of marriage can be sought from the court in cases of void or voidable marriages. Void marriages include marriages within the prohibited degrees of relationship, bigamous marriages, marriages where the formalities have not been complied with in certain respects and marriages between persons who are not respectively male and female or where either party is aged under 16.

Voidable marriages include cases of incapacity or wilful refusal to consummate, cases where a party did not validly consent to the marriage whether as a result of duress, mistake as to identity or as to the nature of the ceremony, unsoundness of mind or otherwise, cases where a party was suffering from a mental disorder of such a kind as to be unfit for marriage and cases where, unknown to the applicant, the other party was suffering from an infectious venereal disease or, at the time of the marriage, was pregnant by a third party.

A void marriage is treated as having never existed. When a decree is granted in respect of a voidable marriage, it operates so as to annul the marriage only from the time the decree is made absolute.

Protection of children

A range of legislation makes provision for the care or protection of children who may be in moral or physical danger through neglect, ill-treatment, bad associations, etc. Further details of the main provisions made are given in chapter one. Other legislation covers a variety of offences, including the following: it is an offence to encourage prostitution or unlawful intercourse with a child under 16; or to allow children aged four to 16 to live in or frequent a brothel; to use a child for begging; to give a child under the age of five intoxicating liquor; and to sell cigarettes, tobacco or cigarette papers to a person apparently under 16. Children under 12 should not be left in a room with an unprotected heating appliance. Children under 14 are not allowed in the bar of licensed premises and the sale of intoxicating liquor is prohibited to those under 16 although when a meal is served, certain drinks, e.g., cider, may be sold to those over 16. The Protection of Children Act 1978 created new offences relating to the taking, distributing and showing of indecent photographs and films of children and young people under 16. There are also protective measures concerning the employment of children, details of which are given in Chapter five.

Parental responsibility

In recent years, the question of whether or not a child's parents were married has become of lesser importance. However a number of differences remain:

Children of unmarried parents

Where a child's parents were not married to each other at the time of his or her birth, only the mother automatically has parental responsibility; the father may acquire it by several means, including a 'parental responsibility agreement' with the mother, or by an order of the court giving him parental responsibility under Section 4 of the Children Act 1989. In considering these applications, the court must treat the welfare of the child as paramount.

The mother may divest herself of her parental rights and duties to her child by placing him or her for adoption. Where the parents were not married to each other at the time of the child's birth, the agreement of the father to the child's adoption is required only if he has parental responsibility through an order or agreement. If no such order has been made before making an adoption order, the court must satisfy itself either that the father does not intend to apply for an order or that any such application would be likely to be refused.

Registration of birth

When the parents of a child are unmarried, there is no obligation on the father of the child to give information concerning the birth of the child to the registrar, but he is encouraged to sign the birth register jointly with the mother: if he does not do this, there are other ways in which the registrar may enter his name on the register. For example, the father may ask for this to be done by producing a declaration, in the prescribed form, acknowledging that he is the father of the child, together with a statutory declaration by the mother acknowledging his paternity. Where no one has been registered as the father of the child, the birth may be registered in the manner prescribed in the Births and Deaths Registration Act 1953 (Section 10A) and with the authority of the Registrar General.

The Adoption and Children Bill

The Bill is progressing through parliament (June 2002). It makes provision for an unmarried father to acquire parental responsibility for his child by registering or re-registering the child's birth with the mother. Parental responsibility acquired in this way can only be brought to an end by a court order. The Bill also provides that a step-parent who is married to a parent may acquire parental responsibility for the child by agreement. If agreement is not given, the step parent may apply to the court for a parental responsibility order. An agreement or order can only be brought to an end by an order of the court.

Maintenance and property rights

Private maintenance agreements should, wherever possible, contain admission of paternity by the man and be properly drawn up in case it is necessary to use them as evidence in subsequent court proceedings. A solicitor's help may be necessary for this. Advice can be obtained from citizens advice bureaux or from one of the voluntary organisations which exists to help lone parent families listed at the end of Chapter One. Public funding is available for most family matters and details may be obtained from a solicitor.

The Family Law Reform Act 1987 provides that, in dispositions of property made after 4 April 1988 whether made during the lifetime of the benefactor or in his or her will or codicil, references to any relationship between two persons will, unless a contrary intention appears, be construed without regard to whether or not the father and mother of either of them were married at any time. The Act provides that the same principle should apply in respect of succession rights on intestacy. The Inheritance (Provision for Family and Dependants) Act 1975 treats all children equally, regardless of whether their parents have ever been married to each other. A child whose parents were not married to each other at the time of the birth cannot inherit a peerage, title or dignity of honour. The law in Scotland relating to legal rights in the parents' estates differs substantially from that in England and Wales.

Legitimation

Under the Legitimacy Act 1976, which applies to England and Wales only, a child whose parents were not married to each other at the time of his or her birth is, in general, legitimated by virtue of his or her parents' subsequent marriage. The parents of a legitimated child must apply for re-registration of his or her birth within three months of their marriage. The Legitimacy Act 1976 also provides that a child of a void marriage is deemed to be legitimate, provided that either or both parents reasonably believed the marriage to be valid at the time of conception.

British Citizenship

The British Nationality Act 1981, which came into force on 1 January 1983, made important changes in British nationality law. It preserved, however, the basic rule that a child of unmarried parents cannot acquire British citizenship through his or her father. The significance of this restricted definition of 'father' that is, the relationship is taken to exist only between a man and any 'legitimate' child born to him, is now potentially greater than was formerly the case. This is because there is no longer any automatic right to British citizenship by birth in the United Kingdom: a child's claim to British citizenship depends on the parent's citizenship status. The child born to unmarried parents has, therefore, only one parent through whom s/he can claim citizenship, irrespective of where s/he was born. If the parents marry and their marriage serves to legitimate the child in British law, citizenship can then be acquired through either parent.

International child abduction

The Child Abduction and Custody Act 1985 enabled the UK to ratify the Hague Convention of 1980 on the civil aspects of international child abduction and the European Convention of 1980 on recognition and enforcement of decisions concerning custody of children. The Hague Convention provides for the expeditious return of children to the country of their habitual residence when they are wrongfully removed to, or retained in, another contracting state. The European Convention provides for orders relating to children made in the UK jurisdictions to be enforced in all contracting states in certain circumstances.

One or both conventions are in force between the UK and the following countries: Argentina, Australia, Austria, Bahamas, Belgium, Belize, Bosnia and Herzegovina, Burkina Faso, Canada,

Chile, Colombia, Croatia, Cyprus, Czech Republic, Denmark, Ecuador, Federal Republic of Yugoslavia, Finland, France, Georgia, Germany, Greece, Honduras, Hon Kong, Hungary, Iceland, Republic of Ireland, Israel, Italy, Liechtenstein, Luxembourg, Macao, Macedonia, Malta, Mauritius, Mexico, Monaco, Netherlands, New Zealand, Norway, Panama, Poland, Portugal, Romania, Slovakia, Slovenia, South Africa, Spain, St Kitts and Nevis, Sweden, Switzerland, Turkmenistan, Turkey, United States of America, Venezuela and Zimbabwe. Each country must set up a central authority and applications are normally dealt with through these authorities. The central authorities for the UK are as follows: in England and Wales, the **Child Abduction Unit**, Official Solicitor's Department, 81 Chancery Lane, London WC2A 1DD. Tel: 020 7911 7045/7047; in Scotland, the **Scottish Courts Administration,** Hayweight House, 23 Lauriston Street, Edinburgh EH3 9DQ; and in Northern Ireland, the **Northern Ireland Courts Service,** Windsor House, 9-15 Bedford Street, Belfast BT7 1LT Tel: 020 9022 8594. The central authority for the Isle of Man is HM Attorney General, Attorney General's Chambers, Douglas, Isle of Man Tel: 01624 685452. Further information and application forms may be obtained from any of these authorities.

CONSUMER LAW

There are a number of trading offences on which local authorities can take legal action, but many common shopping problems involve civil law rights which individual consumers can enforce, if necessary, by taking traders to court. Help and advice is available from citizens advice bureaux, consumer advice centres and local trading standards or consumer protection departments. Unless otherwise shown, either all the legislation summarised below applies in Scotland and Northern Ireland as well as in England and Wales or there is equivalent legislation which provides similar rights.

The Office of Fair Trading

This office is headed by the Director General of Fair Trading, whose responsibilities are set out in the Fair Trading Act 1973 and other legislation. The Office cannot intervene in individual disputes between consumers and traders, although it does publish a range of general consumer advice pamphlets, available free of charge from many consumer advice agencies or direct from the **Office of Fair Trading,** PO Box 366, Hayes UB3 1XB Tel: 0870 6060321.

In order to protect consumers from unfair trading practices, the Director General can suggest changes in the law, take action against traders who persistently neglect their obligations and encourage trade associations to adopt codes of practice. As the licensing authority under the Consumer Credit Act 1974 *(see below),* the Director General can refuse to license, or can remove the licence, of a trader found to be unfit and can also bar unfit persons from estate agency work under the Estate Agents Act 1979, which imposes obligations on estate agents regarding the way they conduct their business. The Control of Misleading Advertisements Regulations 1988 give the Director General powers to apply to the High Court for an injunction to stop the publication of certain advertisements considered misleading, should this be considered as in the public interest. These responsibilities exclude advertisements on radio and television and most investment advertising. The Director General also has responsibilities in connection with monopolies and other trade practices which may be restrictive or anti-competitive and gives advice to the Secretary of State for Trade and Industry on major merger proposals. The Director General's powers now extend, under the Unfair Terms in Consumer Contracts Regulations 1999, to stopping the use of unfair standard terms in contracts between businesses and consumers and preventing anyone recommending such terms. Other bodies now have powers under the Regulations.

Consumer protection

Whether buying goods or using services, consumers are protected by the law. The Trade Descriptions Act 1968 is designed to protect the consumer against the application of false or misleading descriptions to goods and services, while the Consumer Protection Act 1987 provides protection for damage caused by defective products and against misleading indications of the price of goods, services or accommodation. In England and Wales, consumer protection law is enforced by local authorities. The situation differs somewhat in Scotland, where any court action would be undertaken by the procurators fiscal, and in Northern Ireland, where the Trading Standards Department is part of central government.

The purchase by a consumer of goods from a retailer is a form of contract and it is the retailer, rather than the manufacturer, who is responsible for the quality of those goods. Should they prove to be faulty and the faults were not drawn to the buyer's attention before purchase, then, under the Sale of Goods Act 1979, the consumer is entitled to some or all of the money back. The amount will depend on how serious the faults are and how soon they are notified. No sales 'conditions' can take these rights away. The Supply of Goods and Services Act 1982 extends similar protection to the consumer in respect of goods that have been hired, acquired in exchange or supplied as part of a service and the care and skill with which that service is carried out. Although the Act does not apply in Scotland, similar rights exist under common law. A consumer with a complaint should first approach the trader; if the trader denies responsibility, a claim for damages can be made through the County Court, the Sheriff Court in Scotland. In all parts of the UK, there are special procedures to deal with small claims. If the trader belongs to a trade association which supports a code of practice, it may be possible to settle a dispute by arbitration under the code as an alternative to going to court. In some sectors, such as banking, insurance and building societies, there are ombudsmen who may be able to help settle disputes and many public utilities now have regulators who can deal with consumer problems. These include:

Financial Ombudsman Service incorporates the Insurance Ombudsman Bureau, the Office of the Banking Ombudsman, and the Office of the Building Society Ombudsman. South Key Plaza, 183 Marsh Way, Docklands, London E14 9SR. Tel: 0845 600 6666.

Office of Electricity Regulation (OFFER), Head Office, Hagley House, 83-85 Hagley Road, Edgbaston, Birmingham B16 8QG Tel: 0121 456 2100; London Regional Office, 11 Belgrave Road, London SW1V 1RB Tel: 020 7233 6366; **OFFER Scotland,** Regent Court, 70 West Regent Street, Glasgow G2 2QZ Tel: 0141 331 2200; **OFFER Northern Ireland,** Brookmount Buildings, 42 Fountain Street, Belfast BT1 5EE Tel: 020 9031 1575;

Office of Gas Supply (OFGAS), Stockley House, 130 Wilton Road, London SW1V 1LQ Tel: 020 7828 0898;

Office of Telecommunications (OFTEL), Export House, 50 Ludgate Hill, London EC4M 7JJ Tel: 020 7634 8700.

Office of Water Services (OFWAT), Centre City Tower, 7 Hill Street, Birmingham B5 4UA Tel: 0121 625 1300.

The Unfair Contract Terms Act 1977 protects the consumer from certain 'exclusion clauses' which traders use in contracts and notices. It makes ineffective any clause which a firm may put in its forms or notices to try to exclude or limit its liabilities for death or injury caused by negligence. In addition, any clause about 'not accepting responsibility' for other loss or damage caused through negligence will only be effective if the firm can prove in court that the clause is 'reasonable'. The Act also makes it impossible for the wording of a guarantee to limit manufacturers' liability for loss or damage arising from a defect in the goods caused by their negligence. The DTI has announced plans to change the Regulations and to give concurrent powers to some statutory bodies and to the Consumers' Association.

Standard terms in consumer contracts are also subject to a new test of unfairness in the Unfair Terms in Consumer Contracts Regulations 1999. A contract term is unfair if it creates a significant imbalance in the contracting parties' rights and obligations, to the detriment of the consumer, contrary to the requirements of good faith. If a term is unfair, it cannot be enforced against the consumer, although the rest of the contract continues if possible. Ultimately, the fairness of a term is for the courts to decide.

The Director General of Fair Trading can act against businesses using unfair terms by taking court action if necessary. These powers are aimed at stopping unfair terms being used in future contracts but cannot be used to intervene to obtain redress for individual consumers.

A new structure for consumer safety law was introduced in the Consumer Protection Act 1987. It is a criminal offence to supply consumer goods that are not reasonably safe, as defined in the Act, and local trading standards officers are able to take swift action against unsafe products. Such things as nightdresses, toys, electrical products, prams and pushchairs and cooking utensils are covered by a range of specific regulations. Under the Act, anyone injured by a defective product has a greater prospect of being able to claim financial compensation by suing the manufacturer, without having to prove that the supplier has been negligent.

Consumer credit and hire

The Consumer Credit Act 1974 protects the consumer in most aspects of credit and hire. Almost all consumer credit and hire transactions including credit sale, hire purchase, credit token, conditional sale, pawnbroking and moneylending agreements are covered up to a value of £25,000. The Act and its regulations specify the information which must be given (and the manner in which it is done), having regard to the particular type of the agreement. The legislation does not apply where the debtor or hirer is an incorporated body. Responsibility for administering the Act lies with the Director General of Fair Trading but, apart from licensing (see below), day to day enforcement is largely in the hands of local trading standards departments.

Cancellation

Where there have been face-to-face discussions of an agreement prior to its signature, and provided it is signed off trade premises, the Consumer Credit Act provides a statutory 'cooling-off' period of at least five days following the receipt of either the copy of the agreement, which must be given within seven days of the consumer signing it, or a separate notice of cancellation rights; one or the other must be sent by the creditor. At any time between signing the agreement and the end of that period, the consumer can cancel the agreement without penalty.

Early settlement

The Act gives a right of early settlement and lays down the formula which determines the minimum rebate to be given to debtors. There are special provisions relating to hire purchase agreements.

Extortionate credit

A consumer may apply to a court if s/he thinks the terms of a credit bargain are extortionate. If the court finds in the applicant's favour, it can take any one of a number of alternative actions up to and including setting aside the whole of the bargain. There is no financial limit to the bargains which may be referred to a court relating to the early termination of hire purchase and similar agreements (with the termination the consumer returns the goods rather than paying for them early).

Moneylending and pawnbroking

All moneylending or pawnbroking agreements within the financial limit, etc., made since 19 May 1985 are controlled by the Consumer Credit Act and its regulations.

Licensing

Under the Consumer Credit Act 1974, most traders who provide some form of credit (including hire purchase or those who hire out goods) must be licensed. Banks, finance houses, television rental firms, money lenders and pawnbrokers all come within the types of business that can be covered. Moreover, unless their licence specifically permits them to 'canvass off trade premises', traders cannot call on people uninvited to sell goods or services on credit or to hire-out goods. The doorstep selling of loans unconnected with goods is illegal.

Licences are also required for debt collecting, debt adjusting and debt counselling, credit brokerage and for credit reference agencies. Wherever a licence is required, trading without one is a criminal offence. Any agreement which is regulated by the Consumer Credit Act, made by a person trading without a licence, cannot be enforced against a debtor unless it has been validated by the Office of Fair Trading. Details of licence applications are kept on a register which is open to public inspection. The register is housed at the **Consumer Credit Licensing Branch,** Office of Fair Trading, Craven House, 40 Uxbridge Road, Ealing, London W5 2BS Tel: 020 7211 8608.

Credit tokens

It is an offence to give out credit tokens such as credit cards, which may be used to obtain credit facilities, unless they have been requested in writing.

Credit reference agencies

People have the right to be given the name and address of any credit reference agency which collects information about people's financial standing, and which has been consulted about them, up to 28 days after last contacting the trader about credit or hire. They can also obtain a copy of the information held on them by the agency (for a fee of £2) and can amend incorrect information.

Equal liability

Under the Consumer Credit Act, in circumstances where a prior arrangement exists between the retailer and a third-party credit grantor, whoever provides credit for the purchase of goods or services is equally liable with the seller, where the buyer has a claim against the seller, for any breach of contract or misrepresentation. This applies to credit agreements in which the cash price of any single item is over £100 and not more than £30,000. The consumer might well find this useful if the seller has become bankrupt, gone into liquidation or refuses to co-operate. Where the consumer is buying on hire-purchase, the company providing the credit is in law the seller and complaints should in theory be taken to the company first. Provided that the supplier of the goods is still trading, however, this is the preferable first point of contact.

Brokers' fees

A broker who arranges a loan of not more than £25,000, or a home mortgage for any amount, cannot charge a fee, commission or other charge of more than £5 for the service unless the loan agreement is completed within six months. If more than £5 is paid, the excess must be returned. On a loan in excess of £25,000 secured on land, however, the broker is entitled to recover costs (such as survey fees) paid out to third parties.

Credit advertisements

Most advertisements offering credit or hire facilities are controlled by regulations made under the Consumer Credit Act. The idea is that such advertisements should give a fair and reasonably comprehensive indication of the nature and true cost of the credit terms being offered.

Debt

Under the Administration of Justice Act 1970, the power of committal to prison for failure to pay a debt was abolished, with certain exceptions. These include all maintenance orders and certain Crown debts, income tax, corporation tax, capital gains tax, inheritance tax and social security contributions. In these cases, the court may make an 'attachment of earnings' order instead of an order for committal to prison. The Attachment of Earnings Act 1971 provides for the High Court, County Courts and magistrates' courts to make orders to secure payment of certain debts. The order operates as an instruction to the debtor's employer to make periodical deductions from the debtor's earnings and pay them into court.

Although creditors are entitled to remind someone who is in debt about the payments due, they must not resort to improper methods, such as telephoning during unsocial hours or repeatedly at work, contacting a person's employer, or parking a van marked 'debt collectors' outside a person's residence. Similarly, they must not claim falsely that criminal proceedings will be taken if debts are not paid. In fact, creditors only use court action as a last resort and imprisonment is not normal, unless non-attendance, in extreme circumstances, is regarded as contempt of court.

Debt Counselling

There are an increasing number of local organisations which offer debt counselling. Information about these, as well as general advice on the problem, can be obtained from local citizens advice bureaux. **The Money Advice Association,** Kempton House, Dysart Road, Grantham, NG31 7LE. Tel: 01476 594970. Fax: 01476 591204, works to promote the development of money advice services. It offers training and support for money advisers and provides policy feedback to the government and other bodies on matters affecting the financial situation of people in debt. Membership is open to money advisers. A quarterly journal, 'Quarterly Account', is published. The Association offers a Corporate Subscriber Package to representatives of industry and creditors. Email: office@m-a-a.org.uk. Web: www.m-a-a.org.uk.

Data Protection

Under the Data Protection Act 1984, anyone who keeps personal data on computer, or who runs a computer bureau which provides services in respect of personal data, must register with the Data Protection Registrar. Registration costs £75, covering three years, and application forms are available from the Registrar's office. Any person or organisation not registered may be liable for a fine of up to £5,000. The Register is available for inspection by members of the public and a copy of any section is obtainable for a small fee. Individuals may apply to organisations for a copy of the data which is held about them and have a right of rectification or erasure of any inaccurate data. **The Data Protection Registrar** is at Wycliffe House, Water Lane, Wilmslow, Cheshire SK9 5AF Tel: 01625 545700. Fax: 01625 524510.

COMPLAINTS AND COMPENSATION

Parliamentary Commissioner (Ombudsman)

The Parliamentary Commissioner Act 1967 provides for the appointment of a Parliamentary Commissioner for Administration to investigate complaints of injustice experienced because of governmental maladministration. Complaints can only be referred to the Ombudsman by Members of Parliament. The Act normally excludes from investigation matters which might be referred to a statutory tribunal, or for which there is a remedy by way of the courts. It applies to England, Scotland, Wales and, with certain modifications, to Northern Ireland. The Commissioner has similar powers to those of the High Court for obtaining evidence, conducts investigations in private and reports to the MP concerned the results of the investigations or any reasons for not making an investigation. A special report on the case is made to each House of Parliament if the Commissioner finds that an injustice has not been, or will not be, remedied.

Legal Services Ombudsman

The Courts and Legal Services Act 1990 provided for the appointment of a Legal Services Ombudsman to investigate allegations that complaints against lawyers have not been properly investigated by the relevant professional body. Referrals to the Ombudsman should, unless there are special reasons, be made within three months of the professional bodies final decision. Where the Ombudsman decides to investigate such a complaint, the original ground of complaint to the professional body may also be examined. The Ombudsman has powers equivalent to a High Court judge for obtaining evidence and, on completion of an investigation, makes a written report to the complainant, the lawyer and the relevant professional body. These reports may include recommendations that the professional body reconsider the case and take further action; that either the professional body, or the person in respect of whom the complaint was made, compensate the complainant for any loss, inconvenience or distress caused by the handling of the complaint or as a result of the matter complained of; or that the person or professional body to whom a recommendation to pay compensation applies make a separate payment to the complainant by way of reimbursement of the cost, or part of the cost, of making the allegation. The Ombudsman also has the power to make binding compensation awards. The Ombudsman must be told within three months of making the report of any action taken, or to be taken, in the light of the recommendations. Where a practitioner or professional body refuses to comply with a recommendation, the Ombudsman has the power to require them to publicise their reasons for non-compliance. The address is **The Legal Services Ombudsman,** 22 Oxford Court, Oxford Street, Manchester M2 3WQ Tel: 0161 236 9532 Fax: 0161236 2651. Lo Call No: 0845 6010794. E-mail enquiries.olso@gtnet.gov.uk.

Health Service Commissioner

Since 1974, the Parliamentary Commissioner has also been responsible for dealing with complaints arising under the National Health Service, as Health Service Commissioner. Any member of the public may approach the Commissioner directly by complaining in writing, normally within one year of the matter occurring.

Local Authority Commissioner

Two Commissions for Local Administration, one for England and one for Wales, were established under the Local Government Act 1974 to investigate complaints from the public about injustice caused by maladministration in local government. The English Commission at present consists of three Local Commissioners, each of whom will investigate complaints arising in a particular area of the country, and the Parliamentary Commissioner for Administration.

Complaints intended for reference to a Local Commissioner should be made in writing to a member of the authority complained about, together with a request that it should be sent to the Local Commissioner. Complaints must be made within 12 months of the matter occurring. Certain matters are not open to investigation. These include matters which have been taken to a tribunal or court of law, complaints about court proceedings or the police, personnel matters and certain education matters. All investigations are conducted in private, but any report produced about the authority which has been investigated must be made public. Further information can be obtained from **The Commission for Local Administration in England Local Ombudsman,** 21 Queen Anne's Gate, London SW1H 9BU Tel: 020 7222 5622 and **The Commission for Local Administration in Wales,** Derwen House, Court Road, Bridgend, Mid Glamorgan CF31 1BN Tel: 01656 61325/6. An explanatory leaflet, 'Your Local Ombudsman', produced by the English Commission, contains a general guide to the complaints procedure as well as a specimen form of complaint. The Welsh Commission publishes a leaflet, 'Your Local Authority Ombudsmen in Wales'.

Criminal Injuries Compensation Authority

In 1964 the Government established a non departmental public body - the Criminal Injuries Compensation Board (CICB) to administer compensation throughout Great Britain on the basis of common law damages to victims of a crime of violence. The Scheme was introduced to provide an acknowledgement of society's sympathy for such victims. In 1996 the Criminal Injuries Compensation Authority (CICA) was established to administer the tariff based scheme which came into effect for all applications received on or after 1 April 1996. The staff of the Board became the staff of the Authority at that time. The CICB ceased to exist after 31 March 2000 when all applications under consideration transferred to the CICA. From 1 April 2001 all new applications received will be considered under the revised Criminal Injuries Compensation Scheme. CICA, Morley House, 26-30 Holborn Viaduct, London EC1A 2JQ. Tel: 020 7842 6800. Fax: 020 7436 0804. For all general enquiries email: enquiries.cica@gtnet.gov.uk. Web: www.cica.gov.uk

Help may be obtained from the **National Association of Victim Support Schemes,** Cranmer House, 39 Brixton Road, London SW9 6DZ Tel: 020 7735 9166. This organisation co-ordinates and develops local victim support schemes, whose trained volunteers offer information, advice and support to victims of crime. There is a 24-hour Victims' Helpline for victims of crime and their families on Tel: 020 7729 1252.

A freephone Accident Line Tel: 0500 192939, under the auspices of the Law Society, gives easy access to free specialist legal advice for people who have suffered injury through an accident.

EUROPEAN COMMUNITY LAW

European Community (EC) legislation affects people in Great Britain. If countries and companies ignore EC law, individuals and groups in this country have the right of petition to the European Parliament. The President of the Parliament and the European Parliament's Ombudsman have a duty to ensure that EC law is upheld throughout the Community.

The EC Commission has established a relay for legal advice within the member states, the **AIRE (Advice on Individuals' Rights in Europe) Centre.** They can answer any practical questions on Community law affecting people's lives, by post or telephone, and supply up-to-date free information. The UK address is The Aire Centre, 74 Eurolink Business Centre, 39 Effra Road, London SW2 1BZ Tel: 020 7924 0927 Fax: 020 7733 6786.

The European Parliament UK Office is at 2 Queen Anne's Gate, London SW1H 9AA Tel: 020 7227 4300 and the addresses of individual MEPs can be obtained from the office. **The European Commission Representation in the United Kingdom** is based at 8 Storey's Gate, London SW1P 3AT *England;* 9-15 Bedford Street, Belfast BT2 7EG *Northern Ireland;* 4 Cathedral Road, Cardiff CF1 9SG *Wales;* and 9 Alva Street, Edinburgh EH2 4PH *Scotland.*

LAW AND LEGAL SERVICES

ARSCOTTS
48 Albany Villas, Hove, Brighton & Hove BN3 2RW
Tel: 01273 735289 ***Fax:*** 01273 325091
Docx: 59281 HOVE
Email: enquiries@arscotts,co.uk
Web: www.arscotts.co.uk

BARTLETT GOODING & WEELEN
Old Bank House, High Street, Castle Cary, Somerset BA7 7AW
Tel: 01963 350888 ***Fax:*** 01963 351107
Email: robin.weelen@bgw.uk.com
Web: www.bgw.uk.com

BENDLES
22 Portland Square, Carlisle, Cumbria CA1 1PE
Tel: 01228 522215 ***Fax:*** 01228 515442
Docx: 63010 CARLISLE
Email: BendlesSol@aol.com

BEVERIDGE GAUNTLETT
Rosebank Chambers, Rosebank Parade, Yateley, Hampshire GU46 7RN
Tel: 01252 877533 ***Fax:*** 01252 877371
Docx: 94357YATELEY
Email: solicitors@bevlett.fsnet.co.uk

BOOTH & MIDDLETON
366 Manchester Road, Hollinwood, Oldham, Greater Manchester OL9 7NS
Tel: 0161 624 5665 ***Fax:*** 0161 627 5128
Email: info@boothmiddleton.fg.co.uk

BROMLEY HYDE & ROBINSON
50 Wellington Road, Ashton-under-Lyne, Greater Manchester OL6 6XL
Tel: 0161 330 6821 ***Fax:*** 0161 343 1719
Docx: 25616 ASHTON-UNDER-LYNE
Email: bromleys@bromleys.co.uk
Web: www.bromleys.demon.co.uk

COLES MILLER
260-264 Charminster Road, Bournemouth BH8 9RS
Tel: 01202 511512 ***Fax:*** 01202 530957
Docx: 122753 BOURNEMOUTH 10
Email: office@coles-miller.co.uk

DANIEL & CRUTTWELL
The Family Law Centre, 21-22 Bath Street, Frome, Somerset BA11 1DL
Tel: 01373 463311 ***Fax:*** 01373 461765
Docx: 43801 FROME
Email: info@danielcruttwell.co.uk

DREW JONES
17 Queens Road, Coventry, West Midlands CV1 3EG
Tel: 024 7655 5511 ***Fax:*** 024 7655 5577
Docx: 706791 COVENTRY 9
Email: law@drewjones.co.uk
Web: www.drewjones.co.uk

FORRESTERS
117 Duke Street, Barrow-in-Furness, Cumbria LA14 1XA
Tel: 01229 820297 ***Fax:*** 01229 870017
Docx: 63906 BARROW IN FURNESS
Email: mail@forrestsolicitors.co.uk

FOSTER & PARTNERS
1st Floor Office Suite, 48 Corn Street, Bristol BS1 1HQ
Tel: **0117 922 0229** *Fax:* **0117 929 8621**
Docx: **7867 BRISTOL 1**

Email: **pfoster@fostersbristol.co.uk**
We are one of the leading firms of solicitors specialising in public law relating to children in the South West. We deal with all aspects of childrens law and care proceedings.

FRENCH & CO
6 Derby Terrace, Nottingham NG7 1ND
Tel: 0115 955 1111 ***Fax:*** 0115 955 1187
Docx: 10098 NOTTINGHAM
Email: ian@frenchandco.co.uk
Specialists in community care, social security, education and public law.

GWYNNES
Upper Chambers, 37 Sherwood Row, The Telford Centre, Telford, Shropshire TF3 4BW
Tel: 01952 291292 ***Fax:*** 01952 290677
Docx: 28086 TELFORD
Email: Info@Gwynnes.com
Web: www.gwynnes.com

HARTLEY & WORSTENHOLME
10 Gillygate, Pontefract, West Yorkshire WF8 1PQ
Tel: 01977 732222 ***Fax:*** 01977 600343
Docx: 22256 PONTEFRACT
Email: info@hartley-worstenholme.co.uk
Web: www.hartley-worstenholme.co.uk

JOHNS & SAGGAR
193/195 Kentish Town Road, London NW5 2JU
Tel: 020 7267 6744 ***Fax:*** 020 7284 2355
Docx: 46473 KENTISH TOWN
Email: johnsandsaggar@lineone.net
Specialist accredited lawyers in children and family law specialist lawyers in all housing matters.

KTP SOLICITORS
KTP Chambers, Dinas Isaf Industrial Estate, Williamstown, Pontypridd, Rhondda Cynon Taff CF40 1NY
Tel: 01443 424800 ***Fax:*** 01443 441194
Email: ktpsolicitors@aol.com

MOWBRAY WOODWARDS
3 Queen Square, Bath, Bath & North East Somerset BA1 2HG
Tel: 01225 485700 ***Fax:*** 01225 445064
Docx: 8023 BATH
Email: admin@mowbraywoodwards.co.uk

MYERS EBNER & DEANER
Medway House, 103 Shepherds Bush Road, London W6 7LP
Tel: 020 7602 4631 ***Fax:*** 020 7602 7603
Docx: 46756 HAMMERSMITH 3
Email: Myeblaw@aol.com

NAUNTON LYNCH HALL
Oakley Lodge, 20 Liverpool Gardens, Worthing, West Sussex BN11 1RY
Tel: 01903 234556 ***Fax:*** 01903 212162
Docx: 3746 WORTHING
Email: nlh@dial.pipex.com

northainley
halliwell

NORTH AINLEY HALLIWELL
34-42 Clegg Street, Oldham, Greater Manchester OL1 1PS
Tel: 0161 624 5614 ***Fax:*** 0161 678 8380
Docx: 23605 OLDHAM
Email: law@northainley.co.uk
Web: www.northainley.co.uk

PALMERS
Bank Chambers, 51 The Strand, Walmer, Deal, Kent
Tel: 01304 380572 ***Fax:*** 01304 373639
Docx: 32260DEAL
Email: palmers@freenet.co.uk

P ROBINSON
Imperial Buildings, 2 Halford Street, Leicester LE1 1JB
Tel: 0116 262 1462 ***Fax:*** 0116 251 6618
Docx: 10838 LEICESTER 1
Email: rpr@globenet.co.uk

ROBINSON JARVIS & ROLF
Portland House, 18 Melville Street, Ryde, Isle of Wight PO33 2AP
Tel: 01983 562201 ***Fax:*** 01983 616602
Docx: 56652 RYDE IOW ***Email:*** ryde@rjr.co.uk
Web: www.rjr.co.uk

RUSSELL-COOKE
2 Putney Hill, Putney, London SW15 6AB
Tel: 020 8789 9111 ***Fax:*** 020 8780 1194
Docx: 59456 PUTNEY
Email: helpdesk@russell-cooke.co.uk

SHARPLES & CO
62 Gloucester Road, Bishopston, Bristol BS7 8BH
Tel: 0117 942 8214 ***Fax:*** 0117 942 0498
Email: enquiries@sharples-solicitors.com
Web: www.sharples-solicitors.com
Court of Protection Receiverships undertaken by this family firm (Est. 1973) with STEP/Solicitors for the Elderly membership

STUART SMITH & BURNETT
16 Wellington Road, Bridlington, East Riding of Yorkshire YO15 2BG
Tel: 01262 678128 ***Fax:*** 01262 400012
Docx: 61900 BRIDLINGTON
Email: burnetts@lineone.net

SYDNEY MITCHELL
Chattock House, 346 Stratford Road, Shirley, Solihull, West Midlands B90 3DN
Tel: 0121 746 3300 ***Fax:*** 0121 745 7650
Docx: 13856 SHIRLEY 2
Email: enquiries@sydneymitchell.co.uk
Web: www.sydneymitchell.co.uk
Specialists in Family Law work. Areas include divorce, separation agreement and mediation, children matters, injunctions, property disputes, CSA calculation, Financial Issues. Offices also in Sheldon (0121 722 2969) and City Centre (0121 698 2200). Legal Aid Franchise in family work.

T V EDWARDS
Park House, 29 Mile End Road, Tower Hamlets, London E1 4TP
Tel: 020 7791 1050 ***Fax:*** 020 7790 5101
Docx: 300700 TOWER HAMLETS

THOMPSON SMITH & PUXON
4-5 North Hill, Colchester, Essex CO1 1EB
Tel: **01206 574431** *Fax:* **01206 563174**
Docx: **3617 COLCHESTER**
Email: **info@tsplegal.com**
Web: **www.tsplegal.com**

CHAPTER TEN

Information, Advice, Help and Useful Addresses

INTRODUCTION

The tremendous growth in the provision and complexity of the statutory social services during this century, and particularly since 1948, has produced a range of services which is vast and comprehensive, but which at the same time can be confusing to the individual or family in need of help. Recent government policy has created further changes, as services previously provided by statutory bodies are being contracted out to the voluntary sector or to private agencies. This increase in the provision of statutory and non-statutory services, and the level of change within them, has been accompanied by a growing number of organisations which aim to provide information and advice about the services, or to act as advocates in assisting people to have access to services and rights. This chapter is concerned with the agencies which exist to advise the public, and professional or voluntary workers, on how the services described in this Guide can be obtained. It also includes some contact points in the voluntary sector for people running services or hoping to develop them.

INFORMATION AND ADVICE CENTRES

Information about local services is available from the following places:

Post offices are often a useful source of information and advice on queries arising from the daily functions of issuing pensions, allowances, benefits, licences, etc. The addresses of statutory and voluntary organisations may also be obtained from telephone directories and other local directories.

Public libraries frequently have information about social services in general and in particular have details of local services.

Local authority council offices usually have an information service which can provide details of all the authority's services and other local statutory and voluntary agencies. Some local authorities have set up their own information services. This kind of service is usually found in the town hall or council offices. Although similar to CABx in providing information, particularly in relation to local government matters, they are normally more limited in the functions of advice-giving and acting on behalf of the client.

Advice centres

For more complex or technical problems, there are a number of general and specialist advice services, including the following:

Citizens Advice Bureaux (CABx). The CAB Service is the world's largest independent advice-giving agency. CABx provide free, confidential and impartial advice and information on all subjects, ranging from debt and benefits and employment rights to problems with immigration, housing, consumer goods and services and family and personal worries. The CAB Service draws on its experience of client problems to exercise a responsible influence on the development of social policies and services, both locally and nationally. Advice is delivered from the main bureaux, and there are more than a thousand outreach venues. There are more than 26,000 people in the CAB service, 82% of whom are volunteers. Every CAB adviser undergoes rigorous and comprehensive training. Advisers use a national information system which provides accurate information on every subject and is updated monthly from the central office. Many CABx run regular legal advice sessions. The service is committed to equal opportunities for clients and staff, improving accessibility to CAB premises and providing more services to meet the needs of ethnic minority groups. CABx are supported by their National Association, which has a central office, a divisional office in London, area offices throughout England and Wales and the Northern Ireland Association of CABx. CABx in Scotland belong to a separate organisation, Citizens Advice Scotland. The full updated list of CABx is to be found at the end of this chapter.

The National Association of Citizens Advice Bureaux (NACAB), Myddelton House, 115-123 Pentonville Road, London N1 9LZ Tel: 020 7833 2181 provides member bureaux with the support necessary to deliver an effective service to clients, including training, information services and bureau development grants. It is responsible for national social policy work and monitors national enquiry trends. The address of any CAB is in the local telephone directory or library, or available from NACAB. Details of CABx in the Greater London area can be obtained from the London Region, 136 City Road, London EC1V 2NJ Tel: 020 7251 2000.

Independent advice centres

are able to tailor their services and build up areas of specialist expertise according to the needs of their communities. **The Federation of Information Advice Centres (FIAC)** (National Office), 4 Deans Court, St Pauls Church Yard, London EC4V 5AA Tel: 020 7489 1800 Fax: 020 7489 1804 acts as a co-ordinating, resource and service agency for such centres throughout the UK. They can provide ready access to nearly 1000 independent advice centres, including those which are able to provide language skills, many giving support and advice in connection with tribunals and housing benefit appeals. See also www.fiac.org.uk.

Law Centres

There are now at least 55 Law Centres, set up in urban areas and usually financed by central or local government. Law Centres can handle a case from beginning to end, including representation in court or at a tribunal. The services are normally free and the centre will make it clear in any cases where a charge has to be made. All Law Centres employ at least one full-time salaried lawyer and most employ community workers as well. As Law Centres vary in the services they provide, it is advisable to make enquiries at a local Centre before referring someone for particular help. The Law Centres Federation, Duchess House, 18-19 Warren Street, London W1T 5LR, Tel: 020 7387 8570, Fax: 020 7387 8368, E-mail: info@lawcentres.org.uk, Website: www.lawcentres.org.uk; the regional office at Manchester Office, Law Centres Federation, 3rd Floor Elizabeth House, 16 St Peter's Square, Manchester M2 3DF Tel: 0161 236 5333, Fax: 0161 236 9777 will give information about the availability of law centres in any given area and a full list is given in the *Charities Digest* published by Waterlow Professional Publishing Tel: 020 7490 0049, Fax: 020 7608 1163.

Legal advice centres

are normally advice-giving only, offering only a limited amount, if any, of further assistance. There is no charge for the service. The centres are staffed by volunteer lawyers. Specialist legal advice is available from a number of voluntary organisations and many of these are listed elsewhere in this book, alongside the sections on their areas of expertise: child care, welfare rights, etc.

Consumer advice centres

have been established by some local authorities. They are staffed by trained workers who provide consumer information and advice to the general public. This includes advising on the purchase of goods and services, carrying out surveys of prices and giving advice about making complaints under the consumer protection laws. Consumer advice is also available from www.which.net and the following voluntary organisations:

Consumers Association, 2 Marylebone Road, London NW1 4DF Tel: 020 7830 6000 conducts an extensive programme of comparative testing of goods and investigation of services; its news and test reports are published in its monthly magazine 'Which?' and other publications. Legal advice on consumer problems is obtainable via the 'Which Personal Service' for an annual subscription and a 'Tax-saving Guide' is issued each year.

National Consumer Council, 20 Grosvenor Gardens, London SW1W 0DH Tel: 020 7730 3469. Web: www.ncc.org.uk.

Welsh Consumer Council, 5th Floor, Longcross Court, 47 Newport Road, CF24 0WL. Tel: 029 2025 5454 Web: www.wales-consumer.org.uk.

Scottish Consumer Council, 100 Queen Street, Glasgow G1 3DN Tel: 0141 226 5261 Web: www.scotconsumer.org.uk.

General Consumer Council for Northern Ireland, Elizabeth House, 116 Holywood Road, Belfast BT4 1NY Tel: 028 9067 2488 Web: www.gccni.org.uk.

The Council's role is to bring about change which benefits consumers. They carry out research, publish reports, seek to influence both the public and private sectors, and campaign for a fair deal. In addition to our specific duties in relation to energy, transport and food, they investigate and speak out on the important consumer issues of the day. They handle individual complaints about transport, coal and natural gas but not about other problems.

Problems and concerns arising from utility companies (gas, electricity, water, telecommunications) are covered in chapter 9 under consumer law; the section also includes help on taking up problems with banks and building societies.

Housing advice centres are provided by local authorities to deal with queries and problems arising from all aspects of housing matters. A list of housing aid or advice centres is available in London and elsewhere from the **Resource Information Service**, The Basement, 38 Great Pulteney Street, London W1F 9NU, Tel: 020 7494 2408 Web: www.ris.org.uk and for outside London from **Shelter,** 88 Old Street, London EC1V 9JU Tel: 020 7505 4699 **ShelterLine** Tel: 0808 800 4444 (24 hr freephone) For specific housing enquiries.

INDIVIDUALS WHO GIVE ADVICE

Some people seek general advice and help with problems from their GP, clergyman, priest or local police; that is, from people who through their work are in constant touch with the general public and therefore may be expected to know about local services. Two sources of help with problems which should not be overlooked in this context are the local Member of Parliament and local councillors.

MPs can help particularly in disputes between the individual and statutory authorities, with problems such as housing, disagreements over statutory benefit and allowances, difficulties with government services, or even voluntary or commercial organisations. An MP can intervene directly, and often to great effect, with the administration or organisation involved, or with the Minister responsible. Where appropriate s/he may refer the matter to the Parliamentary Commissioner who, in turn, has the power to examine and take action on complaints of injustice involving government departments. Many MPs hold a regular evening or weekend surgery for constituents to discuss problems. The time and place of the surgery can most easily be obtained from the office of the member's local party. Alternatively, an MP may be contacted by a letter addressed to him or her at the House of Commons, Westminster SW1A 0AA. An MP's advice and help are freely available to all constituents, whatever their political affiliation. Care should be taken to approach the MP in whose constituency the individual lives.

Most local councillors make themselves readily available to residents in their ward for advice and help on local problems. The councillor can help by acting as an intermediary between the individual and the local authority in those areas which are the local authority's responsibility. A councillor may be contacted through the Council.

RIGHTS, REDRESS AND STANDARDS OF SERVICE

At various points in earlier chapters, advice is given about where to seek help if something goes seriously wrong in the provision of a service. The Citizen's Charter was established to regulate standards and is based on 'six principles of public service':

- setting and monitoring standards, publicising the standards and the performance of public bodies against them;
- making readily available information in plain language about public services, their cost and quality;
- providing choice in public services where practicable and carrying out regular consultation with users;
- courteous and helpful service from public servants;
- remedies when things go wrong, including well publicised complaints procedures;
- value for money in the delivery of services.

Service First - The New Charter Programme, Service First Unit, Horse Guards Road, London SW1P 3AL was launched in June 1998 by the incoming Labour Government to enhance the Citizens' Charter. The emphasis was revised to include the following four themes: response, quality, effectiveness and working together.

Liberty (National Council for Civil Liberties), 21 Tabard Street, London SE1 4LA Tel: 020 7403 3888 Fax: 020 7407 5354 Web: www.liberty-human-rights.org.uk, campaigns to defend and extend civil liberties in the UK, particularly in respect of minority groups, publishes factsheets and guides to civil rights and provides limited advice *on written request only* on specific civil rights issues.

The Scottish Human Rights Centre, 146 Holland Street, Glasgow G2 4NG Tel: 0141 332 5960 Web: www.scottishhumanrightscentre.org.uk Advice line open 2pm - 5pm.

PERSONAL SUPPORT AND COUNSELLING

Throughout the Guide, reference has been made to voluntary services in specific fields. Where more general counselling is needed, the following organisations may be important starting points:

British Association for Counselling and Psychotherapy, 1 Regent Place, Rugby, Warwickshire CV21 2PJ Tel: 01788 550899 Fax: 01788 562189 Web: www.bacp.co.uk, acts as a national resource centre for counsellors. Membership is open to organisations and individuals who are either engaged in counselling or sympathetic to it. It publishes annual directories of counselling and psychotherapy resources and training.

Samaritans, The Upper Mill, Kingston Road, Ewell, Surrey KT17 2AF Tel: 020 8394 8300 Fax: 020 8394 8301 Web: www.samaritans.org.uk. There are over 200 Samaritan branches in the United Kingdom and Eire, offering a confidential 24-hour service to people in distress. Samaritans are voluntary workers who offer a befriending service to suicidal or despairing people.

OTHER LOCAL SOURCES OF ADVICE AND SUPPORT

In each chapter of this book under specific subject headings, voluntary organisations are named which provide services or take up issues in particular fields. Help can be obtained in finding local services, or in getting assistance in starting such services, from Councils for Voluntary Service (CVS), which exist in a large proportion of district council areas. They are independent charities whose role is to support and develop other voluntary services and create links and liaison between the statutory and voluntary sectors. A full list is given in the *Charities Digest* published by Waterlow Professional Publishing, Paulton House, 8 Shepherdess Walk, London N1 7LB Tel: 020 7490 0049.

There are a number of organisations whose role includes the support and development of voluntary services and voluntary organisations and who are involved in fostering practical and policy links between statutory and voluntary services. These include:

London Voluntary Service Council, 356 Holloway Road, London N7 6PA Tel: 020 7700 8107 Fax: 020 7700 8108, which works on London-wide issues and supports voluntary organisations covering London and the CVS in London boroughs. **KENTE,** an independent group of African, Caribbean and Asian organisations working in the field of care, can be contacted at the same address.

National Association of Councils for Voluntary Service, 3rd Floor, Arundel Court, 177 Arundel Street, Sheffield S1 2NU Tel: 0114 278 6636 Web: www.nacvs.org.uk, which can provide information on local Councils for Voluntary Service in England.

Northern Ireland Council for Voluntary Action, 61 Duncairn Gardens, Belfast BT15 2GB. Tel: 028 9087 7777 Web: www.nicva.org.

Scottish Council for Voluntary Organisations, Mansfield Traquair Centre, 15 Mansfield Place EH3 6BB Tel: 0131 556 3882 Web: www.scvo.org.uk.

Wales Council for Voluntary Action, Baltic House, Mount Stuart Square, Cardiff Bay, Cardiff CF10 5FH. Tel: 029 2043 1700 Web: www.wcva.org.uk.

National Council for Voluntary Organisations (NCVO), Head Office, Regent's Wharf, 8 All Saints Street, London N1 9RL Tel: 020 7713 6161 Web: www.ncvo-vol.org.uk covering England.

PUBLIC BODIES WEBSITES

Public bodies are organisations set up by government ministers either to promote independent advice or to deliver some aspect of public service.

www.learndirect.co.uk
www.disability.gov.uk
www.dataprotection.gov.uk
www.eoc.org.uk (The Equal Opportunities Council)
www.hse.gov.uk/index.htm (Health & Safety Commission)

GOVERNMENT DEPARTMENT WEBSITES

The Department of Health - www.doh.gov.uk
The Department for Education and Skills - www.dfes.gov.uk
The Office of the Deputy Prime Minister - www.odpm.gov.uk
The Department for Transport - www.dft.gov.uk
The Department for Work and Pensions - www.dwp.gov.uk
The Department of Trade and Industry - www.dti.gov.uk
The Home Office - www.homeoffice.gov.uk
The Lord Chancellor's Department - www.lcd.gov.uk
The Department of Environment, Food and Rural Affairs - www.defra.gov.uk
The Northern Ireland Office - www.nio.gov.uk
The Scotland Office - www.scottishsecretary.gov.uk

Further Reading

Official publications

The Stationery Office (HMSO www.hmso.gov.uk) publishes and sells most official publications. These include Bills, Acts of Parliament, Command Papers and the Papers of Committees set up to enquire into matters of public interest. Booksellers will order Stationery Office publications, or they can be obtained from the following addresses:

- Belfast; 16 Arthur Street, Belfast BT1 4GD Tel: 028 9089 5130
- Birmingham; 68-69 Bull Street, Birmingham B4 6AD Tel: 0121 236 9696
- Cardiff; 18-19 High Street, Cardiff CF10 1PT
- Edinburgh; 71 Lothian Road, Edinburgh EH3 9AZ Tel: 0870 606 5566
- London; 123 Kingsway, London WC2B 6PQ Tel: 020 7242 6393
- Manchester; 9-21 Princess Street, Albert Square, Manchester M60 8AS Tel: 0161 834 7201

They can also be bought by post from:

- National Publishing, The Stationery Office, St. Crispin's House, Duke Street, Norwich NR3 1PD Tel: 0870 600 5522 (orders and subscriptions) Fax: 020 7873 8200 (Fax orders)

Reference books and directories

by title:

- ***A-Z Care Homes Guide 2002*** (London: Tomorrow's Guides Ltd, 2002)
- ***Benefits: a housing and supplementary benefits guide for people without a permanent home*** (London: CHAR Campaign for Single Homeless people, 1986 -)
- ***The British Tax System***, J A Kay & M A King, Clarendon Press
- ***The British Tax System***, John Kay, Oxford University Press
- ***Binley's Directory of NHS Management***, Binley's
- ***Butterworths Personal Tax***, Frank Akers-Douglas, Butterworths Law
- ***Butterworths Personal Tax: Self-Assessment and Simplification: Complete Set***, Frank Akers-Douglas and John Snelgrove, Butterworths Tolley
- ***Check your Tax and Money Facts: 2002-2003***, Graham M Kitchen FCA, W Foulsham & Co Ltd
- ***Clarke Hall & Morrison on Children***, 2 vols, annual publication (London: Butterworth)
- ***The "Daily Mail" Income Tax Guide 1999-2000***, ed. Kenneth R Tingley, Orion Business
- ***The "Daily Telegraph" Tax Guide 2001***, David B Genders, HarperCollins
- ***Directory of Catholic diocesan children's societies and other caring services in England and Wales*** (London: Catholic Child Welfare Council)
- ***Directory of British Associations*** (Beckenham: CBD Research Ltd, 1965)

- ***Directory of Services for Elderly People in the UK*** (Longman Community Information Guides)
- ***Directory of Technical and Further Education*** (London: Pitman, 1995 -)
- ***Directory of Vocational and Further Education*** (London: Pitman, 1996)
- ***Disability Rights Handbook; a guide to income benefits and certain aids and services for handicapped people of all ages***, annual publication (London: Disability Alliance)
- ***A Guide to UK Pensions Law***, The Nabarro Nathanson Pensions Department, Butterworths Law
- ***National Welfare Benefits Handbook***, annual publication (London: Child Poverty Action Group)
- ***Pensions and Insurance on Family Breakdown***, David Salter MA LLM (Norton Rose M5 Group Editor), Family Law
- ***Personal Finance***, Arthur J Keowne, Prentice Hall
- ***Rights Guide for Home Owners***, 11th edn. (CPAG, 1996), also published by Shelter
- ***Rights Guide to Non-Means-Tested Benefits*** (London: CPAG, 1996)
- ***Students' Money Matters***, Gwenda Thomas, Trotman
- ***Taxation Simplified***, Clive Steward, Management Books 2000
- ***Tolley's Taxation of Personal Benefits***, Ure, Frith, Sleziak and Templeton, Tolley Publishing
- ***Voluntary Agencies Directory 2002***, annual publication (London: National Council for Voluntary Organisations)
- ***Welfare Benefits Handbook 2002/2003***, ed. C. George, CPAG
- ***Willard's NHS Handbook*** (ed. Peter Marry) JMH Publishing Ltd
- ***Your Rights: 1992-2003***, Sally West, Age Concern Books (Age Concern England)
- ***Your Rights; for pensioners***, annual publication (Age Concern England)
- ***Your Rights; for pensioners***, annual publication (Age Concern Scotland)
- ***Your Taxes and Savings: A Guide for Older People*** from Age Concern England.

by author:

- Brown, Lesley, ***If only I'd known that a year ago...a guide for newly disabled people, their families and friends*** (London: RADAR Promotions, 1999)
- Couch, Forrester and Irwin, ***Access in London: a guide for people who have problems getting around*** (London: Quiller, 1998)
- Darnbrough and Kinrade, ***Directory for Disabled People; a handbook of information for everyone involved with disability***, 7th edn. (Hemel Hempstead: Prentice Hall / RADAR, 1995)
- Smith and Noble, ***Education Divides: Poverty and Schooling in the 1990s*** (London: Child Poverty Action Group, 1998)

- Tonge, Kate and Self, Roger, ***Tolley's Social Security and State Benefits Handbook*** (London: Butterworths Tolley, 2000)

- Baxter, A, ed., ***Directory of Grant Making Trusts 2001-2002*** (Tunbridge, Kent: Charities Aid Foundation,)

- Woodworth, David, ed., ***International Directory of Voluntary Work***, 5th rev.edn. (Vacation-Work, 1993)

Guides produced by the Careers Research Advisory Centre (CRAC):

- ***CIOLA Directory; careers information officers in local authorities*** (CRAC) (Cambridge: Hobsons)

- ***Claims, benefits and rights; the job hunter's survival guide to job forms and documents*** (Cambridge: published for CRAC by Hobsons)

- ***CRAC Degree Course Guides*** (Cambridge: Hobsons)

- ***CRAC Directory of Further Education*** (Cambridge: Hobsons)

- ***CRAC Directory of Graduate Studies*** (Cambridge: Hobsons)

Citizens Advice Bureaux

This comprehensive list is available from the National Association of Citizens' Advice Bureaux website - www.nacab.org.uk

CHANNEL ISLANDS

Jersey
The Annexe, St Pauls Community Centre, New St, St Helier, JE2 3WP
Tel: 01534 724 942

ENGLAND

BATH & NORTH EAST SOMERSET

Bath
2 Edgar Buildings, Bath, BA1 2EE
Tel: 01225 463333

North East Somerset
Town Hall, The Island, Midsomer Norton, Bath, BA3 2HQ
Tel: 01761 418599

BEDFORDSHIRE

Bedford & District
38 Mill Street, Bedford, MK40 3HD
Tel: 01234 354384

Dunstable
Grove House, 76 High Street North, Dunbstable, LU6 1LF
Tel: 01582 661384

Leighton-Linslade
Bossard House, West Street, Leighton Buzzard, LU7 1DA
Tel: 01525 373878

Luton
24-26 King Street, Luton, LU1 2DP
Tel: 01582 486632

Mid-Bedfordshire (Ampthill)
10 Bedford Street, Ampthill, MK45 2NB
Tel: 01525 404511

BLACKPOOL

Blackpool
6 - 10 Whitegate Drive, Lockwood Avenue, Devonshire Square, Blackpool, FY3 9AQ

Poulton-Le-Fylde
Westbourne Hse, 3 Lockwood Avenue, Poulton-le-Fylde, FY6 7AB
Tel: 01253 893483

BOURNEMOUTH

Bournemouth
West Wing Town Hall, Bourne Avenue, Bournemouth, BH2 6DX
Tel: 01202 292561

BRACKNELL FOREST

Bracknell
42 The Broadway, Bracknell, RG12 1AG
Tel: 08450 505161

BRIGHTON & HOVE

Brighton and Hove
39-41 Surrey Street, Brighton, BN1 3PB
Tel: 0845 1203710

BRISTOL

Bristol
12 Broad Street, Bristol, BS1 2HL
Tel: 0117 921 1664

Kingswood & District
117 High Street, Staple Hill, Kingswood, Bristol, BS16 5HF
Tel: 0117 956 9174

South Gloucestershire
Kennedy Way, Yate, Bristol, BS17 4DQ
Tel: 01454 845515

BUCKINGHAMSHIRE

Amersham
47 Hill Avenue, Amersham, HP6 5BX
Tel: 01494 433262

Aylesbury
2 Pebble Lane, Aylesbury, HP20 2JH
Tel: 0870 1264056

Buckingham Winslow & District
Wheeldon House, Market Hill, Buckingham, MK18 1JX
Tel: 01280 816707

Chesham
5 Market Square, Chesham, HP5 1HG
Tel: 01494 784279

High Wycombe
8 Easton Street, High Wycombe, HP11 1NP
Tel: 01494 264045

CAMBRIDGESHIRE

Cambridge
72-74 Newmarket Road, Cambridge, CB5 8DZ
Tel: 01223 361418

Ely
70 Market Street, Ely, CB7 4LS
Tel: 01353 661416

Fenland
12 Church Mews, Wisbech, PE13 1HL
Tel: 01945 464367

Huntingdon
4 George Street, Huntingdon, PE18 6AD
Tel: 01480 388900

St Neots
28 New Street, St Neots, PE19 1AJ
Tel: 01480 388905

Whitemoor
Visitors Centre, Longhill Road, March, PE15 0PR
Tel: 01354 660653

CHESHIRE

Birchwood
46 Benson Road, Birchwood, Warrington, WA3 7PQ
Tel: 01925 824952

Cheadle & Gatley
Cheadle Library, Ashfield Road, Cheadle, Cheshire SK8 1BB
Tel: 0161 428 3153

Chester
Folliott House, 53 Northgate Street, Chester, CH1 2HQ
Tel: 01244 320808

Crewe
50 Victoria Street, Crewe, CW1 2JE
Tel: 01270 212401

Ellesmere Port
10 Shrewsbury Road, Ellesmere Port, Ellesmere Port, CH65 8AP
Tel: 0151 355 3428

Lymm
Whitbarrow Road, Lymm, WA13 9AG
Tel: 01925 753247

Macclesfield
Sunderland House, Sunderland Street, Macclesfield, SK11 6JF
Tel: 01625 426303

Marple
Council Offices, Memorial Park, Marple, SK6 6BB
Tel: 0161 427 6023

Nantwich
The Gables, Beam Street, Nantwich, CW5 5NF
Tel: 01270 625565

Northwich
48 Chester Way, Northwich, CW9 5JA
Tel: 01606 42393

Runcorn
Ground Floor, Grosvenor House, Runcorn, WA7 2ER
Tel: 01928 710000

Sale
73 Chapel Road, Sale, M33 1EG
Tel: 0161 973 9175

Warrington
21 Rylands Street, Warrington, WA1 1EJ
Tel: 01925 574538

Widnes
Unit 6 Victoria Square, Shopping Centre, Lugsdale Rd, Widnes, WA8 6DJ
Tel: 0151 495 3207

Winsford
The Brunner Guildhall, High Street, Winsford, CW7 2AU
Tel: 01606 594497

CO. DURHAM

Chester-Le-Street
1a Front Street, Chester-Le-Street DH3 3BQ
Tel: 0191 389 3000

Derwentside
94 Front Street Stanley DH9 0HU
Tel: 01207 237858

Durham
Millenium Place, Durham, DH1 1WA
Tel: 0191 384 2638

Easington & District
Rear 14 Upper Yoden Way, Town Centre, Peterlee, SR8 1AX
Tel: 0191 586 2639

Spennymoor
Town Hall, High Street, Spennymoor, DL16 6DG
Tel: 01388 420146

Teesdale District
Woodleigh, Flatts Road, Barnard Castle, DL12 8AA
Tel: 01833 631486

Wear Valley
Four Clocks, Resource Centre, 154a Newgate Street, Bishop Auckland DL14 7EN
Tel: 01388 606661

CORNWALL

Bodmin (North Cornwall)
CAB Offices, Shire Hall, Mount Folly Sq, Bodmin, PL31 2DQ
Tel: 01208 74835

Bude Holsworthy & District
Neetside, Bude, EX23 8LB
Tel: 01288 354531

Camborne (Kerrier)
The Community Centre, South Terrace, Camborne, TR14 8SU
Tel: 0845 1203702

Carrick (Truro)
The Library, Union Place, Truro, TR1 1EP
Tel: 01872 278960

Falmouth
Mulberry Passage, Market Strand, Falmouth, TR11 3DB
Tel: 01326 313340

Liskeard
Duchy House, 21 Dean Stree, Liskeard, PL14 4AB
Tel: 01579 344444

Newquay
The Public Library, Marcus Hill, Newquay, TR7 1BD
Tel: 01637 871645

Penzance (Penwith)
The Guildhall, St Johns Road, Penzance, TR18 2QR
Tel: 01736 365438

Saltash
Ground Floor, 18 Belle Vue Road, Saltash, PL12 6ES
Tel: 01752 845515

St Austell
28 Market Hill, St Austell, PL25 5QA
Tel: 01726 63131

CUMBRIA

Barrow-In-Furness
Ramsdon Hall, Abbey Road, Barrow-in-Furness, LA14 5QW
Tel: 01229 823093

Carlisle
Carlyle's Court, St Mary's Gate, Carlisle, CA3 8RN
Tel: 01228 633900

Cumbria Rural
The Library, Ellerthwaite Road, Windermere, LA23 2AJ
Tel: 015394 46464

Kendal
Blackhall Road, Kendal, LA9 4BT
Tel: 01539 720112

Millom & District
Entrance B Advice Centre, St Georges Road, Millom, LA18 5BA
Tel: 01229 772395

Penrith
2 Sandgate, Penrith, CA11 7TP
Tel: 01768 863564

Ulverston & North Lonsdale
Town Hall Annexe, Theatre Street, Ulverston, LA12 7AQ
Tel: 01229 585585

Whitehaven
3 Duke Street, Whitehaven, CA28 7EW
Tel: 01946 693321

Workington
Vulcans Lane, Workington, CA14 2BT
Tel: 01900 604735

DARLINGTON

Darlington
Bennet House, 14 Horsemarket, Darlington, DL1 5PT
Tel: 01325 380755

DERBY

Derby
Progressive Buildings, Sitwell Street, Derby, DE1 2JT
Tel: 01332 343120

DERBYSHIRE

Chesterfield
6-8 Broad Pavement, Chesterfield, S40 1RP
Tel: 01246 209164

High Peak
High Peak CAB, Bradford Community House, Market Street, Glossop, SK13 8AR
Tel: 01457 855869

Matlock
29 Bank Road, Matlock, DE4 3NF
Tel: 01629 583539

North East Derbyshire
126 High Street, Clay Cross, Chesterfield, S45 9EE
Tel: 01246 863550

South Derbyshire
Voluntary Services Centre, 48 Grove Street, Swadlincote, DE11 9DD
Tel: 01283 210107

Staveley
Staveley Hall, Church Street, Staveley, Chesterfield, S43 3TN
Tel: 01246 473668

DEVON

Barnstaple
Ground Floor, Belle Meadow Court, Albert Lane, Barnstaple, EX32 8RJ
Tel: 01271 377077

Bideford
28a Bridgeland Street, Bideford, EX39 2PZ
Tel: 01237 473161

Exeter
Wat Tyler House, 3 King William Street, Exeter, EX4 6PD
Tel: 01392 201210

Exmouth
Town Hall, St Andrews Road, Exmouth, EX8 1AW
Tel: 01395 264645

Honiton (East Devon)
Honiton Library & Info Centre, 48-50 New Street, Honiton, EX14 1BS
Tel: 01404 44213

Ilfracombe
The Candar, Ilfracombe, EX34 9ER
Tel: 01271 863549

Mid Devon District
28 Gold Street, Tiverton, EX16 6PY
Tel: 01884 253688

Newton Abbot
Bank House Centre, 5b Bank Street, Newton Abbot, TQ12 2JL
Tel: 01626 203141

Okehampton
The Ockment Centre, North Street, Okehampton, EX20 1AR
Tel: 01837 52574

Paignton
29 Palace Avenue, Paignton, TQ3 3EQ
Tel: 01803 521726

Tavistock
Kingdon House, North Street, Tavistock, PL19 0AN
Tel: 01822 612359

Teignmouth
Teignmouth Library, Fore Street, Teignmouth, TQ14 8DY
Tel: 01626 776770

Torquay
11 Castle Road, Torquay, TQ1 3BB
Tel: 01803 297799

DORSET

Blandford
Nightingale Centre, 6/7 East Street, Blandford DT11 7ED
Tel: 01258 455066

Bridport
45 South Street, Bridport, DT6 3NY
Tel: 01308 456594

Christchurch
2 Sopers Lane, Christchurch, BH23 1JG
Tel: 01202 482023

Dorchester & District
1 Acland Road, Dorchester, DT1 1JW
Tel: 01305 262220

East Dorset
Hanham Road, Wimborne, BH21 1AS
Tel: 01202 884738

North Dorset
The Courtyard, Newbury Court, Gillingham, SP8 4QX
Tel: 01747 822117

Purbeck
2 Mill Lane, Wareham, BH20 4RA
Tel: 01929 551257

Sherborne
Manor House, Newland, Sherborne, DT9 3JL
Tel: 01935 815681

Weymouth & Portland
2 Mulberry Terrace, Great George Street, Weymouth, DT4 8NQ
Tel: 01305 782798

EAST RIDING OF YORKSHIRE

Boothferry District
80 Pasture Road, Goole, DN14 6HE
Tel: 01405 762054

East Yorkshire
5a Prospect Arcade, Bridlington, YO15 2AL
Tel: 01262 605660

Holderness
44 Hull Road, Withernsea, HU19 2EG
Tel: 01964 613745

EAST SUSSEX

Bexhill & Rother
Voluntary Services Centre, 38 Sackville Road, Bexhill-on-Sea, TN39 3JE
Tel: 01424 215055

Crowborough
THorpe House, Croft Road, Crowborough, TN6 1DL
Tel: 01892 655303

Eastbourne
66 Grove Road, Eastbourne, BN21 4UH
Tel: 01323 417177

Hailsham
Southview, Western Road, Hailsham, BN27 3DN
Tel: 01323 842336

Hastings
24 Cornwallis Terrace, Hastings, TN34 1EB
Tel: 0870 1264101

Lewes
3 North Street, Lewes, BN7 2PA
Tel: 01273 473082

Seaford
23 Church Street, Seaford, BN25 1HD
Tel: 01323 890875

Uckfield
Eden House, The Office Village, River Way, Uckfield, TN22 1SL
Tel: 01825 764940

ESSEX

Barking
55 Ripple Road, Barking, IG11 7NT
Tel: 020 8594 6715

Basildon
The Basildon Centre, St Martins Square, Basildon, SS14 1DL
Tel: 01268 522210

Billericay
Burghstead Lodge, 143 High Street, Billericay, CM12 9AB
Tel: 01277 651858

Braintree
2 St Michaels Road, Braintree, CM7 1EX
Tel: 01376 324129

Brentwood
10 Crown Street, Brentwood, CM14 4BA
Tel: 01277 222888

CAB Tendring-Clacton-on-Sea
92 Pier Avenue, Clacton-on-Sea, CO15 1NJ
Public Tel: 08707 510952

CAB Tendring-Harwich
24 Kingsway, Dovercourt, Harwich, CO12 3AB
Tel: 01255 502462

Castle Point
168 Long Road, Canvey Island, SS8 0JP
Tel: 01268 511889

Chelmsford
47 Broomfield Road, Chelmsford, CM1 1SY
Tel: 01245 257144

Colchester
Winsleys House, High Street, Colchester, CO1 1UG
Tel: 01206 765331

Dagenham
339 Heathway, Dagenham, RM9 5AF
Tel: 020 8592 1084

Epping
50a Hemnall Street, Epping, CM16 4LS
Tel: 01992 574989

Harlow
Harlow Advice Centre, 2 Eastgate Street, The High, Harlow, CM20 1ND
Tel: 01279 424400

Hornchurch
59a Billet Lane, Hornchurch, RM11 1AX
Tel: 01708 445983

Loughton
St Marys Parish Centre, High Road, Loughton, IG10 1BB
Tel: 020 8502 0031

Maldon
St Cedds House, Princes Road, Maldon, CM9 5NY
Tel: 01621 841195

Rayleigh
Civic Suite, Hockley Road, Rayleigh, SS6 8EB
Tel: 01268 770782

Redbridge
Second Floor, South Broadway Centre, 1 CranBrook Rd, Ilford, IG1 4DU
Tel: 020 8514 1314

Rochford
Rochford Day Centre, Back Lane, Rochford, SS4 1AY
Tel: 01702 545552

Romford
9 Victoria Road, Romford, RM1 2JT
Tel: 0870 120 4200

Southend
1 Church Road, Southend-on-Sea, SS1 2AL
Tel: 01702 610610

Thurrock
1 New Road, Grays, RM17 6NG
Tel: 01375 381023

Uttlesford
Barnard's Yard, Saffron Walden, CB11 4EB
Tel: 01799 526582

Waltham Abbey
Side Entrance, Town Hall, Waltham Abbey, EN9 1DE
Tel: 01992 710353

Wickford
Gibraltar Walk, High Street, Wickford, SS12 9AX
Tel: 01268 732094

Witham
Public Hall, Collingwood Road, Witham, CM8 2DY
Tel: 01376 516222

GLOUCESTERSHIRE

Cheltenham & District
14 Royal Crescent, Cheltenham, GL50 3DA
Tel: 01242 522491

Cirencester
2-3 The Mews, Cricklade Street, Cirencester, GL7 1HY
Tel: 01285 652908

Forest of Dean
Town House, Lords Hill Walk, Coleford, GL16 8BD
Tel: 01594 833717

GLOMAS
Voluntary Resource Centre, Sandford Park, College Rd, Cheltenham, GL53 7HX

Gloucester & District
75-81 Eastgate Street, Gloucester, GL1 1PN
Tel: 01452 528017; 01452 527202

Stroud & District
Unit 8, 1st Floor, Brunel Mall, London Road, Stroud, GL5 2BP
Tel: 01453 762084

GREATER MANCHESTER

Altrincham
The Town Hall, Market Street, Altrincham, WA14 1PG
Tel: 0161 928 1129

Atherton
York Street, Atherton, Manchester, M46 9JD
Tel: 01942 873849

Blackley
251 Charlestown Road, Blackley, Manchester, M9 7BD
Tel: 0161 795 3530

Bolton & District
26-28 Mawdsley Street, Bolton, BL1 1LF
Tel: 0870 126 4039

Eccles
40 - 44 Church Street, Eccles, Manchester, M30 0DF
Tel: 0161 789 1540

Failsworth
1 Ashton Road West, Failsworth, M35 0EQ
Tel: 0161 633 4291

Gorton
111 Wellington Street, Gorton, Manchester, M18 8TX
Tel: 0161 231 1607

Harpurhey
Unit A, Harpurhey District Centre, Manchester, M9 1DH
Tel: 0161 205 6291

Hazel Grove
5 Hatherlow Lane, Hazel Grove, Stockport, SK7 4EP
Tel: 0161 456 3335

Hindley
152 Market Street, Hindley, Wigan, WN2 3AY
Tel: 01942 255069

Hope Hospital
Stott Lane, Salford, M6 8HD
Tel: 0161 787 4713

Hulme
Claremont Resource Centre, Rolls Crescent, Hulme, Manchester, M15 5FS
Tel: 0161 226 6729

Irlam & Cadishead
595 Liverpool Road, Irlam, Manchester, M44 5BE
Tel: 0161 775 1849

Leigh
6 The Avenue, Leigh, WN7 1ES
Tel: 01942 708708

Longsight
384 Dickenson Road, Longsight, Manchester, M13 0WQ
Tel: 0161 224 4300

Lower Broughton
Lucy St, Lower Broughton, Salford, M7 1ZP
Tel: 0161 792 1609

Manchester Central
Swan Buildings, 20 Swan Street, Manchester, M4 5JW
Tel: 0161 834 9844

Middleton
Milton Street, Middleton, Manchester, M24 5TU
Tel: 0161 284 4666

Old Trafford
139 Stamford Street, Old Trafford, Manchester, M16 9LT
Tel: 0161 232 1816

Oldham
1-2 Ashcroft Court, Peter Street Oldham, OL1 1HP
Tel: 0845 1203703

Partington
Council Offices, Central Road, Partington, Manchester, M31 4FY
Tel: 0161 775 4256

Prestwich
7 Fairfax Road, Prestwich, M25 5AS
Tel: 0161 773 7835

Radcliffe
1 Blackburn Street, Radcliffe, Manchester, M26 1NN
Tel: 0161 723 3767

Rochdale
104-106 Drake Street, Rochdale, OL16 1PQ
Tel: 0161 284 4666

Salford City
25a Hankinson Way, Salford Precint, Salford, M6 5JA
Tel: 0161 848 8865

Salford No 6
Advice and Information for Young People, 6 Trafford Road, Salford, M5 2TD
Tel: 0161 848 0666

Salford Mental Health Services
Prestwich Psychiatric Hospital, Bury New Road, Prestwich, Manchester, M25 3BL
Tel: 0161 772 3506

Stockport
39 Greek Street, Stockport, SK3 8AX
Tel: 0161 480 3264; 0161 480 421

Stretford
Stretford Library, 55 Bennett Street, Stretford, Manchester, M32 8SG
Tel: 0161 912 5170

Swinton
95 Chorley Road, Swinton, Manchester, M27 4AA
Tel: 0161 794 5028

Tameside District
9 George Street, Ashton-under-Lyne, OL6 6AQ
Tel: 0161 330 2156

Urmston
2 Moorfield Walk, Crofts Bank Road, Urmston, Manchester, M41 0TT
Tel: 0161 748 4469

Walkden
1 Memorial Road, Worsley, M28 3AQ
Tel: 0161 790 5489

Withington
Withington Methodist Church, 439 Wimslow Road, Manchester, M20 4AN
Tel: 0161 445 7376

Wythenshawe
Alpha House, Rowlands Way, Wythenshawe, Manchester, M22 5RG

HAMPSHIRE

Aldershot
Princes Gardens, Aldershot, GU11 1BJ
Tel: 01252 322097

Alton
7 Cross & Pillory Lane, Alton, GU34 1HL
Tel: 01420 84399

Andover & District
Ground Floor, East Wing, Wessex Chambers, Andover, SP10 2BN
Tel: 01264 365534

Ash
Ash Hill Road, Ash, Aldershot, GU12 5DP
Tel: 01252 315569

Basingstoke
The Library, 19/20 Westminster House, Potters Walk, Basingstoke, RG21 7LS
Tel: 01256 322814

Bishops Waltham
The Library, Bank Street, Bishop's Waltham, SO32 1AN
Tel: 01489 896376

Eastleigh
101 Leigh Road, Eastleigh, SO50 9DR
Tel: 023 8061 3949

Fareham
2nd Floor, County Library Building, Osborne Road, Fareham, PO16 7EN
Tel: 01329 233412

Farnborough
Elles Hall, Meudon Avenue, Farnborough, GU14 7LE
Tel: 01252 542708

Fleet & District
Civic Offices, Harlington Way, Fleet, GU51 4AE
Tel: 01252 617922

Gosport
2 Thorngate Way, Gosport, PO12 1HR
Tel: 023 9252 2224

Havant
21a East Street, Havant, PO9 1AA
Tel: 023 9271 7700

Leigh Park
Leigh Park Community Centre, Dunsbury Way, Leigh Park, Havant, PO9 5BG
Tel: 023 9271 7700

Lymington
91-92 High Street, Lymington, SO41 9AP
Tel: 01590 672685

New Milton
Stannington, 14 Spencer Road, New Milton, BH25 6BZ
Tel: 01425 612679

New Forest North
5 Fridays Court, High Street, Ringwood, BH24 1AB
Tel: 01425 473330

Petersfield
The Old Surgery, 18 Heath Road, Petersfield, GU31 4DZ
Tel: 01730 264887

Romsey & District
5 Abbey Walk, Church Street, Romsey, SO51 8JQ

Tadley
Franklin Avenue, Tadley, RG26 4ET
Tel: 0118 981 7660

Waterlooville
Swiss Cottage, 9 St Georges Walk, Waterlooville, PO7 7TU
Tel: 023 9271 7700

Waterside
The Grove, 25 St Johns Street, Hythe, SO45 6BZ
Public Tel: 0870 126 4089

Whitehill & Bordon
Forest Community Centre, Pinehill Road, Bordon, GU35 0BS
Tel: 01420 477747

Winchester
The Winchester Centre, 68 St Georges Street, Winchester, SO23 8AH
Tel: 01962 848000

Yateley & District (Hampshire)
Royal Oak Close, Yateley, GU46 7UD
Tel: 01252 878410

HARTLEPOOL

Hartlepool
87 Park Road, Hartlepool, TS26 9HP

HEREFORDSHIRE

Herefordshire CAB
1a St Owen Street, Hereford, HR1 2JB
Tel: 01432 266456

Leominster & District
11 Corn Street, Leominster, HR6 8LR
Tel: 0870 1264091

Ross-On-Wye
St.Mary's Church Hall, Ross-on-Wye, HR9 5HP

HERTFORDSHIRE

Abbots Langley
The Old Stables St Lawrences Vicarage, High St, Abbots Langley, WD5 0AS
Tel: 01923 267949

Bishops Stortford
74 South Street, Bishop's Stortford, CM23 3AZ
Public Tel: 08701 264083

Broxbourne (Cheshunt)
Bishops College, Old Building Level 4, Cheshunt, EN8 9XP
Tel: 01992 635858

Broxbourne (Hoddesdon)
The Spinning Wheel, 30 High Street, Hoddesdon, EN11 8BP
Tel: 01992 460976

Buntingford
North Entrance, The Manor Ho, 21 High St, Buntingford, SG9 9AB
Tel: 01763 272024

Bushey
8 Rudolph Road, Bushey, Watford, WD2 3DU
Tel: 020 8950 8726

Elstree & Borehamwood
Community Centre, 2 Allum Lane, Elstree, Borehamwood, WD6 3PJ
Tel: 020 8953 4643

Hatfield
1st Floor, Queensway House, Queensway, Hatfield, AL10 0LW
Tel: 01707 262607

Hemel Hempstead
19 Hillfield Road, Hemel Hempstead, HP2 4AA
Tel: 01442 213368

Hertford
Tooke House, 20 Bull Plain, Hertford, SG14 1DT
Tel: 01992 581441

Hitchin
Thomas Bellamy House, Bedford Road, Hitchin, SG5 1HL
Tel: 01462 622999

Letchworth
Old Grammar School, Broadway, Letchworth, SG6 3TD
Tel: 01462 685393

New Barnet
30 Station Road, New Barnet, Barnet, EN5 1PL
Tel: 020 8449 0975

Oxhey & District
4 Bridlington Road, South Oxhey, Watford, WD19 7AF
Tel: 020 8421 0911

Potters Bar
Wyllyotts Centre, 1 Wyllyotts Place, Dukes Lane, Potters Bar, EN6 2JD

Rickmansworth
Northway House, High Street, Rickmansworth, WD3 1EH
Tel: 01923 720424

Royston
Town Hall, Royston, SG8 7DA
Tel: 01763 238020

St Albans
64 London Road, St Albans, AL1 1NG

Stevenage
Swingate House, Danestrete, Stevenage, SG1 1AF
Tel: 01438 369491

Ware & District
Meade House, 85 High Street, Ware, SG12 9AD
Tel: 01920 463495

Watford
St Marys Churchyard, High Street, Watford, WD1 2BE
Tel: 01923 234949

ISLE OF WIGHT

Newport
Exchange House, St Cross Lane, Newport, PO30 5BZ
Tel: 01983 522611

KENT

Ashford
Seabrooke House, 10 Norwood Street, Ashford, TN23 1QT
Tel: 01233 626185

Bexleyheath
8 Brampton Road, Bexleyheath, DA7 4EY
Tel: 020 8303 5100

Broadstairs
Pierremont Gardens, High Street, Broadstairs, CT10 1JH
Tel: 01843 869350

Bromley Town
Community House, South Street, Bromley, BR1 1RH

Canterbury
3 Westgate Hall Road, Off St Peters, Canterbury, CT1 2BT
Tel: 01227 761493

Chatham
The White House, Riverside, Chatham, ME4 4SL
Public Tel: 0870 1264095

Cranbrook & District
Council Offices, High Street, Cranbrook, TN17 3LU
Tel: 01580 713561

Dartford
Enterprise House, 8 Essex Road, Dartford, DA1 2AU
Tel: 01322 224686

Deal
26 Victoria Road, Deal, CT14 7BJ

Dover
Maison Dieu Gardens, Maison Dieu Road, Dover, CT16 1RW
Tel: 01304 202567

Edenbridge
68 High Street, Edenbridge, TN8 5AR
Tel: 01732 865131

Erith
1 Walnut Tree Road, Erith, DA8 1RA
Tel: 01322 340481

Faversham
43 Stone Street, Faversham, ME13 8PH
Tel: 01795 536996

Folkestone (Shepway)
20 Church Street, Folkestone, CT20 1SE
Tel: 01303 220709

Gravesham
8 & 9 Parrock Street, Gravesend, DA12 1ET
Tel: 01474 361239

Herne Bay
185/187 High Street, Herne Bay, CT6 5AF
Tel: 01227 363312

Maidstone
2 Bower Terrace, Tonbridge Road, Maidstone, ME16 8RY
Tel: 01622 688133

Malling
Clouts Memorial Institute, 9 High Street, West Malling, ME19 6QH
Tel: 01732 845501

Medway District CAB Service, Gillingham Bureau
46 Green Street, Off High Street, Gillingham, ME7 5TJ
Public Tel: 0870 1264095

Orpington
309a High Street, Orpington, BR6 0NN

Paddock Wood
The Wesley Centre, Commercial Rd, Paddock Wood, Tonbridge, TN12 6DS
Tel: 01892 832977

Rochester
The Guildhall, 17 High Street, Rochester, ME1 1PY
Public Tel: 0870 1264095

Sevenoaks
Buckhurst Lane, Next to the Library, Sevenoaks, TN13 1HW
Tel: 01732 454443

Sittingbourne
17a Station Street, Sittingbourne, ME10 3DU
Tel: 01795 473652

Swanley & District
16 High Street, Swanley, BR8 8BG
Tel: 01322 664949

Tenterden
Town Hall, High Street, Tenterden, TN30 6AN
Tel: 01580 762371

Thanet
Old Town Hall, Market Street, Margate, CT9 1EU
Tel: 01843 225973

Tonbridge
Castle Lodge, Castle Street, Tonbridge, TN9 1BH
Tel: 01732 350099

Tunbridge Wells
31 Monson Road, Tunbridge Wells, TN1 1LS
Tel: 01892 538388

Whitstable
St Marys Hall, Oxford Street, Whitstable, CT5 1DD
Tel: 01227 264363

KINGSTON UPON HULL

Bransholme
18-20 Madron Close, Barnstaple Road, Bransholme, Hull, HU7 4PR
Tel: 01482 838392

Hull & District CAB
2 Charlotte Street Mews, Hull, HU1 3BQ
Public Tel: 01482 224608

LANCASHIRE

Ashton-In-Makerfield
Old Town Hall, Bryn St, Ashton-in-Makerfield, Wigan, WN4 9AX
Tel: 01942 725668

Bacup
4 Rochdale Road, Bacup, OL13 9NZ
Tel: 01706 873367

Barnoldswick
10 Rainall Road, Barnoldswick, Lancashire, BB18 5AF
Tel: 01282 814814

Blackburn with Darwen
St Johns Centre, Victoria Street, Blackburn, BB1 6DW
Tel: 01254 671211

Burnley
47 Parker Lane, Burnley, BB11 2BU
Tel: 01282 424655

Bury
Unit 19 The Business Centre, Kay Street, Bury, BL9 6BU
Tel: 0161 761 5355

Chorley, South Ribble
35-39 Market Street, Chorley, PR7 2SW
Tel: 01257 279807

Colne
2 Duke Street, Colne, BB8 0SU
Tel: 01282 867188

Fleetwood
43 Lord Street, Fleetwood, FY7 6DU
Tel: 01253 873091

Haslingden
1-3 Burgess Street, Haslingden, Rossendale, BB4 5QT
Tel: 01706 227515

Heywood
46 Market Street, Heywood, OL10 4LY
Tel: .... 0161 284 4666 - District Line

Hyndburn
New Era Centre, Paradise Street, Accrington, BB5 1PB
Public Tel: 01254 394210

Kirkham & Rural Fylde
Council Offices, Moor Street, Kirkham, Preston, PR4 2AU
Tel: 01772 682588

Lancaster
87 King Street, Lancaster, LA1 1RH
Public Tel: 0870 1264035

Lytham St Annes
Ashton Gardens Gate House, 5 St Georges Road, Lytham St Annes, FY8 2AE
Tel: 01253 720710

Morecambe
Oban House, 87-89 Queen Street, Morecambe, LA4 5EN
Tel: 01524 400400

Nelson
61/63 Every Street, Nelson, BB9 7LT
Public Tel: 01282 616750

Preston
Town Hall Annexe, Birley Street, Preston, PR1 2QE
Tel: 01772 822416

Ribble Valley
19-21 Wesleyan Row, Parson Lane, Clitheroe, BB7 2JY
Tel: 01200 428966

Royton
Macauley House, 1 Macanley Street, Royston, Oldham, OL2 6QP
Tel: 0161 633 4291

Skelmersdale (West Lancs)
128 Sandy Lane, Skelmersdale, WN8 8LH
Tel: 01695 723110

Todmorden
Calderdale Citizens Advice Bureau (Todmorden), Burnley Road, Todmorton OL14 7BX
Tel: 01706 813234

Wigan
Gerard Winstanley House, Crawford Street, Wigan, WN1 1NG
Tel: 01942 234292

Wyre District (Thornton Cleveleys)
99 Victoria Road West, Thornton Cleveleys, Blackpool, FY5 3LD
Tel: 01253 850658

LEICESTER

Leicester
2a New Walk, Off King Street, Leicester, LE1 6TF
Tel: 0116 255 4212

LEICESTERSHIRE

Charnwood
John Storer House, Ward's End, Loughborough, LE11 3HA
Tel: 01509 267374

Harborough District
11a St Marys Road, Market Harborough, LE16 7DS
Tel: 01858 466850

Hinckley
The Chestnuts, 25 Mount Road, Hinckley, LE10 1AD
Public Tel: 0870 751943

Lutterworth
Information Centre, Church Gate, Lutterworth, LE17 4AN
Tel: 01455 557375

Melton
3a Park Road, Melton Mowbray, LE13 1TT
Tel: 01664 565882

Oadby & Wigston
Wigston Library, Bull Head Street, Wigston, LE18 1PA
Tel: 0116 2887861

LINCOLNSHIRE

Boston
The Len Medlock, Voluntary Centre, St Georges Rd, Boston, PE21 8YB
Tel: 08450 525252

East Lindsey
20 Algitha Road, Skegness, PE25 2AG
Public Tel: 08450 525252

Grantham & District
26 St Catherines Road, Grantham, NG31 6TT
Tel: 08450 525252

Lincoln & District
Beaumont Lodge, Beaumont Fee, Lincoln, LN1 1UL
Tel: 08450 525252

Sleaford & District
The Advice Centre, Money's Yard, Carre Street, Sleaford, NG34 7TW
Tel: 08450 525252

South Holland
24 The Crescent, Spalding, PE11 1AF
Tel: 08450 525252

Stamford & District
39 High Street, Stamford, PE9 2BB
Tel: 08450 525252

West Lindsey
26 North Street, Gainsborough, DN21 2HU
Tel: 08450 525252

LONDON

Balham & Tooting
215 Balham High Road, London, SW17 7BQ
Tel: 020 8333 6960

Battersea
14 York Road, London, SW11 3QA
Tel: 020 8333 6960

Beckenham & Penge
20 Snowdown Close, Avenue Road, Penge, SE20 7RU
Tel: 020 8778 0921

Bermondsey
8 Market Place, Southwark Park Road, London, SE16 3UQ
Tel: 020 7231 1118

Brent
270-272 High Road, Willesden, London, NW10 2EY
Tel: 0845 050 5250

Brentford & Chiswick
Town Hall, Heathfield Terrace, London, W4 4JN
Tel: 020 8994 4846

Camden Borough Office
118-122 Gratton Road, KentishTown, London, NW5 4BA

Catford
120 Rushey Green, Catford, London, SE6 4HQ
Tel: 0870 126 4037

Chelsea
Old Town Hall, Kings Road,London, SW3 5EE
Tel: 020 7351 2114

City of London
32 Ludgate Hill, London, EC4M 7DR
Tel: 020 7236 1156

Dalston
491-493 Kingsland Road, Dalston, London, E8 4AU
Tel: 0870 126 4013

Edmonton
Edmonton Methodist Church, Fore Street, Edmonton, London, N9 0PN
Tel: 020 8807 4253

Eltham
181 High Street, Eltham, London, SE9 1TS
Tel: 020 8850 6044

Finchley
Hertford Lodge Annexe, East End Road, Finchley, London, N3 3QE
Tel: 0870 1264018

Fulham
The Pavilion, 1 Mund Street, London, W14 9LY
Tel: 020 7385 1322

Grahame Park
The Concourse, Grahame Park, London, NW9 5XA
Tel: 020 8205 4141

Greenwich Money Advice Service
Old Town Hall, Polytechnic Street, London, SE18 6PN
Tel: 020 8317 8266

Hendon
40-42 Church End, Hendon, London, NW4 4JT
Tel: 0870 1288080

Holborn
3rd Floor Holborn Library, 32-38 Theobalds Road, London, WC1X 8PA
Tel: 0845 050 5152

Kensington (London)
140 Ladbroke Grove, London, W10 5ND
Tel: 0870 7510930

Kentish Town
242 Kentish Town Road, Kentish Town, London, NW5 2AB
Tel: 0845 050 5152

Kilburn
200 Kilburn High Road, Kilburn, London, NW6 4JD
Tel: 0845 050 5152

Lewisham Money Advice Service
Deptford Business Park, 8 Evelyn Court, Grinstead Road, London, SE8 5AD
Tel: 020 8694 7647

Leytonstone
Greater London House, 547-551 High Road, Leytonstone, E11 4PB
Tel: 020 8988 9620

Mare Street
236-238 Mare Street, Hackney, London, E8 1HE
Tel: 0870 126 4013

Newham
Stratford Advice Arcade, 107-9 The Grove, Stratford, E15 1HP
Tel: 0870 1264097

Paddington
441 Harrow Road, Paddington, London, W10 4RE
Tel: 0870 1264040

Palmers Green
Town Hall, Green Lanes, Palmers Green, London, N13 4XD
Tel: 020 8882 5940

Peckham
97 Peckham High Street, London, SE15 5RS
Tel: 020 7639 4471

Pimlico
140 Tachbrook Street, London, SW1V 2NE
Tel: 0870 1264040

Putney & Roehampton
228 Upper Richmond Road, London, SW15 6TG
Tel: 020 8333 6960

Royal Courts of Justice
Royal Courts Of Justice, Strand, London, WC2A 2LL
Tel: 020 7947 6880

Sheen
Sheen Lane Centre, Sheen Lane, London, SW14 8LP
Tel: 020 8876 1513

St Marylebone
Westminster Council House, 97-113 Marylebone Road, London, NW1 5PT
Tel: 020 7641 1157

Streatham
Ilex House, 1 Barrhill Road, London, SW2 4RJ
Tel: 020 8674 8993

Sydenham
299 Kirkdale, Sydenham, London, SE26 4QD
Tel: 0870 1264037

Tottenham
Tottenham Town Hall, Town Hall Approach Road, London, N15 4RY
Tel: 020 8376 3700

Tower Hamlets East
86 Bow Road, London, E3 4DL
Tel: 020 8980 3728

Turnpike Lane
14a Willoughby Road, London, N8 0JJ
Tel: 020 8352 0202

Upper Street (Highbury)
135 Upper Street, Islington, London, N1 1QP
Tel: 020 7359 0619

Walthamstow
167 Hoe Street, Walthamstow, London, E17 3AL
Tel: 0870 1264026

Whitechapel
Unit 32, Greatorex Street, London, E1 5NP
Tel: 020 7247 4172

Woolwich
Old Town Hall, Polytechnic Street, Woolwich, London, SE18 6NP
Tel: 020 8854 9607

MERSEYSIDE

Anfield
36/38 Breckfield Rd North, Anfield, Liverpool, L5 4NH
Tel: 0151 285 1081

Bebington CAB Ltd
57 New Chester Road, New Ferry, Bedington, Wirral, CH62 1AB
Tel: 0151 645 8793

Birkenhead (Charity) Ltd
50 Argyle Street, Birkenhead, CH41 6AF
Tel: 0151 647 6517

Bootle
297 Knowsley Road, Bootle, L20 5DF
Tel: 0151 922 1114

Crosby
Prince Street, Waterloo, Crosby, Liverpool, L22 5PB
Tel: 0151 928 9702

Formby
11 Duke Street, Formby, Liverpool, L37 4AN
Tel: 01704 875078

Garston
Garston Community House, Garston Village, 2 Speke Rd, Liverpool, L19 2PA
Tel: 0151 427 5337

Heswall
Hillcroft, Rocky Lane, Heswall, Wirral, CH60 0BY
Tel: 0151 342 6371

Knowsley Central (Huyton)
Community Centre, Lathen Road, Huyton, Liverpool, L36 9XZ
Tel: 0151 489 5098

Knowsley District
10a Church Street, Prescott, L34 3LA

Knowsley North (Kirkby)
2 Newton Gardens, Kirby, Knowsley, Liverpool, L32 8RR
Tel: 0151 546 2284

Knowsley South (Halewood)
5-21 Raven Court, Leather Lane, Halewood, Liverpool, L26 0UP

Liverpool City
State House, 1st Floor, 22 Dale Street, Liverpool, L2 4TR
Tel: 0151 285 8989

Liverpool County Court Service
Queen Elizabeth II Law Courts, 4th Floor, Derby Square, Liverpool, L2 1XA
Tel: .... 0151 473 7373 ext. 4156

Netherley
Unit G, Belle Vale Shop Centre, Childwall Valley, Liverpool, L25 2RQ
Tel: 0151 487 0027

Southport
24 Wright Street, Southport, PR9 0TL
Tel: 01704 531456

Speke Advice Service
Damwood Hall, North Parade, Speke, Liverpool, L24 2SB
Tel: 0151 486 8545

St Helens
Waterlook Street, St Helens, WA10 1DY
Tel: 01744 22935

Toxteth
15 High Park Street, Toxteth, Liverpool, L8 8DX
Tel: 0151 280 8484

Wallasey
237-243 Liscard Road, Wallasey, CH44 5TH
Tel: 0151 639 7858

Walton
131 County Road, Walton, Liverpool, L4 3QF
Tel: 0151 525 1639

Wavertree CAB Ltd
242 Picton Road, Wavertree, Liverpool, L15 4LP
Tel: 0151 522 1406

West Kirby
1-3 Acacia Grove, West Kirby, Wirral, CH48 4DD
Tel: 0151 625 9802

MIDDLESBROUGH

Middlesbrough
3 Bolckow Street, Middlesbrough, TS1 1TH
Tel: 01642 864455

MIDDLESEX

Enfield Town
10 Little Park Gardens, Enfield, EN2 6PQ
Tel: 020 8363 0928

Feltham
Peoples Centre, High Street, Feltham, TW13 4AH
Tel: 020 8707 0077

Harrow
Civic Centre, Station Road, Harrow, HA1 2XH
Tel: 0870 1264460

Hayes
Hayes One Stop, 49-50 Station Road, Hayes, UB3 4BE
Tel: 0870 1264021

Hounslow
45 Treaty Centre, Hounslow, TW3 1ES
Tel: 020 8570 2983

Ruislip
9 Eastcote Road, Ruislip, HA4 8BD
Tel: 0870 1264021

Staines
Community Link, Knowle Green, Staines, TW18 1XA
Tel: 01784 444220

Sunbury & Shepperton
1b Staines Road West, Sunbury-on-Thames, TW16 7AB
Tel: 01932 765041

Twickenham
The Advice Centre, 61 Heath Road, Twickenham, TW1 4AW
Tel: 020 8892 5917

Uxbridge
Link 1a Civic Centre, High Street, Uxbridge, UB8 1UW
Tel: 0870 1264021

MILTON KEYNES

Bletchley
3/5 The Concourse, Brunel Centre, Bletchley, MK2 2ES
Tel: 01908 378569

Milton Keynes Central
Acorn House, 361 Midsummer Boulevard, Milton Keynes, MK9 3HP
Tel: 0870 1264050

NORFOLK

Dereham
Assembly Rooms, Ruthem Place, Dereham, NR19 2TX
Tel: 01362 697776

Diss Eye & Harleston
Shelfanger Road, Diss, IP22 4EH
Tel: 01379 651333

Fakenham & District
The Community Centre, Oak Street, Fakenham, NR21 9DY
Tel: 01328 856040

Great Yarmouth
2 Stonecutters Way, Great Yarmouth, NR30 1HF
Tel: 01493 856665

Holt
Kerridge Way, Holt, NR25 6DN
Tel: 01263 713849

Kings Lynn
Thoresby College, Queen Street, Kings Lynn, PE30 1HX
Tel: 01553 774719

Marham
5 Woodview Road, Upper Marham, King's Lynn, PE33 9JX
Tel: 01760 338347

NMA Money Advice Ltd
Unit 12, Capital House, Heigham Street, Norwich, NR2 4TE
Tel: 01603 763980

North Walsham & District
New Road, North Walsham, NR28 9DE
Tel: 01692 402570

Norwich
The Advice Arcade, 4 Guildhall Hill, Norwich, NR2 1JH
Tel: 01603 765783

Thetford
15 Earls Street, Thetford, IP24 2AB
Tel: 01842 752777

Watton
The Cabin, Harvey Street, Watton, IP25 6EB
Tel: 01953 882746

Wymondham, Attleborough & District CAB
14 The Bridewell, Norwich Road, Wymondham, NR18 0NS
Tel: 01953 603977

NORTH EAST LINCOLNSHIRE

Grimsby, Cleethorpes & District
4 Town Hall Street, Grimsby, DN31 1HN
Tel: 01472 232200

NORTH LINCOLNSHIRE

Scunthorpe
12 Oswald Road, Scunthorpe, DN15 7PT
Tel: 01724 848645

NORTH SOMERSET

North Somerset
Roselawn, Walliscote Grove Road, Weston-Super-Mare, BS23 1UT
Tel: 01934 621908

NORTH YORKSHIRE

Craven
St Andrews Church Hall, Newmarket Street, Skipton, BD23 2JE
Tel: 01756 700210

Hambleton
227 High Street, Northallerton, DL7 8SE
Tel: 01609 770309

Harrogate
Victoria Park House, 18 Victoria Avenue, Harrogate, HG1 5QY
Tel: 01423 503576

Richmondshire
23 Newbiggin, Richmond, DL10 4DX
Tel: 01748 823978

Ripon
5 Duck Hill, Ripon, HG4 1BL
Tel: 01765 603297

Ryedale
Ryedale Community House, Wentworth Street, Malton, YO17 7BN
Tel: 01653 692740

Scarborough & District
62 Roscoe Street, Scarborough, YO12 7BY
Tel: 01723 368710

Selby
16 Park Street, Selby, YO8 4PW
Tel: 01757 702031

Whitby
Church House, Flowergate, Whitby, YO21 3BA
Tel: 01904 605157

NORTHAMPTONSHIRE

Corby
No. 1 Corby Advice Centre, George Street, Corby, NN17 1QG
Tel: 01536 203552

Daventry & District
The Abbey, Market Square, Daventry, NN11 4BH
Tel: 01327 706464

East Northants (Rushden)
Bakehouse Office, 46 Duck Street, Rushden, NN10 9SD

Kettering
The Oasis Centre, 10 Market Street, Kettering, NN16 0AH
Tel: 01536 482321

Northampton
72a St Giles Street, Northampton, NN1 1JW
Tel: 01604 636000

Wellingborough
Rear Of Layton House, High Street, Wellingborough, NN8 4HR
Tel: 01933 274343

NORTHUMBERLAND

Alnwick & District
The Bondgate Centre, 22 Bondgate Without, Alnwick, NE66 1PN
Tel: 01665 604135

Berwick
5 Tweed Street, Berwick-upon-Tweed, TD15 1NG
Tel: 01289 330222

Blyth Valley
Eric Tolhurst Centre, 3-13 Quay Street, Blyth, NE24 2AS
Tel: 01670 367779

Castle Morpeth
Tower Buildings, 9 Oldgate, Morpeth, NE61 1PY
Tel: 01670 518814

Debt Advice within Northumberland
The Fourways, Bridge Street, Amble, NE65 0DR

Tynedale
The Community Centre, Gilesgate, Hexham, NE46 3NP
Tel: 01434 605254

Wansbeck
Station Villa, Kenilworth Road, Ashington, NE63 8AA
Tel: 01670 818360

NOTTINGHAM

Eastwood & District
Library & Information Ctr, Nottingham Road, Eastwood, Nottingham, NG16 3GB
Tel: 01773 718065

Nottingham & District
24-30 Castle Gate, Nottingham, NG1 7AT
Tel: 0115 958 5280

NOTTINGHAMSHIRE

Ashfield
22 Market Street, Sutton-in-Ashfield, NG17 1AG
Tel: 01623 557686

Bassetlaw
Central Avenue, Worksop, S80 1EJ
Tel: 01909 476049

Beeston
Albion Street, Beeston, Nottingham, NG9 2PA
Tel: 0870 126 4027

Mansfield
Suites 22-24, Brunts Business Centre, Block B Samuel Brunts Way, Mansfield, NG18 2AH
Tel: 01623 627163

Newark & District
2 Castlegate, Newark, NG24 1AX
Tel: 01636 704391

Ollerton & District
5 Forest Court, Forest Road, New Ollerton, Newark, NG22 9PL
Tel: 01623 861808

OXFORDSHIRE

Abingdon
The Old Abbey House, Abbey Close, Abingdon, OX14 3JD
Tel: 01235 521894

Banbury
Cornhill House, 26 Cornhill, Banbury, OX16 5NG
Tel: 08450 505162

Bicester
The Garth, Launton Road, Bicester, OX6 0JB
Tel: 01869 321076

Didcot & District
Civic Hall, Britwell Road, Didcot, OX11 7JN
Tel: 01235 813632

Henley & District
32 Market Place, Henley-on-Thames, RG9 2AH

Oxford
95 St Aldates, Oxford, OX1 1DA
Tel: 01865 247578

Thame
Market House, North Street, Thame, OX9 3HH
Tel: 01844 214827

Witney
33a High Street, Witney, OX28 6HP
Tel: 01993 705691

PETERBOROUGH

Peterborough
Alma House, 41a Park Road, Peterborough, PE1 2TH
Tel: 0870 1264024

PLYMOUTH

Plymouth & Devonport
Virginia House Settlement, 1st Floor, 40 Looe Street, Plymouth, PL4 0EB
Tel: 01752 207088

POOLE

Poole
54 Lagland Street, Poole, BH15 1QG
Tel: 01202 678517

PORTSMOUTH

Portsmouth
Drummond House, Dugald Drummond Street, Portsmouth, PO1 2BB
Tel: 023 9282 8621

READING

Reading
21 Chatham Street, Reading, RG1 7JF
Tel: 0118 958059

Reading Community Welfare Rights Unit
17 Chatham Street, Reading, RG1 7JF
Tel: 0118 950 5292

REDCAR & CLEVELAND

Redcar & Cleveland
88 Westgate, Guisborough, TS14 6AP
Tel: 01642 488423

RUTLAND

Rutland
56 High Street, Oakham, LE15 6AL
Tel: 01572 723012

SHROPSHIRE

Bridgnorth & District
Whitburn Street, Bridgnorth, WV16 4QT
Tel: 01746 763838

Madeley
The Peoples Centre, Madeley, Telford, TF7 5AU
Tel: 01952 585824

North Shropshire (Market Drayton)
Lord Clive Chambers, St Marys Street, Market Drayton, TF9 1AA
Tel: 01630 657137

Oswestry & Border
16 Lower Brook Street, Oswestry, SY11 2HJ
Tel: 01691 654425

Shrewsbury
The Roy Fletcher Centre, 12-17 Cross Hill, Shrewsbury, SY1 1JE
Tel: 01743 357855

South Shropshire
Marsdens Hill, Portcullis Lane, Ludlow, SY8 1PZ
Tel: 01584 876454

Telford Town Centre
Meeting Point House, Southwater Square, Telford, TF3 4HS
Tel: 01952 291101

Wellington
35 Church Street, Wellington, TF1 1DG
Tel: 01952 223232

SLOUGH

Slough
27 Church Street, Slough, SL1 1PL
Tel: 01753 522004

SOMERSET

Frome
St Johns Cottage, Church Steps, Frome, BA11 1PL
Tel: 01373 465496

Mid Somerset
The Amulet, 5 Market Place, Shepton Mallet, BA4 5AG
Tel: 01749 343010

Sedgemoor
The Lions, West Quay, Bridgwater, TA6 3DD
Tel: 01278 455236

South Somerset (Yeovil)
Petters House, Petters Way, Yeovil, BA20 1SH
Tel: 01935 421167

Taunton
Sussex Lodge, 44 Station Road, Taunton, TA1 1NS
Tel: 01823 282235

SOUTH YORKSHIRE

Askern & District
59 Manor Road, Askern, DN6 0BE
Tel: 01302 701339

Barnsley
1 Shambles Street, Barnsley, S70 2SQ
Tel: 01226 206492

Doncaster
The Guildhall Advice Ctre, Old Guildhall Yard, Frenchgate, Doncaster, DN1 1QW
Tel: 01302 735225

Mexborough & District
The Lindsay Centre, Hallgate, Mexborough, S64 0JT
Tel: 01709 585827

Pitsmoor
28-30 Spital Hill, Sheffield, S4 7LG
Tel: 0114 275 5376

Rotherham
The Rain Building, Eastwood Lane, Rotherham, S65 1EQ
Tel: 01709 513523

Sharrow
416 - 418 London Road, Sheffield, S2 4ND
Tel: 0114 258 3322

Sheffield Debt Support Unit
237 London Road, Sheffield, S2 4NF
Tel: 0114 255 5455

Sheffield Mental Health
The Carlisle Centre, Nether Edge Hospital, Osbourne Road, Sheffield, S11 9BJ
Tel: 0114 271 8025

South East Sheffield
77 Queen Street, Mosborough, Sheffield, S20 5BP
Tel: 0114 248 0043

Stainforth
14 Church Road, Stainforth, DN7 5AA
Tel: 01302 842845

Thorne CAB
5a Browns Lane, Thorne, Doncaster, DN8 5AF
Tel: 01405 814064

SOUTHAMPTON

Southampton
3 Kings Park Road, Southampton, SO15 2AT
Tel: ...... 023 8022 1406 & 023 8033 3868

Totton & District
91 Junction Road, Totton, Southampton, SO40 3BU
Tel: 0870 1264089

STAFFORDSHIRE

Biddulph
10 Tunstall Road, Biddulph, Stoke-on-Trent, ST8 6HH
Tel: 01782 519332

Burntwood & District
Wade House, 7 Cannock Road, Burntwood, WS7 8JS
Tel: 01543 674170

Burton-Upon-Trent
Voluntary Services Center, Union Street Car Park, Burton-on-Trent, DE14 1AA
Tel: 01283 510993

Cannock
48 Allport Road, Cannock, WS11 1DZ
Tel: 01543 502236

Cheadle
Council Offices, Leek Road, Cheadle, ST10 1JF
Tel: 01538 753189

Coalville & District
Residents Association House, Dimmelow Street, Coalville, ST1 1HL
Tel: 01782 219472

Kidsgrove
Claire House, Liverpool Road, Kidsgrove, Stoke-on-Trent, ST7 4EH
Tel: 01782 786529

Leek
20 St Edward Street, Leek, ST13 5DS
Tel: 01538 373243

Lichfield
29 Levetts Fields, Lichfield, WS13 6HY
Tel: 01543 252730

Newcastle-Under-Lyme
25-27 Well Street, Newcastle under Lyme, ST5 1BP
Tel: 0870 1264049

Rugeley
7 Brook Square, Rugeley, WS15 2DU
Tel: 01889 577042

South Staffordshire
Civic Centre, Gravel Hill, Wombourne, WV5 9HA

Stafford
Stafford District, Vol Services Centre, 131-141 North Walls, Stafford, ST16 3AD
Tel: 01785 258673

Stoke-on-Trent District
Advice House, Cheapside, Hanley, Stoke-on-Trent, ST1 1HL
Tel: 01782 219427

Stone
St Marys Chambers, 19 Station Road, Stone, ST15 8JT
Tel: 01785 814806

Tamworth
1st Floor The Phillip Dix, Centre, Corporation Street, Tamworth, B79 7DN
Tel: 01827 709645

Uttoxeter
Rear Annexe, Town Hall, High Street, Uttoxeter, ST14 7HN
Tel: 01889 568500

STOCKTON-ON-TEES

Stockton & District Adv & Inf Srvc
Bath Lane, Stockton-on-Tees, TS18 2EQ
Tel: 01642 607445

SUFFOLK

Beccles
1 Ballygate, Beccles, NR34 9NA
Tel: 01502 717715

Brandon
11 High Street, Brandon, IP27 0AQ
Tel: 01842 811511

Bury St Edmunds
Risbygate Centre, 90 Risbygate Street, Bury St Edmunds, IP33 1SQ
Tel: 01284 753675

Felixstowe
2-6 Orwell Road, Felixstow, Suffolk, IP11 7HD
Tel: 01394 275958

Halesworth
25 Market Place, Halesworth, IP19 8AY
Tel: 01986 874541

Haverhill
4 Swan Lane, Haverhill, CB9 9EQ
Tel: 01440 704012

Ipswich & District
19 Tower Street, Ipswich, IP1 3BE
Tel: 01473 219777

Leiston
Council Offices, Main Street, Leiston, IP16 4ER
Tel: 01728 832193

Lowestoft
The Advice Centre, 36 Gordon Road, Lowestoft, NR32 1NL
Tel: 01502 518510

Mid-Suffolk
Oak Cottage, 5 Milton Road South, Stowmarket, IP14 1EZ
Tel: 01449 676060

Mildenhall
Willow House, 40 St Andrews St, Mildenhall, Bury St Edmunds, IP28 7HB
Tel: 01638 712094

Newmarket
Foley Gate, Wellington Street, Newmarket, CB8 0HY
Tel: 01638 665999

Saxmundham
26b High Street, Saxmundham, IP17 1AB
Tel: 01728 603057

Sudbury
Belle Vue, Newton Road, Sudbury, CO10 2RG
Tel: 01787 374671

SURREY

Addington
1a Overbury Crescent, New Addington, Croydon, CR0 0LR
Tel: 01689 846890

Beddington & Wallington
16 Stanley Park Road, Wallington, SM6 0EU
Tel: 020 8669 3435

Camberley
Rear of Library, Knoll Road, Camberley, GU15 3SY
Tel: 01276 684342

Caterham & Warlingham
Soper Hall, Harestone Valley Road, Caterham, CR3 6YN
Tel: 01883 344777

Chessington & Hook
Library Court, Elm Road, Chessington, KT9 1AF
Tel: 0870 1264019

Cranleigh
Village Way, Cranleigh, GU6 8AF
Tel: 01483 273378

Croydon Money Advice Unit
Strand House, Zion Road, Thornton Heath, CR7 8RG
Tel: 020 8683 5210

Dorking
231 High Street, Dorking, RH4 1RT
Tel: 01306 876805

Epsom & Ewell
The Pines, 2 The Parade, Epsom, KT18 5DH
Tel: 01372 720205

Esher & District
Harry Fletcher House, High Street, Esher, KT10 9RN
Tel: 01372 464770

Farnham
Bright House, Off East Street, Farnham, GU9 7SB
Tel: 01252 716319

Godalming & District
10 Queen Street, Godalming, GU7 1BD
Tel: 01483 428212

Guildford
15 - 21 Haydon Place, Guildford, GU1 4LL
Tel: 01483 576699

Haslemere
Well Lane House, Well Lane, High Street, Haslemere, GU27 2LB
Tel: 01428 643413

Heathlands
Beech House, Church Road, Frimley, GU16 5AD

Horley
Albert Rooms, 92 Albert Road, Horley, RH6 7HZ
Tel: 0870 75710947

Kingston CABX Service
Neville House, Kinston-upon-Thames, KT1 1BW
Tel: 020 8255 6060

Leatherhead
The Georgion House, Swan Mews, Leatherhead, KT22 8AE
Tel: 01372 375522

Malden & Coombe
Blagdon Road, New Malden, KT3 4AF
Tel: 0870 1264019

Merton Money Advice Service
326 London Road, Mitcham, CR4 3ND
Tel: 020 8640 3194

Mitcham
326 London Road, Mitcham, CR4 3ND
Tel: 020 8288 0450

Morden
7 Crown Parade, Crown Lane, Morden, SM4 5DA
Tel: 020 8715 0707

North Cheam
320 Malden Road, North Cheam, SM3 8EP
Tel: 020 8770 4851

Oxted
The Portacabin, Ellice Road Car Park, Oxted, RH8 0PY
Tel: 01883 715525

Redhill, Reigate & Banstead
24 Cromwell Road, Redhill, RH1 1RT
Tel: 0870 1264072

Richmond
Linfield House, 26 Kew Road, Richmond, TW9 2NA
Tel: 020 8940 2501

Runnymede
Civic Offices, Station Road, Addleston, KT15 2AH
Tel: 01932 842666

St Helier
5-6 Rose Hill Court Parade, St Helier Avenue, Morden, SM4 6JS
Tel: 020 8640 4170

Surrey Welfare Rights Unit
Portesbery Road, Camberley, GU15 3SZ

Sutton
The Central Library, Sutton, SM1 1EA
Tel: 020 8643 5291

Thornton Heath
Strand House, Zion Road, Thornton Heath, CR7 8RG
Tel: 020 8684 2263

Walton Weybridge & Hersham
Elm Grove, Hersham Road, Walton-on-Thames, KT12 1LH
Tel: 01932 248660

Woking
Provencial House, 26 Commercial Way, Woking, GU21 1EN
Tel: 01483 763840

SWINDON

Swindon
Faringdon Road, Swindon, SN1 5AR
Tel: 0845 0505155

TYNE & WEAR

Gateshead
5 Regent Terrace, Gateshead, NE8 1LU
Tel: 0191 477 1392

Newcastle City
St Cuthberts's Chambers, 35 Nelson Street, Newcastle-upon-Tyne, NE1 5AN
Tel: 0191 232 0832

North Tyneside
1 Roxburgh Terrace, Whitley Bay, NE26 1DR
Tel: 0191 200 7777

South Tyneside
Edinburgh Buildings, 2 Station Approach, South Shields, NE33 1HR
Tel: 0191 456 0157

Washington
The Elms, 19 Front Street, Concord, Washington, NE37 2BA
Tel: 0191 416 6848

Wearside CAB Money Advice Unit
Unit 6, St Ignatius Close, Hendon, Sunderland, SR2 8BD
Tel: 0191 565 5135

WARWICKSHIRE

Bedworth
Old Market Tavern, 25 Congreve Walk, Bedworth, CV12 8LX
Tel: 024 7631 1119

North Warwickshire
Coleshill House, Coleshill Road, Atherstone, CV9 1BW
Tel: 0870 7510928

Nuneaton
Barlow House, Back Street, Nuneaton, CV11 4HG
Tel: 024 7634 4708

Rugby
1st Floor, Chestnut House, 32 North Street, Rugby, CV21 2AG
Tel: 0178 8541080

Stratford-Upon-Avon
7a Rother Street, Stratford-upon-Avon, CV37 6LU
Tel: 01789 293299

Warwick District
10, Hamilton Terrace, Leamington Spa, CV32 4LY
Tel: 01926 457900

WEST BERKSHIRE

West Berkshire
16 Bartholomew Street, Newbury, RG14 5LL
Tel: 01635 552050

WEST MIDLANDS

Acocks Green
York House, 26 Station Road, Acocks Green, Birmingham, B27 6DN
Tel: 0121 683 5671

Bilston
William Leigh House, 15 Walsall Street, Bilston, WV14 0AT
Tel: 01902 572000

Birmingham City Centre
Gazette Buildings, 168 Corporation Street, Birmingham, B4 6TF
Tel: 0121 248 4950

Birmingham District CABx
Room 232, 2nd Floor, Gazette Buildings, 168 Corporation Street, Birmingham, B4 6TF
Tel: 0121 6875345

Birmingham District Health Units
North GP Unit, 2 South Cottages, Farthing Lane, Sutton Coldfield B72 1RN

Brierley Hill
Cottage Street, Brierley Hill, DY5 1RE
Tel: 01384 816200

Chelmsley Wood
Stephenson Drive, Chelmsley Wood, Birmingham, B37 5TA
Tel: 0870 7510955

Coventry
4th Floor Coventry Point, Market Way, Coventry, CV1 1EA
Tel: 0845 1202920

Cradley Heath
Cradley Heath Community Ctr, Cradley Heath, B64 4JG
Tel: 01384 636988

Dudley
Marlborough House, 11 St. James's Road, Dudley, DY1 1JG
Tel: 01384 816066

Halesowen
Halesowen Health Centre, Birmingham Street, Halesowen, B63 3HN

Handsworth
171 Churchill Parade, Birchfield Road, Birmingham, B19 1LL
Tel: 0121 250 6500

Kingstanding
404 Kingstanding Road, Kingstanding, Birmingham, B44 8LD
Tel: 0121 683 6883

Low Hill
The Bungalow, Rear of Dale House, Showell Circus, Wolverhampton, WV10 9BG
Tel: 01902 305446

Northfield
734-740 Bristol Rd South, Northfield, Birmingham, B31 2NN
Tel: 0121 683 5755

Oldbury
Municipal Buildings, Halesowen Street, Oldbury, Warley, B69 2AB
Tel: 0121 552 2022

Shirley
Shirley Centre, 274 Stratford Rd, Shirley, B90 3AD
Tel: 0121 745 3148

Smethwick
370-372 High Street, Smethwick, B66 3PJ
Tel: 0121 558 8500

Solihull
The Priory, Church Hill Road, Solihull, B91 3LF
Tel: 0121 705 2211

Stourbridge
69 Market Street, Stourbridge, DY8 1AQ
Tel: 01384 816222

Sutton Coldfield
North GP Unit, 2 South Cottage, Sutton Coldfield, B72 1NR
Tel: 0121 687 5320

Tipton
Neptune Health Park, Sedgley Road West, Tipton, DY4 8LX
Tel: 0121 607 6411

Walsall
139-144 Lichfield Street, Walsall, WS1 1SE
Tel: 01922 700600

West Bromwich
22 Lombard Street, West Bromwich, B70 8RT
Tel: 0121 553 4423

Wolverhampton
26 Snow Hill, Wolverhampton, WV2 4AD
Tel: 01902 572200

Yardley
202-204 Church Road, Yardley, Birmingham, B25 8UT
Tel: 0121 784 6455

WEST SUSSEX

Bognor Regis
Town Hall, Clarence Road, Bognor Regis, PO21 1LD
Tel: 0845 120 3700

Burgess Hill
Delmon House, 38 Church Road, Burgess Hill, RH15 9AE
Tel: 01444 241252

Chichester & District
Bell House, 6 Theatre Lane, Chichester, PO19 1SR
Tel: 01243 784231

Crawley
The Tree, 103 High Street, Crawley, RH10 1DD
Tel: 01293 529717

East Grinstead
Cantelupe House, Cantelupe Road, East Grinstead, RH19 3BZ
Tel: 01342 321638

Haywards Heath
Oaklands, Paddockhall Road, Haywards Heath, RH16 1HG
Tel: 01444 459866

Horsham
Lower Tanbridge Way, Horsham, RH12 1PJ
Tel: 0870 126 4080

Lancing & Sompting
Parish Hall, South Street, Lancing, BN15 8AJ
Tel: 01903 755585

Littlehampton
14-16 Anchor Springs, Littlehampton, BN17 6BP
Tel: 01903 724010

Shoreham & Southwick
Volunteer Centre, Pond Road, Shoreham-by-Sea, BN43 5WU
Tel: 01273 453756

Worthing & District
1 North Street, Worthing, BN11 1DU
Tel: 01903 232116

WEST YORKSHIRE

Batley
Town Hall Annexe, Brunswick Street, Batley, WF17 5DT
Tel: 01924 326066

Bradford (W Yorks)
17 Canal Road, Bradford, BD1 4AT
Tel: 01274 201919

Brighouse
1 Hall Street, Brighouse, HD6 1JY
Tel: 01484 714066

Chapeltown
Willow House, New Roscoe Bldgs, Cross Francis St, Leeds, LS7 4BZ
Tel: 0113 262 9479

Dewsbury
Units 5/6, Empire House,Wakefield Old Road, Dewsbury, WF12 8DJ
Tel: 01924 324252

Elland
Providence U R Church, Huddersfield Road, Elland, HX5 9AH
Tel: 01422 376080

Halifax
37 Harrison Road, Halifax, HX1 2AF
Tel: 01422 342917

Hebden Bridge
New Oxford House, Albert Street, Hebden Bridge, HX7 8AH
Tel: 01422 842848

Keighley & District
The Library Annexe, Spencer Street, Keighley, BD21 3BN
Tel: 01535 605454

Leeds
31 New York Street, Leeds, LS2 7DT
Tel: 0113 245 7679

Otley
Courthouse Street, Otley, LS21 1BG
Tel: 01943 466976

Pontefract
1St Floor, Horsefair House, Horsefair, Pontefract, WF8 1DE
Tel: 01977 793768

Shipley
6 Windsor Road, Shipley, BD18 3EQ
Tel: 01274 532475

South Elmsall
Westfield Resource & Enterprise Centre, Westfield Lane, South Elmsall, Pontefract, WF9 2PU
Tel: 01977 642179

South Kirklees CAB
6-8 St Peters Street, Huddersfield, HD1 1DH
Tel: 01484 425240

Spen Valley
The Town Hall, Church Street, Cleckheaton, BD19 3RH
Tel: 01274 877607

Wakefield
Ground Floor, 27 King Street, Wakefield, WF1 2SR
Tel: 01924 372563

Wakefield District
District Office, 1st Floor, 27 King Street, Wakefield, WF1 2SR
Tel: 01924 378066

WILTSHIRE

Kennet
Commercial Road, Devizes, SN10 1EH
Tel: 01380 722242

North Wiltshire
3 Avon Reach, Monkton Hill, Chippenham, SN15 1EE
Tel: 0870 1203707

Salisbury & District
18 College Street, Salisbury, SP1 3AL
Tel: 01722 327222

West Wiltshire District CAB
Central Car Park, Warminster, BA14 9BT
Tel: 0870 1203737

WINDSOR & MAIDENHEAD

Maidenhead
Redcote House, Holmanleaze, Maidenhead, SL6 8AW
Tel: 01628 621006

WOKINGHAM

Wokingham & District
Wellington House, Wellington Road, Wokingham, RG40 2AG
Tel: 0118 989 0389

WORCESTERSHIRE

Bromsgrove & District
50-52 Birmingham Road, Bromsgrove, B61 0DD
Tel: 01527 831480

Malvern Hills District
The Grange, Grange Road, Malvern, WR14 3HA
Tel: 01684 563611

Redditch
Central Chambers, 20 Unicorn Hill, Redditch, B97 4QU
Tel: 01527 666664

Worcester
The Hopmarket, The Foregate, Worcester, WR1 1DL
Tel: 01905 611371

Wychavon (Evesham)
110 High Street, Evesham, WR11 4EJ
Tel: 01386 443737

Wyre Forest
21-22 New Road, Kidderminster, DY10 1AF
Tel: 01562 823593

YORK

York
3 Blossom Street, York, YO24 1AU
Tel: 01904 636066

NORTHERN IRELAND

BELFAST

Antrim Road
211 Antrim Road, Belfast, BT15 2GW
Tel: 028 9075 2114

Central Belfast
6 Callender Street, Belfast, BT1 5BN
Tel: 028 9024 3196

East Belfast
342 Newtownards Road, Belfast, BT4 1HE
Tel: 028 9073 9447

Falls
8 Springfield Road, Belfast, BT12 7AG
Tel: 028 9031 0318

Shankill
179 Shankill Road, Belfast, BT13 1FP
Tel: 028 9032 7702

Suffolk/Andersontown
208 Andersonstown Road, Belfast, BT11 9EB
Tel: 028 9030 1916

CO. ANTRIM

Antrim
10D High Street, Antrim, BT41 1AN
Tel: 028 9442 8176

Ballymena
28 Mount Street, Ballymena, BT43 6BW
Tel: 028 2564 4398

Carrickfergus
65 North Street, Carrickfergus, BT38 7AE
Tel: 028 9335 1808

Glengormley
1st Floor, 3b Ballyclare Road, Glengormley, Newtown Abbey, BT36 5EU
Tel: 028 9084 4592

Larne
Park Lodge, 49 Victoria Road, Larne, BT40 1RT
Tel: 028 2826 0379

Lisburn
Bridge Community Centre, 50 Railway Street, Lisburn, BT28 1XG
Tel: 028 9266 2251

Rathcoole
Dunanney Centre, Rathmullan Dr, Rathcoole, Newtownabbey, BT37 9DQ
Tel: 028 9085 2271

CO. ARMAGH

Armagh
9 McCrums Court, Armagh, BT61 7RS
Tel: 028 3752 4041

Craigowon District
Town Hall, 7 Edward Street, Portadown, BT62 3LX
Tel: 028 3835 3260

Lurgan
The Town Hall, 6 Union Street, Lurgan, BT66 6AS
Tel: 028 3832 3571

CO. DOWN

Ards
North Down & Ards Comm, Health Care Unit, 39 Regent Street, Newtownards, BT23 4AD
Tel: 028 9181 9257

Banbridge
The Old Town Hall, Scarva Street, Banbridge, BT32 3DA
Tel: 028 4062 2201

Bangor
Hamilton House, 1A Springfield Avenue, Bangor, BT20 5BY
Tel: 028 9127 0009

Downpatrick
2nd Floor, Maghinis House, 8-10 Irish Street, Downpatrick, BT30 6BP
Tel: 028 4461 4110

Holywood
Queens Hall, Sullivan Place, Holywood, BT18 9JF
Tel: 028 9042 8288

Newry
2nd Fl, River House, 41c The Mall, Newry, BT34 1AN
Tel: 028 3026 2934

CO. FERMANAGH

Fermanagh
Belmore Mews, 2 New Street, Enniskillen, BT74 6AH
Tel: 028 6632 4334

CO. LONDONDERRY

Coleraine
24 Lodge Road, Coleraine, BT52 1NB
Tel: 028 7034 4817

Londonderry
1-3 Guildhall Street, Londonderry, BT48 6BJ
Tel: 028 7136 2444

CO. TYRONE

Cookstown & Magherafelt
Cookstown Office, 15 Molesworth Street, Cookstown, BT80 NX
Tel: 028 8676 6126

Dungannon
5-6 Feeneys Lane, Dungannon, BT70 1TX
Tel: 028 8772 5299

Strabane
17 Dock Street, Strabane, BT82 8EE
Tel: 028 7138 2665

SCOTLAND

ABERDEEN

Aberdeen
47 Market Street, Aberdeen, AB11 5PZ
Tel: 01224 586255

ABERDEENSHIRE

Banff & Buchan
Marischal Chambers, Drummers Corner, Peterhead, AB42 6ZP
Tel: 01779 471515

ANGUS

Angus (Arbroath)
11 Millgate, Arbroath, DD11 1NN
Tel: 01241 870661

Angus (Forfar)
175 East High Street, Forfar, DD8 2HH
Tel: 01307 467097

Angus (Montrose)
38 Murray Street, Montrose, DD10 8LB
Tel: 01674 673263

CLACKMANNANSHIRE

Alloa
47 Drysdale Street, Alloa, FK10 1JA
Tel: 01259 723880

DUMFRIES & GALLOWAY

Annan
19a Bank Street, Annan, DG12 6AA
Tel: 01461 201012

Castle Douglas
3 St Andrew Street, Castle Douglas, Kirkcudbrightshire, DG7 3AH
Tel: 01556 502190

Dumfries
81-85 Irish Street, Dumfries, DG1 2PQ
Tel: 01387 252456

Stranraer
23 Lewis Street, Stranraer, DG9 7AB
Tel: 01776 706355

DUNDEE

Dundee
97 Seagate, Dundee, DD1 2ER
Tel: 01382 27171/2

EAST AYRSHIRE

East Ayrshire
3 John Dickie Street, Kilmarnock, KA1 1HW
Tel: 01563 544744

Kilbirnie
43 Main Street, Kilbirnie, KA25 7BX
Tel: 01505 682830

EAST DUNBARTONSHIRE

Barrhead
216 Main Street, Barrhead, Glasgow, G78 1SN
Tel: 0141 881 2032

East Dunbartonshire
5 Dalrymple Court, Townhead, Kirkintilloch, G66 3AA
Tel: 0141 578 0160

EAST KILBRIDE

24 Cornwall Way, East Kilbride, G74 1JR
Tel: 01355 263698

EAST LOTHIAN

Haddington
38 Market Street, Haddington, EH41 3JE
Tel: 01620 824471

Musselburgh
141 High Street, Musselburgh, EH21 7DD
Tel: 0131 653 2748

EDINBURGH

Edinburgh (Central)
58 Dundas Street, Edinburgh, EH3 6QZ
Tel: 0131 557 1500

Edinburgh (Gorgie/Dalry)
Fountainbridge Library, 137 Dundee Street, Edinburgh, EH11 1BG
Tel: 0131 474 8080

Edinburgh (Leith)
166 Gt Junction Street, Edinburgh, EH6 5LJ
Tel: 0131 554 8144

Edinburgh (Pilton)
Unit 20, Edinburgh Shopping Court, 661 Ferry Rd, Edinburgh, EH4 2TX
Tel: 0131 332 9434

Edinburgh (Portobello)
191 Portobello High St, Portobello, Edinburgh, EH15 1EU
Tel: 0131 669 5903

Edinburgh Sheriff Court
27 Chambers Street, Edinburgh, EH1 1LB

FALKIK

Denny & Dunipace
24 Duke Street, Denny, FK6 6DD
Tel: 01324 823118

Falkirk
Old Sheriff Court, Hope Street, Falkirk, FK1 5AR
Tel: 01324 628406

Grangemouth & Bo'ness
1 Kerse Road, Grangemouth, FK3 8HW
Tel: 01324 483467

GLASGOW

Glasgow (Albion Street)
48 Albion Street, Glasgow, G1 1LH

Glasgow (Bridgeton)
35 Main Street, Bridgeton Cross, Glasgow, G40 1QB
Tel: 0141 554 0336

Glasgow (Castlemilk)
27 Dougrie Drive, Castlemilk, Glasgow, G45 9AD
Tel: 0141 634 0338/9

Glasgow (Drumchapel)
49 Dunkenny Square, Drumchapel, Glasgow, G15 8NE
Tel: 0141 944 2612

Glasgow (Easterhouse)
46 Shandwick Square, Glasgow, G34 9DS
Tel: 0141 771 2328

Glasgow (Maryhill)
1145 Maryhill Road, Glasgow, G20 9AZ
Tel: 0141 946 6373

Glasgow (Parkhead)
1361-1363 Gallowgate, Glasgow, G31 4DN
Tel: 0141 554 0004

Rutherglen & Cambuslang
School House, 2 McCallum Avenue, (Corner of Hamilton Road), Rutherglen, Glasgow, G73 3AL
Tel: 0141 647 5100

HIGHLAND

Caithness
7a Brabster Street, Thurso, KW14 7AP
Tel: 01847 894243

Inverness
103 Academy Street, Inverness, IV1 1LX
Tel: 01463 235345

Lochaber
The Orange Room, Lochaber College, An-Aird, Fort William, PH33 3PH
Tel: 01345 381537

Nairn
6 High Street, Nairn, IV12 4BJ
Tel: 01667 456677

Ross & Cromarty
Balallan, 4 Novar Road, Alness, IV17 0QG
Tel: 01349 883333

Skye & Lochalsh
The Green, Portree, IV51 9BT

MIDLOTHIAN

Dalkeith
8 Buccleuch Street, Dalkeith, EH22 1HA
Tel: 0131 663 3688

Penicuik
14a John Street, Penicuik, EH26 8AB
Tel: 01968 675259

MORAY

Moray
30-32 Batchen Street, Elgin, IV30 1BH
Tel: 01343 550088

NORTH AYRSHIRE

Arran
Park Terrace, Lamlash, Isle of Arran, KA27 8NB
Tel: 01770 600210

Irvine
66 High Street, Irvine, KA12 0BA
Tel: 01294 278051

Largs
36 Boyd Street, Largs, KA30 8LE
Tel: 01475 673586

North Ayrshire Citizens Advice Service
Administration Office, 98 Dockhead Street, Saltcoats, KA21 5EL
Tel: 01294 467848

Saltcoats
18-20 Countess Street, Saltcoats, KA21 5HW
Tel: 01294 202328

NORTH LANARKSHIRE

Airdrie
Resource Centre, 14 Anderson Street, Airdrie, ML6 0AA
Tel: 01236 754109

Bellshill
6 Hamilton Road, Bellshill, Strathclyde, ML4 1AQ
Tel: 01698 748615

Coatbridge
Unit 10 Fountain Business, Centre, Ellis Street, Coatbridge, ML5 3AA
Tel: 01236 421447/8

Cumbernauld
2 Annan House, 3rd Floor, Town Centre, Cumbernauld, G67 1DP
Tel: 01236 723201

Motherwell & Wishaw
32 Civic Square, Motherwell, ML1 1TP
Tel: 01698 259389

ORKNEY ISLANDS

Orkney
Anchor Buildings, 6 Bridge Street, Kirkwall, KW15 1HR
Tel: 01856 875266

PERTH & KINROSS

Perth
4 - 12 New Row, Perth, PH1 5QB
Tel: 01738 624301/2

RENFREWSHIRE

Paisley
45 George Street, Paisley, PA1 2JY
Tel: 0141 889 2121

SCOTTISH BORDERS

Central Borders
25 Albert Place, Galashiels, TD1 3DL
Tel: 01896 753889

Peebles
42 Old Town, Peebles, EH45 8JF
Tel: 01721 72122

Roxburgh
15a High Street, Hawick, TD9 9BZ
Tel: 01450 74266

SHETLAND ISLANDS

Shetland Islands
45 Commercial Street, Lerwick, ZE1 0AB
Tel: 01595 694696

STIRLING

Clydesdale
10 - 12 Wide Close, Lanark, ML11 7LX
Tel: 01555 664301

Hamilton
Almada Tower, 67 Almada Street, Hamilton, ML3 0HQ
Tel: 01698 283477

Stirling
The Norman MacEwan Centre, Cameronian Street, Stirling, FK8 2DX
Tel: 01786 470239

UIST (WESTERN ISLES)

Uist
27 Windfield Way, Balivanich, Isle of Benbecula, HS7 5LH
Tel: 01870 602421

WEST DUNBARTONSHIRE

Clydebank
32 Alexander Street, Clydebank, G81 1RZ
Tel: 0141 952 7921

Dumbarton
6/14 Bridge Street, Dumbarton, G82 1NT
Tel: 01389 765345

WEST LOTHIAN

Livingston
Suite 7 Shiel House, Shiel Walk, Craigshill, Livingston, EH54 5EH
Tel: 01506 432977

WESTERN ISLES

Barra (Western Isles)
Castlebay, Castlebay, HS9 5XD
Tel: 01871 810608

Harris (Western Isles)
Pier Road, Tarbert, HS3 3BG
Tel: 01859 502431

Lewis (Western Isles)
2 Bells Road, Stornoway, HS1 2QT
Tel: 01851 705727

WALES

ANGLESEY

Llangefni
4/10 Ffordd Yr Efail, Llangefni, LL77 7ER
Tel: 0845 1203708

BLAENAU GWENT

Abertillery
The Council Offices, Mitre Street, Abertillery, NP13 1AE
Tel: 01495 212424

BRIDGEND

Bridgend
1b Merthyr Mawr Road, Bridgend, CF31 3NH
Tel: 01656 654951

Maesteg
Council Offices, Talbot Street, Maesteg, CF34 9DA
Tel: 01656 734662

CAERPHILLY

Bargoed & District
41b Hanbury Road, Bargoed, CF81 8QU
Tel: 01443 83112

Blackwood
2 Hall Street, Blackwood, NP2 0NR
Tel: 01495 224456

Caerphilly
Park Lane, Caerphilly, CF83 1AA
Tel: 029 2088 2105

Risca
Park Road, Risca, NP11 6BJ
Tel: 01633 614731

CARDIFF

Cardiff
71 Bridge Street, Cardiff, CF10 2EE
Tel: 08701 264028

CARMARTHENSHIRE

Ammanford
14 Iscennen Road, Ammanford, SA18 3BG
Tel: 01269 591091

Carmarthen
113 Lammas Street, Carmarthen, SA31 3AP
Tel: 01267 234488

Llanelli
4a Cowell Street, Llanelli, SA15 1UU
Tel: 01554 759626

CEREDIGION

Aberystwyth
12 Cambrain Place, Aberystwyth, SY23 1NT
Tel: 01970 612817

Cardigan
Napier Street, Cardigan, SA43 1ED
Tel: 01239 613707

CONWY

Abergele
Bridge Street, Abergele, LL22 7HA
Tel: 01492 825627

Colwyn Bay
Basement Offices, The Metropole, Penrhyn Rd, Colwyn Bay, LL29 8LG
Tel: 01492 531310

Llandudno
5 Tudor Court, Adelphi Street, Llandudno, LL30 1BU
Tel: 01492 878818

DENBIGHSHIRE

Denbigh
The Church Institute, Lenten Pool, Denbigh, LL16 3LG
Tel: 01745 814336

Llangollen
9 Oak Street, Llangollen, LL20 8NR
Tel: 01978 860983

Prestatyn
1 Nant Hall Road, Prestatyn, LL19 9LR
Tel: 01745 855400

Rhyl
11 Water Street, Rhyl, LL18 1SP
Tel: 01745 334568

Ruthin
Town Hall, Wynnstay Road, Ruthin, LL15 1YN
Tel: 01824 703483

FLINTSHIRE

Flint
65 Church Street, Flint, CH6 5AF
Tel: 01352 733187

Flintshire District Office
Citizens Advice Bureau, The Annex, Terrig House, Chester St, Mold, CH7 1EG
Tel: 01352 753520

Holywell
The Old Library, Post Office Lane, Holywell, CH8 7LH
Tel: 01352 711262

Mold
The Annexe Terrig House, Chester Street, Mold, CH7 1EG
Tel: 01352 753520

GWYNEDD

Bangor & South Anglesey
60 Deniol Road, Bangor, LL57 2RF
Tel: 0870 7502350

Caernarfon
41 Pool Street, Caernarfon, LL55 2AE
Tel: 0870 7502350

Meirionnydd
Mill Street, Dolgellau, LL40 1EY
Tel: 0870 7502350

Pwllheli
Liverpool House, 12 Penlab Street, Pwllheli, 5DH 5RT
Tel: 0870 7502350

Ynys Mon
6 Victoria Terrace, Holyhead, LL65 1UT
Tel: 0870 1203708

MERTHYR TYDFIL

Merthyr Tydfil
Tramroadside North, Merthyr Tydfil, CF47 0AP
Tel: 01685 379997

MONMOUTHSHIRE

Abergavenny
26a Monk Street, Abergavenny, NP7 5NP
Tel: 01873 735865

Chepstow
The Gate House, High Street, Chepstow, NP6 5LH
Tel: 01291 623437

Monmouth
23a Whitecross Street, Monmouth, NP5 3BY
Tel: 01600 712590

NEATH PORT TALBOT

Neath
44 Alfred Street, Neath, SA11 1EH
Tel: 01639 635545

Port Talbot
36 Forge Road, Port Talbot, SA13 1NU
Tel: 01639 895057

Caldicot
The Cross, Caldicot, Newport, NP6 4HY
Tel: 01291 423840

NEWPORT

Newport
8 Corn Street, Newport, NP20 1DJ
Tel: 01633 265688

Haverfordwest
19 Cartlett, Haverfordwest, SA61 2LH
Tel: 01437 765216

PEMBROKESHIRE

Pembroke Dock
10 Meyrick Street, Pembroke Dock, SA72 6UT
Tel: 01646 683805

POWYS

Brecon
12 Castle Street, Brecon, LD3 9BU
Tel: 01874 624595

Machynlleth & District
The Care Centre, Forge Road, Machynlleth, SY20 8EQ
Tel: 0870 1264067

Montgomeryshire
Ladywell House, Frolic St Entrance, Park Street, Newtown, SY16 1QS
Tel: 01686 626557

Radnor
The Old Town Hall, Temple Street, Llandrindod Wells, LD1 5DL
Tel: 01597 823508

Ystradgynlais
47 Commercial Street, Ystradgynlais, Swansea, SA9 1JH
Tel: 01639 849427

RHONDDA CYNON TAFF

Cynon Valley
Old Library, Duffryn Road, Mountain Ash, CF45 4DA
Tel: 01443 475633

Pontypridd
5 Gelliwastad Road, Pontypridd, CF37 2BP
Tel: 01443 409963

SWANSEA

Swansea
208 High Street, Swansea, SA1 1PE
Tel: 01792 652902

TORFAEN

Cwmbran
21 Caradoc Road, Cwmbran, NP44 1PP
Tel: 01633 482464

Pontypool
Castle Mews,George Street, Pontypool, NP4 6BU
Tel: 01495 757421

VALE OF GLAMORGAN

Barry
119 Broad Street, Barry, CF62 7TZ
Tel: 01446 733310

Cowbridge
Rear of 79 Eastgate, Cowbridge, CF71 7AA
Tel: 01446 775411

Llantwit Major
The Old School, Wine Street, Llantwit Major, CF61 1RZ
Tel: 01446 796594

Penarth
West House Cottage, Stanwell Road, Penarth, CF64 2YG
Tel: 0845 050 5163

WREXHAM

Wrexham
35 Grosvenor Road, Wrexham, LL11 1BT
Tel: 01978 364639